AI for Game Developers

Other resources from O'Reilly

AI for Game Developers

David M. Bourg and Glenn Seemann

O'REILLY®

Beijing · Cambridge · Farnham · Köln · Paris · Sebastopol · Taipei · Tokyo

AI for Game Developers
by David M. Bourg and Glenn Seemann

Published by O'Reilly Media, Inc., 1005 Gravenstein Highway North, Sebastopol, CA 95472.

O'Reilly books may be purchased for educational, business, or sales promotional use. Online editions are also available for most titles (*safari.oreilly.com*). For more information, contact our corporate/institutional sales department: (800) 998-9938 or *corporate@oreilly.com*.

Editors:	Nathan Torkington and Tatiana Apandi Diaz
Production Editor:	Darren Kelly
Cover Designer:	Ellie Volckhausen
Interior Designer:	David Futato
Production Services:	TechBooks, Inc.

Printing History:

July 2004:	First Edition.

RepKover™. This book uses RepKover™, a durable and flexible lay-flat binding.

ISBN: 0-596-00555-5
[M]

Table of Contents

Preface

Recent advances in 3D visualization and physics-based simulation technology, at both the software and hardware levels, have enabled game developers to create compelling, visually immersive gaming environments. The next step in creating even more immersive games is improved artificial intelligence (AI). Advances in computing power, and in hardware-accelerated graphics in particular, are helping to free up more CPU cycles that can be devoted to more sophisticated AI engines for games. Further, the large number of resources—academic papers, books, game industry articles, and web sites—devoted to AI are helping to put advanced AI techniques within the grasp of every game developer, not just those professionals who devote their careers to AI.

With that said, wading through volumes of technical papers, text books, and web sites can be a daunting task for upcoming game AI developers. This book pulls together the information novices need so that they can get a jump-start in the field of game AI development. We present relevant theory on a wide range of topics, which we support with code samples throughout the book.

Many general game development books cover AI to some extent, however their treatment of the technology tends to be limited. This is probably because such books have to cover a lot of different topics and cannot go into great depth on any particular one. Although several very good books do focus on game AI (we list many of them in the "Additional Resources" section of this Preface), most of them are geared toward experienced AI developers and they focus on relatively specific and advanced topics. Therefore, novices likely would require companion resources that cover some of the more fundamental aspects of game AI in more detail. Still other books cover some specific game AI techniques in great detail, but are restricted to covering just those techniques.

Our book covers a wide range of game AI topics at a level appropriate for novice developers. So, if you are new to game programming or if you are an experienced game programmer who needs to get up to speed quickly on AI techniques such as finite state machines, fuzzy logic, and neural networks, among others, this book is for you.

Assumptions This Book Makes

Because this book is targeted for beginner game AI developers, we don't assume you have any AI background. We do, however, assume you know how to program using C/C++. We also assume you have a working knowledge of the basic vector math used in games, but we have included a brief vector math refresher in the Appendix in case your skills are a little rusty.

About This Book

We didn't hope to (nor did we attempt to) cover every aspect of game AI in this book; far too many techniques and variations of techniques are used for an even larger variety of game types, specific game architectures, and in-game scenarios. Instead, we present a mix of both deterministic (traditional) and nondeterministic (newer) AI techniques aimed squarely at beginner AI developers. Here's a summary of what we cover:

Chapter 1, *Introduction to Game AI*

> Here, we define game AI and discuss the current state of the art as well as the future of this technology.

Chapter 2, *Chasing and Evading*

> We cover basic techniques for chasing and evading as well as more advanced techniques for intercepting. We also cover techniques applicable to both tile-based and continuous game environments.

Chapter 3, *Pattern Movement*

> Pattern movement techniques are common to many video games and developers have been using them since the early days of gaming. You can use these techniques to preprogram certain behaviors such as the patrolling of a guard or the swooping in of a spacecraft.

Chapter 4, *Flocking*

> The flocking method we examine in this chapter is an example of an A-life algorithm. In addition to creating cool-looking flocking behavior, A-life algorithms form the basis of more advanced group movement.

Chapter 5, *Potential Function Based Movement*

> Potential-based movement is relatively new in game AI applications. The cool thing about this method is that it can handle chasing, evading, swarming, and collision avoidance simultaneously.

Chapter 6, *Basic Pathfinding and Waypoints*

Game developers use many techniques to find paths in and around game environments. In this chapter, we cover several of these methods, including waypoints.

Chapter 7, *A* Pathfinding*

No treatment of pathfinding is complete without addressing the workhorse algorithm of pathfinding; therefore, we devote this whole chapter to the A* algorithm.

Chapter 8, *Scripted AI and Scripting Engines*

Programmers today often write scripting engines and hand off the tools to level designers who are responsible for creating the content and defining the AI. In this chapter, we explore some of the techniques developers use to apply a scripting system in their games, and the benefits they receive.

Chapter 9, *Finite State Machines*

Finite state machines are the nuts and bolts of game AI. This chapter discusses the fundamentals of finite state machines and how to implement them.

Chapter 10, *Fuzzy Logic*

Developers use fuzzy logic in conjunction with or as a replacement for finite state machines. In this chapter, you'll learn the advantages fuzzy techniques offer over traditional logic techniques.

Chapter 11, *Rule-Based AI*

Technically, fuzzy logic and finite state machines fall under the general heading of rules-based methods. In this chapter, we cover these methods as well as other variants.

Chapter 12, *Basic Probability*

Game developers commonly use basic probability to make their games less predictable. Such cheap unpredictability enables developers to maintain substantial control over their games. Here, we cover basic probability for this purpose as well as lay the groundwork for more advanced methods.

Chapter 13, *Decisions Under Uncertainty—Bayesian Techniques*

Bayesian techniques are probabilistic techniques, and in this chapter we show how you can use them for decision making and for adaptation in games.

Chapter 14, *Neural Networks*

Game developers use neural networks for learning and adaptation in games—in fact, for anything from making decisions to predicting the behavior of players. We cover the most widely used neural network architecture, in detail.

Chapter 15, *Genetic Algorithms*

> Genetic algorithms offer opportunities for evolving game AI. Although developers don't often use genetic algorithms in games, their potential for specific applications is promising, particularly if they are combined with other methods.

Appendix, *Vector Operations*

> This appendix shows you how to implement a C++ class that captures all of the vector operations that you'll need when writing 2D or 3D simulations.

All the chapters in this book are fairly independent of each other. Therefore, you generally can read the chapters in any order you want, without worrying about missing material in earlier chapters. The only exception to this rule is Chapter 12, on basic probability. If you don't have a background in probability, you should read this chapter before reading Chapter 13, on Bayesian methods.

Also, we encourage you to try these algorithms for yourself in your own programs. If you're just getting started in game AI, which we assume you are if you're reading this book, you might want to begin by applying some of the techniques we present in simple arcade-style or board games. You also might consider programming a *bot* using extensible AI tools that are increasingly becoming standard for first-person shooter games. This approach will give you the opportunity to try out your AI ideas without having to program all the other non-AI aspects of your game.

Conventions Used in This Book

The following typographical conventions are used in this book:

Plain text

> Indicates menu titles, menu options, menu buttons, and keyboard accelerators (such as Alt and Ctrl).

Italic

> Indicates new terms, URLs, email addresses, filenames, file extensions, pathnames, directories, and Unix utilities.

`Constant width`

> Indicates commands, options, switches, variables, attributes, keys, functions, types, classes, namespaces, methods, modules, properties, parameters, values, objects, events, event handlers, XML tags, HTML tags, macros, the contents of files, or the output from commands.

`Constant width bold`

> Shows commands or other text that should be typed literally by the user.

Constant width italic

    Shows text that should be replaced with user-supplied values.

Bold

    Variables shown in bold are vectors as opposed to scalar variables, which are shown in regular print.

Additional Resources

Although we attempt to cover a wide range of AI techniques in this book, we realize we can't compress within these pages everything there is to know about AI in game development. Therefore, we've compiled a short list of useful AI web and print resources for you to explore should you decide to pursue game AI further.

Here are some popular web sites related to game development and AI that we find helpful:

- The Game AI Page at *http://www.gameai.com*
- AI Guru at *http://www.aiguru.com*
- Gamasutra at *http://www.gamasutra.com*
- GameDev.net at *http://www.gamedev.net*
- AI Depot at *http://ai-depot.com*
- Generation5 at *http://www.generation5.org*
- The American Association for Artificial Intelligence at *http://www.aaai.org*

Each web site contains information relevant to game AI as well as additional links to other sources of information on AI.

Here are several print resources that we find helpful (note that these resources include both game and nongame AI books):

- *Probabilistic Reasoning in Intelligent Systems: Networks of Plausible Inference* by Judea Pearl (Morgan Kaufmann Publishers, Inc.)
- *Bayesian Artificial Intelligence* by Kevin Korb and Ann Nicholson (Chapman & Hall/CRC)
- *Bayesian Inference and Decision,* Second Edition by Robert Winkler (Probabilistic Publishing)
- *AI Game Programming Wisdom* by Steve Rabin, ed. (Charles River Media)
- *AI Techniques for Game Programming* by Mat Buckland (Premier Press)
- *Practical Neural Network Recipes in C++* by Timothy Masters (Academic Press)
- *Neural Networks for Pattern Recognition* by Christopher Bishop (Oxford University Press)
- *AI Application Programming* by M. Tim Jones (Charles River Media)

Using Code Examples

This book is designed to help you get your job done. In general, you can use the code in this book in your programs and documentation. You do not need to contact us for permission unless you're reproducing a significant portion of the code. For example, writing a program that uses several chunks of code from this book does not require permission. Selling or distributing a CD-ROM of examples from O'Reilly books does require permission. Answering a question by citing this book and quoting example code does not require permission. Incorporating a significant amount of example code from this book into your product's documentation does require permission.

We appreciate, but do not require, attribution. An attribution usually includes the title, author, publisher, and ISBN. For example: "*AI for Game Developers,* by David M. Bourg and Glenn Seemann. Copyright 2004 O'ReillyMedia, Inc., 0-596-00555-5."

If you feel your use of code examples falls outside fair use or the permission given here, feel free to contact us at *permissions@oreilly.com.*

How to Contact Us

Please address comments and questions concerning this book to the publisher:

> O'Reilly Media, Inc.
> 1005 Gravenstein Highway North
> Sebastopol, CA 95472
> (800) 998-9938 (in the United States or Canada)
> (707) 829-0515 (international or local)
> (707) 829-0104 (fax)

We have a web page for this book, where we list errata, examples, and any additional information. You can access this page at:

> *http://www.oreilly.com/catalog/ai*

To comment or ask technical questions about this book, send email to:

> *bookquestions@oreilly.com*

For more information about our books, conferences, Resource Centers, and the O'Reilly Network, see our web site at:

> *http://www.oreilly.com*

Acknowledgments

We'd like to thank our editors, Nathan Torkington and Tatiana Diaz, for their skill, insight, and patience. We'd also like to express our appreciation to O'Reilly for giving us the opportunity to write this book. Further, special thanks go to all the production and technical staff at O'Reilly, and to the technical reviewers, chromatic, Graham Evans, and Mike Keith, for their thoughtful and expert comments and suggestions. Finally, we'd like to thank our respective wives, Helena and Michelle, for their support and encouragement and for putting up with our repeatedly saying, "I have to work on the book this weekend." We can't forget to thank our respective children, who always remind us that it's OK to play. On that note, remember that the most important goal of good AI in games is to make games more fun. Play on!

CHAPTER 1

Introduction to Game AI

In the broadest sense, most games incorporate some form of artificial intelligence (AI). For instance, developers have used AI for years to give seemingly intelligent life to countless game characters, from the ghosts in the classic arcade game *Pac Man* to the bots in the first-person shooter *Unreal,* and many others in between. The huge variety of game genres and game characters necessitates a rather broad interpretation as to what is considered game AI. Indeed, this is true of AI in more traditional scientific applications as well.

Some developers consider tasks such as pathfinding as part of game AI. Steven Woodcock reported in his "2003 Game Developer's Conference AI Roundtable Moderator's Report" that some developers even consider collision detection to be part of game AI.* Clearly, some wide-ranging interpretations of game AI exist.

We're going to stick with a broad interpretation of game AI, which includes everything from simple chasing and evading, to pattern movement, to neural networks and genetic algorithms. Game AI probably best fits within the scope of *weak* AI (see the sidebar "Defining AI"). However, in a sense you can think of game AI in even broader terms.

In games, we aren't always interested in giving nonplayer characters human-level intellect. Perhaps we are writing code to control nonhuman creatures such as dragons, robots, or even rodents. Further, who says we always have to make nonplayer characters smart? Making some nonplayer characters dumb adds to the variety and richness of game content. Although it is true that game AI is often called upon to solve fairly complex problems, we can employ AI in attempts to give nonplayer characters the appearance of having different personalities, or of portraying emotions or various dispositions—for example, scared, agitated, and so on.

---

*Steven Woodcock maintains an excellent Web site devoted to game AI at *http://www.gameai.com.*

Defining AI

The question "what is artificial intelligence?" is not easy to answer. If you look up *artificial intelligence* in a dictionary, you'll probably find a definition that reads something like this: "The ability of a computer or other machine to perform those activities that are normally thought to require intelligence." This definition comes from *The American Heritage Dictionary of the English Language, Fourth Edition* (Houghton Mifflin Company). Still other sources define artificial intelligence as the process or science of creating intelligent machines.

From another perspective it's appropriate to think of AI as the intelligent behavior exhibited by the machine that has been created, or perhaps the artificial brains behind that intelligent behavior. But even this interpretation is not complete. To some folks, the study of AI is not necessarily for the purpose of creating intelligent machines, but for the purpose of gaining better insight into the nature of human intelligence. Still others study AI methods to create machines that exhibit some limited form of intelligence.

This begs the question: "what is intelligence?" To some, the litmus test for AI is how close it is to human intelligence. Others argue that additional requirements must be met for a machine to be considered intelligent. Some people say intelligence requires a conscience and that emotions are integrally tied to intelligence, while others say the ability to solve a problem requiring intelligence if it were to be solved by a human is not enough; AI must also learn and adapt to be considered intelligent.

AI that satisfies all these requirements is considered *strong AI*. Unlike strong AI, *weak AI* involves a broader range of purposes and technologies to give machines specialized intelligent qualities. Game AI falls into the category of weak AI.

The bottom line is that the definition of game AI is rather broad and flexible. Anything that gives the illusion of intelligence to an appropriate level, thus making the game more immersive, challenging, and, most importantly, fun, can be considered game AI. Just like the use of real physics in games, good AI adds to the immersiveness of the game, drawing players in and suspending their reality for a time.

Deterministic Versus Nondeterministic AI

Game AI techniques generally come in two flavors: *deterministic* and *nondeterministic*.

Deterministic

Deterministic behavior or performance is specified and predictable. There's no uncertainty. An example of deterministic behavior is a simple chasing algorithm. You can explicitly code a nonplayer character to move toward some target point by advancing along the x and y coordinate axes until the character's x and y coordinates coincide with the target location.

Nondeterministic

Nondeterministic behavior is the opposite of deterministic behavior. Behavior has a degree of uncertainty and is somewhat unpredictable (the degree of uncertainty depends on the AI method employed and how well that method is understood). An example of nondeterministic behavior is a nonplayer character learning to adapt to the fighting tactics of a player. Such learning could use a neural network, a Bayesian technique, or a genetic algorithm.

Deterministic AI techniques are the bread and butter of game AI. These techniques are predictable, fast, and easy to implement, understand, test, and debug. Although they have a lot going for them, deterministic methods place the burden of anticipating all scenarios and coding all behavior explicitly on the developers' shoulders. Further, deterministic methods do not facilitate learning or evolving. And after a little gameplay, deterministic behaviors tend to become predictable. This limits a game's play-life, so to speak.

Nondeterministic methods facilitate learning and unpredictable gameplay. Further, developers don't have to explicitly code all behaviors in anticipation of all possible scenarios. Nondeterministic methods also can learn and extrapolate on their own, and they can promote so-called *emergent* behavior, or behavior that emerges without explicit instructions. The flocking and neural network algorithms we'll consider in this book are good examples of emergent behavior.

Developers traditionally have been a bit wary of AI that is nondeterministic, although this is changing. Unpredictability is difficult to test and debug—how can you test all possible variations of player action to make sure the game doesn't do something silly in some cases? Game developers face an ever-shortening development cycle that makes developing and testing new technology to production-ready standards extremely difficult. Such short development periods make it difficult for developers to understand cutting-edge AI technologies fully and to see their implications in a mass-market commercial game.

At least until recently, another factor that has limited game AI development is the fact that developers have been focusing most of their attention on graphics quality. As it turns out, such focus on developing better and faster graphics techniques, including hardware acceleration, might now afford more resources to be allocated toward developing better, more sophisticated AI. This fact, along with the pressure to produce the next hit game, is encouraging game developers to more thoroughly explore nondeterministic techniques. We'll come back to this point a little later.

Established Game AI

Perhaps the most widely used AI technique in games is *cheating*. For example, in a war simulation game the computer team can have access to all information on its human opponents—location of their base; the types, number, and location of units, etc.—without having to send out scouts to gather such intelligence the way a human player must. Cheating in this manner is common and helps give the computer an edge against intelligent human players. However, cheating can be bad. If it is obvious to the player that the computer is cheating, the player likely will assume his efforts are futile and lose interest in the game. Also, unbalanced cheating can give computer opponents too much power, making it impossible for the player to beat the computer. Here again, the player is likely to lose interest if he sees his efforts are futile. Cheating must be balanced to create just enough of a challenge for the player to keep the game interesting and fun.

Of course, cheating isn't the only well-established AI technique. *Finite state machines* are a ubiquitous game AI technique. We cover them in detail in Chapter 9, but basically the idea is to enumerate a bunch of actions or states for computer-controlled characters and execute them or transition between them using if-then conditionals that check various conditions and criteria.

Developers commonly use *fuzzy logic* in fuzzy state machines to make the resulting actions somewhat less predictable and to reduce the burden of having to enumerate huge numbers of if-then rules. Rather than have a rule that states *if distance = 10 and health = 100 then attack,* as you might in a finite state machine, fuzzy logic enables you to craft rules using less precise conditions, such as *if close and healthy then attack aggressively.* We cover fuzzy logic in Chapter 10.

Effective and efficient pathfinding is a fundamental task that nonplayer characters must accomplish in all sorts of games. Nonplayer character units in a war simulation must be able to navigate over terrain and avoid barriers to reach the enemy. Creatures in a first-person shooter must be able to navigate through dungeons or buildings to reach or escape from the player. The scenarios are endless, and it's no wonder that AI developers give pathfinding tremendous attention. We cover general pathfinding techniques in Chapter 6 and the venerable A* algorithm in Chapter 7.

These are only a few of the established game AI techniques; others include scripting, rules-based systems, and some artificial life (A-life) techniques, to name a few. A-life techniques are common in robotic applications, and developers have adapted and used them with great success in video games. Basically, an A-life system is a synthetic system that exhibits natural behaviors. These behaviors are emergent and develop as a result of the combined effect of lower-level algorithms. We'll see examples of A-life as well as other techniques throughout this book.

The Future of Game AI

The next big thing in game AI is learning. Rather than have all nonplayer character behavior be predestined by the time a game ships, the game should evolve, learn, and adapt the more it's played. This results in a game that grows with the player and is harder for the player to predict, thus extending the play-life of the game. It is precisely this unpredictable nature of learning and evolving games that has traditionally made AI developers approach learning techniques with a healthy dose of trepidation.

The techniques for learning and reacting to character behavior fall under the non-deterministic AI we talked about earlier, and its difficulties apply here too. Specifically, such nondeterministic, learning AI techniques take longer to develop and test. Further, it's more difficult to really understand what the AI is doing, which makes debugging more difficult. These factors have proven to be serious barriers for widespread use of learning AI techniques. All this is changing, though.

Several mainstream games, such as *Creatures, Black & White, Battlecruiser 3000AD, Dirt Track Racing, Fields of Battle,* and *Heavy Gear,* used nondeterministic AI methods. Their success sparked a renewed interest in learning AI methods such as decision trees, neural networks, genetic algorithms, and probabilistic methods.

These successful games use nondeterministic methods in conjunction with more traditional deterministic methods, and use them only where they are needed and only for problems for which they are best suited. A neural network is not a magic pill that will solve all AI problems in a game; however, you can use it with impressive results for very specific AI tasks within a hybrid AI system. This is the approach we advocate for using these nondeterministic methods. In this way, you can at least isolate the parts of your AI that are unpredictable and more difficult to develop, test, and debug, while ideally keeping the majority of your AI system in traditional form.

Throughout this book we cover both traditional game AI techniques as well as relatively new, up-and-coming AI techniques. We want to arm you with a thorough understanding of what has worked and continues to work for game AI. We also want you to learn several promising new techniques to give you a head start toward the future of game AI.

CHAPTER 2
Chasing and Evading

In this chapter we focus on the ubiquitous problem of chasing and evading. Whether you're developing a spaceship shooter, a strategy simulation, or a role-playing game, chances are you will be faced with trying to make your game's nonplayer characters either chase down or run from your player character. In an action or arcade game the situation might involve having enemy spaceships track and engage the player's ship. In an adventure role-playing game it might involve having a troll or some other lovely creature chase down your player's character. In first-person shooters and flight simulations you might have to make guided missiles track and strike the player or his aircraft. In any case, you need some logic that enables nonplayer character predators to chase, and their prey to run.

The chasing/evading problem consists of two parts. The first part involves the decision to initiate a chase or to evade. The second part involves effecting the chase or evasion—that is, getting your predator to the prey, or having the prey get as far from the predator as possible without getting caught. In a sense, one could argue that the chasing/evading problem contains a third element: obstacle avoidance. Having to avoid obstacles while chasing or evading definitely complicates matters, making the algorithms more difficult to program. Although we don't cover obstacle avoidance in this chapter, we will come back to it in Chapters 5 and 6. In this chapter we focus on the second part of the problem: effecting the chase or evasion. We'll discuss the first part of the problem—decision making—in later chapters, when we explore such topics as state machines and neural networks, among others.

The simplest, easiest-to-program, and most common method you can use to make a predator chase its prey involves updating the predator's coordinates through each game loop such that the difference between the predator's coordinates and the prey's coordinates gets increasingly small. This algorithm pays no attention to the predator and prey's respective headings (the direction in which they're traveling) or their speeds. Although this method is relentlessly effective in that the predator constantly moves toward its prey unless it's impeded by an obstacle, it does have its limitations, as we'll discuss shortly.

In addition to this very basic method, other methods are available to you that might better serve your needs, depending on your game's requirements. For example, in games that incorporate real-time physics engines you can employ methods that consider the positions and velocities of both the predator and its prey so that the predator can try to intercept its prey instead of relentlessly chasing it. In this case the relative position and velocity information can be used as input to an algorithm that will determine appropriate force actuation—steering forces, for example—to guide the predator to the target. Yet another method involves using potential functions to influence the behavior of the predator in a manner that makes it chase its prey, or more specifically, makes the prey attract the predator. Similarly, you can use such potential functions to cause the prey to run from or repel a predator. We cover potential functions in Chapter 5.

In this chapter we explore several chase and evade methods, starting with the most basic method. We also give you example code that implements these methods in the context of tile-based and continuous-movement environments.

Basic Chasing and Evading

As we said earlier, the simplest chase algorithm involves correcting the predator's coordinates based on the prey's coordinates so as to reduce the distance between their positions. This is a very common method for implementing basic chasing and evading. (In this method, evading is virtually the opposite of chasing, whereby instead of trying to decrease the distance between the predator and prey coordinates, you try to increase it.) In code, the method looks something like that shown in Example 2-1.

Example 2-1. Basic chase algorithm

```
if (predatorX > preyX)
    predatorX--;
else if (predatorX < preyX)
    predatorX++;

if (predatorY > preyY)
    predatorY--;
else if (predatorY < preyY)
    predatorY++;
```

In this example, the prey is located at coordinates preyX and preyY, while the predator is located at coordinates predatorX and predatorY. During each cycle through the game loop the predator's coordinates are checked against the prey's. If the predator's x-coordinate is greater than the prey's x-coordinate, the predator's x-coordinate is decremented, moving it closer to the prey's x-position. Conversely, if the predator's x-coordinate is less than the prey's, the predator's x-coordinate is incremented. Similar logic applies to the predator's y-coordinate based on the prey's y-coordinate. The end result is that the predator will move closer and closer to the prey each cycle through the game loop.

Using this same methodology, we can implement evading by simply reversing the logic, as we illustrate in Example 2-2.

Example 2-2. Basic evade algorithm

```
if (preyX > predatorX)
    preyX++;
else if (preyX < predatorX)
    preyX--;

if (preyY > predatorY)
    preyY++;
else if (preyY < predatorY)
    preyY--;
```

In *tile-based games* the game domain is divided into discrete tiles—squares, hexagons, etc.—and the player's position is fixed to a discrete tile. Movement goes tile by tile, and the number of directions in which the player can make headway is limited. In a *continuous environment*, position is represented by floating-point coordinates, which can represent any location in the game domain. The player also is free to head in any direction.

You can apply the approach illustrated in these two examples whether your game incorporates tile-based or continuous movement. In tile-based games, the *x*s and *y*s can represent columns and rows in a grid that encompasses the game domain. In this case, the *x*s and *y*s would be integers. In a continuous environment, the *x*s and *y*s—and *z*s if yours is a 3D game—would be real numbers representing the coordinates in a Cartesian coordinate system encompassing the game domain.

There's no doubt that although it's simple, this method works. The predator will chase his prey with unrelenting determination. The sample program *AIDemo2-1*, available for download from this book's web site (*http://www.oreilly.com/catalog/ai*), implements the basic chase algorithm in a tile-based environment. The relevant code is shown in Example 2-3.

Example 2-3. Basic tile-based chase example

```
if (predatorCol > preyCol)
    predatorCol--;
else if (predatorCol < preyCol)
    predatorCol++;

if (predatorRow> preyRow)
    predatorRow--;
else if (predatorRow<preyRow)
    predatorRow++;
```

Notice the similarities in Examples 2-3 and 2-1. The only difference is that in Example 2-3 rows and columns are used instead of floating-point *x*s and *y*s.

The trouble with this basic method is that often the chasing or evading seems almost too mechanical. Figure 2-1 illustrates the path the troll in the sample program takes as he pursues the player.

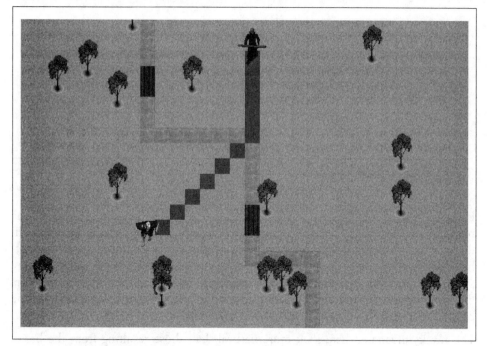

Figure 2-1. Basic tile-based chase

As you can see, the troll first moves diagonally toward the player until one of the coordinates, the horizontal in this case, equals that of the player's.* Then the troll advances toward the player straight along the other coordinate axis, the vertical in this case. Clearly this does not look very natural. A better approach is to have the troll move directly toward the player in a straight line. You can implement such an algorithm without too much difficulty, as we discuss in the next section.

Line-of-Sight Chasing

In this section we explain a few chasing and evading algorithms that use a line-of-sight approach. The gist of the line-of-sight approach is to have the predator take a straight-line path toward the prey; the predator always moves directly toward the prey's current position. If the prey is standing still, the predator will take a straight line path. However, if the prey is moving, the path will not necessarily be a straight line. The predator still will attempt to move directly toward the current position of the prey, but by the time he catches up with the moving prey, the path he would have taken might be curved, as illustrated in Figure 2-2.

---

* In square tile-based games, characters appear to move faster when moving along a diagonal path. This is because the length of the diagonal of a square is SQRT(2) times longer than its sides. Thus, for every diagonal step, the character appears to move SQRT(2) times faster than when it moves horizontally or vertically.

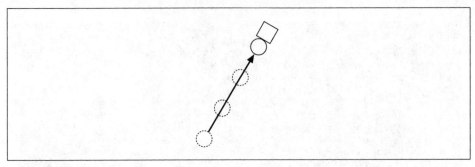

Figure 2-2. Line-of-sight chasing

In Figure 2-2, the circles represent the predator and the diamonds represent the prey. The dashed lines and shapes indicate starting and intermediate positions. In the scenario on the left, the prey is sitting still; thus the predator makes a straight-line dash toward the prey. In the scenario on the right, the prey is moving along some arbitrary path over time. At each time step, or cycle through the game loop, the predator moves toward the current position of the prey. As the prey moves, the predator traces out a curved path from its starting point.

The results illustrated here look more natural than those resulting from the basic-chase algorithm. Over the remainder of this section, we'll show you two algorithms that implement line-of-sight chasing. One algorithm is specifically for tiled environments, while the other applies to continuous environments.

Line-of-Sight Chasing in Tiled Environments

As we stated earlier, the environment in a tile-based game is divided into discrete tiles. This places certain limitations on movement that don't necessarily apply in a continuous environment. In a continuous environment, positions usually are represented using floating-point variables. Those positions are then mapped to the nearest screen pixel. When changing positions in a continuous environment, you don't always have to limit movement to adjacent screen pixels. Screen pixels typically are small enough so that a small number of them can be skipped between each screen redraw without sacrificing motion fluidity.

In tile-based games, however, changing positions is more restrictive. By its very nature, tile-based movement can appear jaggy because each tile is not mapped to a screen pixel. To minimize the jaggy and sometimes jumpy appearance in tile-based games, it's important to move only to adjacent tiles when changing positions. For games that use square tiles, such as the example game, this offers only eight possible directions of movement. This limitation leads to an interesting problem when a predator, such as the troll in the example, is chasing its target. The troll is limited to only eight possible directions, but mathematically speaking, none of those directions can accurately represent the true direction of the target. This dilemma is illustrated in Figure 2-3.

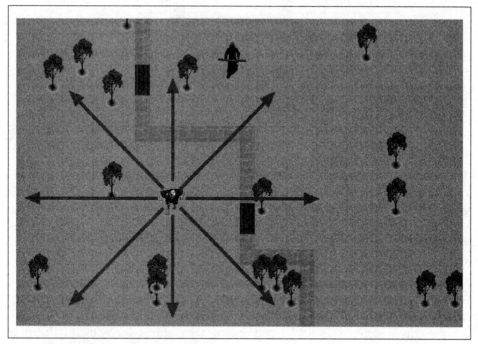

Figure 2-3. Tile-based eight-way movement

As you can see in Figure 2-3, none of the eight possible directions leads directly to the target. What we need is a way to determine which of the eight adjacent tiles to move to so that the troll appears to be moving toward the player in a straight line.

As we showed you earlier, you can use the simple chasing algorithm to make the troll relentlessly chase the player. It will even calculate the shortest possible path to the player. So, what's the disadvantage? One concerns aesthetics. When viewed in a tile-based environment, the simple chase method doesn't always appear to produce a visually straight line. Figure 2-4 illustrates this point.

Another reason to avoid the simple chase method is that it can have undesirable side effects when a group of predators, such as a pack of angry trolls, are converging on the player. Using the simple method, they would all walk diagonally to the nearest axis of their target and then walk along that axis to the target. This could lead to them walking single file to launch their attack. A more sophisticated approach is to have them walk directly toward the target from different directions.

It's interesting to note that both paths shown in Figure 2-4 are the same distance. The line-of-sight method, however, appears more natural and direct, which in turn makes the troll seem more intelligent. So, the objective for the line-of-sight approach

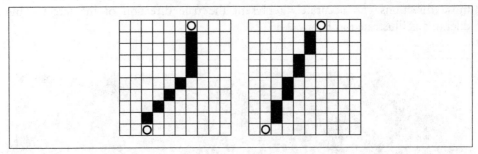

Figure 2-4. Simple chase versus line-of-sight chase

is to calculate a path so that the troll appears to be walking in a straight line toward the player.

The approach we'll take to solve this problem involves using a standard line algorithm that is typically used to draw lines in a pixel environment. We're essentially going to treat the tile-based environment as though each tile was in fact a giant screen pixel. However, instead of coloring the pixels to draw a line on the screen, the line algorithm is going to tell us which tiles the troll should follow so that it will walk in a straight line to its target.

Although you can calculate the points of a line in several ways, in this example we're going to use Bresenham's line algorithm. Bresenham's algorithm is one of the more efficient methods for drawing a line in a pixel-based environment, but that's not the only reason it's useful for pathfinding calculations. Bresenham's algorithm also is attractive because unlike some other line-drawing algorithms, it will never draw two adjacent pixels along a line's shortest axis. For our pathfinding needs, this means the troll will walk along the shortest possible path between the starting and ending points. Figure 2-5 shows how Bresenham's algorithm, on the left, might compare to other line algorithms that can sometimes draw multiple pixels along the

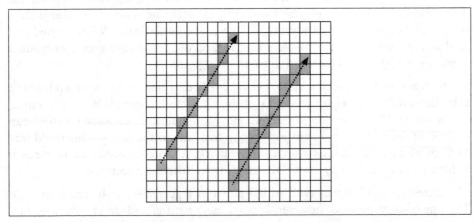

Figure 2-5. Bresenham versus alternate line algorithm

shortest axis. If an algorithm that generated a line such as the one shown on the right is used, the troll would take unnecessary steps. It still would still reach its target, but not in the shortest and most efficient way.

As Figure 2-5 shows, a standard algorithm such as the one shown on the right would mark every tile for pathfinding that mathematically intersected the line between the starting and ending points. This is not desirable for a pathfinding application because it won't generate the shortest possible path. In this case, Bresenham's algorithm produces a much more desirable result.

The Bresenham algorithm used to calculate the direction of the troll's movement takes the starting point, which is the row and column of the troll's position, and the ending point, which is the row and column of the player's position, and calculates a series of steps the troll will have to take so that it will walk in a straight line to the player. Keep in mind that this function needs to be called each time the troll's target, in this case the player, changes position. Once the target moves, the precalculated path becomes obsolete, and therefore it becomes necessary to calculate it again. Examples 2-4 through 2-7 show how you can use the Bresenham algorithm to build a path to the troll's target.

Example 2-4. BuildPathToTarget function

```
void ai_Entity::BuildPathToTarget (void)
{
    int nextCol=col;
    int nextRow=row;
    int deltaRow=endRow-row;
    int deltaCol=endCol-col;
    int stepCol, stepRow;
    int currentStep, fraction;
```

As Example 2-4 shows, this function uses values stored in the ai_Entity class to establish the starting and ending points for the path. The values in col and row are the starting points of the path. In the case of the sample program, col and row contain the current position of the troll. The values in endRow and endCol contain the position of the troll's desired location, which in this case is the player's position.

Example 2-5. Path initialization

```
for (currentStep=0;currentStep<kMaxPathLength; currentStep++)
{
    pathRow[currentStep]=-1;
        pathCol[currentStep]=-1;
}

currentStep=0;
pathRowTarget=endRow;
pathColTarget=endCol;
```

In Example 2-5 you can see the row and column path arrays being initialized. This function is called each time the player's position changes, so it's necessary to clear the old path before the new one is calculated.

Upon this function's exit, the two arrays, pathRow and pathCol, will contain the row and column positions along each point in the troll's path to its target. Updating the troll's position then becomes a simple matter of traversing these arrays and assigning their values to the troll's row and column variables each time the troll is ready to take another step.

Had this been an actual line-drawing function, the points stored in the path arrays would be the coordinates of the pixels that make up the line.

The code in Example 2-6 determines the direction of the path by using the previously calculated deltaRow and deltaCol values.

Example 2-6. Path direction calculation

```
if (deltaRow < 0) stepRow=-1; else stepRow=1;
if (deltaCol < 0) stepCol=-1; else stepCol=1;
deltaRow=abs(deltaRow*2);
deltaCol=abs(deltaCol*2);

pathRow[currentStep]=nextRow;
pathCol[currentStep]=nextCol;
currentStep++;
```

It also sets the first values in the path arrays, which in this case is the row and column position of the troll.

Example 2-7 shows the meat of the Bresenham algorithm.

Example 2-7. Bresenham algorithm

```
if (deltaCol >deltaRow)
    {
     fraction = deltaRow *2-deltaCol;
     while (nextCol != endCol)
      {
       if (fraction >=0)
        {
         nextRow =nextRow +stepRow;
         fraction =fraction -deltaCol;
        }
       nextCol=nextCol+stepCol;
       fraction=fraction +deltaRow;
       pathRow[currentStep]=nextRow;
       pathCol[currentStep]=nextCol;
       currentStep++;
      }
    }
    else
    {
     fraction =deltaCol *2-deltaRow;
     while (nextRow !=endRow)
      {
       if (fraction >=0)
        {
```

```
          nextCol=nextCol+stepCol;
          fraction=fraction —deltaRow;
        }
      nextRow =nextRow +stepRow;
      fraction=fraction +deltaCol;
      pathRow[currentStep]=nextRow;
      pathCol[currentStep]=nextCol;
      currentStep++;
    }
  }
}
```

The initial if conditional uses the values in deltaCol and deltaRow to determine which axis is the longest. The first block of code after the if statement will be executed if the column axis is the longest. The else part will be executed if the row axis is the longest. The algorithm will then traverse the longest axis, calculating each point of the line along the way. Figure 2-6 shows an example of the path the troll would follow using the Bresenham line-of-sight algorithm. In this case, the row axis is the longest, so the else part of the main if conditional would be executed.

Figure 2-6 shows the troll's path, but of course this function doesn't actually draw the path. Instead of drawing the line points, this function stores each row and

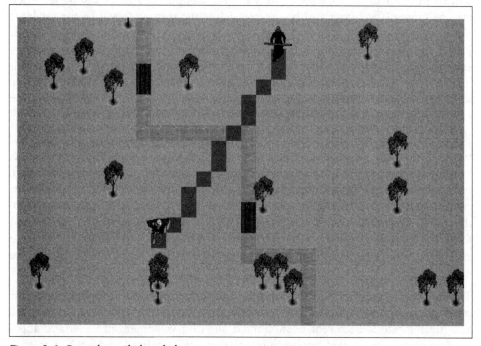

Figure 2-6. Bresenham tile-based chase

column coordinate in the pathRow and pathCol arrays. These stored values are then used by an outside function to guide the troll along a path that leads to the player.

Line-of-Sight Chasing in Continuous Environments

The Bresenham algorithm is an effective method for tiled environments. In this section we discuss a line-of-sight chase algorithm in the context of continuous environments. Specifically, we will show you how to implement a simple chase algorithm that you can use for games that incorporate physics engines where the game entities—airplanes, spaceships, hovercraft, etc.—are driven by applied forces and torques.

The example we'll discuss in this section uses a simple two-dimensional, rigid-body physics engine to calculate the motion of the predator and prey vehicles. You can download the complete source code for this sample program, *AIDemo2-2*, from this book's web site. We'll cover as much rigid-body physics as necessary to get through the example, but we won't go into great detail. For thorough coverage of this subject, refer to *Physics for Game Developers* (O'Reilly).

Here's the scenario. The player controls his vehicle by applying thrust for forward motion and steering forces for turning. The computer-controlled vehicle uses the same mechanics as the player's vehicle does, but the computer controls the thrust and steering forces for its vehicle. We want the computer to chase the player wherever he moves. The player will be the prey while the computer will be the predator. We're assuming that the only information the predator has about the prey is the prey's current position. Knowing this, along with the predator's current position, enables us to construct a line of sight from the predator to the prey. We will use this line of sight to decide how to steer the predator toward the prey. (In the next section we'll show you another method that assumes knowledge of the player's position and velocity expressed as a vector.)

Before getting to the chase algorithm, we want to explain how the predator and prey vehicles will move. The vehicles are identical in that both are pushed about by some applied thrust force and both can turn via activation of steering forces. To turn right, a steering force is applied that will push the nose of the vehicle to the right. Likewise, to turn left, a steering force is applied that will push the nose of the vehicle to the left. For the purposes of this example, we assume that the steering forces are bow thrusters—for example, they could be little jets located on the front end of the vehicle that push the front end to either side. These forces are illustrated in Figure 2-7.

The line-of-sight algorithm will control activation of the steering forces for the predator so as to keep it heading toward the prey at all times. The maximum speed and turning rate of each vehicle are limited due to development of linear and angular drag forces (forces that oppose motion) that are calculated and applied to each vehicle. Also, the vehicles can't always turn on a dime. Their turning radius is a

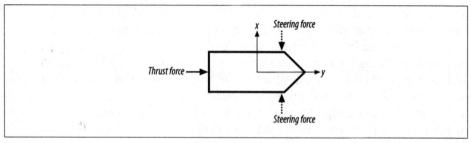

Figure 2-7. Vehicle forces

function of their linear speed—the higher their linear speed, the larger the turning radius. This makes the paths taken by each vehicle look smoother and more natural. To turn on a dime, they have to be traveling fairly slowly.

Example 2-8 shows the function that controls the steering for the predator. It gets called every time step through the simulation—that is, every cycle through the physics engine loop. What's happening here is that the predator constantly calculates the prey's location relative to itself and then adjusts its steering to keep itself pointed directly toward the prey.

Example 2-8. Line-of-sight chase function

```
void    DoLineOfSightChase (void)
{
    Vector  u, v;
    bool    left = false;
    bool    right = false;

    u = VRotate2D(−Predator.fOrientation,
                (Prey.vPosition − Predator.vPosition));

    u.Normalize();

    if (u.x <  -_TOL)
        left = true;
    else if (u.x > _TOL)
        right = true;

    Predator.SetThrusters(left, right);
}
```

As you can see, the algorithm in Example 2-8 is fairly simple. Upon entering the function, four local variables are defined. u and v are Vector types, where the Vector class is a custom class (see Appendix A) that handles all the basic vector math such as vector addition, subtraction, dot products, and cross products, among other operations. The two remaining local variables are a couple of boolean variables, left and right. These are flags that indicate which steering force to turn on; both are set to false initially.

The next line of code after the local variable definitions calculates the line of sight from the predator to the prey. Actually, this line does more than calculate the line of site. It also calculates the relative position vector between the predator and prey in global, earth-fixed coordinates via the code (Prey.vPosition - Predator.vPosition), and then it passes the resulting vector to the function VRotate2D to convert it to the predator's local, body-fixed coordinates. VRotate2D performs a standard coordinate-system transform given the body-fixed coordinate system's orientation with respect to the earth-fixed system (see the sidebar "Global & Local Coordinate Systems"). The result is stored in u, and then u is normalized—that is, it is converted to a vector of unit length.

Global & Local Coordinate Systems

A global (earth-fixed) coordinate system is fixed and does not move, whereas a local (body-fixed) coordinate system is locked onto objects that move around within the global, fixed coordinate system. A local coordinate system also rotates with the object to which it is attached.

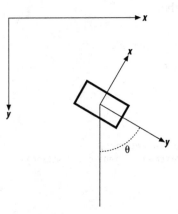

You can use the following equations to convert coordinates expressed in terms of global coordinates to an object's local coordinate system given the object's orientation relative to the global coordinate system:

$$x = X \cos \theta + Y \sin \theta$$
$$y = -X \sin \theta + Y \cos \theta$$

Here, (x, y) are the local, body-fixed coordinates of the global point (X, Y).

What we have now is a unit vector, u, pointing from the predator directly toward the prey. With this vector the next few lines of code determine whether the prey is to the port side, the starboard side, or directly in front of the predator, and steering adjustments are made accordingly. The local y-axis fixed to the predator points in the positive direction from the back to the front of the vehicle—that is, the vehicle always heads along the positive local y-axis.

So, if the x-position of the prey, in terms of the predator's local coordinate system, is negative, the prey is somewhere to the starboard side of the predator and the port steering force should be activated to correct the predator's heading so that it again points directly toward the prey. Similarly, if the prey's x-coordinate is positive, it is somewhere on the port side of the predator and the starboard steering force should be activated to correct the predator's heading. Figure 2-8 illustrates this test to determine which bow thruster to activate. If the prey's x-coordinate is zero, no steering action should be taken.

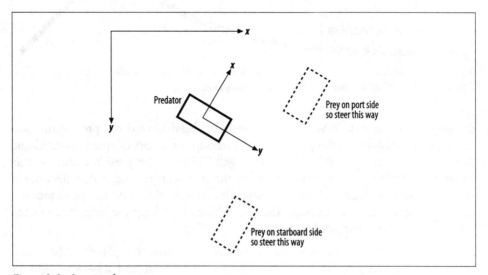

Figure 2-8. Steering force test

The last line of code calls the SetThrusters member function of the rigidbody class for the predator to apply the steering force for the current iteration through the simulation loop. In this example we assume a constant steering force, which can be tuned as desired.

The results of this algorithm are illustrated in Figure 2-9.

Figure 2-9 shows the paths taken by both the predator and the prey. At the start of the simulation, the predator was located in the lower left corner of the window while the prey was located in the lower right. Over time, the prey traveled in a straight line toward the upper left of the window. The predator's path curved as it continuously adjusted its heading to keep pointing toward the moving prey.

Just like the basic algorithm we discussed earlier in this chapter, this line-of-sight algorithm is relentless. The predator will always head directly toward the prey and most likely end up right behind it, unless it is moving so fast that it overshoots

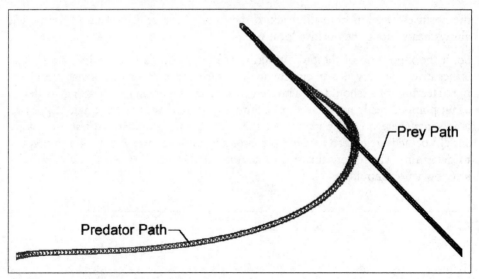

Figure 2-9. Line-of-sight chase in continuous environment

the prey, in which case it will loop around and head toward the prey again. You can prevent overshooting the prey by implementing some sort of speed control logic to allow the predator to slow down as it gets closer to the prey. You can do this by simply calculating the distance between the two vehicles, and if that distance is less than some predefined distance, reduce the forward thrust on the predator. You can calculate the distance between the two vehicles by taking the magnitude of the difference between their position vectors.

If you want the computer-controlled vehicle to evade the player rather than chase him, all you have to do is reverse the greater-than and less-than signs in Example 2-8.

Intercepting

The line-of-sight chase algorithm we discussed in the previous section in the context of continuous movement is effective in that the predator always will head directly toward the prey. The drawback to this algorithm is that heading directly toward the prey is not always the shortest path in terms of range to target or, perhaps, time to target. Further, the line-of-sight algorithm usually ends up with the predator following directly behind the prey unless the predator is faster, in which case it will overshoot the prey. A more desirable solution in many cases—for example, a missile being shot at an aircraft—is to have the predator intercept the prey at some point along the prey's trajectory. This allows the predator to take a path that is potentially shorter in terms of range or time. Further, such an algorithm could potentially allow slower predators to intercept faster prey.

To explain how the intercept algorithm works, we'll use as a basis the physics-based game scenario we described earlier. In fact, all that's required to transform the basic-chase algorithm into an intercept algorithm is the addition of a few lines of code within the chase function. Before getting to the code, though, we want to explain how the intercept algorithm works in principle. (You can apply the same algorithm, building on the line-of-sight example we discussed earlier, in tile-based games too.)

The basic idea of the intercept algorithm is to be able to predict some future position of the prey and to move toward that position so as to reach it at the same time as the prey. This is illustrated in Figure 2-10.

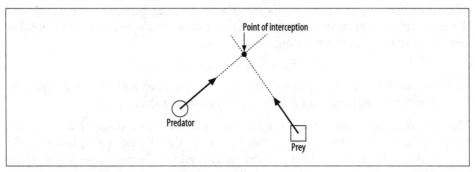

Figure 2-10. Interception

At first glance it might appear that the predicted interception point is simply the point along the trajectory of the prey that is closest to the location of the predator. This is the shortest-distance-to-the-line problem, whereby the shortest distance from a point to the line is along a line segment that is perpendicular to the line. This is not necessarily the interception point because the shortest-distance problem does not consider the relative velocities between the predator and the prey. It might be that the predator will reach the shortest-distance point on the prey's trajectory before the prey arrives. In this case the predator will have to stop and wait for the prey to arrive if it is to be intercepted. This obviously won't work if the predator is a projectile being fired at a moving target such as an aircraft. If the scenario is a role-playing game, as soon as the player sees that the predator is in his path, he'll simply turn away.

To find the point where the predator and prey will meet at the same time, you must consider their relative velocities. So, instead of just knowing the prey's current position, the predator also must know the prey's current velocity—that is, its speed and heading. This information will be used to predict where the prey will be at some time in the future. Then, that predicted position will become the target toward which the predator will head to make the interception. The predator must then continuously monitor the prey's position and velocity, along with its own, and update the predicted interception point accordingly. This facilitates the predator changing course to adapt to any evasive maneuvers the prey might make. This, of course, assumes that the predator has some sort of steering capability.

At this point you should be asking how far ahead in time you should try to predict the prey's position. The answer is that it depends on the relative positions and velocities of both the predator and the prey. Let's consider the calculations involved one step at a time.

The first thing the predator must do is to calculate the relative velocity between itself and the prey. This is called the *closing velocity* and is simply the vector difference between the prey's velocity and the predator's:

$$\mathbf{V}_r = \mathbf{V}_{prey} - \mathbf{V}_{predator}$$

Here the relative, or closing, velocity vector is denoted $\mathbf{V}_r$. The second step involves calculating the *range to close*. That's the relative distance between the predator and the prey, which is equal to the vector difference between the prey's current position and the predator's current position:

$$\mathbf{S}_r = \mathbf{S}_{prey} - \mathbf{S}_{predator}$$

Here the relative distance, or range, between the predator and prey is denoted $\mathbf{S}_r$. Now there's enough information to facilitate calculating the *time to close*.

The time to close is the average time it will take to travel a distance equal to the range to close while traveling at a speed equal to the closing speed, which is the magnitude of the closing velocity, or the relative velocity between the predator and prey. The time to close is calculated as follows:

$$t_c = |\mathbf{S}_r| / |\mathbf{V}_r|$$

The time to close, t_c, is equal to the magnitude of the range vector, $\mathbf{S}_r$, divided by the magnitude of the closing velocity vector, $\mathbf{V}_r$.

Now, knowing the time to close, you can predict where the prey will be t_c in the future. The current position of the prey is $\mathbf{S}_{prey}$ and it is traveling at $\mathbf{V}_{prey}$. Because speed multiplied by time yields average distance traveled, you can calculate how far the prey will travel over a time interval t_c traveling at $\mathbf{V}_{prey}$ and add it to the current position to yield the predicted position, as follows:

$$\mathbf{S}_t = \mathbf{S}_{prey} + (\mathbf{V}_{prey})(t_c)$$

Here, $\mathbf{S}_t$ is the predicted position of the prey t_c in the future. It's this predicted position, $\mathbf{S}_t$, that now becomes the target, or aim, point for the predator. To make the interception, the predator should head toward this point in much the same way as it headed toward the prey using the line-of-sight chase algorithm. In fact, all you need to do is to add a few lines of code to Example 2-8, the line-of-sight chase function, to convert it to an intercepting function. Example 2-9 shows the new function.

Example 2-9. Intercept function

```
void    DoIntercept(void)
{
    Vector  u, v;
    Bool    left = false;
    Bool    right = false;
```

```
Vector    Vr, Sr, St;    // added this line
Double    tc             // added this line

// added these lines:
Vr = Prey.vVelocity − Predator.vVelocity;
Sr = Prey.vPosition − Predator.vPosition;
tc = Sr.Magnitude() / Vr.Magnitude();
St = Prey.vPosition + (Prey.vVelocity * tc);

// changed this line to use St instead of Prey.vPosition:
u = VRotate2D(−Predator.fOrientation,
              (St - Predator.vPosition));

// The remainder of this function is identical to the line-of-
// sight chase function:

u.Normalize();

if (u.x <  -_TOL)
    left = true;
else if (u.x > _TOL)
    right = true;

Predator.SetThrusters(left, right);
}
```

The code in Example 2-9 is commented to highlight where we made changes to adapt the line-of-sight chase function shown in Example 2-8 to an intercept function. As you can see, we added a few lines of code to calculate the closing velocity, range, time to close, and predicted position of the prey, as discussed earlier. We also modified the line of code that calculates the target point in the predator's local co-ordinates to use the predicted position of the prey rather than its current position.

That's all there is to it. This function should be called every time through the game loop or physics engine loop so that the predator constantly updates the predicted interception point and its own trajectory.

The results of this algorithm as incorporated into example *AIDemo2-2* are illustrated in Figures 2-11 through 2-14.

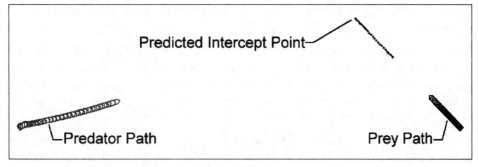

Figure 2-11. Intercept scenario 1—initial trajectories

Figure 2-11 illustrates a scenario in which the predator and prey start out from the lower left and right corners of the window, respectively. The prey moves at constant velocity from the lower right to the upper left of the window. At the same time the predator calculates the predicted interception point and heads toward it, continuously updating the predicted interception point and its heading accordingly. The predicted interception point is illustrated in this figure as the streak of dots ahead of the prey. Initially, the interception point varies as the predator turns toward the prey; however, things settle down and the interception point becomes fixed because the prey is moving at constant velocity.

After a moment the predator intercepts the prey, as shown in Figure 2-12.

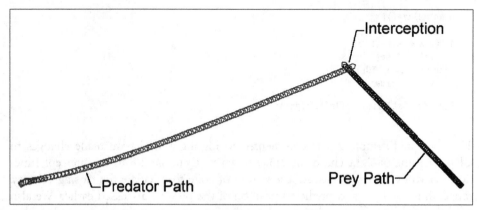

Figure 2-12. Intercept scenario 1—interception

Notice the difference between the path taken by the predator using the intercept algorithm versus that shown in Figure 2-9 using the line-of-sight algorithm. Clearly, this approach yields a shorter path and actually allows the predator and prey to cross the same point in space at the same time. In the line-of-sight algorithm, the predator chases the prey in a roundabout manner, ending up behind it. If the predator was not fast enough to keep up, it would never hit the prey and might get left behind.

Figure 2-13 shows how robust the algorithm is when the prey makes some evasive maneuvers.

Here you can see that the initial predicted intercept point, as illustrated by the trail of dots ahead of the prey, is identical to that shown in Figure 2-11. However, after the prey makes an evasive move to the right, the predicted intercept point is immediately updated and the predator takes corrective action so as to head toward the new intercept point. Figure 2-14 shows the resulting interception.

The interception algorithm we discussed here is quite robust in that it allows the predator to continuously update its trajectory to effect an interception. After experimenting with the demo, you'll see that an interception is made almost all the time.

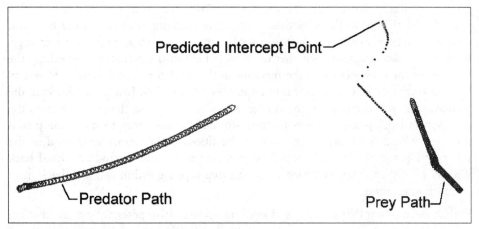

Figure 2-13. Intercept scenario 2—corrective action

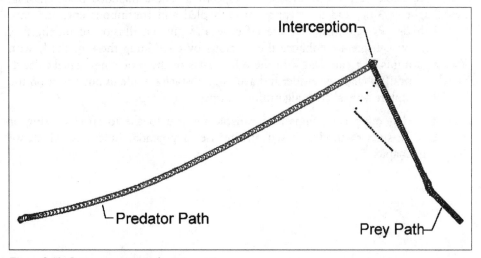

Figure 2-14. Intercept scenario 2—interception

Sometimes interceptions are not possible, however, and you should modify the algorithm we discussed here to deal with these cases. For example, if the predator is slower than the prey and if the predator somehow ends up behind the prey, it will be impossible for the predator to make an interception. It will never be able to catch up to the prey or get ahead of it to intercept it, unless the prey makes a maneuver so that the predator is no longer behind it. Even then, depending on the proximity, the prey still might not have enough speed to effect an interception.

In another example, if the predator somehow gets ahead of the prey and is moving at the same speed or faster than the prey, it will predict an interception point ahead of both the prey and the predator such that neither will reach the interception point—the interception point will constantly move away from both of them. In this case, the best thing to do is to detect when the predator is ahead of the prey and have the predator loop around or take some other action so as to get a better angle on the prey. You can detect whether the prey is behind the predator by checking the position of the prey relative to the predator in the predator's local coordinate system in a manner similar to that shown in Examples 2-8 and 2-9. Instead of checking the x-coordinate, you check the y-coordinate, and if it is negative, the prey is behind the predator and the preditor needs to turn around. An easy way to make the predator turn around is to have it go back to the line-of-sight algorithm instead of the intercept algorithm. This will make the predator turn right around and head back directly toward the prey, at which point the intercept algorithm can kick back in to effect an interception.

Earlier we told you that chasing and evading involves two, potentially three, distinct problems: deciding to chase or evade, actually effecting the chase or evasion, and obstacle avoidance. In this chapter we discussed the second problem of effecting the chase or evasion from a few different perspectives. These included basic chasing, line-of-sight chasing, and intercepting in both tiled and continuous environments. The methods we examined here are effective and give an illusion of intelligence. However, you can greatly enhance the illusions by combining these methods with other algorithms that can deal with the other parts of the problem—namely, deciding when and if to chase or evade, and avoiding obstacles while in pursuit or on the run. We'll explore several such algorithms in upcoming chapters.

Also, note that other algorithms are available for you to use to effect chasing or evading. One such method is based on the use of potential functions, which we discuss in Chapter 5.

CHAPTER 3

Pattern Movement

This chapter covers the subject of pattern movement. *Pattern movement* is a simple way to give the illusion of intelligent behavior. Basically, the computer-controlled characters move according to some predefined pattern that makes it appear as though they are performing complex, thought-out maneuvers. If you're old enough to remember the classic arcade game *Galaga*, you'll immediately know what pattern movement is all about. Recall the alien ships swooping down from the top and in from the sides of the screen, performing loops and turns, all the while shooting at your ship. The aliens, depending on their type and the level you were on, were capable of different maneuvers. These maneuvers were achieved using pattern movement algorithms.

Although *Galaga* is a classic example of using pattern movement, even modern video games use some form of pattern movement. For example, in a role-playing game or first-person shooter game, enemy monsters might patrol areas within the game world according to some predefined pattern. In a flight combat simulation, the enemy aircraft might perform evasive maneuvers according to some predefined patterns. Secondary creatures and nonplayer characters in different genres can be programmed to move in some predefined pattern to give the impression that they are wandering, feeding, or performing some task.

The standard method for implementing pattern movement takes the desired pattern and encodes the control data into an array or set of arrays. The control data consists of specific movement instructions, such as move forward and turn, that force the computer-controlled object or character to move according to the desired pattern. Using these algorithms, you can create a circle, square, zigzag, curve—any type of pattern that you can encode into a concise set of movement instructions.

In this chapter, we'll go over the standard pattern movement algorithm in generic terms before moving on to two examples that implement variations of the standard algorithm. The first example is tile-based, while the second shows how to implement pattern movement in physically simulated environments in which you must consider certain caveats specific to such environments.

Standard Algorithm

The standard pattern movement algorithm uses lists or arrays of encoded instructions, or *control instructions*, that tell the computer-controlled character how to move each step through the game loop. The array is indexed each time through the loop so that a new set of movement instructions gets processed each time through.

Example 3-1 shows a typical set of control instructions.

Example 3-1. Control instructions data structure

```
ControlData {
    double turnRight;
    double turnLeft;
    double stepForward;
    double stepBackward;
    };
```

In this example, turnRight and turnLeft would contain the number of degrees by which to turn right or left. If this were a tile-based game in which the number of directions in which a character could head is limited, turnRight and turnLeft could mean turn right or left by one increment. stepForward and stepBackward would contain the number of distance units, or tiles, by which to step forward or backward.

This control structure also could include other instructions, such as fire weapon, drop bomb, release chaff, do nothing, speed up, and slow down, among many other actions appropriate to your game.

Typically you set up a global array or set of arrays of the control structure type to store the pattern data. The data used to initialize these pattern arrays can be loaded in from a data file or can be hardcoded within the game; it really depends on your coding style and on your game's requirements.

Initialization of a pattern array, one that was hardcoded, might look something such as that shown in Example 3-2.

Example 3-2. Pattern initialization

```
Pattern[0].turnRight = 0;
Pattern[0].turnLeft = 0;
Pattern[0].stepForward = 2;
Pattern[0].stepBackward = 0;

Pattern[1].turnRight = 0;
Pattern[1].turnLeft = 0;
Pattern[1].stepForward = 2;
Pattern[1].stepBackward = 0;

Pattern[2].turnRight = 10;
Pattern[2].turnLeft = 0;
```

```
Pattern[2].stepForward = 0;
Pattern[2].stepBackward = 0;

Pattern[3].turnRight = 10;
Pattern[3].turnLeft = 0;
Pattern[3].stepForward = 0;
Pattern[3].stepBackward = 0;

Pattern[4].turnRight = 0;
Pattern[4].turnLeft = 0;
Pattern[4].stepForward = 2;
Pattern[4].stepBackward = 0;

Pattern[5].turnRight = 0;
Pattern[5].turnLeft = 0;
Pattern[5].stepForward = 2;
Pattern[5].stepBackward = 0;

Pattern[6].turnRight = 0;
Pattern[6].turnLeft = 10;
Pattern[6].stepForward = 0;
Pattern[6].stepBackward = 0;
          .
          .
          .
```

In this example, the pattern instructs the computer-controlled character to move forward 2 distance units, move forward again 2 distance units, turn right 10 degrees, turn right again 10 degrees, move forward 2 distance units, move forward again 2 distance units, and turn left 10 degrees. This specific pattern causes the computer-controlled character to move in a zigzag pattern.

To process this pattern, you need to maintain and increment an index to the pattern array each time through the game loop. Further, each time through the loop, the control instructions corresponding to the current index in the pattern array must be read and executed. Example 3-3 shows how such steps might look in code.

Example 3-3. Processing the pattern array

```
void    GameLoop(void)
{
    .
    .
    .

    Object.orientation + = Pattern[CurrentIndex].turnRight;
    Object.orientation - = Pattern[CurrentIndex].turnLeft;
    Object.x + = Pattern[CurrentIndex].stepForward;
    Object.x - = Pattern[CurrentIndex].stepBackward;

    CurrentIndex++;

    .
    .
    .

}
```

As you can see, the basic algorithm is fairly simple. Of course, implementation details will vary depending on the structure of your game.

It's also common practice to encode several different patterns in different arrays and have the computer select a pattern to execute at random or via some other decision logic within the game. Such techniques enhance the illusion of intelligence and lend more variety to the computer-controlled character's behavior.

Pattern Movement in Tiled Environments

The approach we're going to use for tile-based pattern movement is similar to the method we used for tile-based line-of-sight chasing in Chapter 2. In the line-of-sight example, we used Bresenham's line algorithm to precalculate a path between a starting point and an ending point. In this chapter, we're going to use Bresenham's line algorithm to calculate various patterns of movement. As we did in Chapter 2, we'll store the row and column positions in a set of arrays. These arrays can then be traversed to move the computer-controlled character, a troll in this example, in various patterns.

In this chapter, paths will be more complex than just a starting point and an ending point. Paths will be made up of line segments. Each new segment will begin where the previous one ended. You need to make sure the last segment ends where the first one begins to make the troll moves in a repeating pattern. This method is particularly useful when the troll is in a guarding or patrolling mode. For example, you could have the troll continuously walk around the perimeter of a campsite and then break free of the pattern only if an enemy enters the vicinity. In this case, you could use a simple rectangular pattern.

You can accomplish this rectangular pattern movement by simply calculating four line segments. In Chapter 2, the line-of-sight function cleared the contents of the row and column path arrays each time it was executed. In this case, however, each line is only a segment of the overall pattern. Therefore, we don't want to initialize the path arrays each time a segment is calculated, but rather, append each new line path to the previous one. In this example, we're going to initialize the row and column arrays before the pattern is calculated. Example 3-4 shows the function that we used to initialize the row and column path arrays.

Example 3-4. Initialize path arrays

```
void    InitializePathArrays(void)
{
    int i;

    for (i=0;i<kMaxPathLength;i++)
        {
            pathRow[i] = -1;
            pathCol[i] = -1;
        }
}
```

As Example 3-4 shows, we initialize each element of both arrays to a value of −1. We use -1 because it's not a valid coordinate in the tile-based environment. Typically, in most tile-based environments, the upper leftmost coordinate is (0,0). From that point, the row and column coordinates increase to the size of the tile map. Setting unused elements in the path arrays to −1 is a simple way to indicate which elements in the path arrays are not used. This is useful when appending one line segment to the next in the path arrays. Example 3-5 shows the modified Bresenham line-of-sight algorithm that is used to calculate line segments.

Example 3-5. Calculate line segment

```
void ai_Entity::BuildPathSegment(void)

{
    int i;
    int nextCol=col;
    int nextRow=row;
    int deltaRow=endRow-row;
    int deltaCol=endCol-col;
    int stepCol;
    int stepRow;
    int currentStep;
    int fraction;
    int i;

    for (i=0;i<kMaxPathLength;i++)
        if ((pathRow[i]==−1) && (pathCol[i]==1))
            {
                currentStep=i;
                break;
            }

    if (deltaRow < 0) stepRow=−1; else stepRow=1;
    if (deltaCol < 0) stepCol=−1; else stepCol=1;
    deltaRow=abs(deltaRow*2);
    deltaCol=abs(deltaCol*2);

    pathRow[currentStep]=nextRow;
    pathCol[currentStep]=nextCol;
    currentStep++;
    if (currentStep>=kMaxPathLength)
        return;

    if (deltaCol > deltaRow)
        {
            fraction = deltaRow * 2 - deltaCol;
            while (nextCol != endCol)
                {
                    if (fraction >= 0)
                        {
                            nextRow += stepRow;
                            fraction = fraction - deltaCol;
                        }
```

```
                    nextCol = nextCol + stepCol;
                    fraction = fraction + deltaRow;
                    pathRow[currentStep]=nextRow;
                    pathCol[currentStep]=nextCol;
                    currentStep++;
                    if (currentStep>=kMaxPathLength)
                        return;
                }
        }
    else
        {
            fraction = deltaCol * 2 - deltaRow;
            while (nextRow != endRow)
                {
                    if (fraction >= 0)
                        {
                            nextCol = nextCol + stepCol;
                            fraction = fraction - deltaRow;
                        }
                    nextRow = nextRow + stepRow;
                    fraction = fraction + deltaCol;
                    pathRow[currentStep]=nextRow;
                    pathCol[currentStep]=nextCol;
                    currentStep++;
                    if (currentStep>=kMaxPathLength)
                        return;
                }
        }
}
```

For the most part, this algorithm is very similar to the line-of-sight movement algorithm shown in Example 2-7 from Chapter 2. The major difference is that we replaced the section of code that initializes the path arrays with a new section of code. In this case, we want each new line segment to be appended to the previous one, so we don't want to initialize the path arrays each time this function is called. The new section of code determines where to begin appending the line segment. This is where we rely on the fact that we used a value of -1 to initialize the path arrays. All you need to do is simply traverse the arrays and check for the first occurrence of the value -1. This is where the new line segment begins. Using the function in Example 3-6, we're now ready to calculate the first pattern. Here, we're going to use a simple rectangular patrolling pattern. Figure 3-1 shows the desired pattern.

As you can see in Figure 3-1, we highlighted the vertex coordinates of the rectangular pattern, along with the desired direction of movement. Using this information, we can establish the troll's pattern using the BuildPathSegment function from Example 3-5. Example 3-6 shows how the rectangular pattern is initialized.

Example 3-6. Rectangular pattern

```
entityList[1].InitializePathArrays();
entityList[1].BuildPathSegment(10, 3, 18, 3);
```

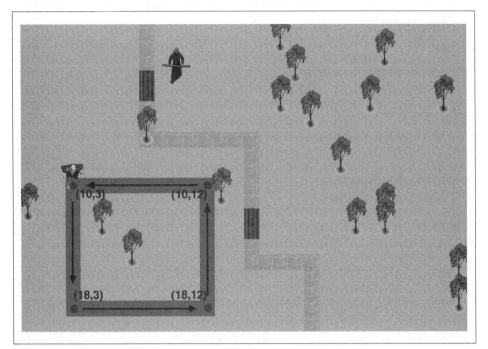

Figure 3-1. Rectangular pattern movement

```
entityList[1].BuildPathSegment(18, 3, 18, 12);
entityList[1].BuildPathSegment(18, 12, 10, 12);
entityList[1].BuildPathSegment(10, 12, 10, 3);
entityList[1].NormalizePattern();
entityList[1].patternRowOffset = 5;
entityList[1].patternColOffset = 2;
```

As you can see in Example 3-6, you first initialize the path arrays by calling the function `InitializePathArrays`. Then you use the coordinates shown in Figure 3-1 to calculate the four line segments that make up the rectangular pattern. After each line segment is calculated and stored in the path arrays, we make a call to `NormalizePattern` to adjust the resulting pattern so that it is represented in terms of relative coordinates instead of absolute coordinates. We do this so that the pattern is not tied to any specific starting position in the game world. Once the pattern is built and normalized, we can execute it from anywhere. Example 3-7 shows the `NormalizePattern` function.

Example 3-7. NormalizePattern function

```
void ai_Entity::NormalizePattern(void)
{
    int i;
    int rowOrigin=pathRow[0];
    int colOrigin=pathCol[0];
```

```
    for (i=0;i<kMaxPathLength;i++)
        if ((pathRow[i]==-1) && (pathCol[i]==-1))
            {
                pathSize=i-1;
                break;
            }

    for (i=0;i<=pathSize;i++)
        {
            pathRow[i]=pathRow[i]-rowOrigin;
            pathCol[i]=pathCol[i]-colOrigin;
        }
}
```

As you can see, all we do to normalize a pattern is subtract the starting position from all the positions stored in the pattern arrays. This yields a pattern in terms of relative coordinates so that we can execute it from anywhere in the game world.

Now that the pattern has been constructed we can traverse the arrays to make the troll walk in the rectangular pattern. You'll notice that the last two coordinates in the final segment are equal to the first two coordinates of the first line segment. This ensures that the troll walks in a repeating pattern.

You can construct any number of patterns using the BuildPathSegment function. You simply need to determine the vertex coordinates of the desired pattern and then calculate each line segment. Of course, you can use as few as two line segments or as many line segments as the program resources allow to create a movement pattern. Example 3-8 shows how you can use just two line segments to create a simple back-and-forth patrolling pattern.

Example 3-8. Simple patrolling pattern

```
entityList[1].InitializePathArrays();
entityList[1].BuildPathSegment(10, 3, 18, 3);
entityList[1].BuildPathSegment(18, 3, 10, 3);
entityList[1].NormalizePattern();
entityList[1].patternRowOffset = 5;
entityList[1].patternColOffset = 2;
```

Using the line segments shown in Example 3-8, the troll simply walks back and forth between coordinates (10,3) and (18,3). This could be useful for such tasks as patrolling near the front gate of a castle or protecting an area near a bridge. The troll could continuously repeat the pattern until an enemy comes within sight. The troll could then switch to a chasing or attacking state.

Of course, there is no real limit to how many line segments you can use to generate a movement pattern. You can use large and complex patterns for such tasks as patrolling the perimeter of a castle or continuously marching along a shoreline to guard against invaders. Example 3-9 shows a more complex pattern. This example creates a pattern made up of eight line segments.

Example 3-9. Complex patrolling pattern

```
entityList[1].BuildPathSegment(4, 2, 4, 11);
entityList[1].BuildPathSegment(4, 11, 2, 24);
entityList[1].BuildPathSegment(2, 24, 13, 27);
entityList[1].BuildPathSegment(13, 27, 16, 24);
entityList[1].BuildPathSegment(16, 24, 13, 17);
entityList[1].BuildPathSegment(13, 17, 13, 13);
entityList[1].BuildPathSegment(13, 13, 17, 5);
entityList[1].BuildPathSegment(17, 5, 4, 2);
entityList[1].NormalizePattern();
entityList[1].patternRowOffset = 5;
entityList[1].patternColOffset = 2;
```

Example 3-9 sets up a complex pattern that takes terrain elements into consideration. The troll starts on the west bank of the river, crosses the north bridge, patrols
to the south, crosses the south bridge, and then returns to its starting point to the
north. The troll then repeats the pattern. Figure 3-2 shows the pattern, along with
the vertex points used to construct it.

As Figure 3-2 shows, this method of pattern movement allows for very long and
complex patterns. This can be particularly useful when setting up long patrols
around various terrain elements.

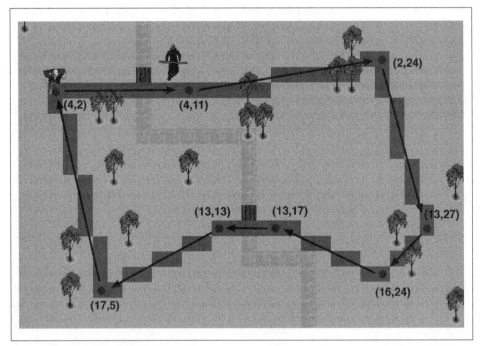

Figure 3-2. Complex tile pattern movement

Although the pattern method used in Figure 3-2 can produce long and complex patterns, these patterns can appear rather repetitive and predictable. The next method we'll look at adds a random factor, while still maintaining a movement pattern. In a tile-based environment, the game world typically is represented by a two-dimensional array. The elements in the array indicate which object is located at each row and column coordinate. For this next pattern movement method, we'll use a second two-dimensional array. This pattern matrix guides the troll along a predefined track. Each element of the pattern array contains either a 0 or a 1. The troll is allowed to move to a row and column coordinate only if the corresponding element in the pattern array contains a 1.

The first thing you must do to implement this type of pattern movement is to set up a pattern matrix. As Example 3-10 shows, you start by initializing the pattern matrix to all 0s.

Example 3-10. Initialize pattern matrix

```
for (i=0;i<kMaxRows;i++)
    for (j=0;j<kMaxCols;j++)
        pattern[i][j]=0;
```

After the entire pattern matrix is set to 0, you can begin setting the coordinates of the desired movement pattern to 1s. We're going to create a pattern by using another variation of the Bresenham line-of-sight algorithm that we used in Chapter 2. In this case, however, we're not going to save the row and column coordinates in path arrays. We're going to set the pattern matrix to 1 at each row and column coordinate along the line. We can then make multiple calls to the pattern line function to create complex patterns. Example 3-11 shows a way to set up one such pattern.

Example 3-11. Pattern Setup

```
BuildPatternSegment(3, 2, 16, 2);
BuildPatternSegment(16, 2, 16, 11);
BuildPatternSegment(16, 11, 9, 11);
BuildPatternSegment(9, 11, 9, 2);
BuildPatternSegment(9, 6, 3, 6);
BuildPatternSegment(3, 6, 3, 2);
```

Each call to the BuildPatternSegment function uses the Bresenham line algorithm to draw a new line segment to the pattern matrix. The first two function parameters are the row and column of the starting point, while the last two are the row and column of the ending point. Each point in the line becomes a 1 in the pattern matrix. This pattern is illustrated in Figure 3-3.

Figure 3-3 highlights each point where the pattern matrix contains a 1. These are the locations where the troll is allowed to move. You'll notice, however, that at certain points along the track there is more than one valid direction for the troll. We're going to rely on this fact to make the troll move in a less repetitive and predictable fashion.

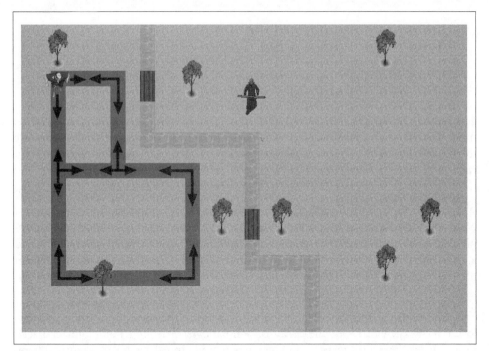

Figure 3-3. Track pattern movement

Whenever it's time to update the troll's position, we'll check each of the eight surrounding elements in the pattern array to determine which are valid moves. This is demonstrated in Example 3-12.

Example 3-12. Follow pattern matrix

```
void ai_Entity::FollowPattern(void)

{
    int i,j;
    int possibleRowPath[8]={0,0,0,0,0,0,0,0};
    int possibleColPath[8]={0,0,0,0,0,0,0,0};
    int rowOffset[8]={-1,-1,-1, 0, 0, 1, 1, 1};
    int colOffset[8]={-1, 0, 1,-1, 1,-1, 0, 1};

    j=0;
    for (i=0;i<8;i++)
        if (pattern[row+rowOffset[i]][col+colOffset[i]]==1)
            if (!(((row+rowOffset[i])==previousRow) &&
                ((col+colOffset[i])==previousCol)))
                {
                    possibleRowPath[j]=row+rowOffset[i];
                    possibleColPath[j]=col+colOffset[i];
                    j++;
                }
```

```
i=Rnd(0,j-1);
previousRow=row;
previousCol=col;

row=possibleRowPath[i];
col=possibleColPath[i];
```

You start by checking the pattern matrix at each of the eight points around the troll's current position. Whenever you find a value of 1, you save that coordinate to the possibleRowPath and possibleColPath arrays. After each point is checked, you randomly select a new coordinate from the array of valid points found. The end result is that the troll won't always turn in the same direction when it reaches an intersection in the pattern matrix.

Note that the purpose of the rowOffset and colOffset variables shown in Example 3-12 is to avoid having to write eight conditional statements. Using a loop and adding these values to the row and column position traverses the eight adjacent tiles. For example, the first two elements, when added to the current row and column, are the tiles to the upper left of the current position.

You have to consider one other point when moving the troll. The troll's previous location always will be in the array of valid moves. Selecting that point can lead to an abrupt back-and-forth movement when updating the troll's position. Therefore, you should always track the troll's previous location using the previousRow and previousCol variables. Then you can exclude that position when building the array of valid moves.

Pattern Movement in Physically Simulated Environments

So far in this chapter we discussed how to implement patterned movement in environments where you can instruct your game characters to take discrete steps or turns; but what about physically simulated environments? Surely you can take advantage of the utility of pattern movement in physically simulated environments as well. The trouble is that the benefit of using physically simulated environments—namely, letting the physics take control of movement—isn't conducive to forcing a physically simulated object to follow a specific pattern of movement. Forcing a physically simulated aircraft, for example, to a specific position or orientation each time through the game loop defeats the purpose of the underlying physical simulation. In physically simulated environments, you don't specify an object's position explicitly during the simulation. So, to implement pattern movement in this case, you need to revise the algorithms we discussed earlier. Specifically, rather than use patterns that set an object's position and orientation each time through the game loop, you need to apply appropriate control forces to the object to coax it, or essentially drive it, to where you want it to go.

You saw in the second example in Chapter 2 how we used steering forces to make the predator chase his prey. You can use these same steering forces to drive your physically simulated objects so that they follow some pattern. This is, in fact, an approximation to simulating an intelligent creature at the helm of such a physically simulated vehicle. By applying control forces, you essentially are mimicking the behavior of the driver piloting his vehicle in some pattern. The pattern can be anything—evasive maneuvers, patrol paths, stunts—so long as you can apply the appropriate control forces, such as thrust and steering forces.

Keep in mind, however, that you don't have absolute control in this case. The physics engine and the model that governs the capabilities—such as speed and turning radius, among others—of the object being simulated still control the object's overall behavior. Your input in the form of steering forces and thrust modulation, for example, is processed by the physics engine, and the resulting behavior is a function of all inputs to the physics engine, not just yours. By letting the physics engine maintain control, we can give the computer-controlled object some sense of intelligence without forcing the object to do something the physics model does not allow. If you violate the physics model, you run the risk of ruining the immersive experience realistic physics create. Remember, our goal is to enhance that immersiveness with the addition of intelligence.

To demonstrate how to implement path movement in the context of physically simulated environments, we're going to use as a basis the scenario we described in Chapter 2 for chasing and intercepting in continuous environments. Recall that this scenario included two vehicles that we simulated using a simple two-dimensional rigid-body simulation. The computer controlled one vehicle, while the player controlled the other. In this chapter, we're going to modify that example, demonstration program *AIDemo2-2*, such that the computer-controlled vehicle moves according to predefined patterns. The resulting demonstration program is entitled *AIDemo3-2*, and you can download it from this book's Web site.

The approach we'll take in this example is very similar to the algorithms we discussed earlier. We'll use an array to store the pattern information and then step through this array, giving the appropriate pattern instructions to the computer-controlled vehicle. There are some key differences between the algorithms we discussed earlier and the one required for physics-based simulations. In the earlier algorithms, the pattern arrays stored discrete movement information—take a step left, move a step forward, turn right, turn left, and so on. Further, each time through the game loop the pattern array index was advanced so that the next move's instructions could be fetched. In physics-based simulations, you must take a different approach, which we discuss in detail in the next section.

Control Structures

As we mentioned earlier, in physics-based simulations you can't force the computer-controlled vehicle to make a discrete step forward or backward. Nor can you tell it explicitly to turn left or right. Instead, you have to feed the physics engine control force information that, in effect, pilots the computer-controlled vehicle in the pattern you desire. Further, when a control force—say, a steering force—is applied in physics-based simulations, it does not instantaneously change the motion of the object being simulated. These control forces have to act over time to effect the desired motion. This means you don't have a direct correspondence between the pattern array indices and game loop cycles; you wouldn't want that anyway. If you have a pattern array that contains a specific set of instructions to be executed each time you step through the simulation, the pattern arrays would be huge because the time steps typically taken in a physics-based simulation are very small.

To get around this, the control information contained in the pattern arrays we use here also contains information so that the computer knows how long, so to speak, each set of instructions should be applied. The algorithm works like this: the computer selects the first set of instructions from the pattern array and applies them to the vehicle being controlled. The physics engine processes those instructions each time step through the simulation until the conditions specified in the given set of instructions are met. At that point the next set of instructions from the pattern array are selected and applied. This process repeats all the way through the pattern array, or until the pattern is aborted for some other reason.

The code in Example 3-13 shows the pattern control data structure we set up for this example.

Example 3-13. Pattern movement control data structure

```
struct    ControlData {
    bool    PThrusterActive;
    bool    SThrusterActive;
    double  dHeadingLimit;
    double  dPositionLimit;
    bool    LimitHeadingChange;
    bool    LimitPositionChange;
};
```

Be aware that this control data will vary depending on what you are simulating in your game and how its underlying physics model works. In this case, the vehicle we're controlling is steered only by bow thruster forces. Thus, these are the only two control forces at our disposal with which we can implement some sort of pattern movement.

Therefore, the data structure shown in Example 3-13 contains two boolean members, PThrusterActive and SThrusterActive, which indicate whether each thruster should be activated. The next two members, dHeadingLimit and dPositionLimit, are used to determine how long each set of controls should be applied. For example, dHeadingLimit specifies a desired change in the vehicle's heading. If you want a particular instruction to turn the vehicle 45 degrees, you set this dHeadingLimit to 45.

Note that this is a relative change in heading and not an absolute orientation. If the flag `LimitHeadingChange` is set to `true`, `dHeadingLimit` is checked each time through the simulation loop while the given pattern instruction is being applied. If the vehicle's heading has changed sufficiently relative to its last heading before this instruction was applied, the next instruction should be fetched.

Similar logic applies to `dPositionLimit`. This member stores the desired change in position—that is, distance traveled relative to the position of the vehicle before the given set of instructions was applied. If `LimitPositionChange` is set to `true`, each time through the simulation loop the relative position change of the vehicle is checked against `dPositionChange` to determine if the next set of instructions should be fetched from the pattern array.

Before proceeding further, let us stress that the pattern movement algorithm we're showing you here works with relative changes in heading and position. The pattern instructions will be something such as move forward 100 ft, then turn 45 degrees to the left, then move forward another 100 ft, then turn 45 degrees to the right, and so on. The instructions will be absolute: move forward until you reach position $(x, y)_0$, then turn until you are facing southeast, then move until you reach position $(x, y)_1$, then turn until you are facing southwest, and so on.

Using relative changes in position and heading enables you to execute the stored pattern regardless of the location or initial orientation of the object being controlled. If you were to use absolute coordinates and compass directions, the patterns you use would be restricted near those coordinates. For example, you could patrol a specific area on a map using some form of pattern, but you would not be able to patrol any area on a map with the specific pattern. The latter approach, using absolute coordinates, is consistent with the algorithm we showed you in the previous tile-based example. Further, such an approach is in line with waypoint navigation, which has its own merits, as we discuss in later chapters.

Because we're using relative changes in position and heading here, you also need some means of tracking these changes from one set of pattern instructions to the next. To this end, we defined another structure that stores the changes in state of the vehicle from one set of pattern instructions to the next. Example 3-14 shows the structure.

Example 3-14. State change tracking structure

```
struct   StateChangeData {
    Vector    InitialHeading;
    Vector    InitialPosition;
    double    dHeading;
    double    dPosition;
    int       CurrentControlID;
};
```

The first two members, `InitialHeading` and `InitialPosition`, are vectors that store the heading and position of the vehicle being controlled at the moment a set of pattern instructions is selected from the pattern array. Every time the pattern array index is advanced and a new set of instructions is fetched, these two members must be updated. The next two members, dHeading and dPosition, store the changes in position and heading as the current set of pattern instructions is being applied during the simulation. Finally, CurrentControlID stores the current index in the pattern array, which indicates the current set of pattern control instructions being executed.

Pattern Definition

Now, to define some patterns, you have to fill in an array of ControlData structures with appropriate steering control instructions corresponding to the desired movement pattern. For this example, we set up three patterns. The first is a square pattern, while the second is a zigzag pattern. In an actual game, you could use the square pattern to have the vehicle patrol an area bounded by the square. You could use the zigzag pattern to have the vehicle make evasive maneuvers, such as when Navy ships zigzag through the ocean to make it more difficult for enemy submarines to attack them with torpedoes. You can define control inputs for virtually any pattern you want to simulate; you can define circles, triangles, or any arbitrary path using this method. In fact, the third pattern we included in this example is an arbitrarily shaped pattern.

For the square and zigzag patterns, we set up two global arrays called PatrolPattern and ZigZagPattern, as shown in Example 3-15.

Example 3-15. Pattern array declarations

```
#define _PATROL_ARRAY_SIZE      8
#define _ZIGZAG_ARRAY_SIZE      4

ControlData       PatrolPattern[_PATROL_ARRAY_SIZE];
ControlData       ZigZagPattern[_ZIGZAG_ARRAY_SIZE];

StateChangeData   PatternTracking;
```

As you can see, we also defined a global variable called PatternTracking that tracks changes in position and heading as these patterns get executed.

Examples 3-16 and 3-17 show how each of these two patterns is initialized with the appropriate control data. We hardcoded the pattern initialization in this demo; however, in an actual game you might prefer to load in the pattern data from a data file. Further, you can optimize the data structure using a more concise encoding, as opposed to the structure we used here for the sake of clarity.

Example 3-16. Square patrol pattern initialization

```
    PatrolPattern[0].LimitPositionChange = true;
    PatrolPattern[0].LimitHeadingChange = false;
```

```
PatrolPattern[0].dHeadingLimit = 0;
PatrolPattern[0].dPositionLimit = 200;
PatrolPattern[0].PThrusterActive = false;
PatrolPattern[0].SThrusterActive = false;

PatrolPattern[1].LimitPositionChange = false;
PatrolPattern[1].LimitHeadingChange = true;
PatrolPattern[1].dHeadingLimit = 90;
PatrolPattern[1].dPositionLimit = 0;
PatrolPattern[1].PThrusterActive = true;
PatrolPattern[1].SThrusterActive = false;

PatrolPattern[2].LimitPositionChange = true;
PatrolPattern[2].LimitHeadingChange = false;
PatrolPattern[2].dHeadingLimit = 0;
PatrolPattern[2].dPositionLimit = 200;
PatrolPattern[2].PThrusterActive = false;
PatrolPattern[2].SThrusterActive = false;

PatrolPattern[3].LimitPositionChange = false;
PatrolPattern[3].LimitHeadingChange = true;
PatrolPattern[3].dHeadingLimit = 90;
PatrolPattern[3].dPositionLimit = 0;
PatrolPattern[3].PThrusterActive = true;
PatrolPattern[3].SThrusterActive = false;

PatrolPattern[4].LimitPositionChange = true;
PatrolPattern[4].LimitHeadingChange = false;
PatrolPattern[4].dHeadingLimit = 0;
PatrolPattern[4].dPositionLimit = 200;
PatrolPattern[4].PThrusterActive = false;
PatrolPattern[4].SThrusterActive = false;

PatrolPattern[5].LimitPositionChange = false;
PatrolPattern[5].LimitHeadingChange = true;
PatrolPattern[5].dHeadingLimit = 90;
PatrolPattern[5].dPositionLimit = 0;
PatrolPattern[5].PThrusterActive = true;
PatrolPattern[5].SThrusterActive = false;

PatrolPattern[6].LimitPositionChange = true;
PatrolPattern[6].LimitHeadingChange = false;
PatrolPattern[6].dHeadingLimit = 0;
PatrolPattern[6].dPositionLimit = 200;
PatrolPattern[6].PThrusterActive = false;
PatrolPattern[6].SThrusterActive = false;

PatrolPattern[7].LimitPositionChange = false;
PatrolPattern[7].LimitHeadingChange = true;
PatrolPattern[7].dHeadingLimit = 90;
PatrolPattern[7].dPositionLimit = 0;
PatrolPattern[7].PThrusterActive = true;
PatrolPattern[7].SThrusterActive = false;
```

Example 3-17. Zigzag pattern initialization

```
ZigZagPattern[0].LimitPositionChange = true;
ZigZagPattern[0].LimitHeadingChange = false;
ZigZagPattern[0].dHeadingLimit = 0;
ZigZagPattern[0].dPositionLimit = 100;
ZigZagPattern[0].PThrusterActive = false;
ZigZagPattern[0].SThrusterActive = false;

ZigZagPattern[1].LimitPositionChange = false;
ZigZagPattern[1].LimitHeadingChange = true;
ZigZagPattern[1].dHeadingLimit = 60;
ZigZagPattern[1].dPositionLimit = 0;
ZigZagPattern[1].PThrusterActive = true;
ZigZagPattern[1].SThrusterActive = false;

ZigZagPattern[2].LimitPositionChange = true;
ZigZagPattern[2].LimitHeadingChange = false;
ZigZagPattern[2].dHeadingLimit = 0;
ZigZagPattern[2].dPositionLimit = 100;
ZigZagPattern[2].PThrusterActive = false;
ZigZagPattern[2].SThrusterActive = false;

ZigZagPattern[3].LimitPositionChange = false;
ZigZagPattern[3].LimitHeadingChange = true;
ZigZagPattern[3].dHeadingLimit = 60;
ZigZagPattern[3].dPositionLimit = 0;
ZigZagPattern[3].PThrusterActive = false;
ZigZagPattern[3].SThrusterActive = true;
```

The square pattern control inputs are fairly simple. The first set of instructions corresponding to array element [0] tells the vehicle to move forward by 200 distance units. In this case no steering forces are applied. Note here that the forward thrust acting on the vehicle already is activated and held constant. You could include thrust in the control structure for more complex patterns that include steering and speed changes.

The next set of pattern instructions, array element [1], tells the vehicle to turn right by activating the port bow thruster until the vehicle's heading has changed 90 degrees. The instructions in element [2] are identical to those in element [0] and they tell the vehicle to continue straight for 200 distance units. The remaining elements are simply a repeat of the first three—element [3] makes another 90-degree right turn, element [4] heads straight for 200 distance units, and so on. The end result is eight sets of instructions in the array that pilot the vehicle in a square pattern.

In practice you could get away with only two sets of instructions, the first two shown in Example 3-16, and still achieve a square pattern. The only difference is that you'd have to repeat those two sets of instructions four times to form a square.

The zigzag controls are similar to the square controls in that the vehicle first moves forward a bit, then turns, then moves forward some more, and then turns again.

However, this time the turns alternate from right to left, and the angle through which the vehicle turns is limited to 60 degrees rather than 90. The end result is that the vehicle moves in a zigzag fashion.

Executing the Patterns

In this example, we initialize the patterns in an `Initialize` function that gets called when the program first starts. Within that function, we also go ahead and initialize the `PatternTracking` structure by making a call to a function called `InitializePatternTracking`, which is shown in Example 3-18.

Example 3-18. InitializePatternTracking function

```
void InitializePatternTracking(void)
{
    PatternTracking.CurrentControlID = 0;
    PatternTracking.dPosition = 0;
    PatternTracking.dHeading = 0;

    PatternTracking.InitialPosition = Craft2.vPosition;
    PatternTracking.InitialHeading = Craft2.vVelocity;
    PatternTracking.InitialHeading.Normalize();
}
```

Whenever `InitializePatternTracking` is called, it copies the current position and velocity vectors for `Craft2`, the computer-controlled vehicle, and stores them in the state change data structure. The `CurrentControlID`, which is the index to the current element in the given pattern array, is set to 0, indicating the first element. Further, changes in position and heading are initialized to 0.

Of course, nothing happens if you don't have a function that actually processes these instructions. So, to that end, we defined a function called `DoPattern`, which takes a pointer to a pattern array and the number of elements in the array as parameters. This function must be called every time through the simulation loop to apply the pattern controls and step through the pattern array. In this example, we make the call to `DoPattern` within the `UpdateSimulation` function as illustrated in Example 3-19.

Example 3-19. UpdateSimulation function

```
void UpdateSimulation(void)
{

    .
    .
    .

    if(Patrol)
```

```
    {
        if(!DoPattern(PatrolPattern, _PATROL_ARRAY_SIZE))
            InitializePatternTracking();
    }

    if(ZigZag)
    {
        if(!DoPattern(ZigZagPattern, _ZIGZAG_ARRAY_SIZE))
            InitializePatternTracking();
    }

    .
    .
    .


    Craft2.UpdateBodyEuler(dt);

    .
    .
    .


}
```

In this case, we have two global variables, boolean flags, that indicate which pattern to execute. If Patrol is set to true, the square pattern is processed; whereas if ZigZag is set to true, the zigzag pattern is processed. These flags are mutually exclusive in this example.

Using such flags enables you to abort a pattern if required. For example, if in the midst of executing the patrol pattern, other logic in the game detects an enemy vehicle in the patrol area, you can set the Patrol flag to false and a Chase flag to true. This would make the computer-controlled craft stop patrolling and begin chasing the enemy.

The DoPattern function must be called before the physics engine processes all the forces and torques acting on the vehicles; otherwise, the pattern instructions will not get included in the force and torque calculations. In this case, that happens when the Craft2.UpdateBodyEuler (dt) call is made.

As you can see here in the if statements, DoPattern returns a boolean value. If the return value of DoPattern is set to false, it means the given pattern has been fully stepped through. In that case, the pattern is reinitialized so that the vehicle continues in that pattern. In a real game, you would probably have some other control logic to test for other conditions before deciding that the patrol pattern should be repeated. Detecting the presence of an enemy is a good check to make. Also, checking fuel levels might be appropriate depending on your game. You really can check anything here, it just depends on your game's requirements. This, by the way, ties into finite state machines, which we cover later.

DoPattern Function

Now, let's take a close look at the DoPattern function shown in Example 3-20.

Example 3-20. DoPattern function

```
bool    DoPattern(ControlData *pPattern, int size)
{
    int    i = PatternTracking.CurrentControlID;
    Vector    u;

    // Check to see if the next set of instructions in the pattern
    // array needs to be fetched.
    if(    (pPattern[i].LimitPositionChange &&
        (PatternTracking.dPosition >= pPattern[i].dPositionLimit)) ||
        (pPattern[i].LimitHeadingChange &&
        (PatternTracking.dHeading >= pPattern[i].dHeadingLimit)) )
    {
        InitializePatternTracking();
        i++;
        PatternTracking.CurrentControlID = i;
        if(PatternTracking.CurrentControlID >= size)
            return false;
    }

    // Calculate the change in heading since the time
    // this set of instructions was initialized.
    u = Craft2.vVelocity;
    u.Normalize();
    double P;
    P = PatternTracking.InitialHeading * u;
    PatternTracking.dHeading = fabs(acos(P) * 180 / pi);

    // Calculate the change in position since the time
    // this set of instructions was initialized.
    u = Craft2.vPosition - PatternTracking.InitialPosition;
    PatternTracking.dPosition = u.Magnitude();

    // Determine the steering force factor.
    double f;
    if(pPattern[i].LimitHeadingChange)
        f = 1 - PatternTracking.dHeading /
            pPattern[i].dHeadingLimit;
    else
        f = 1;

    if(f < 0.05) f = 0.05;

    // Apply steering forces in accordance with the current set
    // of instructions.
    Craft2.SetThrusters( pPattern[i].PThrusterActive,
            pPattern[i].SThrusterActive, f);

    return true;
}
```

The first thing DoPattern does is copy the CurrentControlID, the current index to the pattern array, to a temporary variable, i, for use later.

Next, the function checks to see if either the change in position or change in heading limits have been reached for the current set of control instructions. If so, the tracking structure is reinitialized so that the next set of instructions can be tracked. Further, the index to the pattern array is incremented and tested to see if the end of the given pattern has been reached. If so, the function simply returns false at this point; otherwise, it continues to process the pattern.

The next block of code calculates the change in the vehicle's heading since the time the current set of instructions was initialized. The vehicle's heading is obtained from its velocity vector. To calculate the change in heading as an angle, you copy the velocity vector to a temporary vector, u in this case, and normalize it. (Refer to the Appendix for a review of basic vector operations.) This gives the current heading as a unit vector. Then you take the vector dot product of the initial heading stored in the pattern-tracking structure with the unit vector, u, representing the current heading. The result is stored in the scalar variable, P. Next, using the definition of the vector dot product and noting that both vectors involved here are of unit length, you can calculate the angle between these two vectors by taking the inverse cosine of P. This yields the angle in radians, and you must multiply it by 180 and divide by pi to get degrees. Note that we also take the absolute value of the resulting angle because all we're interested in is the change in the heading angle.

The next block of code calculates the change in position of the vehicle since the time the current set of instructions was initialized. You find the change in position by taking the vector difference between the vehicle's current position and the initial position stored in the pattern tracking structure. The magnitude of the resulting vector yields the change in distance.

Next, the function determines an appropriate steering force factor to apply to the maximum available steering thruster force for the vehicle defined by the underlying physics model. You find the thrust factor by subtracting 1 from the ratio of the change in heading to the desired change in heading, which is the heading limit we are shooting for given the current set of control instructions. This factor is then passed to the SetThrusters function for the rigid-body object, Craft2, which multiplies the maximum available steering force by the given factor and applies the thrust to either the port or starboard side of the vehicle.

We clip the minimum steering force factor to a value of 0.05 so that some amount of steering force always is available. Because this is a physically simulated vehicle, it's inappropriate to just override the underlying physics and force the vehicle to a specific heading. You could do this, of course, but it would defeat the purpose of having the physics model in the first place. So, because we are applying steering forces, which act over time to steer the vehicle, and because the vehicle is not fixed to a guide rail, a certain amount of lag exists between the time we turn the steering forces on or off and the response of the vehicle. This means that if we steer hard all the way through the turn, we'll overshoot the desired change in heading. If we were targeting a 90-degree turn, we'd overshoot it a few degrees depending on the underlying physics model. Therefore, to avoid overshooting, we want to start our turn with full force but then gradually reduce the steering force as we get closer to our heading change target. This way, we turn smoothly through the desired change in heading, gradually reaching our goal without overshooting.

Compare this to turning a car. If you're going to make a right turn in your car, you initially turn the wheel all the way to the right, and as you progress through the turn you start to let the wheel go back the other way, gradually straightening your tires. You wouldn't turn the wheel hard over and keep it there until you turned 90 degrees and then suddenly release the wheel, trying not to overshoot.

Now, the reason we clip the minimum steering force is so that we actually reach our change in heading target. Using the "1 minus the change in heading ratio" formula means that the force factor goes to 0 in the limit as the actual change in heading goes to the desired change in heading. This means our change in heading would asymptote to the desired change in heading but never actually get there because the steering force would be too small or 0. The 0.05 factor is just a number we tuned for this particular model. You'll have to tune your own physics models appropriately for what you are modeling.

Results

Figures 3-4 and 3-5 show the results of this algorithm for both the square and zigzag patterns. We took these screenshots directly from the example program available for download.

In Figure 3-4 you can see that a square pattern is indeed traced out by the computer-controlled vehicle. You should notice that the corners of the square are filleted nicely—that is, they are not hard right angles. The turning radius illustrated here is a function of the physics model for this vehicle and the steering force thrust modulation we discussed a moment ago. It will be different for your specific model, and you'll have to tune the simulation as always to get satisfactory results.

Figure 3-5 shows the zigzag pattern taken from the same example program. Again, notice the smooth turns. This gives the path a rather natural look. If this were an aircraft being simulated, one would also expect to see smooth turns.

The pattern shown in Figure 3-6 consists of 10 instructions that tell the computer-controlled vehicle to go straight, turn 135 degrees right, go straight some more, turn 135 degrees left, and so on, until the pattern shown here is achieved.

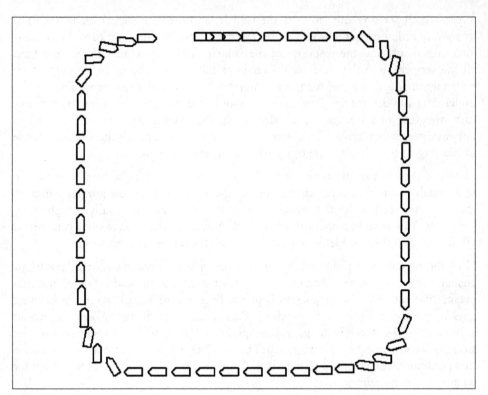

Figure 3-4. Square path

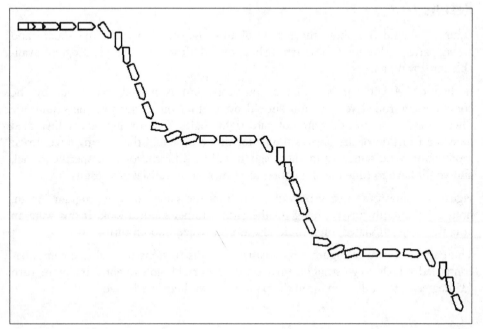

Figure 3-5. Zigzag path

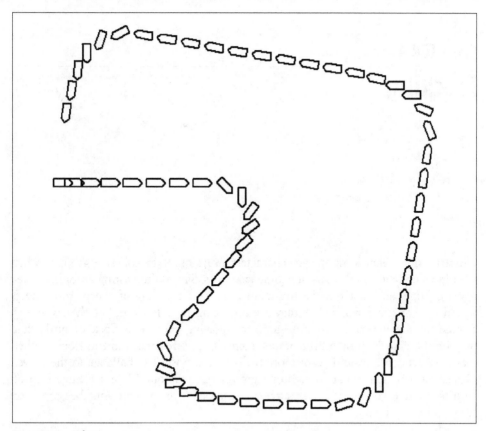

Figure 3-6. Arbitrary pattern

Just for fun, we included an arbitrary pattern in this example to show you that this algorithm does not restrict you to simple patterns such as squares and zigzags. You can encode any pattern you can imagine into a series of instructions in the same manner, enabling you to achieve seemingly intelligent movement.

CHAPTER 4
Flocking

Often in video games, nonplayer characters must move in cohesive groups rather than independently. Let's consider some examples. Say you're writing an online role-playing game, and just outside the main town is a meadow of sheep. Your sheep would appear more realistic if they were grazing in a flock rather than walking around aimlessly. Perhaps in this same role-playing game is a flock of birds that prey on the game's human inhabitants. Here again, birds that hunt in flocks rather than independently would seem more realistic and pose the challenge to the player of dealing with somewhat cooperating groups of predators. It's not a huge leap of faith to see that you could apply such flocking behavior to giant ants, bees, rats, or sea creatures as well.

These examples of local fauna moving, grazing, or attacking in herds or flocks might seem like obvious ways in which you can use flocking behavior in games. With that said, you do not need to limit such flocking behavior to fauna and can, in fact, extend it to other nonplayer characters. For example, in a real-time strategy simulation, you can use group movement behavior for nonplayer unit movement. These units can be computer-controlled humans, trolls, orcs, or mechanized vehicles of all sorts. In a combat flight simulation, you can apply such group movement to computer-controlled squadrons of aircraft. In a first-person shooter, computer-controlled enemy or friendly squads can employ such group movement. You even can use variations on basic flocking behavior to simulate crowds of people loitering around a town square, for example.

In all these examples, the idea is to have the nonplayer characters move cohesively with the illusion of having purpose. This is as opposed to a bunch of units that move about, each with their own agenda and with no semblance of coordinated group movement whatsoever.

At the heart of such group behavior lie basic flocking algorithms such as the one presented by Craig Reynolds in his 1987 SIGGRAPH paper, "Flocks, Herds, and Schools: A Distributed Behavioral Model." You can apply the algorithm Reynolds presented in its original form to simulate flocks of birds, fish, or other creatures, or in modified versions to simulate group movement of units, squads, or air squadrons. In this chapter we're going to take a close look at a basic flocking algorithm and show how you can modify it to handle such situations as obstacle avoidance. For generality, we'll use the term *units* to refer to the individual entities comprising the group—for example, birds, sheep, aircraft, humans, and so on—throughout the remainder of this chapter.

Classic Flocking

Craig Reynolds coined the term *boids* when referring to his simulated flocks. The behavior he generated very closely resembles shoals of fish or flocks of birds. All the boids can be moving in one direction at one moment, and then the next moment the tip of the flock formation can turn and the rest of the flock will follow as a wave of turning boids propagates through the flock. Reynolds' implementation is leaderless in that no one boid actually leads the flock; in a sense they all sort of follow the group, which seems to have a mind of its own. The motion Reynolds' flocking algorithm generated is quite impressive. Even more impressive is the fact that this behavior is the result of three elegantly simple rules. These rules are summarized as follows:

Cohesion
  Have each unit steer toward the average position of its neighbors.

Alignment
  Have each unit steer so as to align itself to the average heading of its neighbors.

Separation
  Have each unit steer to avoid hitting its neighbors.

It's clear from these three rule statements that each unit must be able to steer, for example, by application of steering forces. Further, each unit must be aware of its local surroundings—it has to know where its neighbors are located, where they're headed, and how close they are to it.

In physically simulated, continuous environments, you can steer by applying steering forces on the units being simulated. Here you can apply the same technique we used in the chasing, evading, and pattern movement examples earlier in the book. (Refer to Chapter 2 and, specifically, to Figure 2-7 and surrounding discussion to see how you can handle steering.) We should point out that many flocking algorithms you'll find in other printed material or on the Web use particles to represent the units, whereas here we're going to use rigid bodies such as those we covered in Chapters 2 and 3. Although particles are easier to handle in that you don't have to worry about rotation, it's very likely that in your games the units won't be particles. Instead, they'll be units with a definite volume and a well defined front and back, which makes it important to track their orientations so that while moving around, they rotate to face the direction in which they are heading. Treating the units as rigid bodies enables you to take care of orientation.

For tiled environments, you can employ the line-of-sight methods we used in the tile-based chasing and evading examples to have the units steer, or rather, head toward a specific point. For example, in the case of the cohesion rule, you'd have the unit head toward the average location, expressed as a tile coordinate, of its neighbors. (Refer to the section "Line-of-Sight Chasing" in Chapter 2.)

To what extent is each unit aware of its neighbors? Basically, each unit is aware of its local surroundings—that is, it knows the average location, heading, and separation between it and the other units in the group in its immediate vicinity. The unit does not necessarily know what the entire group is doing at any given time. Figure 4-1 illustrates a unit's local visibility.

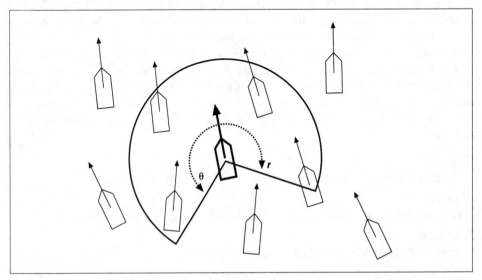

Figure 4-1. Unit visibility

Figure 4-1 illustrates a unit (the bold one in the middle of the figure) with a visibility arc of radius r around it. The unit can see all other units that fall within that arc. The visible units are used when applying the flocking rules; all the other units are ignored. The visibility arc is defined by two parameters—the arc radius, r, and the angle, θ. Both parameters affect the resulting flocking motion, and you can tune them to your needs.

In general, a large radius will allow the unit to see more of the group, which results in a more cohesive flock. That is, the flock tends to splinter into smaller flocks less often because each unit can see where most or all of the units are and steer accordingly. On the other hand, a smaller radius tends to increase the likelihood of the flock to splinter, forming smaller flocks. A flock might splinter if some units temporarily lose sight of their neighbors, which can be their link to the larger flock. When this occurs, the detached units will splinter off into a smaller flock and could perhaps rejoin the others if they happen to come within sight again. Navigating around obstacles also can cause a flock to break up. In this case, a larger radius will help the flock to rejoin the group.

The other parameter, θ, measures the field of view, so to speak, of each unit. The widest field of view is, of course, 360 degrees. Some flocking algorithms use a 360-degree field of view because it is easier to implement; however, the resulting flocking behavior might be somewhat unrealistic. A more common field of view is similar to that illustrated in Figure 4-1, where there is a distinct blind spot behind each unit. Here, again, you can tune this parameter to your liking. In general, a wide field of view, such as the one illustrated in Figure 4-2 in which the view angle is approximately 270 degrees, results in well formed flocks. A narrow field of view, such as the one illustrated in Figure 4-2 in which the view angle is a narrow 45 degrees, results in flocks that tend to look more like a line of ants walking along a path.

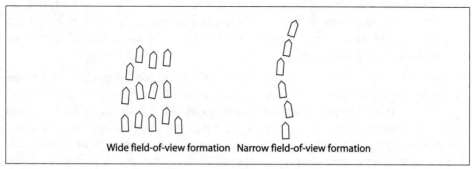

Wide field-of-view formation   Narrow field-of-view formation

Figure 4-2. Wide versus narrow field-of-view flock formations

Both results have their uses. For example, if you were simulating a squadron of fighter jets, you might use a wide field of view. If you were simulating a squad of army units sneaking up on someone, you might use a narrow field of view so that they follow each other in a line and, therefore, do not present a wide target as they make their approach. If you combine this latter case with obstacle avoidance, your units would appear to follow the point man as they sneak around obstacles.

Later, we'll build on the three flocking rules of cohesion, alignment, and separation to facilitate obstacle avoidance and leaders. But first, let's go through some example code that implements these three rules.

Flocking Example

The example we're going to look at involves simulating several units in a continuous environment. Here, we'll use the same rigid-body simulation algorithms we used in the chasing and pattern movement examples we discussed earlier. This example is named *AIDemo4*, and it's available for download from the book's Web site (*http://www.oreilly.com/catalog/ai*).

Basically, we're going to simulate about 20 units that will move around in flocks and interact with the environment and with a player. For this simple demonstration, interaction with the environment consists of avoiding circular objects. The flocking units interact with the player by chasing him.

Steering Model

For this example, we'll implement a steering model that is more or less identical to the one we used in the physics-based demo in Chapter 2. You can refer to Figure 2-8 and the surrounding discussion to refresh your memory on the steering model. Basically, we're going to treat each unit as a rigid body and apply a net steering force at the front end of the unit. This net steering force will point in either the starboard or port direction relative to the unit and will be the accumulation of steering forces determined by application of each flocking rule. This approach enables us to implement any number or combination of flocking rules—each rule makes a small contribution to the total steering force and the net result is applied to the unit once all the rules are considered.

We should caution you that this approach does require some tuning to make sure no single rule dominates. That is, you don't want the steering force contribution from a given rule to be so strong that it always overpowers the contributions from other rules. For example, if we make the steering force contribution from the cohesion rule overpower the others, and say we implement an obstacle avoidance rule so that units try to steer away from objects, if the cohesion rule dominates, the units might stay together. Therefore, they will be unable to steer around objects and might run into or through them. To mitigate this sort of unbalance, we're going to do two things: first, we're going to modulate the steering force contribution from each rule; and second, we're going to tune the steering model to make sure everything is balanced, at least most of the time.

Tuning will require trial and error. Modulating the steering forces will require that we write the steering force contribution from each rule in the form of an equation or response curve so that the contribution is not constant. Instead, we want the steering force to be a function of some key parameter important to the given rule.

Consider the avoidance rule for a moment. In this case, we're trying to prevent the units from running into each other, while at the same time enabling the units to get close to each other based on the alignment and cohesion rules. We want the avoidance rule steering force contribution to be small when the units are far away from each other, but we want the avoidance rule steering force contribution to be relatively large when the units are dangerously close to each other. This way, when the units are far apart, the cohesion rule can work to get them together and form a flock without having to fight the avoidance rule. Further, once the units are in a flock, we want the avoidance rule to be strong enough to prevent the units from colliding in spite of their tendency to want to stay together due to the cohesion and alignment rules. It's clear in this example that separation distance between units is an important parameter. Therefore, we want to write the avoidance steering force as a function of separation distance. You can use an infinite number of functions to accomplish this task; however, in our experience, a simple inverse function works fine. In this case, the avoidance steering force is inversely proportional to the separation distance. Therefore, large separation distances yield small avoidance steering forces, while small separation distances yield larger avoidance steering forces.

We'll use a similar approach for the other rules. For example, for alignment we'll consider the angle between a given unit's current heading relative to the average heading of its neighbors. If that angle is small, we want to make only a small adjustment to its heading, whereas if the angle is large, a larger adjustment is required. To achieve such behavior, we'll make the alignment steering force contribution directly proportional to the angle between the unit's current heading and the average heading of its neighbors. In the following sections, we'll look at and discuss some code that implements this steering model.

Neighbors

As we discussed earlier, each unit in a flock must be aware of its neighbors. Exactly how many neighbors each unit is aware of is a function of the field-of-view and view radius parameters shown in Figure 4-1. Because the arrangement of the units in a flock will change constantly, each unit must update its view of the world each time through the game loop. This means we must cycle through all the units in the flock collecting the required data. Note that we have to do this for each unit to acquire each unit's unique perspective. This neighbor search can become computationally expensive as the number of units grows large. The sample code we discuss shortly is written for clarity and is a good place to make some optimizations.

The example program entitled *AIDemo4*, which you can download from the book's web site (*http://www.oreilly.com/catalog/ai*), is set up similar to the examples we discussed earlier in this book. In this example, you'll find a function called UpdateSimulation that is called each time through the game, or simulation, loop. This function is responsible for updating the positions of each unit and for drawing each unit to the display buffer. Example 4-1 shows the UpdateSimulation function for this example.

Example 4-1. UpdateSimulation function

```
void    UpdateSimulation(void)
{
    double    dt = _TIMESTEP;
    int       i;
```

```
// Initialize the back buffer:
if(FrameCounter >= _RENDER_FRAME_COUNT)
{
    ClearBackBuffer();
    DrawObstacles();
}

// Update the player-controlled unit (Units[0]):
Units[0].SetThrusters(false, false, 1);

if (IsKeyDown(VK_RIGHT))
    Units[0].SetThrusters(true, false, 0.5);

if (IsKeyDown(VK_LEFT))
    Units[0].SetThrusters(false, true, 0.5);

Units[0].UpdateBodyEuler(dt);

if(Units[0].vPosition.x > _WINWIDTH) Units[0].vPosition.x = 0;
if(Units[0].vPosition.x < 0) Units[0].vPosition.x = _WINWIDTH;
if(Units[0].vPosition.y > _WINHEIGHT) Units[0].vPosition.y = 0;
if(Units[0].vPosition.y < 0) Units[0].vPosition.y = _WINHEIGHT;

if(FrameCounter >= _RENDER_FRAME_COUNT)
    DrawCraft(Units[0], RGB(0, 255, 0));

// Update the computer-controlled units:
for(i=1; i<_MAX_NUM_UNITS; i++)
{
    DoUnitAI(i);

    Units[i].UpdateBodyEuler(dt);

    if(Units[i].vPosition.x > _WINWIDTH)
        Units[i].vPosition.x = 0;
    if(Units[i].vPosition.x < 0)
        Units[i].vPosition.x = _WINWIDTH;
    if(Units[i].vPosition.y > _WINHEIGHT)
        Units[i].vPosition.y = 0;
    if(Units[i].vPosition.y < 0)
        Units[i].vPosition.y = _WINHEIGHT;

    if(FrameCounter >= _RENDER_FRAME_COUNT)
    {
        if(Units[i].Leader)
            DrawCraft(Units[i], RGB(255,0,0));
        else {
            if(Units[i].Interceptor)
                DrawCraft(Units[i], RGB(255,0,255));
            else
                DrawCraft(Units[i], RGB(0,0,255));
        }
    }
}
```

```
    }

    // Copy the back buffer to the screen:
    if(FrameCounter >= _RENDER_FRAME_COUNT) {
        CopyBackBufferToWindow();
        FrameCounter = 0;
    } else
        FrameCounter++;
}
```

UpdateSimulation performs the usual tasks. It clears the back buffer upon which the scene will be drawn; it handles any user interaction for the player-controlled unit; it updates the computer-controlled units; it draws everything to the back buffer; and it copies the back buffer to the screen when done. The interesting part for our purposes is where the computer-controlled units are updated. For this task, UpdateSimulation loops through an array of computer-controlled units and, for each one, calls another function named DoUnitAI. All the fun happens in DoUnitAI, so we'll spend the remainder of this chapter looking at this function.

DoUnitAI handles everything with regard to the computer-controlled unit's movement. All the flocking rules are implemented in this function. Before the rules are implemented, however, the function has to collect data on the given unit's neighbors. Notice here that the given unit, the one currently under consideration, is passed in as a parameter. More specifically, an array index to the current unit under consideration is passed in to DoUnitAI as the parameter i.

Example 4-2 shows a snippet of the very beginning of DoUnitAI. This snippet contains only the local variable list and initialization code. Normally, we just brush over this kind of code, but because this code contains a relatively large number of local variables and because they are used often in the flocking calculations, it's worthwhile to go through it and state exactly what each one represents.

Example 4-2. DoUnitAI initialization

```
void    DoUnitAI(int i)
{
        int     j;
        int     N;      // Number of neighbors
        Vector  Pave;   // Average position vector
        Vector  Vave;   // Average velocity vector
        Vector  Fs;     // Net steering force
        Vector  Pfs;    // Point of application of Fs
        Vector  d, u, v, w;
        double  m;
        bool    InView;
        bool    DoFlock = WideView||LimitedView||NarrowView;
        int     RadiusFactor;

        // Initialize:
```

```
Fs.x = Fs.y = Fs.z = 0;
Pave.x = Pave.y = Pave.z = 0;
Vave.x = Vave.y = Vave.z = 0;
N = 0;
Pfs.x = 0;
Pfs.y = Units[i].fLength / 2.0f;
```

.
.
.

}

We've already mentioned that the parameter, i, represents the array index to the
unit currently under consideration. This is the unit for which all the neighbor data
will be collected and the flocking rules will be implemented. The variable, j, is
used as the array index to all other units in the Units array. These are the potential
neighbors to Units[i]. N represents the number of neighbors that are within view of
the unit currently under consideration. Pave and Vave will hold the average position
and velocity vectors, respectively, of the N neighbors. Fs represents the net steering
force to be applied to the unit under consideration. **Pfs** represents the location in
body-fixed coordinates at which the steering force will be applied. d, u, v, and w are
used to store various vector quantities that are calculated throughout the function.
Such quantities include relative position vectors and heading vectors in both global
and local coordinates. m is a multiplier variable that always will be either +1 or -1.
It's used to make the steering forces point in the directions we need—that is, to
either the starboard or port side of the unit under consideration. InView is a flag that
indicates whether a particular unit is within view of the unit under consideration.
DoFlock is simply a flag that indicates whether to apply the flocking rules. In this
demo, you can turn flocking on or off. Further, you can implement three different
visibility models to see how the flock behaves. These visibility models are called
WideView, LimitedView, and NarrowView. Finally, RadiusFactor represents the r parameter
shown in Figure 4-1, which is different for each visibility model. Note the field-
of-view angle is different for each model as well; we'll talk more about this in a
moment.

After all the local variables are declared, several of them are initialized explicitly.
As you can see in Example 4-2, they are, for the most part, initialized to 0. The
variables you see listed there are the ones that are used to accumulate some value—
for example, to accumulate the steering force contributions from each rule, or to
accumulate the number of neighbors within view, and so on. The only one not
initialized to 0 is the vector **Pfs**, which represents the point of application of the
steering force vector on the unit under consideration. Here, **Pfs** is set to represent a
point on the very front and centerline of the unit. This will make the steering force
line of action offset from the unit's center of gravity so that when the steering force
is applied, the unit will move in the appropriate direction as well as turn and face
the appropriate direction.

Upon completing the initialization of local variables, DoUnitAI enters a loop to gather information about the current unit's neighbors, if there are any.

Example 4-3 contains a snippet from DoUnitAI that performs all the neighbor checks and data collection. To this end, a loop is entered, the j loop, whereby each unit in the Units array—except for Units[0] (the player-controlled unit) and Units[i] (the unit for which neighbors are being sought)—is tested to see if it is within view of the current unit. If it is, its data is collected.

Example 4-3. Neighbors

```
    .
    .
    .

for(j=1; j<_MAX_NUM_UNITS; j++)
{
    if(i!=j)
    {
        InView = false;
        d = Units[j].vPosition - Units[i].vPosition;
        w = VRotate2D(-Units[i].fOrientation, d);

        if(WideView)
        {
            InView = ((w.y > 0) || ((w.y < 0) &&
                    (fabs(w.x) >
                    fabs(w.y)*
                    _BACK_VIEW_ANGLE_FACTOR)));
            RadiusFactor = _WIDEVIEW_RADIUS_FACTOR;
        }

        if(LimitedView)
        {
            InView = (w.y > 0);
            RadiusFactor = _LIMITEDVIEW_RADIUS_FACTOR;
        }

        if(NarrowView)
        {
            InView = (((w.y > 0) && (fabs(w.x) <
                    fabs(w.y)*
                    _FRONT_VIEW_ANGLE_FACTOR)));
            RadiusFactor = _NARROWVIEW_RADIUS_FACTOR;
        }

        if(InView)
        {
            if(d.Magnitude() <= (Units[i].fLength *
                            RadiusFactor))
            {
                Pave += Units[j].vPosition;
                Vave += Units[j].vVelocity;
```

```
                N++;
        }
    }


            .
            .
            .

        }
    }


    .
    .
    .
```

After checking to make sure that i is not equal to j—that is, we aren't checking the current unit against itself—the function calculates the distance vector between the current unit, Units[i], and Units[j], which is simply the difference in their position vectors. This result is stored in the local variable, d. Next, d is converted from global coordinates to local coordinates fixed to Units[i]. The result is stored in the vector **w**.

Next, the function goes on to check to see if Units[j] is within the field of view of Units[i]. This check is a function of the field-of-view angle as illustrated in Figure 4-1; we'll check the radius value later, and only if the field-of-view check passes.

Now, because this example includes three different visibility models, three blocks of code perform field-of-view checks. These checks correspond to the wide-field-of-view, the limited-field-of-view, and the narrow-field-of-view models. As we discussed earlier, a unit's visibility influences the group's flocking behavior. You can toggle each model on or off in the example program to see their effect.

The wide-view model offers the greatest visibility and lends itself to easily formed and regrouped flocks. In this case, each unit can see directly in front of itself, to its sides, and behind itself, with the exception of a narrow blind spot directly behind itself. Figure 4-3 illustrates this field of view.

The test to determine whether Units[j] falls within this field of view consists of two parts. First, if the relative position of Units[j] in terms of local coordinates fixed to the current unit, Units[i], is such that its y-coordinate is positive, we know that Units[j] is within the field of view. Second, if the y-coordinate is negative, it could be either within the field of view or in the blind spot, so another check is required. This check looks at the x-coordinate to determine if Units[j] is located within the pie slice-shaped blind spot formed by the two straight lines that bound the visibility arc, as shown in Figure 4-3. If the absolute value of the x-coordinate of Units[j] is greater than some factor times the absolute value of the y-coordinate, we know Units[j] is located on the outside of the blind spot—that is, within the field of view. That factor times the absolute value of the y-coordinate calculation simply

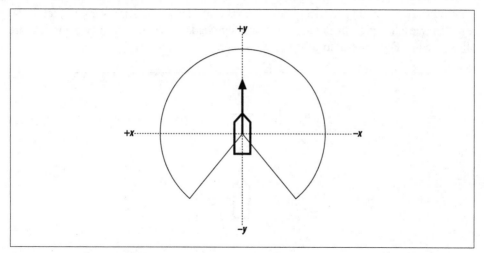

+y

+x

-x

-y

Figure 4-3. Wide field of view

represents the straight lines bounding the field-of-view arc we mentioned earlier. The code that performs this check is shown in Example 4-3, but the key part is repeated here in Example 4-4 for convenience.

Example 4-4. Wide-field-of-view check

```
        .
        .
        .

    if(WideView)
    {
        InView = ((w.y > 0) || ((w.y < 0) &&
                   (fabs(w.x) >
                fabs(w.y)*
                _BACK_VIEW_ANGLE_FACTOR)));
        RadiusFactor = _WIDEVIEW_RADIUS_FACTOR;
    }

        .
        .
        .
```

In the code shown here, the BACK_VIEW_ANGLE_FACTOR represents a field-of-view angle factor. If it is set to a value of 1, the field-of-view bounding lines will be 45 degrees from the x-axis. If the factor is greater than 1, the lines will be closer to the x-axis, essentially creating a larger blind spot. Conversely, if the factor is less than 1, the lines will be closer to the y-axis, creating a smaller blind spot.

You'll also notice here that the RadiusFactor is set to some predefined value, _WIDEVIEW_RADIUS_FACTOR. This factor controls the radius parameter shown in Figure 4-1. By the way, when tuning this example, this radius factor is one of the parameters that require adjustment to achieve the desired behavior.

The other two visibility model checks are very similar to the wide-view model; however, they each represent smaller and smaller fields of view. These two models are illustrated in Figures 4-4 and 4-5.

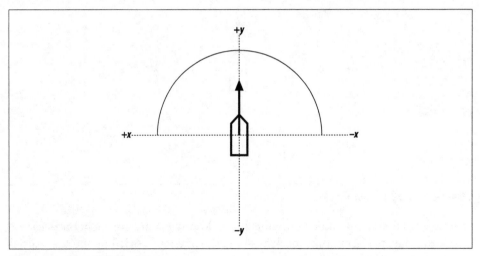

Figure 4-4. Limited field of view

In the limited-view model, the visibility arc is restricted to the local positive y-axis of the unit. This means each unit cannot see anything behind itself. In this case, the test is relatively simple, as shown in Example 4-5, where all you need to determine is whether the y-coordinate of Units[j], expressed in Units[i] local coordinates, is positive.

Example 4-5. Limited-field-of-view check

```
      .
      .
      .

            if(LimitedView)
            {
                InView = (w.y > 0);
                RadiusFactor = _LIMITEDVIEW_RADIUS_FACTOR;
            }
      .
      .
      .

```

The narrow-field-of-view model restricts each unit to seeing only what is directly in front of it, as illustrated in Figure 4-5.

The code check in this case is very similar to that for the wide-view case, where the visibility arc can be controlled by some factor. The calculations are shown in Example 4-6.

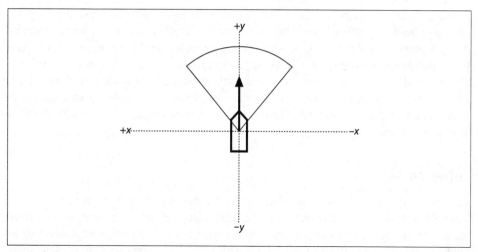

Figure 4-5. Narrow field of view

Example 4-6. Narrow-field-of-view check

```
    .
    .
    .

    if(NarrowView)
    {
        InView = (((w.y > 0) && (fabs(w.x) <
                fabs(w.y)*
            _FRONT_VIEW_ANGLE_FACTOR)));
        RadiusFactor = _NARROWVIEW_RADIUS_FACTOR;
    }

    .
    .
    .
```

In this case, the factor, _FRONT_VIEW_ANGLE_FACTOR, controls the field of view directly in front of the unit. If this factor is equal to 1, the lines bounding the view cone are 45 degrees from the x-axis. If the factor is greater than 1, the lines move closer to the x-axis, effectively increasing the field of view. If the factor is less than 1, the lines move closer to the y-axis, effectively reducing the field of view.

If any of these tests pass, depending on which view model you selected for this demo, another check is made to see if Units[j] is also within a specified distance from Units[i]. If Units[j] is within the field of view and within the specified distance, it is visible by Units[i] and will be considered a neighbor for subsequent calculations.

The last if block in Example 4-3 shows this distance test. If the magnitude of the **d** vector is less than the Units[i]'s length times the RadiusFactor, Units[j] is close enough to Units[i] to be considered a neighbor. Notice how this prescribed separation threshold is specified in terms of the unit's length times some factor. You can use any value here depending on your needs, though you'll have to tune it for your particular game; however, we like using the radius factor times the unit's length because it scales. If for some reason you decide to change the scale (the dimensions) of your game world, including the units in the game, their visibility will scale proportionately and you won't have to go back and tune some new visibility distance at the new scale.

Cohesion

Cohesion implies that we want all the units to stay together in a group; we don't want each unit breaking from the group and going its separate way. As we stated earlier, to satisfy this rule, each unit should steer toward the average position of its neighbors. Figure 4-6 illustrates a unit surrounded by several neighbors. The small dashed circle in the figure represents the average position of the four neighbors that are within view of the unit shown in bold lines with the visibility arc around itself.

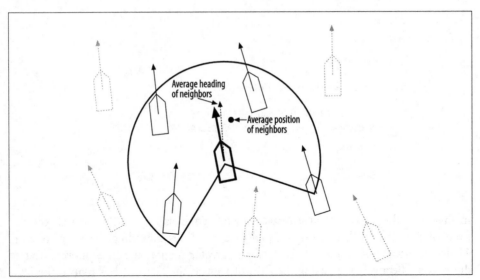

Figure 4-6. Average position and heading of neighbors

The average position of neighbors is fairly easy to calculate. Once the neighbors have been identified, their average position is the vector sum of their respective positions divided by the total number of neighbors (a scalar). The result is a vector representing their average position. Example 4-3 already shows where the positions of the neighbors are summed once they've been identified. The relevant code is repeated here in Example 4-7 for convenience.

Example 4-7. Neighbor position summation

```
        .
        .
        .
     if(InView)
     {
         if(d.Magnitude() <= (Units[i].fLength *
                              RadiusFactor))
         {
             Pave += Units[j].vPosition;
             Vave += Units[j].vVelocity;
             N++;
         }
     }


        .
        .
        .
```

The line that reads `Pave += Units[j].vPosition;` sums the position vectors of all neighbors. Remember, `Pave` and `vPosition` are `Vector` types, and the overloaded operators take care of vector addition for us.

After `DoUnitAI` takes care of identifying and collecting information on neighbors, you can apply the flocking rules. The first one handled is the cohesion rule, and the code in Example 4-8 shows how to do this.

Example 4-8. Cohesion rule

```
        .
        .
        .
     // Cohesion Rule:
     if(DoFlock && (N > 0))
     {
         Pave = Pave / N;
         v = Units[i].vVelocity;
         v.Normalize();
         u = Pave - Units[i].vPosition;
         u.Normalize();
         w = VRotate2D(-Units[i].fOrientation, u);
         if(w.x < 0) m = -1;
         if(w.x > 0) m = 1;
         if(fabs(v*u) < 1)
             Fs.x += m * _STEERINGFORCE * acos(v * u) / pi;

     }
        .
        .
        .
```

Notice that the first thing this block of code does is check to make sure the number of neighbors is greater than zero. If so, we can go ahead and calculate the average position of the neighbors. Do this by taking the vector sum of all neighbor positions, Pave, and dividing by the number of neighbors, N.

Next, the heading of the current unit under consideration, Units[i], is stored in **v** and normalized. It will be used in subsequent calculations. Now the displacement between Units[i] and the average position of its neighbors is calculated by taking the vector difference between Pave and Units[i]'s position. The result is stored in **u** and normalized. **u** is then rotated from global coordinates to local coordinates fixed to Units[i] and the result is stored in **w**. This gives the location of the average position of Units[i]'s neighbors relative to Units[i]'s current position.

Next, the multiplier, m, for the steering force is determined. If the x-coordinate of **w** is greater than zero, the average position of the neighbors is located to the starboard side of Units[i] and it has to turn left (starboard). If the x-coordinate of **w** is less than zero, Units[i] must turn right (port side).

Finally, a quick check is made to see if the dot product between the unit vectors **v** and **u** is less than 1 and greater than minus −1.* This must be done because the dot product will be used when calculating the angle between these two vectors, and the arc cosine function takes an argument between +/-1.

The last line shown in Example 4-8 is the one that actually calculates the steering force satisfying the cohesion rule. In that line the steering force is accumulated in Fs.x and is equal to the direction factor, m, times the prescribed maximum steering force times the angle between the current unit's heading and the vector from it to the average position of its neighbors divided by *pi*. The angle between the current unit's heading and the vector to the average position of its neighbors is found by taking the arc cosine of the dot product of vectors **v** and **u**. This comes from the definition of dot product. Note that the two vectors, **v** and **u**, are unit vectors. Dividing the resulting angle by *pi* yields a scale factor that gets applied to the maximum steering force. Basically, the steering force being accumulated in Fs.x is a linear function of the angle between the current unit's heading and the vector to the average position of its neighbors. This means that if the angle is large, the steering force will be relatively large, whereas if the angle is small, the steering force will be relatively small. This is exactly what we want. If the current unit is heading in a direction far from the average position of its neighbors, we want it to make a harder corrective turn. If it is heading in a direction not too far off from the average neighbor position, we want smaller corrections to its heading.

Alignment

Alignment implies that we want all the units in a flock to head in generally the same direction. To satisfy this rule, each unit should steer so as to try to assume a heading equal to the average heading of its neighbors. Referring to Figure 4-6, the

---

* Refer to the Appendix for a review of the vector dot product operation.

bold unit in the center is moving along a given heading indicated by the bold arrow attached to it. The light, dashed vector also attached to it represents the average heading of its neighbors. Therefore, for this example, the bold unit needs to steer toward the right.

We can use each unit's velocity vector to determine its heading. Normalizing each unit's velocity vector yields its heading vector. Example 4-7 shows how the heading data for a unit's neighbors is collected. The line `Vave += Units[j].vVelocity;` accumulates each neighbor's velocity vector in `Vave` in a manner similar to how positions were accumulated in `Pave`.

Example 4-9 shows how the alignment steering force is determined for each unit. The code shown here is almost identical to that shown in Example 4-8 for the cohesion rule. Here, instead of dealing with the average position of neighbors, the average heading of the current unit's neighbors is first calculated by dividing `Vave` by the number of neighbors, `N`. The result is stored in **u** and then normalized, yielding the average heading vector.

Example 4-9. Alignment rule

```
      .
      .
      .
// Alignment Rule:
if(DoFlock && (N > 0))
{
    Vave = Vave / N;
    u = Vave;
    u.Normalize();
    v = Units[i].vVelocity;
    v.Normalize();
    w = VRotate2D(-Units[i].fOrientation, u);
    if(w.x < 0) m = -1;
    if(w.x > 0) m = 1;
    if(fabs(v*u) < 1)
        Fs.x += m * _STEERINGFORCE * acos(v * u) / pi;
}
      .
      .
      .
```

Next, the heading of the current unit, `Units[i]`, is determined by taking its velocity vector and normalizing it. The result is stored in **v**. Now, the average heading of the current unit's neighbors is rotated from global coordinates to local coordinates fixed to `Units[i]` and stored in vector **w**. The steering direction factor, `m`, is then calculated in the same manner as before. And, as in the cohesion rule, the alignment steering force is accumulated in `Fs.x`.

In this case, the steering force is a linear function of the angle between the current unit's heading and the average heading of its neighbors. Here again, we want small steering corrections to be made when the current unit is heading in a direction fairly close to the average of its neighbors, whereas we want large steering corrections to be made if the current unit is heading in a direction way off from its neighbors' average heading.

Separation

Separation implies that we want the units to maintain some minimum distance away from each other, even though they might be trying to get closer to each other as a result of the cohesion and alignment rules. We don't want the units running into each other or, worse yet, coalescing at a coincident position. Therefore, we'll enforce separation by requiring the units to steer away from any neighbor that is within view and within a prescribed minimum separation distance.

Figure 4-7 illustrates a unit that is too close to a given unit, the bold one. The outer arc centered on the bold unit is the visibility arc we've already discussed. The inner arc represents the minimum separation distance. Any unit that moves within this minimum separation arc will be steered clear of it by the bold unit.

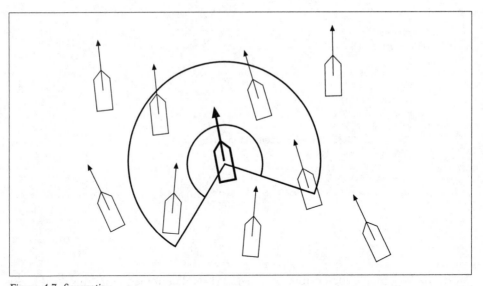

Figure 4-7. Separation

The code to handle separation is just a little different from that for cohesion and alignment because for separation, we need to look at each individual neighbor when determining suitable steering corrections rather than some average property of all the neighbors. It is convenient to include the separation code within the same j loop shown in Example 4-3 where the neighbors are identified. The new j loop, complete with the separation rule implementation, is shown in Example 4-10.

Example 4-10. Neighbors and separation

```
    .
    .
    .

for(j=1; j<_MAX_NUM_UNITS; j++)
{
  if(i!=j)
  {
      InView = false;
      d = Units[j].vPosition - Units[i].vPosition;
      w = VRotate2D(-Units[i].fOrientation, d);

      if(WideView)
      {
          InView = ((w.y > 0) || ((w.y < 0) &&
              (fabs(w.x) >
              fabs(w.y)*_BACK_VIEW_ANGLE_FACTOR)));
          RadiusFactor = _WIDEVIEW_RADIUS_FACTOR;
      }

      if(LimitedView)
      {
          InView = (w.y > 0);
          RadiusFactor = _LIMITEDVIEW_RADIUS_FACTOR;
      }

      if(NarrowView)
      {
          InView = (((w.y > 0) && (fabs(w.x) <
              fabs(w.y)*_FRONT_VIEW_ANGLE_FACTOR)));
          RadiusFactor = _NARROWVIEW_RADIUS_FACTOR;
      }

      if(InView)
      {
          if(d.Magnitude() <= (Units[i].fLength *
                              RadiusFactor))
          {
              Pave += Units[j].vPosition;
              Vave += Units[j].vVelocity;
              N++;
          }
      }

      if(InView)
      {
          if(d.Magnitude() <=
            (Units[i].fLength * _SEPARATION_FACTOR))
          {
              if(w.x < 0) m = 1;
              if(w.x > 0) m = -1;

              Fs.x += m * _STEERINGFORCE *
```

```
                    (Units[i].fLength *
                    _SEPARATION_FACTOR) /
                    d.Magnitude();
             }
          }
       }
    }

    .
    .
    .
```

The last if block contains the new separation rule code. Basically, if the j unit is in view and if it is within a distance of Units[i].fLength *_SEPARATION_FACTOR from the current unit, Units[i], we calculate and apply a steering correction. Notice that d is the distance separating Units[i] and Units[j], and was calculated at the beginning of the j loop.

Once it has been determined that Units[j] presents a potential collision, the code proceeds to calculate the corrective steering force. First, the direction factor, m, is determined so that the resulting steering force is of such a direction that the current unit, Units[i], steers away from Units[j]. In this case, m takes on the opposite sense, as in the cohesion and alignment calculations.

As in the cases of cohesion and alignment, steering forces get accumulated in Fs.x. In this case, the corrective steering force is inversely proportional to the actual separation distance. This will make the steering correction force greater the closer Units[j] gets to the current unit. Notice here again that the minimum separation distance is scaled as a function of the unit's length and some prescribed separation factor. This occurs so that separation scales just like visibility, as we discussed earlier.

We also should mention that even though separation forces are calculated here, units won't always avoid each other with 100% certainty. Sometimes the sum of all steering forces is such that one unit is forced very close to or right over an adjacent unit. Tuning all the steering force parameters helps to mitigate, though not eliminate, this situation. You could set the separation steering force so high as to override any other forces, but you'll find that the units' behavior when in close proximity to each other appears very erratic. Further, it will make it difficult to keep flocks together. In the end, depending on your game's requirements, you still might have to implement some sort of collision detection and response algorithm similar to that discussed in *Physics for Game Developers* (O'Reilly) to handle cases in which two or more units run into each other.

You also should be aware that visibility has an important effect on separation. For example, while in the wide-view visibility model, the units maintain separation very effectively; however, in the narrow-view model the units fail to maintain side-to-side separation. This is because their views are so restricted, they are unaware of other units right alongside them. If you go with such a limited-view model in your games, you'll probably have to use a separate view model, such as the wide-view model, for the separation rule. You can easily change this example to use such a separate model by replacing the last if block's condition to match the logic for determining whether a unit is in view according to the wide-view model.

Once all the flocking rules are implemented and appropriate steering forces are calculated for the current unit, DoUnitAI stores the resulting steering forces and point of application in the current unit's member variables. This is shown in Example 4-11.

Example 4-11. Set Units[i] member variables

```
void DoUnitAI(int i)

    // Do all steering force calculations...
    .
    .
    .

    Units[i].Fa = Fs;
    Units[i].Pa = Pfs;
}
```

Once DoUnitAI returns, UpdateSimulation becomes responsible for applying the new steering forces and updating the positions of the units (see Example 4-1).

Obstacle Avoidance

The flocking rules we discussed so far yield impressive results. However, such flocking behavior would be far more realistic and useful in games if the units also could avoid running into objects in the game world as they move around in a flock. As it turns out, adding such obstacle avoidance behavior is a relatively simple matter. All we have to do is provide some mechanism for the units to see ahead of them and then apply appropriate steering forces to avoid obstacles in their paths.

In this example, we'll consider a simple idealization of an obstacle—we'll consider them as circles. This need not be the case in your games; you can apply the same general approach we'll apply here for other obstacle shapes as well. The only differences will, of course, be geometry, and how you mathematically determine whether a unit is about to run into the obstacle.

To detect whether an obstacle is in the path of a unit, we'll borrow from robotics and outfit our units with virtual *feelers*. Basically, these feelers will stick out in front of the units, and if they hit something, this will be an indication to the units to turn. We'll assume that each unit can see obstacles to the extent that we can calculate to which side of the unit the obstacle is located. This will tell us whether to turn right or left.

The model we just described isn't the only one that will work. For example, you could outfit your units with more than one feeler—say, three sticking out in three different directions to sense not only whether the obstacle is present, but also to which side of the unit it is located. Wide units might require more than one feeler so that you can be sure the unit won't sideswipe an obstacle. In 3D you could use a virtual volume that extends out in front of the unit. You then could test this volume against the game-world geometry to determine an impending collision with an obstacle. You can take many approaches.

Getting back to the approach we'll discuss, take a look at Figure 4-8 to see how our single virtual feeler will work in geometric terms. The vector, **v**, represents the feeler. It's of some prescribed finite length and is collinear with the unit's heading. The large shaded circle represents an obstacle. To determine whether the feeler intersects the obstacle at some point, we need to apply a little vector math.

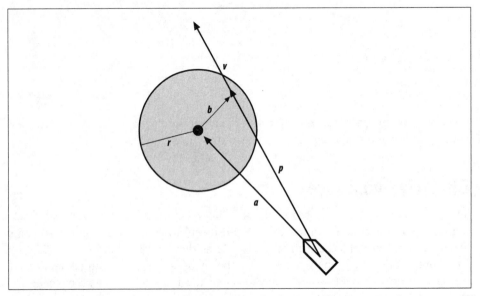

Figure 4-8. Obstacle avoidance

First, we calculate the vector, **a**. This is simply the difference between the unit's and the obstacle's positions. Next, we project **a** onto **v** by taking their dot product. This yields vector **p**. Subtracting vector **p** from **a** yields vector **b**. Now to test whether **v** intersects the circle somewhere we need to test two conditions. First, the magnitude of **p** must be less than the magnitude of **v**. Second, the magnitude of **b** must be less than the radius of the obstacle, r. If both of these tests pass, corrective steering is required; otherwise, the unit can continue on its current heading.

The steering force to be applied in the event of an impending collision is calculated in a manner similar to the flocking rules we discussed earlier. Basically, the required force is calculated as inversely proportional to the distance from the unit to the center of the obstacle. More specifically, the steering force is a function of the prescribed maximum steering force times the ratio of the magnitude of **v** to the magnitude of a. This will make the steering correction greater the closer the unit is to the obstacle, where there's more urgency to get out of the way.

Example 4-12 shows the code that you must add to DoUnitAI to perform these avoidance calculations. You insert this code just after the code that handles the three flocking rules. Notice here that all the obstacles in the game world are looped through and checked to see if there's an impending collision. Here again, in practice you'll want to optimize this code. Also notice that the corrective steering force is accumulated in the same Fs.x member variable within which the other flocking rule steering forces were accumulated.

Example 4-12. Obstacle avoidance

```
    .
    .
    .
Vector    a, p, b;

for(j=0; j<_NUM_OBSTACLES; j++)
{
    u = Units[i].vVelocity;
    u.Normalize();
    v = u * _COLLISION_VISIBILITY_FACTOR *
        Units[i].fLength;

    a = Obstacles[j] - Units[i].vPosition;
    p = (a * u) * u;
    b = p - a;

    if((b.Magnitude() < _OBSTACLE_RADIUS) &&
       (p.Magnitude() < v.Magnitude()))
    {
        // Impending collision...steer away
        w = VRotate2D(-Units[i].fOrientation, a);
        w.Normalize();
        if(w.x < 0) m = 1;
        if(w.x > 0) m = -1;
        Fs.x += m * _STEERINGFORCE *
                (_COLLISION_VISIBILITY_FACTOR *
                Units[i].fLength)/a.Magnitude();
    }
}
    .
    .
    .
```

If you download and run this example, you'll see that even while the units form flocks, they'll still steer well clear of the randomly placed circular objects. It is interesting to experiment with the different visibility models to see how the flocks behave as they encounter obstacles. With the wide-visibility model the flock tends to split and go around the obstacles on either side. In some cases, they regroup quite readily while in others they don't. With the limited- and narrow-visibility models, the units tend to form single-file lines that flow smoothly around obstacles, without splitting.

We should point out that this obstacle avoidance algorithm will not necessarily guarantee zero collisions between units and obstacles. A situation could arise such that a given unit receives conflicting steering instructions that might force it into an obstacle—for example, if a unit happens to get too close to a neighbor on one side while at the same time trying to avoid an obstacle on the other side. Depending on the relative distances from the neighbor and the obstacle, one steering force might dominate the other, causing a collision. Judicious tuning, again, can help mitigate this problem, but in practice you still might have to implement some sort of collision detection and response mechanism to properly handle these potential collisions.

Follow the Leader

Modifications to the basic flocking algorithm aren't strictly limited to obstacle avoidance. Because steering forces from a variety of rules are accumulated in the same variable and then applied all at once to control unit motion, you can effectively layer any number of rules on top of the ones we've already considered.

One such additional rule with interesting applications is a follow-the-leader rule. As we stated earlier, the flocking algorithm we discussed so far is leaderless; however, if we can combine the basic flocking algorithm with some leader-based AI, we can open up many new possibilities for the use of flocking in games.

At the moment, the three flocking rules will yield flocks that seem to randomly navigate the game world. If we add a leader to the mix, we could get flocks that move with greater purpose or with seemingly greater intelligence. For example, in an air combat simulation, the computer might control a squadron of aircraft in pursuit of the player. We could designate one of the computer-controlled aircraft as a leader and have him chase the player, while the other computer-controlled aircraft use the basic flocking rules to tail the leader, effectively acting as wingmen. Upon engaging the player, the flocking rules could be toggled off as appropriate as a dogfight ensues.

In another example, you might want to simulate a squad of army units on foot patrol through the jungle. You could designate one unit as the point man and have the other units flock behind using either a wide-visibility model or a limited one, depending on whether you want them in a bunched-up group or a single-file line.

What we'll do now with the flocking example we've been discussing is add some sort of leader capability. In this case, we won't explicitly designate any particular unit as a leader, but instead we'll let some simple rules sort out who should be or could be a leader. In this way, any unit has the potential of being a leader at any given time. This approach has the advantage of not leaving the flock leaderless in the event the leader gets destroyed or somehow separated from his flock.

Once a leader is established, we could implement any number of rules or techniques to have the leader do something meaningful. We could have the leader execute some prescribed pattern, or chase something, or perhaps evade. In this example, we'll have the leader chase or intercept the user-controlled unit. Further, we'll break up the computer-controlled units into two types: regular units and interceptors. Interceptors will be somewhat faster than regular units and will follow the intercepting algorithms we discussed earlier in this book. The regular units will travel more slowly and will follow the chase algorithms we discussed earlier. You can define or classify units in an infinite number of ways. We chose these to illustrate some possibilities.

Example 4-13 shows a few lines of code that you must add to the block of code shown in Example 4-3; the one that calculates all the neighbor data for a given unit.

Example 4-13. Leader check

```
        .
        .
        .
if(((w.y > 0) &&
    (fabs(w.x) < fabs(w.y)*_FRONT_VIEW_ANGLE_FACTOR)))
    if(d.Magnitude() <=
      (Units[i].fLength * _NARROWVIEW_RADIUS_FACTOR))
        Nf++;
        .
        .
        .


if(InView &&
   (Units[i].Interceptor == Units[j].Interceptor))
{
        .
        .
        .
}
        .
        .
        .
```

The first if block shown here performs a check, using the same narrow-visibility model we've already discussed, to determine the number of units directly in front of and within view of the current unit under consideration. Later, this information will be used to determine whether the current unit should be a leader. Essentially, if no other units are directly in front of a given unit, it becomes a leader and can have other units flocking around or behind it. If at least one unit is in front of and within view of the current unit, the current unit can't become a leader. It must follow the flocking rules only.

The second if block shown in Example 4-13 is a simple modification to the InView test. The additional code checks to make sure the types of the current unit and Units[j] are the same so that interceptor units flock with other interceptor units and regular units flock with other regular units, without mixing the two types in a flock. Therefore, if you download and run this example program and toggle one of the flocking modes on, you'll see at least two flocks form: one flock of regular units and one flock of interceptor units. (Note that the player-controlled unit will be shown in green and you can control it using the keyboard arrow keys.)

Example 4-14 shows how the leader rules are implemented for the two types of computer-controlled units.

Example 4-14. Leaders, chasing and intercepting

```
    .
    .
    .
// Chase the target if the unit is a leader
// Note: Nf is the number of units in front
// of the current unit.
if(Chase)
{
    if(Nf == 0)
        Units[i].Leader = true;
    else
        Units[i].Leader = false;

    if(Units[i].Leader)
    {
        if(!Units[i].Interceptor)
        {
            // Chase
            u = Units[0].vPosition;
            d = u - Units[i].vPosition;
            w = VRotate2D(-Units[i].fOrientation, d);
            if(w.x < 0) m = -1;
            if(w.x > 0) m = 1;
            Fs.x += m*_STEERINGFORCE;
        } else {
            // Intercept
            Vector    s1, s2, s12;
            double    tClose;
            Vector    Vr12;

            Vr12 = Units[0].vVelocity -
                    Units[i].vVelocity;
            s12 = Units[0].vPosition -
                    Units[i].vPosition;
```

```
            tClose = s12.Magnitude() /
                Vr12.Magnitude();

        s1 = Units[0].vPosition +
            (Units[0].vVelocity * tClose);
        Target = s1;
        s2 = s1 - Units[i].vPosition;
        w = VRotate2D(-Units[i].fOrientation, s2);
        if(w.x < 0) m = -1;
        if(w.x > 0) m = 1;
        Fs.x += m*_STEERINGFORCE;
        }
    }
}
.
.
.
```

If you toggle the chase option on in the example program, the Chase variable gets set to true and the block of code shown here will be executed. Within this block, a check of the number of units, Nf, in front of and within view of the current unit is made to determine whether the current unit is a leader. If Nf is set to 0, no other units are in front of the current one and it thus becomes a leader.

If the current unit is not a leader, nothing else happens; however, if it is a leader, it will execute either a chase or an intercept algorithm, depending on its type. These chase and intercept algorithms are the same as those we discussed earlier in the book, so we won't go through the code again here.

These new leader rules add some interesting behavior to the example program. In the example program, any leader will turn red and you'll easily see how any given unit can become a leader or flocking unit as the simulation progresses. Further, having just the two simple types of computer-controlled units yields some interesting tactical behavior. For example, while hunting the player unit, one flock tails the player while the other flock seems to flank the player in an attempt to intercept him. The result resembles a pincer-type maneuver.

Certainly, you can add other AI to the leaders to make their leading even more intelligent. Further, you can define and add other unit types to the mix, creating even greater variety. The possibilities are endless, and the ones we discussed here serve only as illustrations as to what's possible.

CHAPTER 5

Potential Function-Based Movement

In this chapter we're going to borrow some principles from physics and adapt them for use in game AI. Specifically, we're going to use *potential functions* to control the behavior of our computer-controlled game units in certain situations. For example, we can use potential functions in games to create swarming units, simulate crowd movement, handle chasing and evading, and avoid obstacles. The specific potential function we focus on is called the Lenard-Jones potential function. We show you what this function looks like and how to apply it in games.

How Can You Use Potential Functions for Game AI?

Let's revisit the chasing and evading problem we discussed at length in Chapter 2. If you recall, we considered a few different techniques for having a computer-controlled unit chase down or evade a player-controlled unit. Those techniques included the basic chase algorithm, in which the computer-controlled unit always moved directly toward the player, and an intercept algorithm. We can use potential functions to achieve behavior similar to what we can achieve using both of those techniques. The benefit to using potential functions here is that a single function handles both chasing and evading, and we don't need all the other conditionals and control logic associated with the algorithms we presented earlier. Further, this same potential function also can handle obstacle avoidance for us. Although this is convenient, there is a price to be paid. As we'll discuss later, the potential function algorithms can be quite CPU-intensive for large numbers of interacting game units and objects.

Another benefit to the potential function algorithm is that it is very simple to implement. All you have to do is calculate the force between the two units—the computer-controlled unit and the player in this case—and then apply that force to the front end of the computer-controlled unit, where it essentially acts as a steering force. The steering model here is similar to those we discussed in Chapters 2 and 4; however, in this case the force will always point along a line of action connecting the two units under consideration. This means the force can point in any direction relative to the computer-controlled unit, and not just to its left or right. By applying this force to the front end of the unit, we can get it to turn and head in the direction in which the force is pointing. By reversing the direction of this force, we can get a unit to either chase or evade as desired. Note that this steering force contributes to the propulsive force, or the thrust, of the unit, so you might see it speed up or slow down as it moves around.

As you've probably guessed, the examples we'll consider throughout the remainder of this chapter use the physically simulated model that you saw in earlier chapters. In fact, we use the examples from Chapters 2, 3, and 4 with some minor modifications. As before, you can find the example programs on this book's web site (*http://www.oreilly.com/catalog/ai*).

So, What Is a Potential Function?

Entire books have been written concerning potential theory as applied to all sorts of physical phenomena, and in the world of physics well-established relationships exist between potentials (as in potential energy, for example), forces, and work. However, we need not concern ourselves with too much theory to adapt the so-called *Lenard-Jones potential function* to game AI. What's important to us is how this function behaves and how we can take advantage of that behavior in our games.

$$ U = -\frac{A}{r^n} + \frac{B}{r^m} $$

This equation is the Lenard-Jones potential function. Figure 5-1 shows three graphs of this function for different values of the exponents, n and m.

In physics, the Lenard-Jones potential represents the potential energy of attraction and repulsion between molecules. Here, U represents the interatomic potential energy, which is inversely proportional to the separation distance, r, between molecules. A and B are parameters, as are the exponents m and n. If we take the derivative of this potential function, we get a function representing a force. The force function produces both attractive and repulsive forces depending on the proximity of two molecules, or in our case game units, being acted upon. It's this ability to represent both attractive and repulsive forces that will benefit us; however, instead of molecules, we're going to deal with computer-controlled units.

So, what can we do with this ability to attract or repel computer-controlled units? Well, first off we can use the Lenard-Jones function to cause our computer-controlled unit to be attracted to the player unit so that the computer-controlled

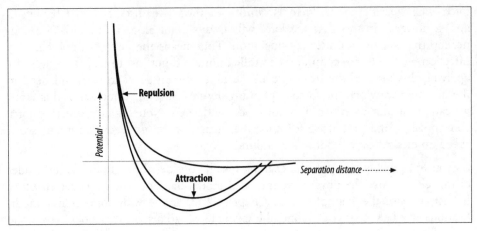

Figure 5-1. Lenard-Jones potential function

unit will chase the player. We also can tweak the parameters of the potential function to cause the computer-controlled unit to be repelled by the player, thus causing it to evade the player. Further, we can give any number of player units various weights to cause some of them to be more attractive or repulsive to the computer-controlled units than others. This will give us a means of prioritizing targets and threats.

In addition to chasing and evading, we can apply the same potential function to cause the computer-controlled units to avoid obstacles. Basically, the obstacles will repel the computer-controlled units when in close proximity, causing them to essentially steer away from them. We even can have many computer-controlled units attract one another to form a swarm. We then can apply other influences to induce the swarm to move either toward or away from a player or some other object and to avoid obstacles along the way.

The cool thing about using the Lenard-Jones potential function for these tasks is that this one simple function enables us to create all sorts of seemingly intelligent behavior.

Chasing/Evading

To show how to implement potential-based chasing (or evading), we need only add a few bits of code to *AIDemo2-2* (see Chapter 2 for more details). In that example program, we simulated the predator and prey units in a continuous environment. The function UpdateSimulation was responsible for handling user interaction and for

Lenard-Jones Potential Function

The following equation shows the Lenard-Jones potential function:

$$U = -\frac{A}{r^n} + \frac{B}{r^m}$$

In solid mechanics, U represents the interatomic potential energy, which is inversely proportional to the separation distance, r, between molecules. A and B are parameters, as are the exponents m and n. To get the interatomic force between two molecules, we take the negative of the derivative of this potential function, which yields:

$$F = -\frac{dV}{dr} = -\frac{nA}{r^{n+1}} + \frac{mB}{r^{m+1}}$$

Here, again, A, B, m, and n are parameters that are chosen to realistically model the forces of attraction and repulsion of the material under consideration. For example, these parameters would differ if a scientist were trying to model a solid (e.g., steel) versus a fluid (e.g., water). Note that the potential function has two terms: one involves $-A/r^n$, while the other involves B/r^m. The term involving A and n represents the attraction force component of the total force, while the term involving B and m represents the repulsive force component.

The repulsive component acts over a relatively short distance, r, from the object, but it has a relatively large magnitude when r gets small. The negative part of the curve that moves further away from the vertical axis represents the force of attraction. Here, the magnitude of the force is smaller but it acts over a much greater range of separation, r.

You can change the slope of the potential or force curve by adjusting the n and m parameters. This enables you to adjust the range over which repulsion or attraction dominates and affords some control over the point of transition. You can think of A and B as the strength of the attraction and repulsion forces, respectively, whereas the n and m represent the attenuation of these two force components.

updating the units every step through the game loop. We're going to add two lines to that function, as shown in Example 5-1.

Example 5-1. Chase/evade demo UpdateSimulation

```
void    UpdateSimulation(void)
{
    double dt = _TIMESTEP;
    RECT r;
```

```
    // User controls Craft1:
    Craft1.SetThrusters(false, false);

    if (IsKeyDown(VK_UP))
        Craft1.ModulateThrust(true);

    if (IsKeyDown(VK_DOWN))
        Craft1.ModulateThrust(false);

    if (IsKeyDown(VK_RIGHT))
        Craft1.SetThrusters(true, false);

    if (IsKeyDown(VK_LEFT))
        Craft1.SetThrusters(false, true);

    // Do Craft2 AI:
    .
    .
    .
    if(PotentialChase)
        DoAttractCraft2();

    // Update each craft's position:
    Craft1.UpdateBodyEuler(dt);
    Craft2.UpdateBodyEuler(dt);

    // Update the screen:
    .
    .
    .
}
```

As you can see, we added a check to see if the PotentialChase flag is set to true. If
it is, we execute the AI for Craft2, the computer-controlled unit, which now uses
the potential function. DoAttractCraft2 handles this for us. Basically, all it does is use
the potential function to calculate the force of attraction (or repulsion) between the
two units, applying the result as a steering force to the computer-controlled unit.
Example 5-2 shows DoAttractCraft2.

Example 5-2. DoAttractCraft2
```
// Apply Lenard-Jones potential force to Craft2
void    DoAttractCraft2(void)
{
    Vector  r = Craft2.vPosition - Craft1.vPosition;
    Vector  u = r;

    u.Normalize();

    double  U, A, B, n, m, d;

    A = 2000;
```

```
B = 4000;
n = 2;
m = 3;
d = r.Magnitude()/Craft2.fLength;
U = -A/pow(d, n) + B/pow(d, m);

Craft2.Fa = VRotate2D( -Craft2.fOrientation, U * u);

Craft2.Pa.x = 0;
Craft2.Pa.y = Craft2.fLength / 2;

Target = Craft1.vPosition;

}
```

The code within this function is a fairly straightforward implementation of the Lenard-Jones function. Upon entry, the function first calculates the displacement vector between Craft1 and Craft2. It does this by simply taking the vector difference between their respective positions. The result is stored in the vector **r** and a copy is placed in the vector **u** for use later. Note that **u** also is normalized.

Next, several local variables are declared corresponding to each parameter in the Lenard-Jones function. The variable names shown here directly correspond to the parameters we discussed earlier. The only new parameter is d. d represents the separation distance, r, divided by the unit's length. This yields a separation distance in terms of unit lengths rather than position units. This is done for scaling purposes, as we discussed in Chapter 4.

Aside from dividing r by d, all the other parameters are hardcoded with some constant values. You don't have to do it like this, of course; you could read those values in from some file or other source. We did it this way for clarity. As far as the actual numbers go, they were determined by tuning—i.e., they all were adjusted by trial and error until the desired results were achieved.

The line that reads U = -A/pow(d, n) + B/pow(d, m); actually calculates the steering force that will be applied to the computer-controlled unit. We used the symbol U here, but keep in mind that what we really are calculating is a force. Also, notice that U is a scalar quantity that will be either negative or positive, depending on whether the force is an attractive or repulsive force. To get the force vector, we multiply it by **u**, which is a unit vector along the line of action connecting the two units. The result is then rotated to a local coordinate system connected to Craft2 so that it can be used as a steering force. This steering force is applied to the front end of Craft2 to steer it toward or away from the target, Craft1. That's all there is to it.

Upon running this modified version of the chase program, we can see that the computer-controlled unit does indeed chase or evade the player unit depending on the parameters we've defined. Figure 5-2 shows some of the results we generated while tuning the parameters.

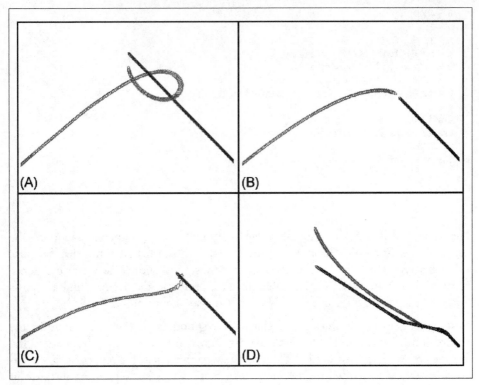

Figure 5-2. Potential chase and evade

In Figure 5-2 (A), the predator heads toward the prey and then loops around as the prey passes him by. When the predator gets too close, it turns abruptly to maintain some separation between the two units. In Figure 5-2 (B), we reduced the strength of the attraction component (we reduced parameter A somewhat), which yielded behavior resembling the interception algorithm we discussed in Chapter 2. In Figure 5-2 (C), we increased the strength of attraction and the result resembles the basic line-of-sight algorithm. Finally, in Figure 5-2 (D), we reduced the attraction force, increased the repulsion force, and adjusted the exponent parameters. This resulted in the computer-controlled unit running from the player.

Adjusting the parameters gives you a great deal of flexibility when tuning the behavior of your computer-controlled units. Further, you need not use the same parameters for each unit. You can give different parameter settings to different units to lend some variety to their behavior—to give each unit its own personality, so to speak.

You can take this a step further by combining this potential function approach with one of the other chase algorithms we discussed in Chapter 2. If you play around with *AIDemo2-2*, you'll notice that the menu selections for Potential Chase and the other chase algorithms are not mutually exclusive. This means you could turn on

Potential Chase and Basic Chase at the same time. The results are very interesting. The predator relentlessly chases the prey as expected, but when it gets within a certain radius of the prey, it holds that separation—i.e., it keeps its distance. The predator sort of hovers around the prey, constantly pointing toward the prey. If the prey were to turn and head toward the predator, the predator would turn and run until the prey stops, in which case the predator would resume shadowing the prey. In a game, you could use this behavior to control alien spacecraft as they pursue and shadow the player's jet or spacecraft. You also could use such an algorithm to create a wolf or lion that stalks its victim, keeping a safe distance until just the right moment. You even could use such behavior to have a defensive player cover a receiver in a football game. Your imagination is the only limit here, and this example serves to illustrate the power of combining different algorithms to add variety and, hopefully, to yield some sort of emergent behavior.

Obstacle Avoidance

As you've probably already realized, we can use the repelling nature of the Lenard-Jones function to our advantage when it comes to dealing with obstacles. In this case, we set the A parameter, the attraction strength, to 0 to leave only the repulsion component. We then can play with the B parameter to adjust the strength of the repulsive force and the m exponent to adjust the *attenuation*—i.e., the radius of influence of the repulsive force. This effectively enables us to simulate spherical, rigid objects. As the computer-controlled unit approaches one of these objects, a repulsive force develops that forces the unit to steer away from or around the object. Keep in mind that the magnitude of the repulsive force is a function of the separation distance. As the unit approaches the object, the force might be small, causing a rather gradual turn. However, if the unit is very close, the repulsive force will be large, which will force the unit to turn very hard.

In *AIDemo5-1*, we created several randomly placed circular objects in the scene. Then we created a computer-controlled unit and set it in motion along an initially random trajectory. The idea was to see if the unit could avoid all the obstacles. Indeed, the unit did well in avoiding the objects, as illustrated in Figure 5-3.

Here, the dark circles represent obstacles, while the swerving lines represent the trails the computer-controlled unit left behind as it navigated the scene. It's clear from this screenshot that the unit makes some gentle turns to avoid objects that are some distance away. Further, it takes some rather abrupt turns when it finds itself in very close proximity to an object. This behavior is very similar to what we achieved in the flocking examples in the previous chapter; however, we achieved the result here by using a very different mechanism.

How all this works is conceptually very simple. Each time through the game loop all the objects, stored in an array, are cycled through, and for each object the repulsion force between it and the unit is calculated. For many objects the force is small, as they might be very far from the unit, whereas for others that are close to the

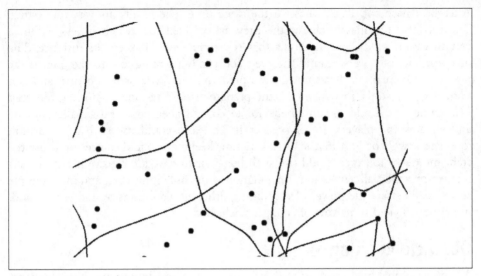

Figure 5-3. Obstacle avoidance

unit the force is much larger. All the force contributions are summed, and the net result is applied as a steering force to the unit. These calculations are illustrated in Example 5-3.

Example 5-3. Obstacle avoidance

```
void    DoUnitAI(int i)
{

        int        j;
        Vector     Fs;
        Vector     Pfs;
        Vector     r, u;
        double     U, A, B, n, m, d;

        Fs.x = Fs.y = Fs.z = 0;
        Pfs.x = 0;
        Pfs.y = Units[i].fLength / 2.0f;

        .
        .
        .

        if(Avoid)
        {
            for(j=0; j<_NUM_OBSTACLES; j++)
            {
                r = Units[i].vPosition - Obstacles[j];
                u = r;
                u.Normalize();

                A = 0;
```

```
            B = 13000;
            n = 1;
            m = 2.5;
            d = r.Magnitude()/Units[i].fLength;
            U = -A/pow(d, n) + B/pow(d, m);

            Fs += VRotate2D( -Units[i].fOrientation,
                             U * u);
        }
    }

    Units[i].Fa = Fs;
    Units[i].Pa = Pfs;
}
```

The force calculation shown here is essentially the same as the one we used in the chase example; however, in this case the A parameter is set to 0. Also, the force calculation is performed once for each object, thus the force calculation is wrapped in a for loop that traverses the Obstacles array.

You need not restrict yourself to circular or spherical obstacles. Although the repulsion force does indeed have a spherical influence, you can effectively use several of these spheres to approximate arbitrarily shaped obstacles. You can line up several of them and place them close to one another to create wall boundaries, and you even can group them using different attenuation and strength settings to approximate virtually any shape. Figure 5-4 shows an example of how to use many small, spherical obstacles to represent a box within which the unit is free to move.

In this case, we simply took example *AIDemo5-1* and distributed the obstacles in a regular fashion to create a box. We used the same algorithm shown in Example 5-3 to keep the unit from leaving the box. The trail shown in Figure 5-4 illustrates the path the unit takes as it moves around the box.

Granted, this is a simple example, but it does illustrate how you can approximate nonspherical boundaries. Theoretically, you could distribute several spherical obstacles around a racetrack to create a boundary within which you want a computer-controlled race car to navigate. These boundaries need not be used for the player, but would serve only to guide the computer-controlled unit. You could combine such boundaries with others that only attract, and then place these strategically to cause the computer-controlled unit to be biased toward a certain line or track around the racecourse. This latter technique sort of gets into waypoints, which we'll address later.

Swarming

Let's consider group behavior as yet another illustration of how to use potential functions for game AI. Specifically, let's consider swarming. This is similar to flocking, however the resulting behavior looks a bit more chaotic. Rather than a flock of

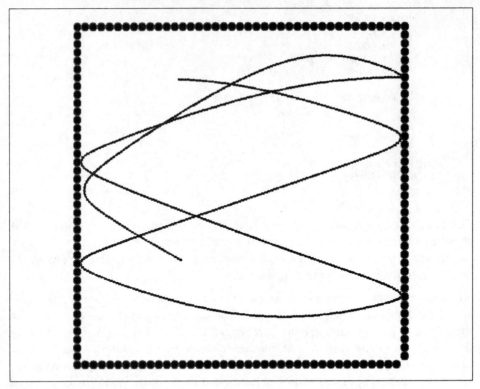

Figure 5-4. Boxed in

graceful birds, we're talking about something more like an angry swarm of bees. Using potential functions, it's easy to simulate this kind of behavior. No rules are required, as was the case for flocking. All we have to do is calculate the Lenard-Jones force between each unit in the swarm. The attractive components of those forces will make the units come together (cohesion), while the repulsive components will keep them from running over each other (avoidance).

Example 5-4 illustrates how to create a swarm using potential functions.

Example 5-4. Swarming

```
void    DoUnitAI(int i)
{

        int         j;
        Vector  Fs;
        Vector  Pfs;
        Vector  r, u;
        double  U, A, B, n, m, d;

        // begin Flock AI
```

```
Fs.x = Fs.y = Fs.z = 0;
Pfs.x = 0;
Pfs.y = Units[i].fLength / 2.0f;


if(Swarm)
{
    for(j=1; j<_MAX_NUM_UNITS; j++)
    {
        if(i!=j)
        {
            r = Units[i].vPosition -
                Units[j].vPosition;
            u = r;
            u.Normalize();

            A = 2000;
            B = 10000;
            n = 1;
            m = 2;
            d = r.Magnitude()/
                    Units[i].fLength;
            U = -A/pow(d, n) +
                    B/pow(d, m);

            Fs += VRotate2D(
                        -Units[i].fOrientation,
                        U * u);
        }
    }
}

Units[i].Fa = Fs;
Units[i].Pa = Pfs;
// end Flock AI


}
```

Here, again, the part of this code that calculates the force acting between each unit with every other unit is the same force calculation we used in the earlier examples. The main difference here is that we have to calculate this force between each and every unit. This means we'll have nested loops that index the Units array calculating the forces between Units[i] and Units[j], so long as i is not equal to j. Clearly this can result in a great many computations as the number of units in the swarm gets large. Later we'll discuss a few things that you can do to optimize this code.

For now, take a look at Figure 5-5, which illustrates the resulting swarming behavior.

It's difficult to do justice to the swarm with just a snapshot, so you should download the example program and try it for yourself to really see what the swarm looks like. In any case, Figure 5-5 (A) illustrates how the units have come together. Figure

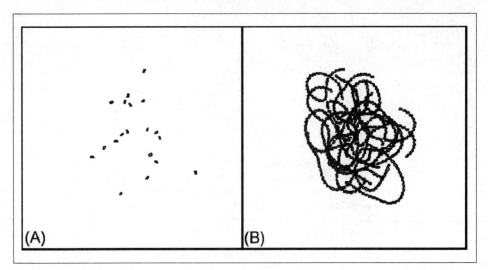

Figure 5-5. Swarm

5-5 (B) shows the paths each unit took. Clearly, the paths swirl and are intertwined. Such behavior creates a rather convincing-looking swarm of bees or flies.

You also can combine the chase and obstacle avoidance algorithms we discussed earlier with the swarming algorithm shown in Example 5-4. This would allow your swarms to not only swarm, but also to chase prey and avoid running into things along the way. Example 5-5 highlights what changes you need to make to the function shown in Example 5-4 to achieve swarms that chase prey and avoid obstacles.

Example 5-5. Swarming with chasing and obstacle avoidance

```
void    DoUnitAI(int i)
{

        int         j;
        Vector   Fs;
        Vector   Pfs;
        Vector   r, u;
        double   U, A, B, n, m, d;

        // begin Flock AI
        Fs.x = Fs.y = Fs.z = 0;
        Pfs.x = 0;
        Pfs.y = Units[i].fLength / 2.0f;


        if(Swarm)
        {
            for(j=1; j<_MAX_NUM_UNITS; j++)
            {
                if(i!=j)
```

```
            {
                r = Units[i].vPosition -
                    Units[j].vPosition;
                u = r;
                u.Normalize();

                A = 2000;
                B = 10000;
                n = 1;
                m = 2;
                d = r.Magnitude()/
                    Units[i].fLength;
                U = -A/pow(d, n) +
                    B/pow(d, m);

                Fs += VRotate2D(
                            -Units[i].fOrientation,
                            U * u);
            }
        }
    }

    if(Chase)
    {
        r = Units[i].vPosition - Units[0].vPosition;
        u = r;
        u.Normalize();

        A = 10000;
        B = 10000;
        n = 1;
        m = 2;
        d = r.Magnitude()/Units[i].fLength;
        U = -A/pow(d, n) + B/pow(d, m);

        Fs += VRotate2D( -Units[i].fOrientation, U * u);
    }

    if(Avoid)
    {
        for(j=0; j<_NUM_OBSTACLES; j++)
        {
            r = Units[i].vPosition - Obstacles[j];
            u = r;
            u.Normalize();

            A = 0;
            B = 13000;
            n = 1;
            m = 2.5;
            d = r.Magnitude()/Units[i].fLength;
            U = -A/pow(d, n) + B/pow(d, m);

            Fs += VRotate2D( -Units[i].fOrientation,
                        U * u);
```

```
        }
    }
    Units[i].Fa = Fs;
    Units[i].Pa = Pfs;
    // end Flock AI

}
```

Here, again, the actual force calculation is the same as before, and in fact we simply cut and pasted the highlighted blocks of code from the earlier examples into this one.

Swarms are not the only things for which you can use this algorithm. You also can use it to model crowd behavior. In this case, you'll have to tune the parameters to make the units move around a little more smoothly rather than erratically, like bees or flies.

Finally, we should mention that you can combine leaders with this algorithm just as we did in the flocking algorithms in the previous chapter. In this case, you need only designate a particular unit as a leader and have it attract the other units. Interestingly, in this scenario as the leader moves around, the swarm tends to organize itself into something that resembles the more graceful flocks we saw in the previous chapter.

Optimization Suggestions

You've probably already noticed that the algorithms we discussed here can become quite computationally intensive as the number of obstacles or units in a swarm increases. In the case of swarming units, the simple algorithm shown in Examples 5-4 and 5-5 is of order N^2 and would clearly become prohibitive for larger numbers of units. Therefore, optimization is very important when actually implementing these algorithms in real games. To that end, we'll offer several suggestions for optimizing the algorithms we discussed in this chapter. Keep in mind that these suggestions are general in nature and their actual implementation will vary depending on your game architecture.

The first optimization you could make to the obstacle avoidance algorithm is to simply not perform the force calculation for objects that are too far away from the unit to have any influence on it. What you could do here is put in a quick check on the separation distance between the given obstacle and the unit, and if that distance is greater than some prescribed distance, skip the force calculation. This potentially could save many division and exponent operations.

Another approach you could take is to divide your game domain into a grid containing cells of some prescribed size. You could then assign each cell an array to store indices to each obstacle that falls within that cell. Then, while the unit moves around, you can readily determine which cell it is in and perform calculations only between the unit and those obstacles contained within that cell and the immediately adjacent cells. Now, the actual size and layout of the cells would depend on your specific game, but generally such an approach could produce dramatic savings if your game domain is large and contains a large number of obstacles. The tradeoff here is, of course, increased memory requirements to store all the lists, as well as some additional bookkeeping baggage.

You could use this same grid-and-cell approach to optimize the swarming algorithm. Once you've set up a grid, each cell would be associated with a linked list. Then, each time through the game loop, you traverse the unit's array once and determine within which cell each unit lies. You add a reference to each unit in a cell to that particular cell's linked list. Then, instead of going through nested loops, comparing each unit with every other unit, you need only traverse the units in each cell's list, plus the lists for the immediately adjacent cells. Here, again, bookkeeping becomes more complicated, but the savings in CPU usage could be dramatic. This optimization technique is commonly applied in computational fluid dynamics algorithms and effectively reduces order N^2 algorithms to something close to order N.

One final suggestion we can offer is based on the observation that the force between each pair of units is equal in magnitude but opposite in direction. Therefore, once you've calculated the force between the pair of units i and j, you need not recalculate it for the pair j and i. Instead, you apply the force to i and the negative of the force to j. You'll of course have to do some bookkeeping to track which unit pairs you've already addressed so that you don't double up on the forces.

CHAPTER 6
Basic Pathfinding and Waypoints

Many different types of pathfinding problems exist. Unfortunately, no one solution is appropriate to every type of pathfinding problem. The solution depends on the specifics of the pathfinding requirements for any given game. For example, is the destination moving or stationary? Are obstacles present? If so, are the obstacles moving? What is the terrain like? Is the shortest solution always the best solution? A longer path along a road might be quicker than a shorter path over hills or swampland. It's also possible that a pathfinding problem might not even require reaching a specific destination. Perhaps you just want a game character to move around or explore the game environment intelligently. Because there are so many types of pathfinding problems, it wouldn't be appropriate to select just one solution. The A* algorithm, for example, although an ideal solution for many pathfinding problems, isn't appropriate for every situation. This chapter explores some of the techniques you can use for situations in which the A* algorithm might not be the best solution. We'll cover the venerable A* algorithm in Chapter 7.

Basic Pathfinding

At its most basic level, *pathfinding* is simply the process of moving the position of a game character from its initial location to a desired destination. This is essentially the same principle we used in the basic chasing algorithm we showed you in Chapter 2. Example 6-1 shows how you can use this algorithm for basic pathfinding.

Example 6-1. Basic pathfinding algorithm

```
if(positionX > destinationX)
    positionX--;
else if(positionX < destinationX)
    positionX++;

if(positionY > destinationY)
```

```
        positionY--;
else if(positionY < destinationY)
        positionY++;
```

In this example, the position of the game character is specified using the `positionX` and `positionY` variables. Each time this code is executed, the `positionX` and `positionY` coordinates are either increased or decreased so that the game character's position moves closer to the `destinationX` and `destinationY` coordinates. This is a simple and fast solution to a basic pathfinding problem. However, like its chasing algorithm counterpart from Chapter 2, it does have some limitations. This method produces an unnatural-looking path to the destination. The game character moves diagonally toward the goal until it reaches the point where it is on the same x- or y-axis as the destination position. It then moves in a straight horizontal or vertical path until it reaches its destination. Figure 6-1 illustrates how this looks.

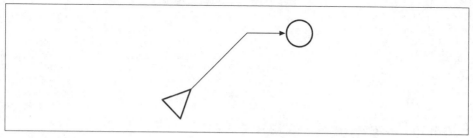

Figure 6-1. Simple path movement

As Figure 6-1 shows, the game character (the triangle) follows a rather unnatural path to the destination (the circle). A better approach would be to move in a more natural line-of-sight path. As with the line-of-sight chase function we showed you in Chapter 2, you can accomplish this by using the Bresenham line algorithm. Figure 6-2 illustrates how a line-of-sight path using the Bresenham line algorithm appears relative to the basic pathfinding algorithm shown in Example 6-1.

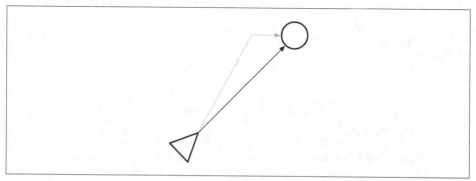

Figure 6-2. Line-of-sight path movement

As you can see in Figure 6-2, the line-of-sight approach produces a more natural-looking path. Although the line-of-sight method does have some advantages, both of the previous methods produce accurate results for basic pathfinding. They are both simple and relatively fast, so you should use them whenever possible. However, the two previous methods aren't practical in many scenarios. For example, having obstacles in the game environment, such as in Figure 6-3, can require some additional considerations.

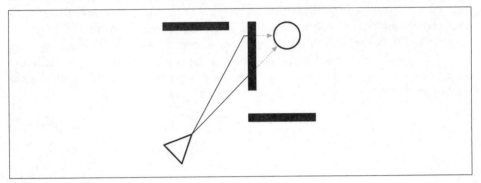

Figure 6-3. Problems with obstacles

Random Movement Obstacle Avoidance

Random movement can be a simple and effective method of obstacle avoidance. This works particularly well in an environment with relatively few obstacles. A game environment with sparsely placed trees, such as the one shown in Figure 6-4, is a good candidate for the random movement technique.

As Figure 6-4 shows, the player is not in the troll's line of sight. However, because so few obstacles are in the environment, when you simply move the troll in almost any direction the player will enter the troll's line of sight. In this scenario, a CPU-intensive pathfinding algorithm would be overkill. On the other hand, if the game environment were composed of many rooms with small doorways between each room, the random movement method probably wouldn't be an ideal solution. Example 6-2 shows the basic algorithm used for random movement obstacle avoidance.

Example 6-2. Random movement obstacle avoidance algorithm

```
if Player In Line of Sight
   {
      Follow Straight Path to Player
   }
```

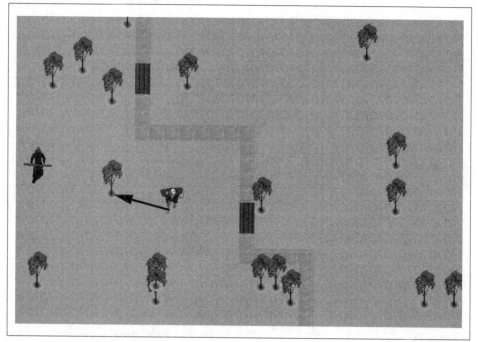

Figure 6-4. Random movement

```
else
    {
        Move in Random Direction
    }
```

As the algorithm in Example 6-2 shows, if the player is in the computer-controlled adversary's line of sight, a straight line-of-sight path is followed. If an obstacle is present, the computer-controlled character is moved in a random direction. Because so few obstacles are in the scene, it's likely that the player will be in the line of sight the next time through the game loop.

Tracing Around Obstacles

Tracing around obstacles is another relatively simple method of obstacle avoidance. This method can be effective when attempting to find a path around large obstacles, such as a mountain range in a strategy or role-playing game. With this method, the computer-controlled character follows a simple pathfinding algorithm in an attempt to reach its goal. It continues along its path until it reaches an obstacle. At that point it switches to a tracing state. In the tracing state it follows the edge of the obstacle in an attempt to work its way around it. Figure 6-5 illustrates how a hypothetical

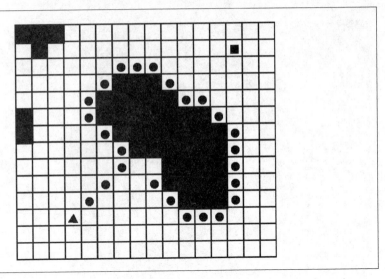

Figure 6-5. Basic tracing

computer-controlled character, shown as a triangle, would trace a path around an obstacle to get to its goal, shown as a square.

Besides showing a path around the obstacle, Figure 6-5 also shows one of the problems with tracing: deciding when to stop tracing. As Figure 6-5 shows, the outskirts of the obstacle were traced, but the tracing went too far. In fact, it's almost back to the starting point. We need a way to determine when we should switch from the tracing state back to a simple pathfinding state. One way of accomplishing this is to calculate a line from the point the tracing starts to the desired destination. The computer-controlled character will continue in the tracing state until that line is crossed, at which point it reverts to the simple pathfinding state. This is shown in Figure 6-6.

Tracing the outskirts of the obstacle until the line connecting the starting point and desired destination is crossed ensures that the path doesn't loop back to the starting point. If another obstacle is encountered after switching back to the simple pathfinding state, it once again goes into the tracing state. This continues until the destination is reached.

Another method is to incorporate a line-of-sight algorithm with the previous tracing method. Basically, at each step along the way, we utilize a line-of-sight algorithm to determine if a straight line-of-sight path can be followed to reach the destination. This method is illustrated in Figure 6-7.

As Figure 6-7 shows, we follow the outskirts of the obstacle, but at each step we check to see if the destination is in the computer-controlled character's line of sight. If so, we switch from a tracing state to a line-of-sight pathfinding state.

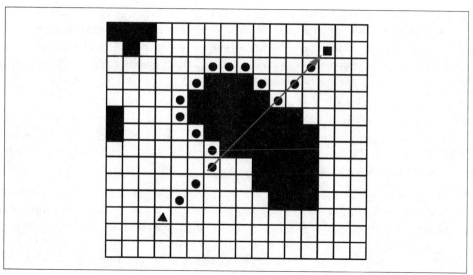

Figure 6-6. Improved tracing

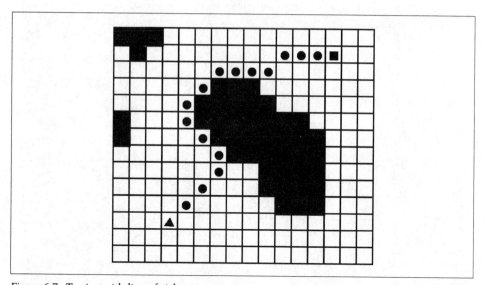

Figure 6-7. Tracing with line of sight

Breadcrumb Pathfinding

Breadcrumb pathfinding can make computer-controlled characters seem very intelligent because the player is unknowingly creating the path for the computer-controlled character. Each time the player takes a step, he unknowingly leaves an invisible marker, or breadcrumb, on the game world. When a game character comes in contact with a breadcrumb, the breadcrumb simply begins following the trail. The game character will follow in the footsteps of the player until the player is reached. The complexity of the path and the number of obstacles in the way are irrelevant. The player already has created the path, so no serious calculations are necessary.

The breadcrumb method also is an effective and efficient way to move groups of computer-controlled characters. Instead of having each member of a group use an expensive and time-consuming pathfinding algorithm, you can simply have each member follow the leader's breadcrumbs.

Figure 6-8 shows how each step the player takes is marked with an integer value. In this case, a maximum of 15 steps are recorded. In a real game, the number of breadcrumbs dropped will depend on the particular game and how smart you want the game-controlled characters to appear. In this example, a troll randomly moves about the tile-based environment until it detects a breadcrumb on an adjacent location.

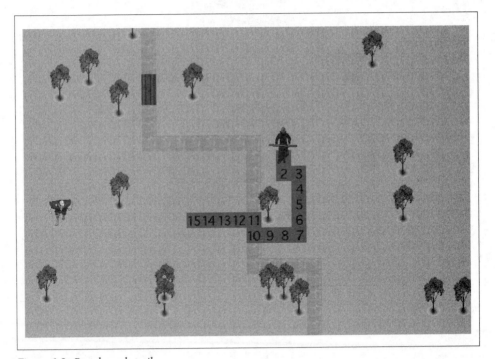

Figure 6-8. Breadcrumb trail

Of course, in a real game, the player never sees the breadcrumb trail. It's there exclusively for the game AI. Example 6-3 shows the class we use to track the data associated with each game character.

Example 6-3. ai_Entity class

```
#define  kMaxTrailLength  15

class  ai_Entity
{
    public:
    int  row;
    int  col;
    int  type;
    int  state;
    int  trailRow[kMaxTrailLength];
    int  trailCol[kMaxTrailLength];

    ai_Entity();
    ~ai_Entity();

};
```

The initial #define statement sets the maximum number of player steps to track. We then use the kMaxTrailLength constant to define the bounds for the trailRow and trailCol arrays. The trailRow and trailCol arrays store the row and column coordinates of the previous 15 steps taken by the player.

As Example 6-4 shows, we begin by setting each element of the trailRow and trailCol arrays to a value of -1. We use -1 because it's a value outside of the coordinate system we are using for this tile-based demo. When the demo first starts, the player hasn't taken any steps, so we need a way to recognize that some of the elements in the trailRow and trailCol arrays haven't been set yet.

Example 6-4. Trail array initialization

```
int  i;

for (i=0;i<kMaxTrailLength;i++)
  {
    trailRow[i]=-1;
    trailCol[i]=-1;
  }
```

As you can see in Example 6-4, we traverse the entire trailRow and trailCol arrays, setting each value to -1. We are now ready to start recording the actual footsteps. The most logical place to do this is in the function that changes the player's position. Here we'll use the KeyDown function. This is where the demo checks the four direction keys and then changes the player's position if a key-down event is detected. The KeyDown function is shown in Example 6-5.

Example 6-5. Recording the player positions

```
void ai_World::KeyDown(int key)
{
    int  i;
```

```
if (key==kUpKey)
    for (i=0;i<kMaxEntities;i++)
        if (entityList[i].state==kPlayer)
            if (entityList[i].row>0)
                {
                    entityList[i].row--;
                    DropBreadCrumb();
                }

if (key==kDownKey)
    for (i=0;i<kMaxEntities;i++)
        if (entityList[i].state==kPlayer)
            if (entityList[i].row<(kMaxRows-1))
                {
                    entityList[i].row++;
                    DropBreadCrumb();
                }

if (key==kLeftKey)
    for (i=0;i<kMaxEntities;i++)
        if (entityList[i].state==kPlayer)
            if (entityList[i].col>0)
                {
                    entityList[i].col--;
                    DropBreadCrumb();
                }

if (key==kRightKey)
    for (i=0;i<kMaxEntities;i++)
        if (entityList[i].state==kPlayer)
            if (entityList[i].col<(kMaxCols-1))
                {
                    entityList[i].col++;
                    DropBreadCrumb();
                }

}
```

The KeyDown function shown in Example 6-5 determines if the player has pressed any of the four direction keys. If so, it traverses the entityList array to search for a character being controlled by the player. If it finds one, it makes sure the new desired position is within the bounds of the tile world. If the desired position is legitimate, the position is updated. The next step is to actually record the position by calling the function DropBreadCrumb. The DropBreadCrumb function is shown in Example 6-6.

Example 6-6. Dropping a breadcrumb

```
void ai_World::DropBreadCrumb(void)

{
    int  i;

    for (i=kMaxTrailLength-1;i>0;i--)
```

```
    {
      entityList[0].trailRow[i]=entityList[0].trailRow[i-1];
      entityList[0].trailCol[i]=entityList[0].trailCol[i-1];
    }
  entityList[0].trailRow[0]=entityList[0].row;
  entityList[0].trailCol[0]=entityList[0].col;

}
```

The DropBreadCrumb function adds the current player position to the trailRow and trailCol arrays. These arrays maintain a list of the most recent player positions. In this case, the constant kMaxTrailLength sets the number of positions that will be tracked. The longer the trail, the more likely a computer-controlled character will discover it and pathfind its way to the player.

The DropBreadCrumb function begins by dropping the oldest position in the trailRow and trailCol arrays. We are tracking only kMaxTrailLength positions, so each time we add a new position we must drop the oldest one. We do this with the initial for loop. In effect, this loop shifts all the positions in the array. It deletes the oldest position and makes the first array element available for the current player position. Next, we store the player's current position in the first element of the trailRow and trailCol arrays.

The next step is to actually make the computer-controlled character detect and follow the breadcrumb trail that the player is leaving. The demo begins by having the computer-controlled troll move randomly about the tiled environment. Figure 6-9 illustrates how the troll moves about the tiled environment in any one of eight possible directions.

Example 6-7 goes on to show how the troll detects and follows the breadcrumb trail.

Example 6-7. Following the breadcrumbs

```
for (i=0;i<kMaxEntities;i++)
  {

    r=entityList[i].row;
    c=entityList[i].col;
    foundCrumb=-1;
    for (j=0;j<kMaxTrailLength;j++)
    {
      if ((r==entityList[0].trailRow[j]) &&
          (c==entityList[0].trailCol[j]))
        {
          foundCrumb=j;
          break;
        }
      if ((r-1==entityList[0].trailRow[j]) &&
          (c-1==entityList[0].trailCol[j]))
        {
```

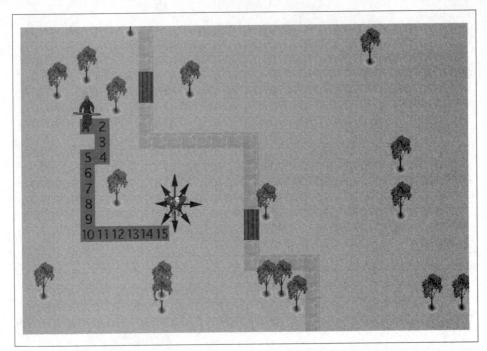

Figure 6-9. Finding the breadcrumbs

```
        foundCrumb=j;
        break;
      }
   if ((r-1==entityList[0].trailRow[j]) &&
      (c==entityList[0].trailCol[j]))
     {
        foundCrumb=j;
        break;
     }
   if ((r-1==entityList[0].trailRow[j]) &&
      (c+1==entityList[0].trailCol[j]))
     {
        foundCrumb=j;
        break;
     }
   if ((r==entityList[0].trailRow[j]) &&
      (c-1==entityList[0].trailCol[j]))
     {
        foundCrumb=j;
        break;
     }
   if ((r==entityList[0].trailRow[j]) &&
      (c+1==entityList[0].trailCol[j]))
     {
        foundCrumb=j;
        break;
     }
```

```
     if ((r+1==entityList[0].trailRow[j]) &&
         (c-1==entityList[0].trailCol[j]))
       {
         foundCrumb=j;
         break;
       }
     if ((r+1==entityList[0].trailRow[j]) &&
         (c==entityList[0].trailCol[j]))
       {
         foundCrumb=j;
         break;
       }
     if ((r+1==entityList[0].trailRow[j]) &&
         (c+1==entityList[0].trailCol[j]))
       {
         foundCrumb=j;
         break;
       }
   }

   if (foundCrumb>=0)
     {
       entityList[i].row=entityList[0].trailRow[foundCrumb];
       entityList[i].col=entityList[0].trailCol[foundCrumb];
     }
   else
     {
       entityList[i].row=entityList[i].row+Rnd(0,2)-1;
       entityList[i].col=entityList[i].col+Rnd(0,2)-1;
     }

   if (entityList[i].row<0)
     entityList[i].row=0;
   if (entityList[i].col<0)
     entityList[i].col=0;

   if (entityList[i].row>=kMaxRows)
     entityList[i].row=kMaxRows-1;
   if (entityList[i].col>=kMaxCols)
     entityList[i].col=kMaxCols-1;
}
```

We begin by traversing the `trailRow` and `trailCol` arrays. These are the arrays that store the most recent row and column player positions. These saved positions are the breadcrumbs left by the player. The actual number of positions saved is set by the `kMaxTrailLength` constant. The goal is to determine if any of the eight positions adjacent to the computer-controlled troll contain a breadcrumb. We use eight `if` statements to compare each adjacent tile to each element in the `trailRow` and `trailCol` arrays. The `for` loop begins at array element 0 because this is the most recent player position. If a breadcrumb is found, its corresponding array index is stored in the `foundCrumb` array index. We then break out of the `for` loop because we know we won't find any breadcrumbs closer to the player position. We know this because the `trailRow` and `trailCol` arrays are ordered from the most recent player position to the oldest player position. Starting the search from the most recent player position also ensures that the troll will follow the breadcrumbs to, rather than away from, the player. It's quite probable that the troll will first detect a breadcrumb somewhere in the middle of the `trailRow` and `trailCol` arrays. We want to make sure the troll follows the breadcrumbs to the player.

Once the `for` loop is finished executing, we check whether a breadcrumb has been found. The `foundCrumb` variable stores the array index of the breadcrumb found. If no breadcrumb is found, it contains its initial value of -1. If `foundCrumb` is greater than or equal to 0, we set the troll's position to the value stored at array index `foundCrumb` in the `trailRow` and `trailCol` arrays. Doing this each time the troll's position needs to be updated results in the troll following a trail to the player's position.

If `foundCrumb` is equal to a value of -1 when we exit the `for` loop, we know that no breadcrumbs were found. In this case, we simply select a random direction in which to move. Hopefully, this random move will put the troll adjacent to a breadcrumb which can be detected and followed the next time the troll's position needs to be updated.

There is another benefit to storing the most recent player positions in the lower `trailRow` and `trailCol` array elements. It is not unusual for a player to backtrack or to move in such a way that his path overlaps with or is adjacent to a previous location. This is illustrated in Figure 6-10.

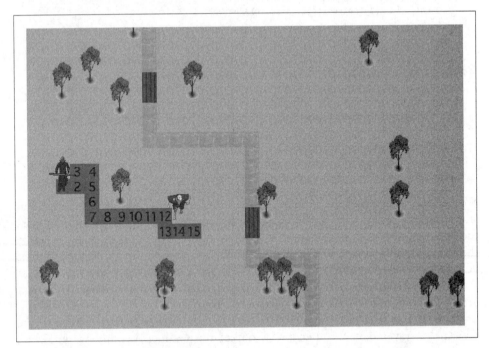

Figure 6-10. Following the shortest path

In this case, the troll isn't going to follow the exact footsteps of the player. In fact, doing so would be rather unnatural. It would probably be obvious to the player that the troll was simply moving in the player's footsteps rather than finding its way to the player in an intelligent way. In this case, however, the troll will always look for the adjacent tile containing the most recent breadcrumb. The end result is that the troll will skip over breadcrumbs whenever possible. For example, in Figure 6-10, the troll would follow array elements {12,11,10,9,8,7,6,2} as it moves to the player's position.

Path Following

Pathfinding is often thought of solely as a problem of moving from a starting point to a desired destination. Many times, however, it is necessary to move computer-controlled characters in a game environment in a realistic way even though they might not have an ultimate destination. For example, a car-racing game would require the computer-controlled cars to navigate a roadway. Likewise, a strategy or role-playing game might require troops to patrol the roads between towns. Like all pathfinding problems, the solution depends on the type of game environment. In a car-racing game the environment probably would be of a continuous nature. In this case the movement probably would be less rigid. You would want the cars to stay on the road, but in some circumstances that might not be possible. If a car tries to make a turn at an extremely high rate of speed, it likely would run off the road. It could then attempt to slow down and steer back in the direction of the road.

You can use a more rigid approach in a tile-based game environment. You can think of this as more of a containment problem. In this scenario the game character is confined to a certain terrain element, such as a road. Figure 6-11 shows an example of this.

In Figure 6-11, all the terrain elements labeled as 2s are considered to be the road. The terrain elements labeled as 1s are considered to be out of bounds. So, this becomes a matter of containing the computer-controlled troll to the road area of the terrain. However, we don't want the troll to simply move randomly on the road. The result would look unnatural. We want the troll to appear as though it's walking along the road. As you'll notice, the road is more than one tile thick, so this isn't just a matter of looking for the next adjacent tile containing a 2 and then moving there. We need to analyze the surrounding terrain and decide on the best move. A tile-based environment typically offers eight possible directions when moving. We examine all eight directions and then eliminate those that are not part of the road. The problem then becomes one of deciding which of the remaining directions to take. Example 6-8 shows how we begin to analyze the surrounding terrain.

Example 6-8. Terrain analysis

```
int   r;
int   c;
int   terrainAnalysis[9];
```

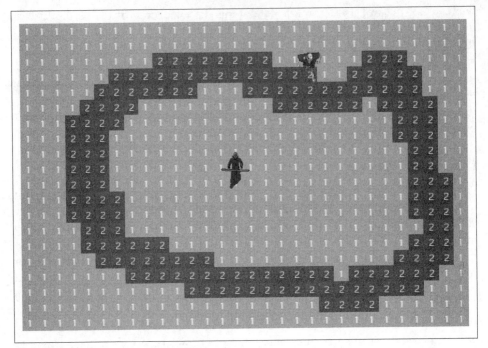

Figure 6-11. Following the road

```
r=entityList[i].row;
c=entityList[i].col;

terrainAnalysis[1]=terrain[r-1][c-1];
terrainAnalysis[2]=terrain[r-1][c];
terrainAnalysis[3]=terrain[r-1][c+1];
terrainAnalysis[4]=terrain[r][c+1];
terrainAnalysis[5]=terrain[r+1][c+1];
terrainAnalysis[6]=terrain[r+1][c];
terrainAnalysis[7]=terrain[r+1][c-1];
terrainAnalysis[8]=terrain[r][c-1];

for (j=1;j<=8;j++)
  if (terrainAnalysis[j]==1)
    terrainAnalysis[j]=0;
  else
    terrainAnalysis[j]=10;
```

We begin defining the terrainAnalysis array. This is where we will store the terrain values from the eight tiles adjacent to the computer-controlled troll. We do this by offsetting the current row and column positions of the troll. After the eight values are stored, we enter a for loop which determines if each value is part of the road. If it's not part of the road, the corresponding terrainAnalysis array element is set to 0. If it is part of the road, the terrainAnalysis element is set to a value of 10.

Now that we know which directions are possible, we want to take the current direction of movement into consideration. We want to keep the troll moving in the same general direction. We want to turn only when we have to, and even then a turn to the left or right is preferable to a complete change in direction. In this demo, we assign a number to each direction so that we can track the current direction. Figure 6-12 shows the numbers assigned to each direction.

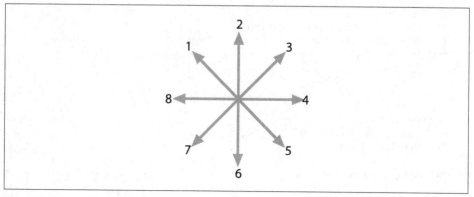

Figure 6-12. Possible directions

We will use the numbers shown in Figure 6-12 to record the direction of the move each time we update the troll's position. This enables us to give added weight to the previous direction whenever it is time to update the troll's position. Example 6-9 shows how this is accomplished.

Example 6-9. Direction analysis

```
if (entityList[i].direction==1)
    {
      terrainAnalysis[1]=terrainAnalysis[1]+2;
      terrainAnalysis[2]++;
      terrainAnalysis[5]--;
      terrainAnalysis[8]++;
    }
if (entityList[i].direction==2)
    {
      terrainAnalysis[1]++;
      terrainAnalysis[2]=terrainAnalysis[2]+2;
      terrainAnalysis[3]++;
      terrainAnalysis[6]--;
    }
if (entityList[i].direction==3)
    {
      terrainAnalysis[2]++;
      terrainAnalysis[3]=terrainAnalysis[3]+2;
      terrainAnalysis[4]++;
      terrainAnalysis[7]--;
    }
```

```
if (entityList[i].direction==4)
  {
    terrainAnalysis[3]++;
    terrainAnalysis[4]=terrainAnalysis[4]+2;
    terrainAnalysis[5]++;
    terrainAnalysis[7]--;
  }
if (entityList[i].direction==5)
  {
    terrainAnalysis[4]++;
    terrainAnalysis[5]=terrainAnalysis[5]+1;
    terrainAnalysis[6]++;
    terrainAnalysis[8]--;
  }
if (entityList[i].direction==6)
  {
    terrainAnalysis[2]--;
    terrainAnalysis[5]++;
    terrainAnalysis[6]=terrainAnalysis[6]+2;
    terrainAnalysis[7]++;
  }
if (entityList[i].direction==7)
  {
    terrainAnalysis[3]--;
    terrainAnalysis[6]++;
    terrainAnalysis[7]=terrainAnalysis[7]+2;
    terrainAnalysis[8]++;
  }
if (entityList[i].direction==8)
  {
    terrainAnalysis[1]++;
    terrainAnalysis[4]--;
    terrainAnalysis[7]++;
    terrainAnalysis[8]=terrainAnalysis[8]+2;
  }
```

Each if statement uses the current direction, stored in entityList[i].direction, to either increase or decrease the values in the terrainAnalysis array. This will make some potential directions more desirable, while making others less desirable. The first if statement, for example, checks for a previous direction of 1, which corresponds to an upper-left movement. If the previous direction was 1, we give added weight to element 1 of the terrainAnalysis array. We do this by incrementing its value by 2. Of course, continuing in the upper-left direction might not be possible. Perhaps that's the edge of the road. So, we have to consider the remaining possibilities. The next two best possibilities would be either moving straight up or directly to the left. We add weight to those two directions by incrementing the terrainAnalysis array elements 2 and 8 by a value of 1. Elements 3, 4, 6, and 7 are considered neutral, so we don't change those elements in the terrainAnalysis array. The final direction, however, is considered undesirable. In this case, direction 5 would be the complete opposite of the current direction. That direction would be our last resort, so we decrease the weight of that element of the terrainAnalysis array by a value of 1. This example is illustrated in Figure 6-13.

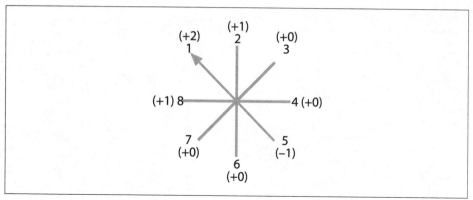

Figure 6-13. Weighting directions

As Figure 6-13 shows, the current direction is 1, or up and left. All things being equal, we want the troll to continue in that direction, so the terrainAnalysis element is weighted with a +2. The two next best possibilities are directions 2 and 8 because those are the least severe turns. Those two are weighted with a +1. All the remaining elements are left as is, except for 5, which is the complete opposite direction. The next step is to choose the best direction. This is demonstrated in Example 6-10.

Example 6-10. Choosing a direction

```
maxTerrain=0;
maxIndex=0;
for (j=1;j<=8;j++)
   if   (terrainAnalysis[j]>maxTerrain)
      {
         maxTerrain=terrainAnalysis[j];
         maxIndex=j;
      }
```

As Example 6-10 shows, we traverse the terrainAnalysis array in search of the most highly weighted of the possible directions. Upon exit from the for loop, the variable maxIndex will contain the array index to the most highly weighted direction. Example 6-11 shows how we use the value in maxIndex to update the troll's position.

Example 6-11. Update position

```
if (maxIndex==1)
  {
    entityList[i].direction=1;
    entityList[i].row--;
    entityList[i].col--;
  }
```

```
if (maxIndex==2)
  {
    entityList[i].direction=2;
    entityList[i].row--;
  }
if (maxIndex==3)
  {
    entityList[i].direction=3;
    entityList[i].row--;
    entityList[i].col++;
  }
if (maxIndex==4)
  {
    entityList[i].direction=4;
    entityList[i].col++;
  }
if (maxIndex==5)
  {
    entityList[i].direction=5;
    entityList[i].row++;
    entityList[i].col++;
  }
if (maxIndex==6)
  {
    entityList[i].direction=6;
    entityList[i].row++;
  }
if (maxIndex==7)
  {
    entityList[i].direction=7;
    entityList[i].row++;
    entityList[i].col--;
  }
if (maxIndex==8)
  {
    entityList[i].direction=8;
    entityList[i].col--;
  }
```

The value in maxIndex indicates the new direction of the troll. We include an if state-ment for each of the possible eight directions. Once the desired direction is found, we update the value in entityList[i].direction. This becomes the previous direction for the next time the troll's position needs to be updated. We then update the entityList[i].row and entityList[i].col values as needed. Figure 6-14 shows the path followed as the troll moves along the road.

As Figure 6-14 shows, the troll continuously circles the road. In a real game, you could make the computer-controlled adversaries continuously patrol the roadways, until they encounter a player. At that point the computer-controlled character's state could switch to an attack mode.

In this example, we used the adjacent tiles to make a weighted decision about direction to move in next. You can increase the robustness of this technique by

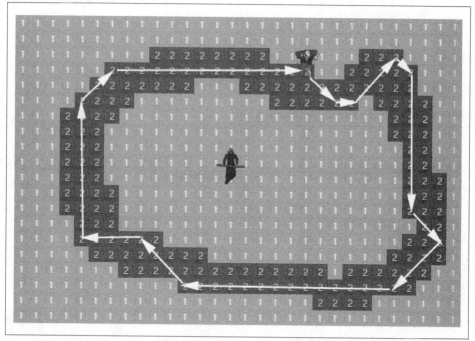

Figure 6-14. Road path

examining more than just the adjacent tiles. You can weight the directions not just on the adjacent tiles, but also on the tiles adjacent to them. This could make the movement look even more natural and intelligent.

Wall Tracing

Another method of pathfinding that is very useful in game development is *wall tracing*. Like path-following, this method doesn't calculate a path from a starting point to an ending point. Wall tracing is more of an exploration technique. It's most useful in game environments made of many small rooms, although you can use it in maze-like game environments as well. You also can use the basic algorithm for tracing around obstacles, as we described in the previous section on obstacle tracing. Games rarely have every computer-controlled adversary simultaneously plotting a path to the player. Sometimes it's desirable for the computer-controlled characters to explore the environment in search of the player, weapons, power-ups, treasure, or anything else a game character can interact with. Having the computer-controlled characters randomly move about the environment is one solution that game developers frequently implement. This offers a certain level of unpredictability, but it also can result in the computer-controlled characters getting stuck in small rooms for long periods of time. Figure 6-15 shows a dungeon-like level that's made up of many small rooms.

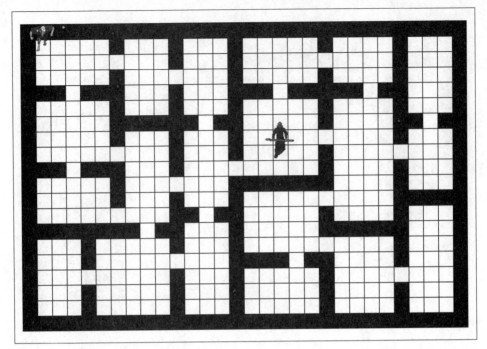

Figure 6-15. Wall tracing

In the example shown in Figure 6-15, we could make the troll move in random directions. However, it would probably take it a while just to get out of the upper-left room. A better approach would be to make the troll systematically explore the entire environment. Fortunately, a relatively simple solution is available. Basically, we are going to use a lefthanded approach. If the troll always moves to its left, it will do a thorough job of exploring its environment. The trick is to remember that the troll needs to move to its left whenever possible, and not necessarily to the left from the point of view of the player. This is illustrated in Figure 6-16.

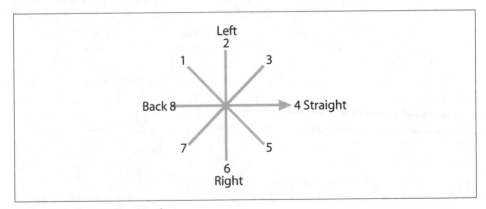

Figure 6-16. Facing player's right

At the start of the demo, the troll is facing right relative to the player's point of view. This is designated as direction 4, as shown in Figure 6-16. This means direction 2 is to the troll's left, direction 6 is to the troll's right, and direction 8 is to the troll's rear. With the lefthanded movement approach, the troll always will try to move to its left first. If it can't move to its left, it will try to move straight ahead. If that is blocked, it will try to move to its right next. If that also is blocked, it will reverse direction. When the demo first starts, the troll will try to move up relative to the player's point of view. As you can see in Figure 6-15, a wall blocks its way, so the troll must try straight ahead next. This is direction 4 relative to the troll's point of view. No obstruction appears straight ahead of the troll, so it makes the move. This lefthanded movement technique is shown in Example 6-12.

Example 6-12. Left-handed movement

```
r=entityList[i].row;
c=entityList[i].col;

if (entityList[i].direction==4)
    {
      if (terrain[r-1][c]==1)
        {
          entityList[i].row--;
          entityList[i].direction=2;
        }
      else if (terrain[r][c+1]==1)
        {
          entityList[i].col++;
          entityList[i].direction=4;
        }
      else if (terrain[r+1][c]==1)
        {
          entityList[i].row++;
          entityList[i].direction=6;
        }
      else if (terrain[r][c-1]==1)
        {
          entityList[i].col--;
          entityList[i].direction=8;
        }
    }
else if (entityList[i].direction==6)
    {
      if (terrain[r][c+1]==1)
        {
          entityList[i].col++;
          entityList[i].direction=4;
        }
      else if (terrain[r+1][c]==1)
        {
          entityList[i].row++;
          entityList[i].direction=6;
        }
```

```
        else if (terrain[r][c-1]==1)
          {
            entityList[i].col--;
            entityList[i].direction=8;
          }
        else if (terrain[r-1][c]==1)
          {
            entityList[i].row--;
            entityList[i].direction=2;
          }
    }

else if (entityList[i].direction==8)
  {
      if (terrain[r+1][c]==1)
        {
          entityList[i].row++;
          entityList[i].direction=6;
        }
      else if (terrain[r][c-1]==1)
        {
          entityList[i].col--;
          entityList[i].direction=8;
        }
      else if (terrain[r-1][c]==1)
        {
          entityList[i].row--;
          entityList[i].direction=2;
        }
      else if (terrain[r][c+1]==1)
        {
          entityList[i].col++;
          entityList[i].direction=4;
        }
  }

else if (entityList[i].direction==2)
  {
      if (terrain[r][c-1]==1)
        {
          entityList[i].col--;
          entityList[i].direction=8;
        }
      else if (terrain[r-1][c]==1)
        {
          entityList[i].row--;
          entityList[i].direction=2;
        }
      else if (terrain[r][c+1]==1)
        {
          entityList[i].col++;
          entityList[i].direction=4;
        }
      else if (terrain[r+1][c]==1)
```

```
    {
        entityList[i].row++;
        entityList[i].direction=6;
    }
}
```

Example 6-12 shows four separate if statement blocks. We need to use a different if block for each of the four possible directions in which the troll can face. This is required because the tile to the troll's left is dependent on the direction it's facing. This fact is illustrated in Figure 6-17.

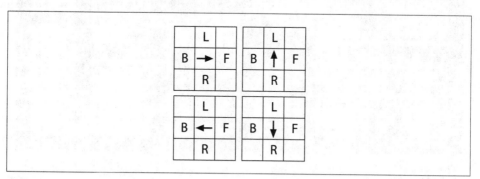

Figure 6-17. Relative directions

As Figure 6-17 shows, if the troll is facing the right relative to the player's point of view, its left is the tile above it. If it's facing up, the tile to its left is actually the tile on the left side. If it's facing left, the tile below it is to its left. Finally, if it's facing down, the tile to the right is the troll's left.

As the first if block shows, if the troll is facing right, designated as direction 4, it first checks the tile to its left by examining terrain[r-1][c]. If this location contains a 1, there is no obstruction. At this point, the troll's position is updated, and just as important, its direction is updated to 2. This means that it's now facing up relative to the player's point of view. The next time this block of code is executed, a different if block will be used because its direction has changed. The additional if statements ensure that the same procedure is followed for each possible direction.

If the first check of terrain[r-1][c] detected an obstruction, the tile in front of the troll would have been checked next. If that also contained an obstruction, the tile to the troll's right would have been checked, followed by the tile to its rear. The end result is that the troll will thoroughly explore the game environment. This is illustrated in Figure 6-18.

As you can see, following the left-handed movement method, the troll enters every room in the game environment. Although this approach is conceptually easy and in

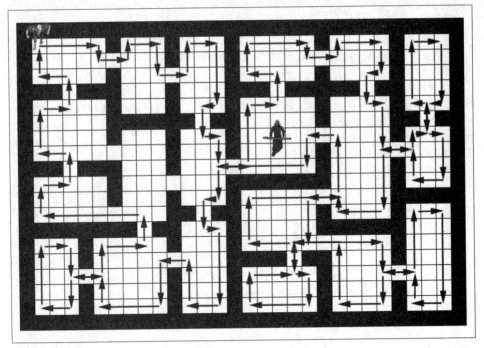

Figure 6-18. Wall-tracing path

most cases very effective, it is not guaranteed to work in all cases. Some geometries will prevent this method from allowing the troll to reach every single room.

Waypoint Navigation

Pathfinding can be a very time-consuming and CPU-intensive operation. One way to reduce this problem is to precalculate paths whenever possible. *Waypoint navigation* reduces this problem by carefully placing nodes in the game environment and then using precalculated paths or inexpensive pathfinding methods to move between each node. Figure 6-19 illustrates how to place nodes on a simple map consisting of seven rooms.

In Figure 6-19, you'll notice that every point on the map is in the line of sight of at least one node. Also, every node is in the line of sight of at least one other node. With a game environment constructed in this way, a game-controlled character always will be able to reach any position on the map using a simple line-of-sight algorithm. The game AI simply needs to know how the nodes connect to one another. Figure 6-20 illustrates how to label and connect each node on the map.

Using the node labels and links shown in Figure 6-20, we can now determine a path from any room to any other room. For example, moving from the room containing

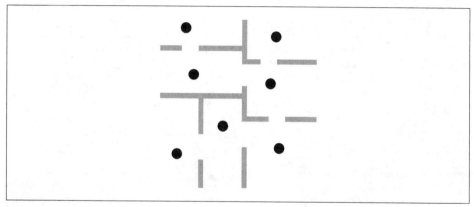

Figure 6-19. Placing nodes

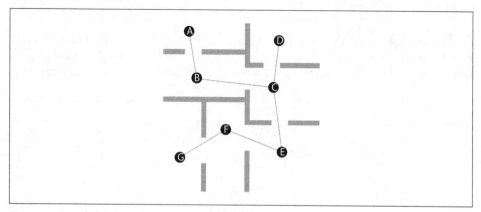

Figure 6-20. Labeling nodes

node *A* to the room containing node *E* entails moving through nodes *ABCE*. The path between nodes is calculated by a line-of-sight algorithm, or it can be a series of precalculated steps. Figure 6-21 shows how a computer-controlled character, indicated by the triangle, would calculate a path to the player-controlled character, indicated by the square.

The computer-controlled character first calculates which node is nearest its current location and in its line of sight. In this case, that is node *A*. It then calculates which node is nearest the player's current location and in the player's line of sight. That is node *E*. The computer then plots a course from its current position to node *A*. Then it follows the node connections from node *A* to node *E*. In this case, that is $A \rightarrow B \rightarrow C \rightarrow E$. Once it reaches the end node, it can plot a line-of-sight path from the final node to the player.

This seems simple enough, but how does the computer know which nodes to follow? In other words, how does the computer know that to get from node *A* to node

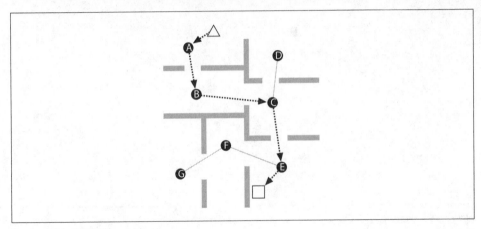

Figure 6-21. Building a path

E, it must first pass through nodes B and C? The answer lies in a simple table format for the data that enables us to quickly and easily determine the shortest path between any two nodes. Figure 6-22 shows our initial empty node connection table.

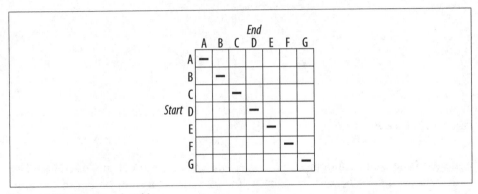

Figure 6-22. Empty node table

The purpose of the table is to establish the connections between the nodes. Filling in the table becomes a simple matter of determining the first node to visit when moving from any starting node to any ending node. The starting nodes are listed along the left side of the table, while the ending notes are shown across the top. We will determine the best path to follow by looking at the intersection on the table between the starting and ending nodes. You'll notice that the diagonal on the table contains dashes. These table elements don't need to be filled in because the starting and ending positions are equal. Take the upper-left table element, for example. Both the starting and ending nodes are A. You will never have to move from node A to node A, so that element is left blank. The next table element in the top row, however, shows a starting node of A and an ending node of B. We now look at Figure 6-21 to determine the first step to make when moving from node A to node B. In this case, the next move is to node B, so we fill in B on the second element of the top row. The next table element shows a starting node of A and an ending node of C. Again, Figure 6-21 shows us that the first step to take is to node B. When filling in the table we aren't concerned with determining the entire path between every two nodes. We only need to determine the first node to visit when moving from any node to any other node. Figure 6-23 shows the first table row completed.

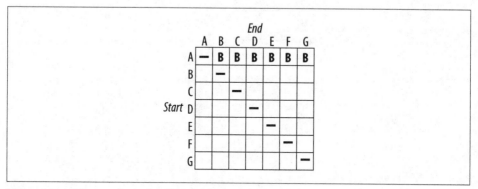

Figure 6-23. Filling in the node table

Figure 6-23 shows us that when moving from node A to any other node, we must first visit node B. Examining Figure 6-21 confirms this fact. The only node connected to node A is node B, so we must always pass through node B when moving from node A to any other node. Simply knowing that we must visit node B when moving from node A to node E doesn't get us to the destination. We must finish filling in the table. Moving to the second row in the table, we see that moving from node B to node A requires a move to node A. Moving from node B to node C requires a move to C. We continue doing this until each element in the table is complete. Figure 6-24 shows the completed node connection table.

End

Start	A	B	C	D	E	F	G
A	—	B	B	B	B	B	B
B	A	—	C	C	C	C	C
C	B	B	—	D	E	E	E
D	C	C	C	—	C	C	C
E	C	C	C	C	—	F	F
F	E	E	E	E	E	—	G
G	F	F	F	F	F	F	—

Figure 6-24. Completed node table

By using the completed table shown in Figure 6-24, we can determine the path to follow to get from any node to any other node. Figure 6-25 shows an example of a desired path. In this figure, a hypothetical computer-controlled character, indicated by the triangle, wants to build a path to the player, indicated by the square.

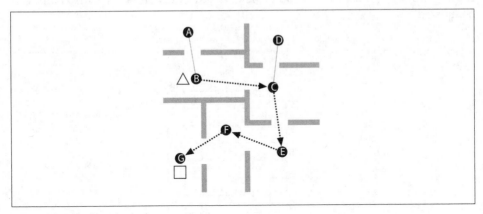

Figure 6-25. Finding the path

To build a path we simply need to refer to the completed node connection table shown in Figure 6-24. As shown in Figure 6-25, we want to build a path from node B to node G. We start by finding the intersection on the table between node B and node G. The table shows node C at the intersection. So, the first link to traverse when moving from node B to node G is B → C. Once we arrive at node C, we refer to the table again to find the intersection between node C and the desired destination, node G. In the case, we find node E at the intersection. We then proceed to move from C → E. We repeat this process until the destination is reached. Figure 6-26 shows the individual path segments that are followed when building a path from node B to node G.

Goal B ➡ G		
B ➡ G	Table intersection ➡ C	Move ➡ C
C ➡ G	Table intersection ➡ E	Move ➡ E
E ➡ G	Table intersection ➡ F	Move ➡ F
F ➡ G	Table intersection ➡ G	Move ➡ G

Figure 6-26. Finding the path

As Figure 6-26 shows, the computer-controlled character needs to follow four path segments to reach its destination.

Each method we discussed here has its advantages and disadvantages, and it's clear that no single method is best suited for all possible pathfinding problems. Another method we mentioned at the beginning of this chapter, the A* algorithm, is applicable to a wide range of pathfinding problems. The A* algorithm is an extremely popular pathfinding algorithm used in games, and we devote the entire next chapter to the method.

CHAPTER 7

A* Pathfinding

In this chapter we are going to discuss the fundamentals of the A* pathfinding algorithm. Pathfinding is one of the most basic problems of game AI. Poor pathfinding can make game characters seem very brainless and artificial. Nothing can break the immersive effect of a game faster than seeing a game character unable to navigate a simple set of obstacles. Handling the problem of pathfinding effectively can go a long way toward making a game more enjoyable and immersive for the player.

Fortunately, the A* algorithm provides an effective solution to the problem of pathfinding. The A* algorithm is probably one of the most, if not *the* most used pathfinding algorithm in game development today. What makes the A* algorithm so appealing is that it is guaranteed to find the best path between any starting point and any ending point, assuming, of course, that a path exists. Also, it's a relatively efficient algorithm, which adds to its appeal. In fact, you should use it whenever possible, unless, of course, you are dealing with some type of special-case scenario. For example, if a clear line of sight exists with no obstacles between the starting point and ending point, the A* algorithm would be overkill. A faster and more efficient line-of-sight movement algorithm would be better. It also probably wouldn't be the best alternative if CPU cycles are at a minimum. The A* algorithm is efficient, but it still can consume quite a few CPU cycles, especially if you need to do simultaneous pathfinding for a large number of game characters. For most pathfinding problems, however, A* is the best choice.Unfortunately, understanding how the A* algorithm works can be difficult for new game developers. In this chapter we step through the inner workings of the A* algorithm to see how it builds a path from a starting point to an ending point. Seeing the step-by-step construction of an A* path should help make it clear how the A* algorithm does its magic.

Defining the Search Area

The first step in pathfinding is to define the search area. We need some way to represent the game world in a manner that allows the search algorithm to search for and find the best path. Ultimately, the game world needs to be represented by points that both the game characters and objects can occupy. It is the pathfinding algorithm's job to find the best path between any two points, avoiding any obstacles. How the actual game world will be represented depends on the type of game. In some cases, the game world might have to be simplified. For example, a game which uses a continuous environment would probably be made up of a very large number of points that the game characters would be able to occupy. The A* algorithm would not be practical for this type of search space. It simply would be too large. However, it might work if the search area could be simplified. This would involve placing nodes throughout the game world. We then would be able to build paths between nodes, but not necessarily between every possible point in the world. This is illustrated in Figure 7-1.

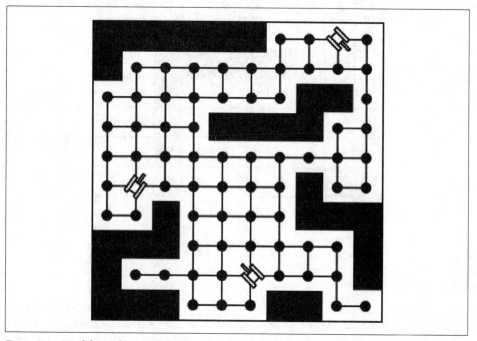

Figure 7-1. Simplifying the search area

The tanks in Figure 7-1 are free to occupy any point in their coordinate system, but for the purposes of pathfinding, the game world is simplified by placing nodes throughout the game environment. These nodes do not correspond directly to every possible tank position. That would require too many nodes. We need to reduce the nodes to a manageable number, which is what we mean when we say we need to simplify the search area.

Of course, we need to maintain a list of the connections between the nodes. The search algorithm needs to know how the nodes connect. Once it knows how they link together, the A* algorithm can calculate a path from any node to any other node. The more nodes placed in the world, the slower the pathfinding process. If pathfinding is taking too many CPU cycles, one alternative is to simplify the search area by using fewer nodes.

On the other hand, a game that uses a tiled world would be a good candidate for the A* algorithm, assuming, of course, that the world isn't unreasonably large. It would be a good candidate because essentially the world already would be divided into nodes. Each tile would be a node in the search area. This is illustrated in Figure 7-2.

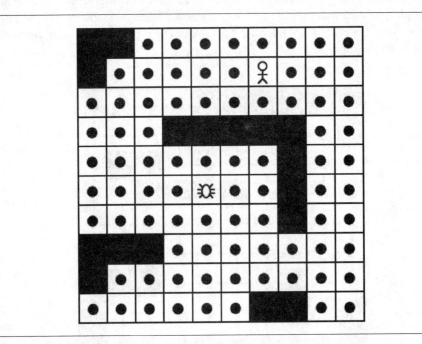

Figure 7-2. Tiled search area

Tiled environments, such as the one shown in Figure 7-2, are well suited to the A* algorithm. Each tile serves as a node in the search area. You don't need to maintain a list of links between the nodes because they are already adjacent in the game world. If necessary, you also can simplify tiled environments. You can place a single node to cover multiple tiles. In the case of very large tiled environments, you can set up the pathfinding algorithm to search only a subset of the world. Think of it as a smaller square within a larger square. If a path cannot be found within the confines of the smaller square, you can assume that no reasonable path exists.

Starting the Search

Once we have simplified the search area so that it's made up of a reasonable number of nodes, we are ready to begin the search. We will use the A* algorithm to find the shortest path between any two nodes. In this example, we will use a small tiled environment. Each tile will be a node in the search area and some nodes will contain obstacles. We will use the A* algorithm to find the shortest path while avoiding the obstacles. Example 7-1 shows the basic algorithm we will follow.

Example 7-1. A* pseudo code

```
add the starting node to the open list
while the open list is not empty
   {
      current node=node from open list with the lowest cost
      if current node = goal node then
         path complete
      else
         move current node to the closed list
         examine each node adjacent to the current node
         for each adjacent node
           if it isn't on the open list
              and isn't on the closed list
                 and it isn't an obstacle then
                    move it to open list and calculate cost
   }
```

Some of the particulars of the pseudo code shown in Example 7-1 might seem a little foreign, but they will become clear as we begin stepping through the algorithm.

Figure 7-3 shows the tiled search area that we will use. The starting point will be the spider near the center. The desired destination will be the human character. The solid black squares represent wall obstacles, while the white squares represent areas the spider can walk on.

Like any pathfinding algorithm, A* will find a path between a starting node and an ending node. It accomplishes this by starting the search at the starting node and then branching out to the surrounding nodes. In the case of this example, it will begin at the starting tile and then spread to the adjacent tiles. This branching out to adjacent tiles continues until we reach the destination node. However, before we start this branching search technique, we need a way to keep track of which tiles need to be searched. This is typically called the *open list* when using the A* algorithm. We begin with just one node in the open list. This is the starting node. We will add more nodes to the open list later. (Note, we'll use the terms *nodes* and *tiles* interchangeably when referring to tiled environments.)

Once we have built the open list, we traverse it and search the tiles adjacent to each tile on the list. The idea is to look at each adjacent tile and determine if it is a valid tile for the path. We basically are checking to see if the adjacent tiles can be walked on by a game character. For example, a road tile would be valid, whereas a wall tile probably would not be valid. We proceed to check each of the eight adjacent tiles and then add each valid tile to the open list. If a tile contains an obstacle, we simply

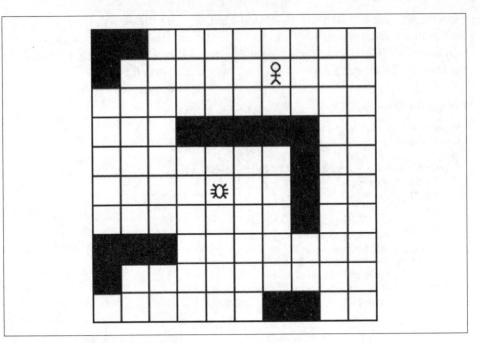

Figure 7-3. Creating a tiled search area

ignore it. It doesn't get added to the open list. Figure 7-4 shows the tiles adjacent to the initial location that need to be checked.

In addition to the open list, the A* algorithm also maintains a *closed list*. The closed list contains the tiles that already were checked and no longer need to be examined. We essentially add a tile to the closed list once all its adjacent tiles have been checked. As Figure 7-5 shows, we have checked each tile adjacent to the starting tile, so the starting tile can be added to the closed list.

So, as Figure 7-5 shows, the end result is that we now have eight new tiles added to the open list and one tile removed from the open list. The description so far shows the basic iteration through a main A* loop; however, we need to track some additional information. We need some way to link the tiles together. The open list maintains a list of adjacent tiles that a character can walk on, but we also need to know how the adjacent tiles link together. We do this by tracking the parent tile of each tile in the open list. A tile's parent is the single tile that the character steps from to get to its current location. As Figure 7-6 shows, on the first iteration through the loop, each tile will point to the starting tile as its parent.

Ultimately we will use the parent links to trace a path back to the starting tile once we finally reach the destination. However, we still need to go through a series of additional iterations before we reach the destination.

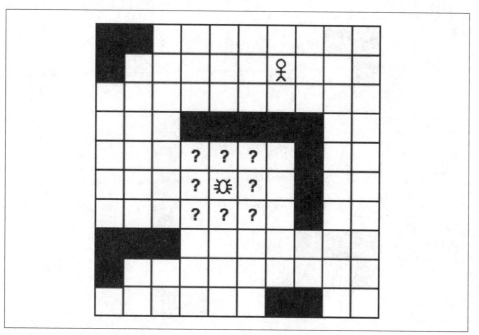

Figure 7-4. Adjacent tiles to consider

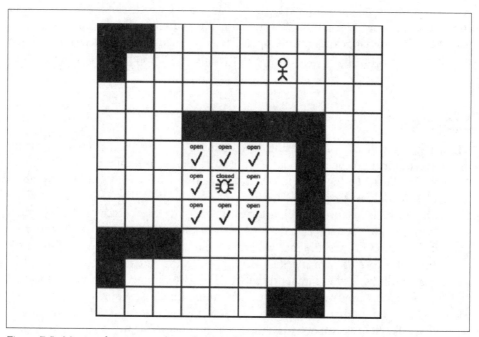

Figure 7-5. Moving the starting tile to the closed list

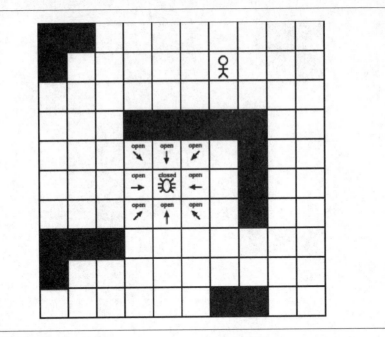

Figure 7-6. Linking to the parents

At this point we begin the process again. We now have to choose a new tile to check from the open list. On the first iteration we had only a single tile on the open list. We now have eight tiles on the open list. The trick now is to determine which member of the open list to check. We determine this by applying a score to each tile.

Scoring

Ultimately, we will use path scoring to determine the best path from the starting tile to the destination tile. To actually score each tile, we basically add together two components. First, we look at the cost to move from the starting tile to any given tile. Next, we look at the cost to move from the given tile to the destination tile. The first component is relatively straightforward. We start our search from the initial location and branch out from there. This makes calculating the cost of moving from the initial location to each tile that we branch out to relatively easy. We simply take the sum of the cost of each tile that leads back to the initial location. Remember, we are saving links to the parents of each tile. Back-stepping to the initial location is a simple matter. However, how do we determine the cost of moving from a given tile to the destination tile? The destination tile is the ultimate goal, which we haven't reached yet. So, how do we determine the cost of a path that we haven't determined yet? Well, at this point, all we can do is guess. This is called the *heuristic*. We essentially make the best guess we can make, given the information we have. Figure 7-7 shows the equation we use for scoring any given tile.

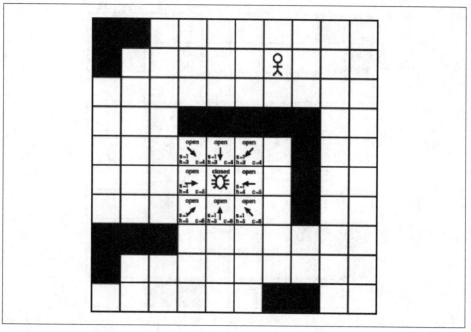

Score = Cost from Start + Heuristic

Figure 7-7. Calculating the path score

So, we calculate each tile's score by adding the cost of getting there from the starting location to the heuristic value, which is an estimate of the cost of getting from the given tile to the final destination.

We use this score when determining which tile to check next from the open list. We will first check the tiles with the lowest cost. In this case, a lower cost will equate to a shorter path. Figure 7-8 shows the score, cost, and heuristic applied to each tile we have checked so far.

Figure 7-8. Initial tile path scores

The *s* value shown in each open tile is the cost of getting there from the starting tile. In this case, each value is 1 because each tile is just one step from the starting tile. The *h* value is the heuristic. The heuristic is an estimate of the number of steps from the given tile to the destination tile. For example, the tile to the upper right of the starting tile has an *h* value of 3. That's because that tile is three steps away from the destination tile. You'll notice that we don't take obstacles into consideration when determining the heuristic. We haven't examined the tiles between the current tile and the destination tile, so we don't really know yet if they contain obstacles. At this point we simply want to determine the cost, assuming that there are no obstacles. The final value is c, which is the sum of s and h. This is the cost of the tile. It represents the known cost of getting there from the starting point and an estimate of the remaining cost to get to the destination.

Previously, we posed the question of which tile to choose first from the open list on the next iteration through the A* algorithm. The answer is the one with the lowest c value. As Figure 7-9 shows, the lowest c value is 4, but we actually have three tiles with that value. Which one should we choose? It doesn't really matter. Let's start with the one to the upper right of the starting tile. Assuming that we are using a (row, column) coordinate system where the upper-left coordinate of the search area is position $(1, 1)$, we are now looking at tile $(5, 6)$.

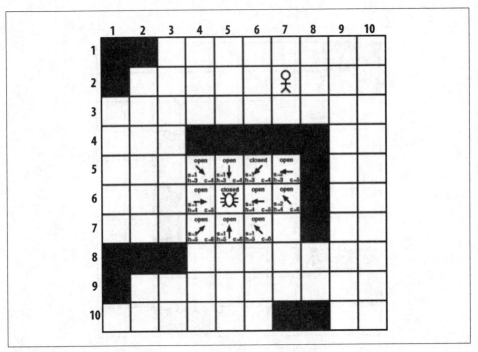

Figure 7-9. Examining tile (5, 6)

The current tile of interest in Figure 7-9 is tile $(5, 6)$, which is positioned to the upper right of the starting location. We now repeat the algorithm we showed you previously where we examine each tile adjacent to the current tile. In the first iteration each tile adjacent to the starting tile was available, meaning they had not yet been examined and they didn't contain any obstacles. However, that isn't the case with this iteration. When looking for adjacent tiles, we will only consider tiles that haven't been examined before and that a game character can walk on. This means we will ignore all tiles on the open list, all tiles on the closed list, or all tiles that contain obstacles. This leaves only two tiles, the one directly to the right of the current tile and the one to the lower right of the current tile. Both tiles are added to the open list. As you can see in Figure 7-9, we create a pointer for each tile added to the open list that points back to its parent tile. We also calculate the *s*, *h*, and *c* values of the new tiles. In this case we calculate the *s* values by stepping back through the parent link. This tells us how many steps we are from the starting point. Once again, the *h* value is the heuristic, which is an estimate of the distance from the given tile to the destination. And once again the *c* value is the sum of *s* and *h*. The final step is to add our current tile, the one at position (5, 6), to the closed list. This tile is no longer of any interest to us. We already examined each of its adjacent tiles, so there is no need to examine it again.

We now repeat the process. We have added two new tiles to the open list and moved one to the closed list. We once again search the open list for the tile with the lowest cost. As with the first iteration, the tile with the lowest cost in the open list has a value of 4. However, this time we have only two tiles in the open list with a cost of 4. As before, it really doesn't matter which we examine first. For this example, we will examine tile (5, 5) next. This is shown in Figure 7-10.

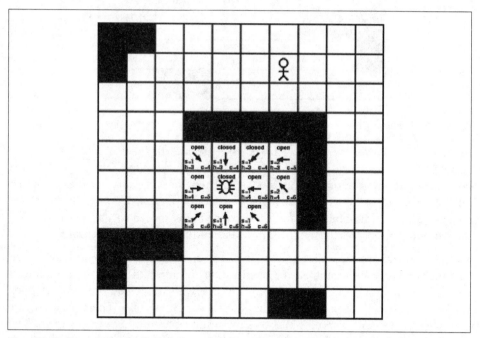

Figure 7-10. Examining tile (5, 5)

As with the previous cases, we examine each tile adjacent to the current tile. However, in this case no available tiles are adjacent to the current tile. They all are either open or closed, or they contain an obstacle. So, as Figure 7-10 shows, we simply have to mark the current tile as closed and then move on.

Now we are down to one single tile in the open list that appears to be superior to the rest. It has a cost of 4, which is the lowest among all the tiles in the open list. It's located at position (5, 4), which is to the upper left of the starting position. As Figure 7-11 shows, this is the tile we will examine next.

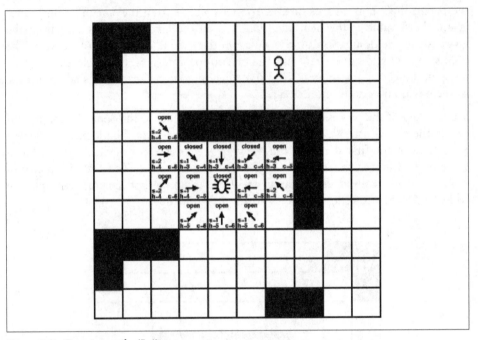

Figure 7-11. Examining tile (5, 4)

As Figure 7-11 shows, we once again examine all the tiles that are adjacent to the current tile. In this case, only three tiles are available: the one to the upper left, the one to the left, and the one to the lower left. The remaining adjacent tiles are either on the open list, are on the closed list, or contain an obstruction. The three new tiles are added to the open list and the current tile is moved to the closed list. We then calculate the scores for the three new tiles and begin the process again.

We have added two new tiles to the open list and moved one to the closed list. The previous time we examined the open list we found that the tile with the lowest cost had a value of 4. This time around the tile with the lowest cost on the open list has a value of 5. In fact, three open tiles have a value of 5. Their positions are (5, 7), (6, 6), and (6, 4). Figure 7-12 shows the result of examining each of them. The actual A* algorithm would only examine one tile at a time and then only check the additional tiles with the same value if no new tiles with lower values were discovered. However, for purposes of this example, we'll show the results of examining all of them.

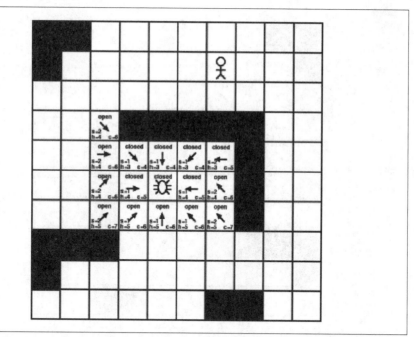

Figure 7-12. Examining all tiles with a cost of 5

As with the previous iterations, each new available tile is added to the open list and each examined tile is moved to the closed list. We also calculate the scores for each new tile. Traversing the open list again tells us that 6 is the lowest score available, so we proceed to examine the tiles with that score. Once again, it doesn't matter which we check first. As with Figure 7-12, we'll assume the worst-case scenario in which the best option is selected last. This will show the results of examining all the tiles with a score of 6. This is illustrated in Figure 7-13.

As Figure 7-13 shows, we examined every tile with a cost of 6. As with the previous iterations, new tiles are added to the open list and the examined tiles are moved to the closed list. Once again, the cost values are calculated for the new tiles. As you can see in Figure 7-13, the value of the heuristic is becoming more apparent. The increases in the heuristics of the tiles on the lower portion of the search area are causing noticeable increases to the total cost values. The tiles in the lower part of the search area are still open, so they still might provide the best path to the destination, but for now there are better options to pursue. The lower heuristic values of the open tiles at the top of the search area are making those more desirable. In fact, traversing the open list reveals that the current lowest-cost tile now has a value of 6. In this case, only one tile has a value of 6, tile (3, 4). Figure 7-14 shows the result of examining tile (3, 4).

Examining tile (3, 4) results in the addition of three new tiles to the open list. Of course, the current tile at position (3, 4) is then moved to the closed list. As Figure

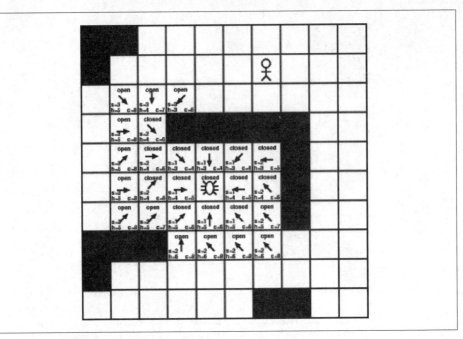

Figure 7-13. Examining all tiles with a cost of 6

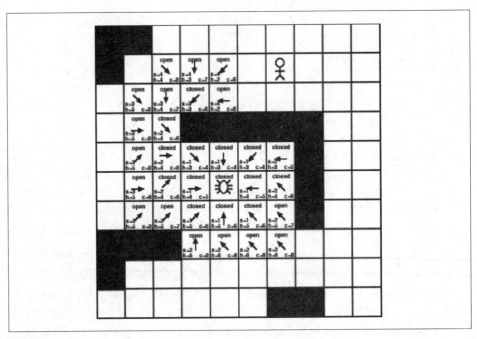

Figure 7-14. Examining tile (3,4)

7-14 shows, most of the tiles on the open list have a cost of 8. Luckily, two of the new tiles added during the previous iteration have a cost of just 6. These are the two tiles we will focus on next. Once again, for purposes of this example, we will assume the worst-case scenario in which it's necessary to examine both. Figure 7-15 illustrates the results of examining these two tiles.

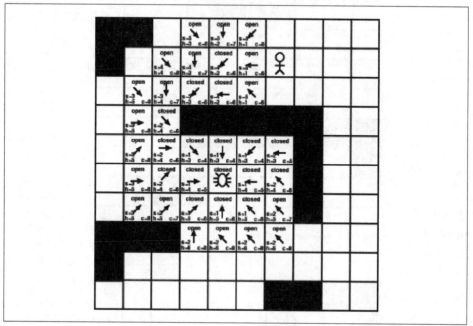

Figure 7-15. Examining tiles (2, 5) and (3, 5)

As Figure 7-15 shows, we are finally nearing the destination tile. The previous iteration produced five new tiles for the open list, three of which have a cost of 6, which is the current lowest value. As with the previous iterations, we will now examine all three tiles with a cost value of 6. This is shown in Figure 7-16.

As Figure 7-16 illustrates, we finally reached the destination. However, how does the algorithm determine when we reached it? The answer is simple. The path is found when the destination tile is added to the open list. At that point it's a simple matter of following the parent links back to the starting point. The only nodes that concern us now are the ones that lead back to the starting node. Figure 7-17 shows the nodes used to build the actual path.

Once the destination is placed in the open list, we know the path is complete. We then follow the parent links back to the starting tile. In this case, that generates a path made up of the points (2, 7), (2, 6), (2, 5), (3, 4), (4, 3), (5, 4), and (6, 5). If you follow the algorithm we showed here, you'll always find the shortest possible path. Other paths of equal length might exist, but none will be shorter.

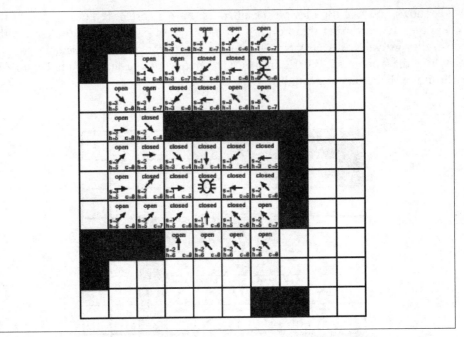

Figure 7-16. Examining tiles (1, 6), (2, 6), and (3, 6)

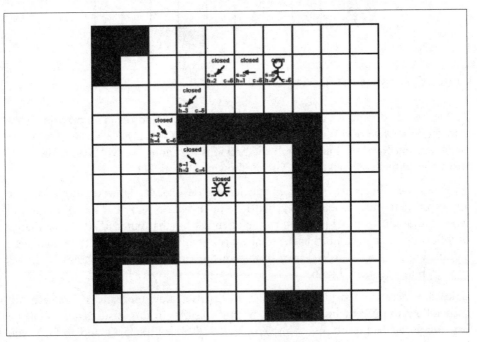

Figure 7-17. The completed path

Finding a Dead End

It's always possible that no valid path exists between any two given points, so how do we know when we have reached a dead end? The simple way to determine if we've reached a dead end is to monitor the open list. If we reach the point where no members are in the open list to examine, we've reached a dead end. Figure 7-18 shows such a scenario.

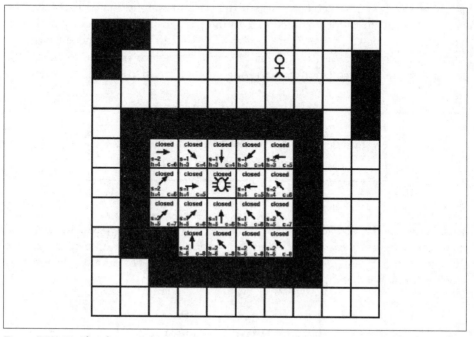

Figure 7-18. Dead end

As Figure 7-18 shows, the A* algorithm has branched out to every possible adjacent tile. Each one has been examined and moved to the closed list. Eventually, the point was reached where every tile on the open list was examined and no new tiles were available to add. At that point we can conclude that we've reached a dead end and that it simply isn't possible to build a path from the starting point to the desired destination.

Terrain Cost

As the previous example shows, path scoring already plays a major role in the A* algorithm. The standard A* algorithm in its most basic form simply determines path cost by the distance traveled. A longer path is considered to be more costly, and hence, less desirable. We often think of a good pathfinding algorithm as one that finds the shortest possible path. However, sometimes other considerations exist.

For example, the shortest path isn't always the fastest path. A game environment can include many types of terrain, all of which can affect the game characters differently. A long walk along a road might be faster than a shorter walk through a swamp. This is where terrain cost comes into play. The previous example shows how we calculate each node's cost by adding its distance from the initial location to the heuristic value, which is the estimated distance to the destination. It might not have been obvious, but the previous example basically did calculate terrain cost. It just wasn't very noticeable because all the terrain was the same. Each step the game character took added a value of 1 to the path cost. Basically, every node had the same cost. However, there's no reason why we can't assign different cost values to different nodes. It requires just a minor change to the cost equation. We can update the cost equation by factoring in the terrain cost. This is shown in Figure 7-19.

Total Cost from Start = Cost from Start + Terrain Cost

Score = Total Cost from Start + Heuristic

Figure 7-19. Scoring with terrain cost

This results in paths that are longer, but that involve easier terrain. In an actual game this can result in a game character getting from point A to point B in a shorter amount of time, even if the actual path is longer. For example, Figure 7-20 shows several hypothetical types of terrain.

	Open Terrain	Cost = 1
 ⚘	Grassland	Cost = 3
 ⚘⚘	Swampland	Cost = 5

Figure 7-20. Types of terrain

The previous example essentially had only open terrain. The cost of moving from one node to another was always 1. As Figure 7-20 shows, we will now introduce two new types of terrain. The first new terrain type is grassland, which has a cost of 3. The second new type of terrain is swampland, which has a cost of 5. In this case, cost ultimately refers to the amount of time it takes to traverse the node. For example, if it takes a game character one second to walk across a node of open terrain, it will take three seconds to walk across a node of grassland, and five seconds to walk across a node of swampland. The actual physical distances might be equal, but the time it takes to traverse them is different. The A* algorithm always searches for the lowest-cost path. If the cost of every node is the same, the result will be the shortest path. However, if we vary the cost of the nodes, the lowest-cost path might no longer be the shortest path. If we equate cost with time, A* will find the fastest path rather than the shortest path. Figure 7-21 shows the same tile layout as the previous example, but with the introduction of the terrain elements shown in Figure 7-22.

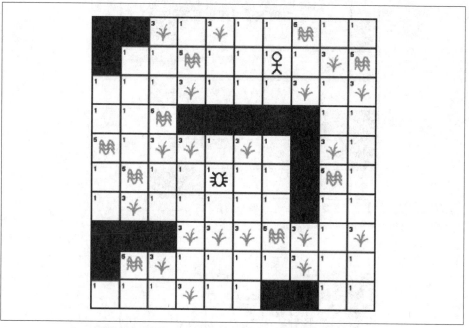

Figure 7-21. Adding different terrain elements

As you can see in Figure 7-21, the obstacles and game characters are in the same locations as they were in the previous example. The only difference now is the addition of terrain cost. We are no longer looking for the shortest physical path. We now want the fastest path. We are going to assume that grassland takes three times longer to traverse than open terrain does, and that swampland takes five times longer. The question is, how will the added terrain cost affect the path? Figure 7-22 shows the path derived from the previous example.

As Figure 7-22 shows, the shortest path was found. However, you'll notice that the path is now over several high-cost terrain elements. There is no question that it's the shortest path, but is there a quicker path? We determine this by using the same A* algorithm we stepped through in the first example, but this time we add the terrain cost to the total cost of each node. Figure 7-23 shows the results of following the entire algorithm to its conclusion.

As you can see in Figure 7-23, this is very similar to how we calculated the path in the previous example. We use the same branching technique where we examine the

Figure 7-22. Original path over terrain elements

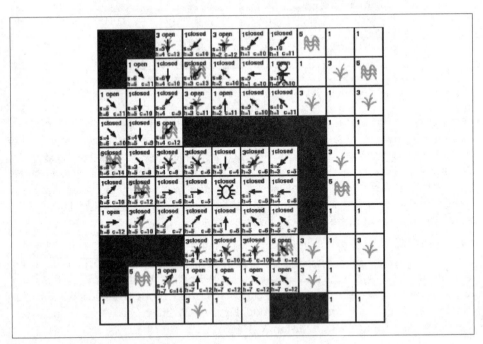

Figure 7-23. Calculating the lowest-cost path

adjacent tiles of the current tile. We then use the same open and closed list to track which tiles need to be examined and which are no longer of interest. The main difference is the *s* value, which is the cost of moving to any given node from the starting node. We simply used a value of 1 for every node in the previous example. We are now adding the terrain cost to the *s* value. The resulting lowest-cost path is shown in Figure 7-24.

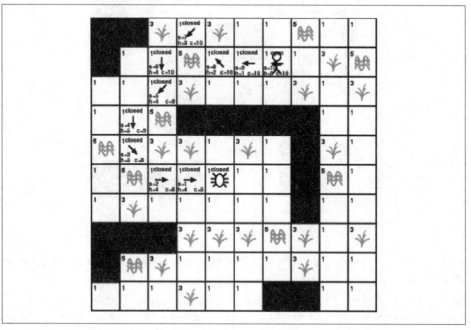

Figure 7-24. The lowest-cost path

As Figure 7-24 shows, the A* algorithm has worked its way around the higher-cost terrain elements. We no longer have the shortest physical path, but we can be assured that no quicker path exists. Other paths might exist that are physically shorter or longer and that would take the same amount of time to traverse, but none would be quicker.

Terrain cost also can be useful when applying the A* algorithm to a continuous environment. The previous examples showed how you can apply the A* algorithm to a tiled environment where all nodes are equidistant. However, equidistant nodes are not a requirement of the A* algorithm. Figure 7-25 shows how nodes could be placed in a continuous environment.

In Figure 7-25, you'll notice that the distance between the nodes varies. This means that in a continuous environment it will take a longer period of time to traverse the distances between the nodes that are farther apart. This, of course, assumes an equivalent terrain between nodes. However, in this case, the cost of moving between

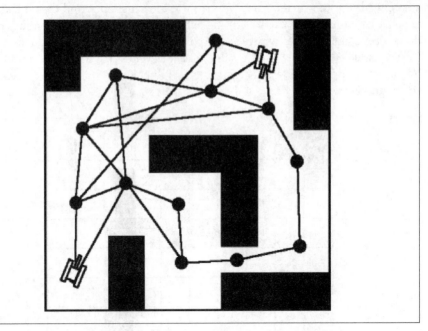

Figure 7-25. Continuous environment node placement

nodes would vary even though the terrain is equivalent. The cost would be equal to the distance between nodes.

We've discussed several different types of costs associated with moving between nodes. Although we tend to think of cost as being either time or distance, other possibilities exist, such as money, fuel, or other types of resources.

Influence Mapping

The previous section showed how different terrain elements can affect how the A* algorithm calculates a path. Terrain cost is usually something that the game designer hardcodes into the game world. Basically, we know beforehand where the grasslands, swamplands, hills, and rivers will be located. However, other elements can influence path cost when calculating a path with A*. For example, nodes that pass through the line of sight of any enemy might present a higher cost. This isn't a cost that you could build into a game level because the position of the game characters can change. *Influence mapping* is a way to vary the cost of the A* nodes depending on what is happening in the game. This is illustrated in Figure 7-26.

As Figure 7-26 shows, we have assigned a cost to each node. Unlike the terrain cost we showed you in the previous section, however, this cost is influenced by the position and orientation of the tank shown at position (8, 4). This influence map

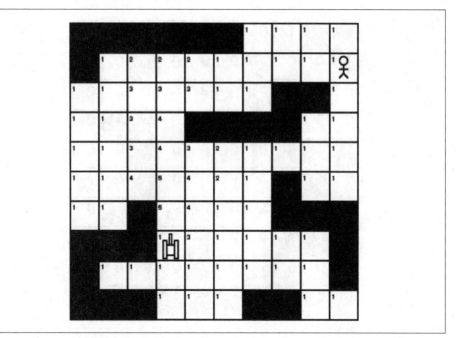

Figure 7-26. Influenced by the enemy firing zone

will change as the tank's position and orientation change. Like the terrain cost from the previous section, the influence map cost will be added to each node's *s* value when calculating possible paths. This will result in the tank's target possibly taking a longer and slower route when building a path. However, the tiles in the line of fire still are passable, just at a higher cost. If no other path is available, or if the alternate paths have a higher cost, the game character will pass through the line of fire.

You can use influence mapping in other ways to make game characters seem smarter. You can record individual game incidents in an influence map. In this case, we aren't using the position and orientation of a game character to build an influence map. We are instead using what the character does. For example, if the player repeatedly ambushes and kills computer-controlled characters at a given doorway, that doorway might increase in cost. The computer could then begin to build alternate paths whenever possible. To the player, this can make the computer-controlled characters seem very intelligent. It will appear as though they are learning from their mistakes. This technique is illustrated in Figure 7-27.

The influence map illustrated in Figure 7-27 records the number of kills the player makes on each node. Each time the player makes a kill, that node increases in cost. For example, there might be a particular doorway where the player has discovered an ambush technique that has led to a series of successful kills. Instead of having

Figure 7-27. Influenced by the number of kills

the computer-controlled adversaries repeatedly pass through the same doorway, you could create perhaps a longer, but less costly path to offset the player's tactical advantage.

Further Information

Steven Woodcock reported in his "2003 Game Developer's Conference AI Roundtable Moderator's Report" that AI developers essentially considered pathfinding solved. Other game AI resources all over the Web echo this sentiment. What developers mean is that proven algorithms are available to solve pathfinding problems in a wide variety of game scenarios and most effort these days is focused on optimizing these methods. The workhorse pathfinding method is by far the A* algorithm. Current development effort is now focused on developing faster, more efficient A* algorithms. *Game Programming Gems* (Charles River Media) and *AI Game Programming Wisdom* (Charles River Media) contain several interesting articles on A* optimizations.

CHAPTER 8

Scripted AI and Scripting Engines

This chapter discusses some of the techniques you can use to apply a scripting system to the problem of game AI, and the benefits you can reap from doing this. At its most basic level, you can think of scripting as a very simple programming language tailored to a specific task related to the game in question. Scripting can be an integral part of the game development process, as it enables the game designers rather than the game programmers to write and refine much of the game mechanics. Players also can use scripting to create or modify their own game worlds or levels. Taken a step further, you can use a scripting system in a massively multiplayer online role-playing game (MMORG) to alter the game behavior while the game is actually being played.

You can take several approaches when implementing a scripting system. A sophisticated scripting system might interface an already existing scripting language, such as Lua or Python, for example, with the actual game engine. Some games create a proprietary scripting language designed for the needs of the individual game. Although it's sometimes beneficial to use those methods, it's easier to have the game parse standard text files containing the scripting commands. Employing this approach, you can create scripts using any standard text editor. In a real game, the scripts can be read in and parsed when the game first starts, or at some other specified time. For example, scripts that control creatures or events in a dungeon can be read in and parsed when the player actually enters the dungeon area.

In the scope of game AI, you can use scripting to alter opponent attributes, behavior, responses, and game events. This chapter looks at all these uses.

Scripting Techniques

The actual scripting language used in a game is ultimately up to the game designers and programmers. It can resemble preexisting languages such as C or C++, or it can take a totally unique approach; perhaps even a graphical rather than a text-based approach. Deciding how the scripting system looks and works depends primarily on who will be using the scripting system. If your target is the end player, a more natural language or graphical approach might be beneficial. If the system is primarily for the designers and programmers, it might not be beneficial to spend your development time on a complex and time-consuming natural language parsing system. A quick and dirty approach might be better.

You also should consider other factors when developing a scripting system. Perhaps you want the script to be easy to read and write for the game designers, but not necessarily for the game players. In this case, you might want to use a form of encryption. You also could develop a script compiler so that the end result is less readable to humans.

In this chapter we create simple scripting commands and save them in standard text files. We want to avoid the need for a complex language parser, but at the same time we have been careful to choose a vocabulary that makes it relatively easy for humans to read and write the scripts. In other words, we use words that accurately reflect the aspect of the game that the script is altering.

Scripting Opponent Attributes

It's common and beneficial to specify all the basic attributes of each AI opponent by using some type of scripting. This makes it easy to tweak the AI opponents throughout the development and testing process. If all the vital data were hardcoded into the program, you would have to recompile for even the most basic change.

In general, you can script opponent attributes such as intelligence, speed, strength, courage, and magical ability. In reality, there is no limit to the possible number or types of attributes you can script. It really comes down to the type of game you're developing. Of course, the game engine ultimately will use these attributes whenever a computer-controlled friend or foe interacts with the player. For example, an opponent that has a higher intelligence attribute would be expected to behave differently from one of lower intelligence. Perhaps a more intelligent opponent would use a more sophisticated pathfinding algorithm to track down a player, while a less intelligent opponent might become easily confused when trying to reach the player.

Example 8-1 shows a basic script you can use to set game attributes.

Example 8-1. Basic script to set attributes

```
CREATURE=1;
INTELLIGENCE=20;
STRENGTH=75;
SPEED=50;
END
```

In this example, our script parser has to interpret five commands. The first, CREATURE, indicates which AI opponent is being set. The next three, INTELLIGENCE, STRENGTH, and SPEED, are the actual attributes being set. The final command, END, tells the script parser that we are finished with that creature. Anything that follows comprises a new and separate block of commands.

It would be just as easy to include the numbers 1,20,75,50 in a file and thus avoid any need for parsing the script text. That approach works and developers use it frequently, but it does have some disadvantages. First, you lose quite a bit of readability. Second, and most important, your scripting system can increase in complexity to the point where specifying attributes by just including their numerical values in a file becomes impractical. Example 8-2 shows how a script can become more complicated by using a conditional statement.

Example 8-2. Conditional script to set attributes

```
CREATURE=1;
If (LEVEL<5)
  BEGIN
     INTELLIGENCE=20;
     STRENGTH=75;
     SPEED=50;
  END
ELSE
  BEGIN
     INTELLIGENCE=40;
     STRENGTH=150;
     SPEED=100;
  END
END
```

As shown in Example 8-2, we now have conditional statements that initialize the creature attributes to different values depending on the current game level.

Basic Script Parsing

Now that we've shown what a basic attribute script looks like, we're going to explore how a game reads and parses a script. As an example, we will use a basic script to set some of the attributes for a troll. We will create a text file called *Troll Settings.txt*. Example 8-3 shows the contents of the troll settings file.

Example 8-3. Basic script to set attributes

```
INTELLIGENCE=20;
STRENGTH=75;
SPEED=50;
```

Example 8-3 is a simple example that sets only three creature attributes. However, we will set up our code so that we can easily add more attributes with very little change to our script parser. Basically, we are going to set up our parser so that it will search a given file for a specified keyword and then return the value associated with the keyword. Example 8-4 shows how this might look in an actual game.

Example 8-4. Basic script to set attributes

```
intelligence[kTroll]=fi_GetData("Troll Settings.txt,
                       "INTELLIGENCE");
strength[kTroll]= fi_GetData("Troll Settings.txt,
                     "STRENGTH");
speed[kTroll]= fi_GetData("Troll Settings.txt,
                   "SPEED");
```

Example 8-4 shows three hypothetical arrays that can store creature attributes. Rather than hardcoding these values into the game, they are loaded from an external script file called *Troll Settings.txt*. The function fi_GetData traverses the external file until it finds the specified keyword. It then returns the value associated with that keyword. The game designers are free to tweak the creature setting without the need to recompile the program code after each change.

Now that we have seen how you can use the fi_GetData function to set the attributes for a troll, let's go a step further. Example 8-5 shows how the function accomplishes its task.

Example 8-5. Reading data from a script

```
int fi_GetData(char filename[kStringLength], char searchFor[kStringLength])

{

FILE    *dataStream;
char    inStr[kStringLength];
char    rinStr[kStringLength];
char    value[kStringLength];
long    ivalue;
int     i;
int     j;

dataStream = fopen(filename, "r" );
if (dataStream != NULL)
   {
      while (!feof(dataStream))
         {
            if (!fgets(rinStr,kStringLength,dataStream))
              {
                 fclose( dataStream );
                 return (0);
              }
```

```
            j=0;
            strcpy(inStr,"");
            for (i=0;i<strlen(rinStr);i++)
              if (rinStr[i]!=' ')
                {
                  inStr[j]=rinStr[i];
                  inStr[j+1]='\0';
                  j++;
                }

            if (strncmp(searchFor, inStr,
                  strlen(searchFor)) == 0)
              {
                j=0;
                for(i=strlen(searchFor);
                  i<kStringLength;
                  i++)
                  {
                    if (inStr[i]==';')
                      break;
                    value[j]=inStr[i];
                    value[j+1]='\0';
                    j++;
                  }
                StringToNumber(value, &ivalue);
                fclose( dataStream );

                return ((int)ivalue);
              }
          }
        fclose( dataStream );
        return (0);
      }
  return (0);
}
```

The function in Example 8-5 begins by accepting two string parameters. The first specifies the name of the script file to be searched and the second is the search term. The function then opens the text file using the specified file name. Once the file is opened, the function begins traversing the script file one text line at a time. Each line is read in as a string.

Notice that each line is read into the variable rinStr, and then it's copied immediately to inStr, but without the spaces. The spaces are eliminated to make the parsing a bit more foolproof. This prevents our script parser from getting tripped up if the script writer adds one or more spaces before or after the search term or attributes. Once we have a script line stored in a string, sans spaces, we can search for the search term.

As you recall, we passed our search term to the fi_GetData function by using the string variable searchFor. At this point in the function, we use the C function strncmp to search inStr for the search term.

If the search term is not found, the function simply proceeds to read the next text line in the script file. However, if it is found, we enter a new loop that copies into a new string named `value` the part of `inStr` that contains the attribute value. The string value is converted to an integer value by calling the outside function `StringToNumber`. The `fi_GetData` function then returns the value in `ivalue`.

This function is written in a very generic way. No search terms are hardcoded into the function. It simply searches the given file for a search term and then returns an integer value associated with it. This makes it easy to add new attributes to our program code.

Also, note that this is one area of game development where it is important to check for errors. This is true particularly if you want players as well as game designers to use the scripting system. You should never assume any of the scripts being parsed are valid. For example, you shouldn't rely on the script writers to keep all the numeric values within legal bounds.

Scripting Opponent Behavior

Directly affecting an opponent's behavior is one of the most common uses of scripting in game AI. Some of the previous examples showed how scripting attributes can have an indirect effect on behavior. This included such examples as modifying a creature's intelligence attribute, which presumably would alter its behavior in the game.

Scripting behavior enables us to directly manipulate the actions of an AI opponent. For this to be useful, however, we need some way for our script to see into the game world and check for conditions that might alter our AI behavior. To accomplish this we can add predefined global variables to our scripting system. The actual game engine, not our scripting language, will assign the values in these variables. They are used simply as a way for the script to evaluate a particular condition in the game world. We will use these global variables in conditional scripting statements. For example, in our scripting system we might have a global boolean variable called `PlayerArmed` which will direct a cowardly troll to ambush only unarmed opponents. Example 8-6 shows how such a script might look.

Example 8-6. Basic behavior script

```
If (PlayerArmed==TRUE)
   BEGIN
     DoFlee();
   END
ELSE
   BEGIN
     DoAttack();
   END
```

In Example 8-6, the script does not assign the value `PlayerArmed`. It represents a value within the game engine. The game engine will evaluate the script and link this behavior to the cowardly troll.

In this example, the value `PlayerArmed` is a simple boolean value that represents nothing more than another boolean value within the game engine. There certainly is nothing wrong with this, but scripting is more useful when you use simple global variables which represent a more complex series of evaluations. For example, in this sample script we checked whether the player was armed. Although that might be useful for an opponent to know, it doesn't necessarily represent how challenging the opponent will be in a fight.

Many factors could contribute to how challenging a potential opponent will be. We can make our scripting system even more powerful if we evaluate these conditions in the game engine and then make the result available to the script as a single global variable. For example, we could use a Bayesian network to evaluate how tough an opponent the player is and then make the result available in a variable such as `PlayerChallenge`. The script shown in Example 8-7 is just as simple as the one in Example 8-6, but it can have a much more sophisticated effect on the gameplay.

Example 8-7. Behavior script

```
If (PlayerChallenge ==DIFFICULT)
   BEGIN
     DoFlee();
   END
ELSE
   BEGIN
     DoAttack();
   END
```

In the case of Example 8-7, `PlayerChallenge` could represent a series of complex evaluations that rank the player. Some of the factors could include whether the player is armed, the type of armor being worn, the current player's health, whether any other players in the area might come to his defense, and so on.

Another aspect of behavior that you can script is AI character movement. We can take a concept, such as pattern movement from Chapter 3, and implement it in a scripting system. For example, it might be useful for the game designer to establish patrol patterns for AI characters. Chapter 3 showed some examples of hardcoded pattern movement. Of course, hardcoding behavior has many disadvantages. It's much more difficult to tweak a game's design if a recompile is needed after every minor change. Figure 8-1 shows an example of a movement pattern that a game designer can implement using a scripting system.

Example 8-8 shows how we can construct a script to achieve the desired behavior.

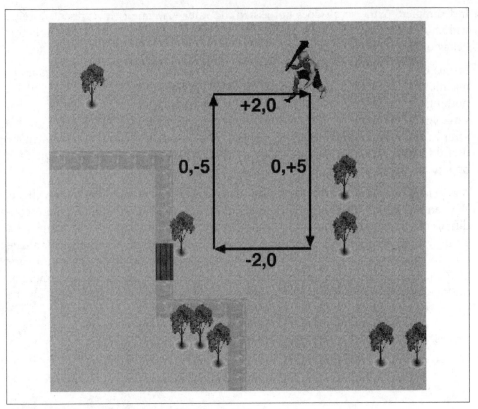

Figure 8-1. Scripted pattern movement

Example 8-8. Pattern movement script

```
If (creature.state==kPatrol)
  begin
    move(0,1);
    move(0,1);
    move(0,1);
    move(0,1);
    move(0,1);
    move(-1,0);
    move(-1,0);
    move(0,-1);
    move(0,-1);
    move(0,-1);
    move(0,-1);
    move(0,-1);
    move(0,1);
    move(0,1);
  end
```

Example 8-8 gives a glimpse of finite state machines from Chapter 9. In the scripting example, if the AI creature is in the patrolling state, it uses the specified movement pattern. Each move is shown as a single unit change from the previous position. See Chapter 3 for a detailed explanation of pattern movement techniques.

Scripting Verbal Interaction

The benefits of scripting go beyond just making an AI opponent more sophisticated and challenging. Many types of games incorporate intelligent behavior in ways that aren't meant to be a direct challenge to the player. A role-playing game, for example, might provide the player with a series of subtle hints meant to move the story along. Scripting is an excellent way to enable the game designer to create a compelling story without the need to alter the actual game program.

Intelligent behavior can make a game more challenging, but verbal responses that are intelligent and appropriate to the situation can go even farther when creating an immersive environment for the player. Verbal interaction can range from helpful hints from a friendly nonplayer character to taunts from an adversary. Verbal interaction seems most intelligent and immersive when it relates to the current game situation. This means the game AI needs to check a given set of game parameters and then respond to them accordingly.

For example, how a player is armed might be one parameter that can be checked. We can then have an adversarial AI character comment on how ineffective that weapon will be once combat starts. This seems more intelligent and immersive because it's not just a random taunt. It applies to the current game situation. It makes it seem as though the computer-controlled characters are aware of what's happening in the game. A quick example of how this script might look is shown in Example 8-9.

Example 8-9. Verbal taunt script

```
If (PlayerArmed ==Dagger)
  Say("What a cute little knife.");

If (PlayerArmed ==Bow)
  Say("Drop the bow now and I'll let you live.");

If (PlayerArmed ==Sword)
  Say("That sword will fit nicely in my collection.");

If (PlayerArmed ==BattleAxe)
  Say("You're too weak to wield that battle axe.");
```

As Example 8-9 shows, knowing a bit about the current game situation can add an immersive effect to gameplay. This is much more effective than simply adding random general taunts.

So, an important aspect of a scripting system is to enable the script writer to see what's happening inside the game engine. The more game elements the script can see, the better. Figure 8-2 shows a hypothetical game scenario in which an evil giant is chasing the player. In this case, the game AI is able to use unique elements of the game state to supply a taunt appropriate to the situation. In this case, we know that the adversary is a giant, the player is a human, and the player is armed with a staff.

Figure 8-2. Giant taunt

Example 8-10 shows how the game AI might can be an appropriate taunt during a battle between a computer-controlled giant and a player-controlled human. In a real game you probably would want to add multiple responses for each given situation and then randomly select among them. This would help prevent the responses from becoming repetitive and predictable.

Example 8-10. Giant taunt script

```
If (Creature==Giant) and (player==Human)
  begin
    if (playerArmed==Staff)
      Say("You will need more than a staff, puny human!");
```

```
if (playerArmed==Sword)
  Say("Drop your sword and I might not crush you!");

if (playerArmed==Dagger)
  Say("Your tiny dagger is no match for my club!");
end
```

Of course, this type of scripting isn't limited to adversarial characters that are out to kill the players. Benevolent computer-controlled characters can use the same techniques. This can help the script writer create an engaging and immersive plot. Example 8-11 shows how a script helps construct a plot and guide the player actions toward the game goals.

Example 8-11. Benevolent AI script

```
If (Creature==FriendlyWizard)
  begin
    if (playerHas==RedAmulet)
      Say("I see you found the Red Amulet.
          Bring it to the stone temple
          and you will be rewarded.");
  end
```

As Example 8-11 shows, a vital piece of information concerning where the amulet should be placed won't be revealed to the player until the amulet is found and the player confronts the friendly wizard.

The previous script examples show how game AI can respond in a given situation, but it's also sometimes necessary for game characters to have some type of verbal interaction with the player. This could be benevolent characters meant to provide the player with helpful information, or perhaps a less-than-honest character meant to intentionally mislead the player.

In this type of scenario, the player needs some mechanism to input text into the game. The game engine then makes the text strings available to the script system, which analyzes the text and provides an appropriate response. Figure 8-3 shows how this might appear in an actual game.

In the case of Figure 8-3, the player would type in the text "What is your name?" and the scripting system would return the text "I am Merlin." Example 8-12 shows a basic script that you could use to accomplish this.

Example 8-12. Basic "What is your name?" script

```
If Ask("What is your name?")
  begin
    Say("I am Merlin.");
  end
```

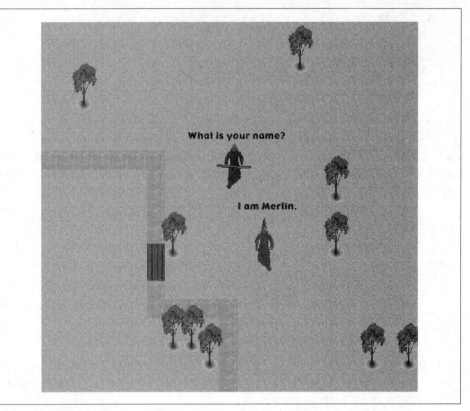

Figure 8-3. Merlin

Of course, Example 8-12 does have one serious flaw. It works only when the player types in the exact text of the question as it appears in the script. In reality, you can form a question in many ways. For example, what happens if the player enters one of the lines of text shown in Example 8-13?

Example 8-13. Example player input

```
What's your name?
Whats your name?
What is your name.
What is thy name?
What is your name, Wizard?
Hello, what is your name?
```

As you can see, the script in Example 8-12 would fail for all the questions shown in Example 8-13, even though it's quite obvious what's being asked. Not only can you ask a question in many ways, but we also have to consider the possibility that the player might not form the question in a correct manner. In fact, you can see that one of the example questions ends in a period rather than a question mark. We could have strict requirements for the player-entered text, but it would have the effect of removing the player from the immersive effect of the game whenever he made the inevitable minor error.

One alternative to checking each literal text string is to create a language parser to decipher each sentence to determine exactly what is being asked. For some games a sophisticated language parser might be appropriate; however, for most games there is a simpler approach. As you saw in Example 8-13, you can form the same question in many ways, but if you'll notice, they all have something in common. They all contain the words "what" and "name." So, instead of checking for each literal text string, we can simply search for and respond to particular keywords. In this case, the scripting engine simply checks for the presence of given keywords within a text string.

As Example 8-14 shows, the script is checking for the presence of two keywords in the player-entered text. Using this approach, the script responds correctly to every question in Example 8-13.

Example 8-14. Keyword scripting

```
If (Ask("what") and Ask("name") )
  begin
    Say("I am Merlin.");
  end
```

Now that we've shown you how to write a typical script to check player input for a given set of keywords, let's look at how the actual game engine checks player input for a given keyword. Example 8-15 shows how to do this.

Example 8-15. Searching for keywords

```
Boolean FoundKeyword(char inputText[kStringLength], char
searchFor[kStringLength])

{
  char   inStr[kStringLength];
  char   searchStr[kStringLength];
  int    i;

  for (i=0;i<=strlen(inputText);i++)
    {
      inStr[i]=inputText[i];
      if (((int)inStr[i]>=65) && ((int)inStr[i]<=90))
        inStr[i]=(char)((int)inStr[i]+32);
    }

  for (i=0;i<=strlen(searchFor);i++)
    {
```

```
        searchStr[i]=searchFor[i];
        if (((int)searchStr[i]>=65) &&
           ((int)searchStr[i]<=90))
           searchStr[i]=(char)((int)searchStr[i]+32);
    }

  if (strstr(inStr,searchStr)!=NULL)
     return (true);

  return (false);

}
```

Example 8-15 shows the actual code in the game engine that is invoked whenever the "Ask" function is called from the game designer's script. This function takes two parameters: inputText, which is the line of text the player entered, and searchFor, which is the keyword we want to search for. The first thing we do in this function is to convert both strings to all lowercase. Like many programming languages, C and C++ are case-sensitive. A string containing the text "Name" is not equal to a string containing the text "name." We can't rely on the player always using capitalization consistently or properly. The simplest solution is to convert all strings to lowercase. That way, it doesn't matter if the player enters all uppercase, all lowercase, or some combination.

Once we have two lowercase strings, we call the C function strstr to compare the text strings. The strstr function searches inStr for the first occurrence of searchStr. If searchStr is not found in inStr, a null pointer is returned.

Scripting Events

Now let's examine some of the other ways scripting can make gameplay more immersive. The previous sections showed how scripts alter the behavior of AI characters. Scripting behavior goes a long way toward making games and AI characters seem more real. However, you can use scripting to make games more entertaining and realistic in other ways as well. In this section we examine how scripts trigger in-game events that might not be related directly to AI characters. For example, perhaps stepping on a particular location will trigger a trap. Example 8-16 shows how this might look in a text-based scripting language.

Example 8-16. Trap event script

```
If (PlayerLocation(120,76))
   Trigger(kExposionTrap);

If (PlayerLocation(56,16))
   Trigger(kPoisonTrap);
```

As Example 8-16 shows, the scripting system can compare the player position to some predetermined value and then trigger a trap if they are equal. Of course, you can make this much more sophisticated by making the triggering mechanism more complex. Perhaps the trap is triggered only if the player is holding a certain item or wearing a particular piece of armor.

Scripting also can be an effective way to add a sense of ambience to gameplay. For example, you can link certain situations or objects to particular sound effects. If the player walks on a dock, a seagull sound effect might be triggered. You could use an entire scripting file solely for linking sound effects to different situations.

Figure 8-4 shows the player standing in a doorway. This would be an excellent situation to link to a creaking-door sound effect.

Figure 8-4. Door Sound script

Example 8-17 shows how the player location or game situation, such as the game time, can trigger relevant sound effects.

Example 8-17. Triggered sound script

```
If (PlayerLocation(kDoorway))
  PlaySound(kCreakingDoorSnd);

If (PlayerLocation(kDock))
  PlaySound (kSeagullSnd);

If (PlayerLocation(kBoat))
  PlaySound (kWavesSnd);

If (GameTime==kNight)
  PlaySound (kCricketsSnd);

If (GameTime==kDay)
  PlaySound (kBirdsSnd);
```

Although this chapter differentiated between the types of AI scripting, in a real game it can be beneficial to use them together. For example, instead of a player action triggering an effect such as a sound effect, perhaps it triggers a specific creature AI patrolling pattern. We also showed examples of how AI creatures can respond to text entered by the player; however, this also can be a very useful way to trigger in-game events. For example, the player could recite a spell that triggers some event.

Further Information

In this chapter we showed you how to implement basic scripting that enables you to alter game AI outside the main game program. Such scripting can be very effective. Indeed, we successfully implemented these techniques in an MMORG to enable game masters to change the game AI and other game parameters in real time. Implementing a full-fledged scripting engine can be very challenging, and it involves additional concepts that we have not yet covered. These concepts include finite state machines and rule-based systems, which we'll get to in Chapters 9 and 11 of this book.

If you decide to pursue scripting even further than we do in this book, you might find the following resources to be particularly helpful:

- *AI Application Programming* by M.Tim Jones (Charles River Media)
- *AI Game Programming Wisdom* by Steve Rabin, ed. (Charles River Media)

In the first reference, author Tim Jones shows how to implement a scripted rule-based system from scratch. His approach combines concepts we covered in this chapter and those we will cover in Chapter 11. The second reference includes seven articles written by game programming veterans focusing specifically on issues related to implementing scripting engines for games.

CHAPTER 9

Finite State Machines

A *finite state machine* is an abstract machine that can exist in one of several different and predefined states. A finite state machine also can define a set of conditions that determine when the state should change. The actual state determines how the state machine behaves.

Finite state machines date back to the earliest days of computer game programming. For example, the ghosts in *Pac Man* are finite state machines. They can roam freely, chase the player, or evade the player. In each state they behave differently, and their transitions are determined by the player's actions. For example, if the player eats a power pill, the ghosts' state might change from chasing to evading. We'll come back to this example in the next section.

Although finite state machines have been around for a long time, they are still quite common and useful in modern games. The fact that they are relatively easy to understand, implement, and debug contributes to their frequent use in game development. In this chapter, we discuss the fundamentals of finite state machines and show you how to implement them.

Basic State Machine Model

The diagram in Figure 9-1 illustrates how you can model a simple finite state machine.

In Figure 9-1, each potential state is illustrated with a circle, and there are four possible states {Si, $S1$, $S2$, $S3$}. Of course, every finite state machine also needs a means to move from one state to another. In this case, the transition functions are illustrated as {$t1$, $t2$, $t3$, $t4$, $t5$}. The finite state machine begins with the initial state Si. It remains is this state until the $t1$ transition function provides a stimulus. Once the stimulus is provided, the state switches to $S1$. At this point, it's easy for you to see which stimulus is needed to move from one state to another. In some cases,

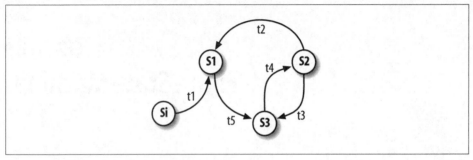

Figure 9-1. Generic finite state machine diagram

such as with *S1*, only the stimulus provided by *t5* can change the machine's state. However, notice that in the case of *S3* and *S2* two possible stimuli result in a state change.

Now that we've shown you a simple state machine model, let's look at a more practical and slightly more complex example. Figure 9-2 shows a finite state machine that might appear in an actual game.

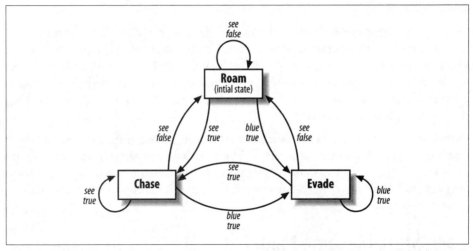

Figure 9-2. Ghost finite state machine diagram

Look closely at Figure 9-2, and you can see that the behavior of the finite state machine models a behavior similar to that of a ghost in *Pac Man*. Each oval represents a possible state. In this case, there are three possible states: roam, evade, and chase. The arrows show the possible transitions. The transitions show the conditions under which the state can change or remain the same.

In this case, the computer-controlled AI opponent begins in the initial rRoam state. Two conditions can cause a change of state. The first is blue=true. In this case, the AI opponent has turned blue because the player has eaten a power pill. This results in a state change from roam to evade. The other condition that can change the state is see=true, which means the game AI can see the player, resulting in a state change from roam to chase. Now it is no longer necessary to roam freely. The game AI can see and chase the player.

The figure also shows that the finite state machine stays in the evade state as long as it's blue. Otherwise, the state changes to chase if the player can be seen. If the player can't be seen, it reverts to the roam state. Likewise, the machine remains in the chase state unless it's blue, in which case it changes to evade. However, if it's chasing the player but loses sight of him or her, it once again reverts to the roam state.

Now that we've shown how you can model this behavior in a finite state machine diagram, let's see how you can set up actual program code to implement this behavior. Example 9-1 shows the code.

Example 9-1. Ghost behavior

```
switch (currentState)
  {

    case kRoam:
      if (imBlue==true) currentState=kEvade;
      else if (canSeePlayer==true) currentState=kChase;
      else if (canSeePlayer==false) currentState=kRoam;
      break;


    case kChase:
      if (imBlue==true) currentState=kEvade;
      else if (canSeePlayer==false) currentState=kRoam;
      else if (canSeePlayer==true) currentState=kChase;
      break;

    case kEvade:
      if (imBlue==true) currentState=kEvade;
      else if (canSeePlayer==true) currentState=kChase;
      else if (canSeePlayer==false) currentState=kRoam;
      break;


  }
```

The program code in Example 9-1 is not necessarily the most efficient solution to the problem, but it does show how you can use actual program code to model the behavior shown in Figure 9-2. In this case, the switch statement checks for three possible states: kRoam, kChase, and kEvade. Each case in the switch statement then checks for the possible conditions under which the state either changes or remains the same. Notice that in each case the imBlue condition is considered to have precedence. If imBlue is true, the state automatically switches to kEvade regardless of any other conditions. The finite state machine then remains in the kEvade state as long as imBlue is true.

Finite State Machine Design

Now we will discuss some of the methods you can use to implement a finite state machine in a game. Finite state machines actually lend themselves very well to game AI development. They present a simple and logical way to control game AI behavior. In fact, they probably have been implemented in many games without the developer realizing that a finite state machine model was being used.

We'll start by dividing the task into two components. First, we will discuss the types of structures we will use to store the data associated with the game AI entity. Then we will discuss how to set up the functions we will use to transition between the machine states.

Finite State Machine Structures and Classes

Games that are developed using a high-level language, such as C or C++, typically store all the data related to each game AI entity in a single structure or class. Such a structure can contain values such as position, health, strength, special abilities, and inventory, among many others. Of course, besides all these elements, the structure also stores the current AI state, and it's the state that ultimately determines the AI's behavior. Example 9-2 shows how a typical game might store a game AI entity's data in a single class structure.

Example 9-2. Game AI structure

```
class AIEntity
  {
    public:
      int type;
      int state;
      int row;
      int column;
      int health;
      int strength;
      int intelligence;
      int magic;
  };
```

In Example 9-2, the first element in the class refers to the entity type. This can be anything, such as a troll, a human, or an interstellar battle cruiser. The next element in the class is the one that concerns us most in this chapter. This is where the AI state is stored. The remaining variables in the structure show typical values that generally are associated with a game AI entity.

The state itself typically is assigned using a global constant. Adding a new state is as simple as adding a new global constant. Example 9-3 shows how you can define such constants.

Example 9-3. State constants

```
#define   kRoam        1
#define   kEvade       2
#define   kAttack      3
#define   kHide        4
```

Now that we've seen how the AI state and vital statistics are grouped in a single class structure, let's look at how we can add transition functions to the structure.

Finite State Machine Behavior and Transition Functions

The next step in implementing a finite state machine is to provide functions that determine how the AI entity should behave and when the state should be changed. Example 9-4 shows how you can add behavior and transition functions to an AI class structure.

Example 9-4. Game AI transition functions

```
class   AIEntity
  {
     public:
        int type;
        int state;
        int row;
        int column;
        int health;
        int strength;
        int intelligence;
        int magic;
        int armed;

        Boolean playerInRange();
        int checkHealth();
  };
```

You can see that we added two functions to the AIEntity class. Of course, in a real game you probably would use many functions to control the AI behavior and alter the AI state. In this case, however, two transition functions suffice to demonstrate how you can alter an AI entity's state. Example 9-5 shows how you can use the two transition functions to change the machine state.

Example 9-5. Changing states

```
if ((checkHealth()<kPoorHealth) && (playerInRange()==false))
  state=kHide;
else if (checkHealth()<kPoorHealth)
  state=kEvade;
else if (playerInRange())
  state=kAttack;
else
  state=kRoam;
```

The first if statement in Example 9-5 checks to see if the AI entity's health is low and if the player is not nearby. If these conditions are true, the creature represented by this class structure goes into a hiding state. Presumably, it remains in this state until its health increases. The second if simply checks for poor health. The fact that we've reached this if statement means the player is nearby. If that wasn't the case, the first if statement would have been evaluated as true. Because the player is nearby, hiding might not be practical, as the player might be able to see the AI entity. In this case, it's more appropriate to attempt to evade the player. The third if statement checks to see if the player is in range. Once again, we know the AI is in good health; otherwise, one of the first two if statements would have been evaluated as true. Because the player is nearby and the AI entity is in good health, the state is changed to attack. The final state option is selected if none of the other options applies. In this case, we go into a default roam state. The creature in this example remains in the roam state until the conditions specified by the transition function indicate that the state should change.

The previous sections showed the basics of setting up a class structure and transition functions for a simple finite state machine. In the next section we go on to implement these concepts into a full-featured finite state machine example.

Ant Example

The objective in this example of our finite state machine is to create a finite state machine simulation consisting of two teams of AI ants. The purpose of the simulation is for the ants to collect food and return it to their home position. The ants will have to follow certain obstacles and rules in the simulation. First, the ants will move randomly in their environment in an attempt to locate a piece of food. Once an ant finds a piece of food, it will return to its home position. When it arrives home, it will drop its food and then start a new search for water rather than food. The thirsty ants will roam randomly in search of water. Once an ant finds water, it will resume its search for more food.

Returning food to the home position also will result in a new ant emerging from the home position. The ant population will continue to grow so long as more food is returned to the home position. Of course, the ants will encounter obstacles along the way. In addition to the randomly placed food will be randomly placed poison. Naturally, the poison has a fatal effect on the ants.

Figure 9-3 presents a finite state diagram that illustrates the behavior of each ant in the simulation.

As Figure 9-3 shows, each ant begins in the initial forage state. From that point, the state can change in only two ways. The state can change to go home with the found food transition function, or it can encounter the found poison transition, which kills the ant. Once food is found, the state changes to go home. Once again, there are

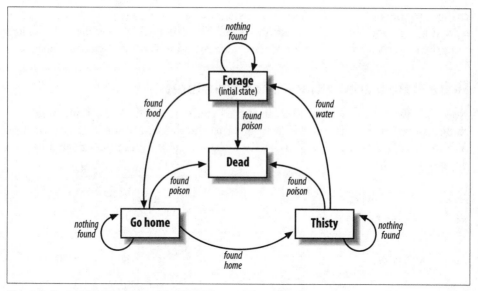

Figure 9-3. Ant finite state machine diagram

only two ways out of this state. One is to meet the objective and find the home position. This is illustrated by the found home transition arrow. The other possible transition is to find poison. Once the home position is found, the state changes to thirsty. Like the previous states, there are two ways to change states. One is to meet the goal by finding water, and the other is to find poison. If the goal is met, the ant returns to the initial forage state.

As you can see, the ants will be in one of several different states as they attempt to perform their tasks. Each state represents a different desired behavior. So, we will now use the previously described rules for our simulation to define the possible states for the AI ants. This is demonstrated in Example 9-6.

Example 9-6. Ant states

```
#define   kForage      1
#define   kGoHome      2
#define   kThirsty     3
#define   kDead        4
```

The first rule for the simulation is that the ants forage randomly for food. This is defined by the kForage state. Any ant in the kForage state moves randomly about its environment in search of food. Once an ant finds a piece of food, it changes to the kGoHome state. In this state, the ant returns to its home position. It no longer forages when in the kGoHome state. It ignores any food it finds while returning home. If the ant successfully returns to its home position without encountering any poison, it changes to the kThirsty state. This state is similar to the forage state, but instead of searching for food the ant searches for water. Once it finds water, the ant changes from the kThirsty state back to the kForage state. At that point the behavior repeats.

Finite State Machine Classes and Structures

Now that we have described and illustrated the basic goal of the finite state machine in our ant simulation, let's move on to the data structure that we will use. As shown in Example 9-7, we'll use a C++ class to store all the data related to each finite state machine ant.

Example 9-7. ai_Entity class

```
#define  kMaxEntities      200


class    ai_Entity
{
  public:
  int          type;
  int          state;
  int          row;
  int          col;

  ai_Entity();
  ~ai_Entity();

};

ai_Entity    entityList[kMaxEntities];
```

As Example 9-7 shows, we start with a C++ class containing four variables. The first variable is type, which is the type of AI entity the structure represents.

If you remember from the previous description, the ant simulation consists of two teams of ants. We will differentiate between them by using the constants in Example 9-8.

Example 9-8. Team constants

```
#define  kRedAnt      1
#define  kBlackAnt    2
```

The second variable in ai_Entity is state. This variable stores the current state of the ant. This can be any of the values defined in Example 9-6; namely, kForage, kGoHome, kThirsty, and kDead.

The final two variables are row and col. The ant simulation takes place in a tiled environment. The row and col variables contain the positions of the ants within the tiled world.

As Example 9-7 goes on to show, we create an array to store each ant's data. Each element in the array represents a different ant. The maximum number of ants in the simulation is limited by the constant, which also is defined in Example 9-7.

Defining the Simulation World

As we stated previously, the simulation takes place in a tiled environment. The world is represented by a two-dimensional array of integers. Example 9-9 shows the constant and array declarations.

Example 9-9. Terrain array

```
#define  kMaxRows    32
#define  kMaxCols    42

int  terrain[kMaxRows][kMaxCols];
```

Each element in the terrain array stores the value of a tile in the environment. The size of the world is defined by the kMaxRows and kMaxCols constants. A real tile-based game most likely would contain a large number of possible values for each tile. In this simulation, however, we are using only six possible values. Example 9-10 shows the constants.

Example 9-10. Terrain values

```
#define  kGround      1
#define  kWater       2
#define  kBlackHome   3
#define  kRedHome     4
#define  kPoison      5
#define  kFood        6
```

The default value in the tile environment is kGround. You can think of this as nothing more than an empty location. The next constant, kWater, is the element the ants search for when in the kThirsty state. The next two constants are kBlackhome and kRedHome. These are the home locations the ants seek out when in the kGoHome state. Stepping on a tile containing the kPoison element kills the ants, changing their states to kDead. The final constant is kFood. When an ant in the kForage state steps on a terrain element containing the kFood element, it changes states from kForage to kGoHome.

Once the variables and constants are declared, we can proceed to initialize the world using the code shown in Example 9-11.

Example 9-11. Initializing the world

```
#define  kRedHomeRow      5
#define  kRedHomeCol      5

#define  kBlackHomeRow    5
#define  kBlackHomeCol    36
```

```
for (i=0;i<kMaxRows;i++)
  for (j=0;j<kMaxCols;j++)
    {
      terrain[i][j]=kGround;
    }

terrain[kRedHomeRow][kRedHomeCol]=kRedHome;
terrain[kBlackHomeRow][kBlackHomeCol]=kBlackHome;

for (i=0;i<kMaxWater;i++)
  terrain[Rnd(2,kMaxRows)-3][Rnd(1,kMaxCols)-1]=kWater;

for (i=0;i<kMaxPoison;i++)
  terrain[Rnd(2,kMaxRows)-3][Rnd(1,kMaxCols)-1]=kPoison;

for (i=0;i<kMaxFood;i++)
  terrain[Rnd(2,kMaxRows)-3][Rnd(1,kMaxCols)-1]=kFood;
```

Example 9-11 starts by initializing the entire two-dimensional world array to the value in kGround. Remember, this is the default value. We then initialize the two home locations. The actual positions are defined in the constants kRedHomeRow, kRedHomeCol, kBlackHomeRow, and kBlackHomeCol. These are the positions the ants move toward when in the kGoHome state. Each ant moves to its respective color.

The final section of Example 9-11 shows three for loops that randomly place the kWater, kPoison, and kFood tiles. The number of each type of tile is defined by its respective constant. Of course, altering these values changes the behavior of the simulation.

Figure 9-4 shows the result of initializing the tiled world. We haven't populated the world yet with any finite state machine ants, but we do have the randomly placed food, water, and poison.

Now that we've initialized the variables associated with the tile, the next step is to begin populating the world with AI ants.

Populating the World

The first thing we need is some means of creating a new AI entity. To accomplish this, we are going to add a new function to the ai_Entity class. Example 9-12 shows the addition to the ai_Entity class.

Example 9-12. ai_Entity class

```
class     ai_Entity
{
  public:
    int        type;
    int        state;
```

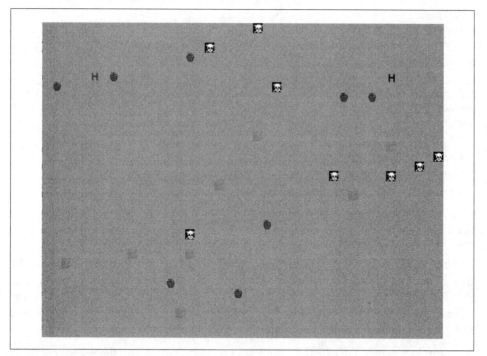

Figure 9-4. Ant world

```
int         row;
int         col;

ai_Entity();
~ai_Entity();

void New (int theType, int theState, int theRow, int theCol);

};
```

The New function is called whenever it is necessary to add a new ant to the world. At the beginning of the simulation we add only two of each color ant to the world. However, we call this function again whenever an ant successfully returns food to the home position. Example 9-13 shows how the actual function is defined.

Example 9-13. New ai_Entity

```
void ai_Entity::New(int  theType, int theState, int theRow, int theCol)

{
  int   i;

  type=theType;
  row=theRow;
```

```
        col=theCol;
        state=theState;


}
```

The New function is rather simple. It initializes the four values in ai_Entity. These include the entity type, state, row, and column. Now let's look at Example 9-14 to see how the New function adds ants to the finite state machine simulation.

Example 9-14. Adding ants

```
entityList[0].New(kRedAnt,kForage,5,5);
entityList[1].New(kRedAnt,kForage,8,5);

entityList[2].New(kBlackAnt,kForage,5,36);
entityList[3].New(kBlackAnt,kForage,8,36);
```

As Example 9-14 shows, the simulation begins by adding four ants to the world. The first parameter passed to the New function specifies the entity type. In this simulation, we start with two red ants and two black ants. The second parameter is the initial state of the finite state machine ants. The final two parameters are the row and column positions of the starting point of each ant.

As Figure 9-5 shows, we added four ants to the simulation using the New function.

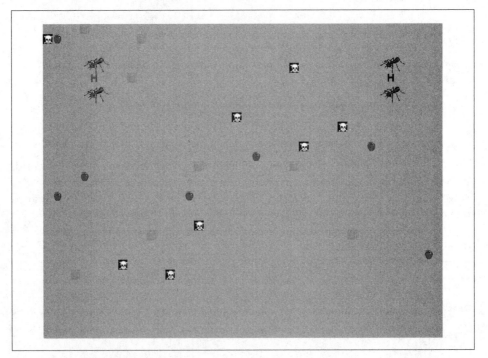

Figure 9-5. Populating the world

Each ant shown in Figure 9-5 begins with its initial state set to kForage. From their initial starting positions they will begin randomly moving about the tiled environment in search of food. In this case, the food is shown as apples. However, if they step on poison, shown as a skull and crossbones, they switch to the kDead state. The squares containing the water pattern are the elements they search for when they are in the kThirsty state.

Updating the World

In the previous section we successfully populated the world with four finite state machine ants. Now we will show you how to run the simulation. This is a critical part of the finite state machine implementation. If you recall, the basic premise of the finite state machine is to link individual and unique states to different types of behavior. This is the part of the code where we actually make each ant behave a certain way depending on its state. This part of the code lends itself to the use of a switch statement, which checks for each possible state. In a real game, this switch statement typically would be called once each time through the main loop. Example 9-15 shows how to use the switch statement.

Example 9-15. Running the simulation

```
for (i=0;i<kMaxEntities;i++)
   {
     switch (entityList[i].state)
        {
           case kForage:
             entityList[i].Forage();
             break;

           case kGoHome:
             entityList[i].GoHome();
             break;

           case kThirsty:
             entityList[i].Thirsty();
             break;

           case kDead:
             entityList[i].Dead();
             break;

        }
   }
```

As Example 9-15 shows, we create a loop that iterates through each element in the entityList array. Each entityList element contains a different finite state machine ant. We use a switch statement to check the state of each ant in entityList. Notice that we have a case statement for each possible state. We then link each state to the desired behavior by calling the appropriate function for each behavior. As you can see in Example 9-16, we need to add four new functions to the ai_Entity class.

Example 9-16. ai_Entity class functions

```
class    ai_Entity
{
  public:
  int            type;
  int            state;
  int            row;
  int            col;

  ai_Entity();
  ~ai_Entity();

  void  New (int theType, int theState, int theRow, int theCol);

  void Forage(void);
  void GoHome(void);
  void Thirsty(void);
  void Dead(void);

};
```

Example 9-16 shows the updated ai_Entity class with the four new behavior functions. Each function is associated with one of the state behaviors.

Forage

The first new function, Forage, is associated with the kForage state. If you recall, in this state the ants randomly move about the world in search of food. Once in the forage state, the ants can switch to a different state in only two ways. The first way is to meet the objective by randomly finding a piece of food. In this case, the state switches to kGoHome. The other way for the ants to switch states is by stepping on poison. In this case, the state switches to kDead. This behavior is implemented in the Forage function, as shown in Example 9-17.

Example 9-17. Forage function

```
void ai_Entity::Forage(void)

{
  int rowMove;
  int colMove;
  int newRow;
  int newCol;
  int foodRow;
```

```
    int foodCol;
    int poisonRow;
    int poisonCol;

    rowMove=Rnd(0,2)-1;
    colMove=Rnd(0,2)-1;

    newRow=row+rowMove;
    newCol=col+colMove;

    if (newRow<1) return;
    if (newCol<1) return;
    if (newRow>=kMaxRows-1) return;
    if (newCol>=kMaxCols-1) return;

    if ((terrain[newRow][newCol]==kGround) ||
        (terrain[newRow][newCol]==kWater))
      {
        row=newRow;
        col=newCol;
      }

    if (terrain[newRow][newCol]==kFood)
      {
        row=newRow;
        col=newCol;
        terrain[row][col]=kGround;
        state=kGoHome;
        do {
          foodRow=Rnd(2,kMaxRows)-3;
          foodCol=Rnd(2,kMaxCols)-3;
        } while (terrain[foodRow][foodCol]!=kGround);
        terrain[foodRow][foodCol]=kFood;
      }

    if (terrain[newRow][newCol]==kPoison)
      {
        row=newRow;
        col=newCol;
        terrain[row][col]=kGround;
        state=kDead;
        do {
          poisonRow=Rnd(2,kMaxRows)-3;
          poisonCol=Rnd(2,kMaxCols)-3;
        } while (terrain[poisonRow][poisonCol]!=kGround);
        terrain[poisonRow][poisonCol]=kPoison;
      }
}
```

The Forage function begins by declaring eight variables. The first two are rowMove and colMove. These two variables contain the distances to move in both the row and column directions. The next two variables are newRow and newCol. These two variables contain the new row and column positions of the ant. The final four variables, foodRow, foodCol, poisonRow, and poisonCol, are the new positions used to replace any food or poison that might get consumed.

We then proceed to calculate the new position. We begin by assigning a random number between -1 and +1 to the rowMove and colMove variables. This ensures that the ant can move in any of the eight possible directions in the tiled environment. It's also possible that both values will be 0, in which case the ant will remain in its current position.

Once we have assigned rowMove and colMove, we proceed to add their values to the current row and column positions and store the result in newRow and newCol. This will be the new ant position, assuming, of course, it's a legal position in the tiled environment. In fact, the next block of if statements checks to see if the new position is within the legal bounds of the tiled environment. If it's not a legal position, we exit the function.

Now that we know the position is legal, we go on to determine what the ant will be standing on in its new position. The first if statement simply checks for kGround or kWater at the new position. Neither of these two elements will cause a change in state, so we simply update the ant row and col with the values in newRow and newCol. The ant is shown in its new position after the next screen update.

The next section shows a critical part of the finite state machine design. This if statement checks to see if the new position contains food. This section is critical because it contains a possible state transition. If the new position does contain food, we update the ant's position, erase the food, and change the state of the ant. In this case, we are changing from kForage to kGoHome. The final do-while loop in this if statement replaces the consumed food with another randomly placed piece of food. If we don't continuously replace the consumed food, the ant population won't be able to grow.

The final part of the Forage function shows another possible state transition. The last if statement checks to see if the new position contains poison. If it does contain poison, the ant's position is updated, the poison is deleted, and the ant's state is changed from kForage to kDead. We then use the do-while loop to replenish the consumed poison.

GoHome

We are now going to move on to the second new behavior function that we added to the ai_Entity class in Example 9-16. This one is called GoHome and it's associated with the kGoHome state. As we stated previously, the ants switch to the kGoHome state once they randomly find a piece of food. They remain in this state until they either successfully return to their home position or step on poison. Example 9-18 shows the GoHome function.

Example 9-18. GoHome function

```
void ai_Entity::GoHome(void)

{
  int   rowMove;
  int   colMove;
  int   newRow;
  int   newCol;
  int   homeRow;
  int   homeCol;
  int   index;
  int   poisonRow;
  int   poisonCol;

  if (type==kRedAnt)
    {
      homeRow=kRedHomeRow;
      homeCol=kRedHomeCol;
    }
  else
    {
      homeRow=kBlackHomeRow;
      homeCol=kBlackHomeCol;
    }

  if (row<homeRow)
    rowMove=1;
  else if (row>homeRow)
    rowMove=-1;
  else
    rowMove=0;

  if (col<homeCol)
    colMove=1;
  else if (col>homeCol)
    colMove=-1;
  else
    colMove=0;

  newRow=row+rowMove;
  newCol=col+colMove;

  if (newRow<1) return;
  if (newCol<1) return;
  if (newRow>=kMaxRows-1) return;
  if (newCol>=kMaxCols-1) return;

  if (terrain[newRow][newCol]!=kPoison)
    {
      row=newRow;
      col=newCol;
    }
```

```
        else
          {
             row=newRow;
             col=newCol;
             terrain[row][col]=kGround;
             state=kDead;
             do {
                poisonRow=Rnd(2,kMaxRows)-3;
                poisonCol=Rnd(2,kMaxCols)-3;
             } while (terrain[poisonRow][poisonCol]!=kGround);
             terrain[poisonRow][poisonCol]=kPoison;
          }


     if ((newRow==homeRow) && (newCol==homeCol))
        {
           row=newRow;
           col=newCol;
           state=kThirsty;
           for (index=0; index <kMaxEntities; index ++)
              if (entityList[index].type==0)
                 {
                    entityList[index].New(type,
                                          kForage,
                                          homeRow,
                                          homeCol);
                    break;
                 }
        }
}
```

The variable declarations in the GoHome function are very similar to those in the
Forage function. In this function, however, we added two new variables, homeRow and
homeCol. We will use these two variables to determine if the ant has successfully
reached its home position. The variable index is used when adding a new ant to the
world. The remaining two variables, poisonRow and poisonCol, are used to replace any
poison that might be consumed.

We start by determining where the home position is located. If you recall, there are
two types of ants, red ants and black ants. Each color has a different home position.
The positions of each home are set in the globally defined constants kRedHomeRow,
kRedHomeCol, kBlackHomeRow, and kBlackHomeCol. We check the entity type to determine
if it's a red ant or a black ant. We then use the global home position constants to
set the local homeRow and homeCol variables. Now that we know where the home is
located, we can move the ant toward that position.

As you might recall, this is a variation of the simple chasing algorithm from Chapter 2. If the ant's current row is less than the home row, the row offset, rowMove,
is set to 1. If the ant's row is greater than the home row, rowMove is set to -1. If
they are equal, there is no need to change the ant's row, so rowMove is set to 0. The

column positions are handled the same way. If the ant's column is less than the home column, colMove is set to 1. If it's greater, it's set to -1. If col is equal to homeCol, colMove is set to 0.

Once we have the row and column offsets, we can proceed to calculate the new row and column positions. We determine the new row position by adding rowMove to the current row position. We determine the new column position by adding colMove to the current column position.

Once we assign the values to newRow and newCol, we check to see if the new position is within the bounds of the tiled environment. It's good practice to always do this, but in this case, it's really not necessary. This function always moves the ants toward their home position, which always should be within the confines of the tiled world. So, the ants always will be confined to the limits of the world unless the global home position constants are changed to something outside the limits of the world.

The first part of the if statement checks to see if the ant did not step on poison. If the new position does not contain poison, the ant's position is updated. If the else portion of the if statement gets executed, we know the ant has, in fact, stepped on poison. In this case, a state change is required—the ant's position is updated, the poison is deleted, and the ant's state is changed from kGoHome to kDead. We then use the do-while loop to replace the consumed poison.

The final if statement in the GoHome function checks to see if the goal was achieved. It uses the values we assigned to homeRow and homeCol to determine if the new position is equal to the home position. If so, the ant's position is updated and the state is switched from kGoHome to kThirsty. This will make the ant assume a new behavior the next time the UpdateWorld function is executed. The final part of the if statement is used to generate a new ant. If you recall, whenever food is successfully returned to the home position, a new ant is spawned. We use a for loop to traverse the entityList and check for the first unused element in the array. If an unused array element is found, we create a new ant at the home position and initialize it to the kForage state.

Thirsty

The next behavior function we added to the ai_Entity class in Example 9-16 is associated with the kThirsty state. As you recall, the ants are switched to the kThirsty state after successfully returning food to their home positions. In this state, the ants randomly move about the world in search of water. Unlike the kForage state, however, the ants don't return to the home position after meeting their goal. Instead, when the ants find water, the state switches from kThirsty back to kForage. As with the previous states, stepping on poison automatically changes the state to kDead.

The third new behavior function we added to the ai_Entity class is called Thirsty, and as the name implies, it's executed when the ants are in the kThirsty state. As we stated previously, the ants switch to the kThirsty state after successfully returning food to their home positions. They remain in the kThirsty state until they find water or until they step on poison. If they find water, they revert to their initial kForage state. If they step on poison, they switch to the kDead state. Example 9-19 shows the Thirsty function.

Example 9-19. Thirsty function

```
void ai_Entity::Thirsty(void)

{
    int   rowMove;
    int   colMove;
    int   newRow;
    int   newCol;
    int   foodRow;
    int   foodCol;
    int   poisonRow;
    int   poisonCol;

    rowMove=Rnd(0,2)-1;
    colMove=Rnd(0,2)-1;

    newRow=row+rowMove;
    newCol=col+colMove;

    if (newRow<1) return;
    if (newCol<1) return;
    if (newRow>=kMaxRows-1) return;
    if (newCol>=kMaxCols-1) return;

    if ((terrain[newRow][newCol]==kGround) ||
        (terrain[newRow][newCol]==kFood))
        {
          row=newRow;
          col=newCol;
        }


    if (terrain[newRow][newCol]==kWater)
        {
          row=newRow;
          col=newCol;
          terrain[row][col]=kGround;
          state=kForage;
          do {
             foodRow=Rnd(2,kMaxRows)-3;
             foodCol=Rnd(2,kMaxCols)-3;
          } while (terrain[foodRow][foodCol]!=kGround);
          terrain[foodRow][foodCol]=kWater;
        }
```

```
    if (terrain[newRow][newCol]==kPoison)
      {
        row=newRow;
        col=newCol;
        terrain[row][col]=kGround;
        state=kDead;
        do {
          poisonRow=Rnd(2,kMaxRows)-3;
          poisonCol=Rnd(2,kMaxCols)-3;
        } while (terrain[poisonRow][poisonCol]!=kGround);
        terrain[poisonRow][poisonCol]=kPoison;
      }

}
```

As you can see in Example 9-19, the Thirsty function begins much like the Forage function. We declare two position offset variables, rowMove and colMove, and two variables for the new ant position, newRow and newCol. The remaining variables, foodRow, foodCol, poisonRow, and poisonCol, are used when replacing consumed food and poison.

We then calculate a random offset for both the row and column positions. Both the rowMove and colMove variables contain a random value between -1 and +1. We add these random values to the current positions to get the new position. The new position is stored in newRow and newCol. The block of if statements determines if the new position is within the bounds of the world. If it's not, we immediately exit the function.

This if statement checks to see if the new position is an empty tile or a tile containing food. In other words, it doesn't contain either of the two elements that would cause a change in state.

The next if statement checks to see if the new position contains water. If it does contain water, the ant's position is updated, the water is deleted, and the ant's state is changed back to the initial kForage state. The do-while loop then randomly places more water.

As in the previous behavior function, the final if statement in the Thirsty function checks to see if the ant stepped on poison. If so, the ant's position is updated, the poison is deleted, and the ant's state is changed to kDead. Once again, the do-while loop is used to replace the consumed poison.

The Results

This completes all four functions associated with the kForage, kThirsty, kGoHome, and kDead states. You can observe the different behaviors and how the finite state machine ants transition from one state to another by running the simulation.

As you can see in Figure 9-6, even though we started with only four ants in the simulation, it doesn't take long for them to overrun the world. In fact, it's interesting to watch how quickly they begin multiplying with the given amount of food, water, and poison.

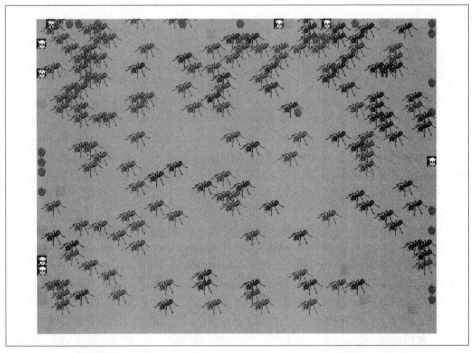

Figure 9-6. Population explosion

It's also interesting to watch how you can affect the population growth, or decline, by simply altering the values shown in Example 9-20.

Example 9-20. Food, water, and poison regulation

```
#define  kMaxWater     15
#define  kMaxPoison     8
#define  kMaxFood      20
```

As Example 9-20 shows, altering the simulation is as simple as modifying a few global constants. For example, decreasing the poison level too much causes a rapid population explosion, while lowering the food supply slows the population growth, but doesn't necessarily cause it to decrease. By adjusting these values, along with the possibility of adding more states and, therefore, more types of behavior, you can make the simulation even more complex and interesting to watch.

Further Information

Finite state machines are ubiquitous in games. It's no surprise that virtually every game development book covers them to some degree. Further, the Internet is full of resources covering finite state machines. Here are just a few Internet resources that discuss finite state machines:

- *http://www.gamasutra.com*
- *http://www.gameai.com*
- *http://www.generation5.org*
- *http://www.aboutai.net*

If you perform an Internet search using the keywords "finite state machine," you're sure to find a few hundred more resources. Also, try performing a search using the keywords "fuzzy state machine." Fuzzy state machines are a popular variant of finite state machines that incorporate probability in state transitions. We cover probability in Chapter 12.

CHAPTER 10
Fuzzy Logic

In 1965 Lotfi Zadeh, a professor at the University of California Berkeley, wrote his original paper laying out fuzzy set theory. We find no better way of explaining what fuzzy logic is than by quoting the father of fuzzy logic himself. In a 1994 interview of Zadeh conducted by Jack Woehr of *Dr. Dobbs Journal*, Woehr paraphrases Zadeh when he says "fuzzy logic is a means of presenting problems to computers in a way akin to the way humans solve them." Zadeh later goes on to say that "the essence of fuzzy logic is that everything is a matter of degree." We'll now elaborate on these two fundamental principles of fuzzy logic.

What does the statement "problems are presented to computers in a way similar to how humans solve them" really mean? The idea here is that humans very often analyze situations, or solve problems, in a rather imprecise manner. We might not have all the facts, the facts might be uncertain, or perhaps we can only generalize the facts without the benefit of precise data or measurements.

For example, say you're playing a friendly game of basketball with your buddies. When sizing up an opponent on the court to decide whether you or someone else should guard him, you might base your decision on the opponent's height and dexterity. You might decide the opponent is tall and quick, and therefore, you'd be better off guarding someone else. Or perhaps you'd say he is very tall but somewhat slow, so you might do fine against him. You normally wouldn't say to yourself something such as, "He's 6 feet 5.5 inches tall and can run the length of the court in 5.7 seconds."

Fuzzy logic enables you to pose and solve problems using linguistic terms similar to what you might use; in theory you could have the computer, using fuzzy logic, tell you whether to guard a particular opponent given that he is very tall and slow, and so on. Although this is not necessarily a practical application of fuzzy logic, it does illustrate a key point—fuzzy logic enables you to think as you normally do while using very precise tools such as computers.

The second principle, that everything is a matter of degree, can be illustrated using the same basketball opponent example. When you say the opponent is tall versus average or very tall, you don't necessarily have fixed boundaries in mind for such distinctions or categories. You can pretty much judge that the guy is tall or very tall without having to say to yourself that if he is more than 7 feet, he's very tall, whereas if he is less than 7 feet, he's tall. What about if he is 6 feet 11.5 inches tall? Certainly you'd still consider that to be very tall, though not to the same degree as if he were 7 feet 4 inches. The border defining your view of tall versus very tall is rather gray and has some overlap.

Traditional Boolean logic forces us to define a point above which we'd consider the guy very tall and below which we'd consider the guy just tall. We'd be forced to say he is either very tall or not very tall. You can circumvent this true or false/on or off characteristic of traditional Boolean logic using fuzzy logic. Fuzzy logic allows gray areas, or degrees, of being very tall, for example.

In fact, you can think of everything in terms of fuzzy logic as being true, but to varying degrees. If we say that something is true to degree 1 in fuzzy logic, it is absolutely true. A truth to degree 0 is an absolute false. So, in fuzzy logic we can have something that is either absolutely true, or absolutely false, or anything in between—something with a degree between 0 and 1. We'll look at the mechanisms that enable us to quantify degrees of truth a little later.

Another aspect of the ability to have varying degrees of truth in fuzzy logic is that in control applications, for example, responses to fuzzy input are smooth. Using traditional Boolean logic forces us to switch response states to some given input in an abrupt manner. To alleviate very abrupt state transitions, we'd have to discretize the input into a larger number of sufficiently small ranges. We can avoid these problems using fuzzy logic because the response will vary smoothly given the degree of truth, or strength, of the input condition.

Let's consider an example. A standard home central air conditioner is equipped with a thermostat, which the homeowner sets to a specific temperature. Given the thermostat's design, it will turn on when the temperature rises higher than the thermostat setting and cut off when the temperature reaches or falls lower than the thermostat setting. Where we're from in Southern Louisiana, our air conditioner units constantly are switching on and off as the temperature rises and falls due to the warming of the summer sun and subsequent cooling by the air conditioner. Such switching is hard on the air conditioner and often results in significant wear and tear on the unit.

One can envision in this scenario a fuzzy thermostat that modulates the cooling fan so as to keep the temperature about ideal. As the temperature rises the fan speeds up, and as the temperature drops the fan slows down, all the while maintaining some equilibrium temperature right around our prescribed ideal. This would be done without the unit having to switch on and off constantly. Indeed, such systems do exist, and they represent one of the early applications of fuzzy control. Other applications that have benefited from fuzzy control include train and subway control and robot control, to name a few.

Fuzzy logic applications are not limited to control systems. You can use fuzzy logic for decision-making applications as well. One typical example includes stock portfolio analysis or management, whereby one can use fuzzy logic to make buy or sell decisions. Pretty much any problem that involves decision making based on subjective, imprecise, or vague information is a candidate for fuzzy logic.

Traditional logic practitioners argue that you also can solve these problems using traditional rules-based approaches and logic. That might be true; however, fuzzy logic affords us the use of intuitive linguistic terms such as near, far, very far, and so on, when setting up the problem, developing rules, and assessing output. This usually makes the system more readable and easier to understand and maintain. Further, Timothy Masters, in his book *Practical Neural Network Recipes in C++*, (Morgan Kauffman) reports that fuzzy-rules systems generally require 50% to 80% fewer rules than traditional rules systems to accomplish identical tasks. These benefits make fuzzy logic well worth taking a look at for game AI that is typically replete with if-then style rules and Boolean logic. With this motivation, let's consider a few illustrative examples of how we can use fuzzy logic in games.

How Can You Use Fuzzy Logic in Games?

You can use fuzzy logic in games in a variety of ways. For example, you can use fuzzy logic to control bots or other nonplayer character units. You also can use it for assessing threats posed by players. Further, you can use fuzzy logic to classify both player and nonplayer characters. These are only a few specific examples, but they illustrate how you can use fuzzy logic in distinctly different scenarios. Let's consider each example in a little more detail.

Control

Fuzzy logic is used in a wide variety of real-world control applications such as controlling trains, air conditioning and heating systems, and robots, among other applications. Video games also offer many opportunities for fuzzy control. You can use fuzzy control to navigate game units—land vehicles, aircraft, foot units, and so on—smoothly through waypoints and around obstacles. You also can accomplish as well as improve upon basic chasing and evading using fuzzy control.

Let's say you have a unit that is traveling along some given heading, but it needs to travel toward some specific target that might be static or on the move. This target could be a waypoint, an enemy unit, some treasure, a home base, or anything else you can imagine in your game. We can solve this problem using deterministic methods similar to those we've already discussed in this book; however, recall that in some cases we had to manually modulate steering forces to achieve smooth turns.

If we didn't modulate the steering forces, the units abruptly would change heading and their motion would appear unnatural. Fuzzy logic enables you to achieve smooth motion without manually modulating steering forces. You also can gain other improvements using fuzzy logic. For example, recall the problem with basic chasing whereby the unit always ended up following directly behind the target moving along one coordinate axis only. Earlier we solved this problem using other methods, such as line-of-sight chasing, interception, or potential functions. Fuzzy logic, in this case, would yield results similar to interception. Basically, we'd tell our fuzzy controller that our intended target is to the far left, or to the left, or straight ahead, or to the right, and so on, and let it calculate the proper steering force to apply to facilitate heading toward the target in a smooth manner.

Threat Assessment

Let's consider another potential application of fuzzy logic in games; one that involves a decision rather than direct motion control.

Say in your battle simulation game the computer team often has to deploy units as defense against a potentially threatening enemy force. We'll assume that the computer team has acquired specific knowledge of an opposing force. For simplicity, we'll limit this knowledge to the enemy force's range from the computer team and the force's size. Range can be specified in terms of near, close, far, and very far, while size can be specified in terms of tiny, small, medium, large, or massive.

Given this information, we can use a fuzzy system to have the computer assess the threat posed by the enemy force. For example, the threat could be considered as no threat, low threat, medium threat, or high threat, upon determination of which the computer could decide on a suitable number of units to deploy in defense. This fuzzy approach would enable us to do the following:

- Model the computer as having less-than-perfect knowledge
- Allow the size of the defensive force to vary smoothly and less predictably

Classification

Let's say you want to rank both player and nonplayer characters in your game in terms of their combat prowess. You can base this rank on factors such as strength, weapon proficiency, number of hit points, and armor class, among many other factors of your choosing. Ultimately, you want to combine these factors so as to yield a ranking such as wimpy, easy, moderate, tough, formidable, etc. For example, a player with high hit points, average armor class, high strength, and low weapons proficiency might get a rank of moderate. Fuzzy logic enables you to determine such a rank. Further, you can use the fuzzy logic system to generate a numerical score representing rank, or rating, which you can input to some other AI process for the game.

Of course, you can accomplish this classification by other means, such as Boolean rules, neural networks, and others. However, a fuzzy system enables you to do it in an intuitive manner with fewer rules and without the need to train the system. You still have to set up the fuzzy rules ahead of time, as in every fuzzy system; however, you have to perform that process only once, and you have the linguistic constructs afforded by fuzzy logic to help you. We'll come back to this later.

Fuzzy Logic Basics

Now that you have an idea of what fuzzy logic is all about and how you can use it in games, let's take a close look at how fuzzy logic works and is implemented. If the concept of fuzzy logic is still a little, well, fuzzy to you at this point, don't worry. The concepts will become much clearer as we go over the details in the next few sections.

Overview

The fuzzy control or inference process comprises three basic steps. Figure 10-1 illustrates these steps.

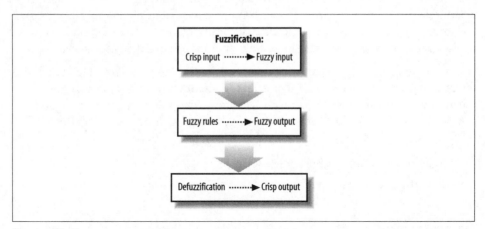

Figure 10-1. Fuzzy process overview

The first part of the process is called the *fuzzification* process. In this step, a mapping process converts *crisp* data (real numbers) to fuzzy data. This mapping process involves finding the degree of membership of the crisp input in predefined fuzzy sets. For example, given a person's weight in pounds, we can find the degree to which the person is underweight, overweight, or at an ideal weight.

Once you have expressed all the inputs to the system in terms of fuzzy set membership, you can combine them using logical, fuzzy rules to determine the degree to which each rule is true. In other words, you can find the strength of each rule or the degree of membership in an output, or action, fuzzy set. For example, given a person's weight and activity level as input variables, we can define rules that look something such as the following:

- If overweight AND NOT active then frequent exercise
- If overweight AND active then moderate diet

These rules combine the fuzzy input variables using logical operators to yield a degree of membership, or degree or truth, of the corresponding output action, which in this case is the recommendation to engage in frequent exercise or go on a moderate diet.

Often, having a fuzzy output such as *frequent exercise* is not enough. We might want to quantify the amount of exercise—for example, three hours per week. This process of taking fuzzy output membership and producing a corresponding crisp numerical output is called *defuzzification*. Let's consider each step in more detail.

Fuzzification

Input to a fuzzy system can originate in the form of crisp numbers. These are real numbers quantifying the input variables—for example, a person weighs 185.3 pounds or a person is 6 feet 1 inch tall. In the fuzzification process we want to map these crisp values to degrees of membership in qualitative fuzzy sets. For example, we might map 185.3 pounds to *slightly overweight* and 6 feet 1 inch to *tall*. You achieve this type of mapping using membership functions, also called *characteristic functions*.

Membership Functions

Membership functions map input variables to a degree of membership, in a fuzzy set, between 0 and 1. If the degree of membership in a given set is 1, we can say the input for that set is absolutely true. If the degree is 0, we can say for that set the input is absolutely false. If the degree is somewhere between 0 and 1, it is true to a certain extent—that is, to a degree.

Before looking at fuzzy membership functions, let's consider the membership function for Boolean logic. Figure 10-2 illustrates such a function.

Here we see that input values lower than x_0 are mapped to false, while values higher than x_0 are mapped to true. There is no in-between mapping. Going back to the weight example, if x_0 equals 170 pounds, anyone weighing more than 170 pounds is *overweight* and anyone weighing less than 170 pounds is *not overweight*. Even if a person weighs 169.9 pounds, he still is considered not overweight. Fuzzy membership functions enable us to transition gradually from false to true, or from *not overweight* to *overweight* in our example.

You can use virtually any function as a membership function, and the shape usually is governed by desired accuracy, the nature of the problem being considered, experience, and ease of implementation, among other factors. With that said, a

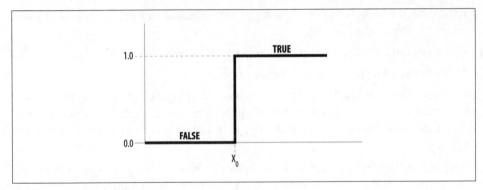

Figure 10-2. Boolean logic membership function

handful of commonly used membership functions have proven useful for a wide variety of applications. We'll discuss those common membership functions in this chapter.

Consider the grade function illustrated in Figure 10-3.

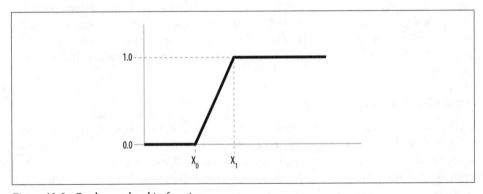

Figure 10-3. Grade membership function

Here you can see the gradual transition from 0 to 1. The range of x-values for which this function applies is called its *support*. For values less than x_0, the degree of membership is 0 or absolutely false, while for values greater than x_1, the degree is 1 or absolutely true. Between x_0 and x_1, the degree of membership varies linearly.

Using the point-slope equation for a straight line, we can write the equation representing the grade membership function as follows:

$$f(x) = \begin{cases} 0; x \leq x_0 \\ \dfrac{x}{x_1 - x_0} - \dfrac{x_0}{x_1 - x_0}; x_0 < x < x_1 \\ 1; x \geq x_1 \end{cases}$$

Going back to the weight example, let's say this function represents the membership for *overweight*. Let x_0 equal 175 and x_1 equal 195. If a person weighs 170 pounds, he is *overweight* to a degree of 0—that is, he is *not overweight*. If he weighs 185 pounds, he is *overweight* to a degree of 0.5—he's somewhat overweight.

Typically, we're interested in the degree to which an input variable falls within a number of qualitative sets. For example, we might want to know the degree to which a person is *overweight*, *underweight*, or at an *ideal* weight. In this case, we could set up a collection of sets, as illustrated in Figure 10-4.

Point-slope Equation for a Straight Line

The equation for a straight line passing through the points (x_0, y_0) and $(x_1\ y_1)$ is:

$$y - y_1 = m(x - x_1)$$

where m is the slope of the line and is equal to:

$$m = \frac{(y_1 - Y_0)}{(x_1 - x_0)}$$

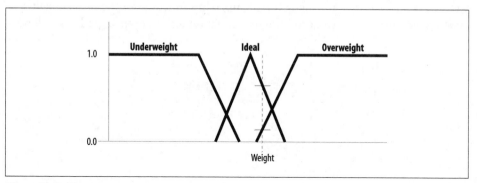

Figure 10-4. Fuzzy sets

With this sort of collection, we can calculate a given input value's membership in each of the three sets—*underweight*, *ideal*, and *overweight*. We might, for a given weight, find that a person is *underweight* to a degree of 0, *ideal* to a degree of 0.75, and *overweight* to a degree of 0.15. We can infer in this case that the person's weight is substantially ideal—that is, to a degree of 75%.

The triangular membership function shown in Figure 10-4 is another common form of membership function. Referring to Figure 10-5, you can write the equation for a triangular membership function as follows:

$$f(x) = \begin{cases} 0; x \le x_0 \\ \dfrac{x}{x_1 - x_0} - \dfrac{x_0}{x_1 - x_0}; x_0 < x < x_1 \\ 1; x = x_1 \\ \dfrac{-x}{x_2 - x_1} + \dfrac{x_2}{x_2 - x_1}; x_1 < x < x_2 \end{cases}$$

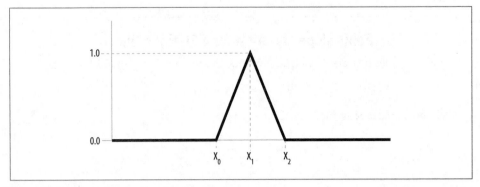

Figure 10-5. Triangular membership function

Figure 10-4 also shows a reverse-grade membership function for the *underweight* set. Referring to Figure 10-6, you can write the equation for the reverse grade as follows:

$$f(x) = \begin{cases} 1; x \le x_0 \\ \dfrac{-x}{x_1 - x_0} + \dfrac{x_1}{x_1 - x_0}; x_0 < x < x_1 \\ 0; x \ge x_1 \end{cases}$$

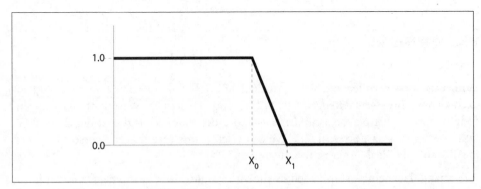

Figure 10-6. Reverse grade membership function

Another common membership function is the trapezoid function, as shown in Figure 10-7.

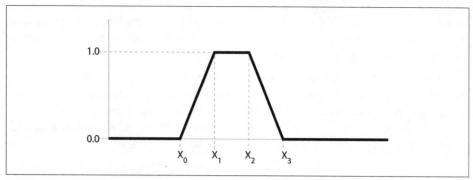

Figure 10-7. Trapezoid membership function

You can write the trapezoid function as follows:

$$f(x) = \begin{cases} 0; x \leq x_0 \\ \dfrac{x}{x_1 - x_0} - \dfrac{x_0}{x_1 - x_0}; x_0 < x < x_1 \\ 1; x_1 \leq x \leq x_2 \\ \dfrac{-x}{x_3 - x_2} + \dfrac{x_3}{x_3 - x_2}; x_2 < x < x_3 \end{cases}$$

Setting up collections of fuzzy sets for a given input variable, as shown in Figure 10-4, is largely a matter of judgment and trial and error. It's not uncommon to tune the arrangement of set membership functions to achieve desirable or optimum results. While tuning, you can try different shapes for each fuzzy set, or you can try using more or fewer fuzzy sets. Some fuzzy logic practitioners recommend the use of seven fuzzy sets to fully define the practical working range of any input variable. Figure 10-8 illustrates such an arrangement.

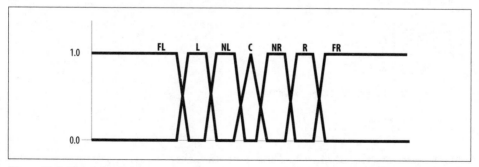

Figure 10-8. Seven fuzzy sets

The seven fuzzy sets shown in Figure 10-8 are *center, near right, right, far right, near left, left,* and *far left.* These categories can be anything, depending on your problem.

For example, to represent the alignment of player and nonplayer characters in your role-playing game, you might have fuzzy sets such as *neutral*, *neutral good*, *good*, *chaotic good*, *neutral evil*, *evil*, and *chaotic evil*.

Notice that each set in Figures 10-4 and 10-8 overlaps immediately adjacent sets. This is important for smooth transitions. The generally accepted rule of thumb is that each set should overlap its neighbor by about 25%.

The membership functions we discussed so far are the most commonly used; however, other functions sometimes are employed when higher accuracy or nonlinearity is required. For example, some applications use Gaussian curves, while others use S-shaped curves. These are illustrated in Figure 10-9. For most applications and games, the piecewise linear functions discussed here are sufficient.

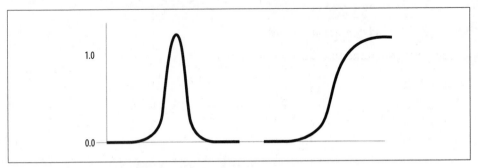

Figure 10-9. Examples of other membership functions

Example 10-1 shows how the various membership functions we've discussed might look in code.

Example 10-1. Fuzzy membership functions

```
double    FuzzyGrade(double value, double x0, double x1)
{
    double result = 0;
    double x = value;

    if(x <= x0)
        result = 0;
    else if(x >= x1)
        result = 1;
    else
        result = (x/(x1-x0))-(x0/(x1-x0));

    return result;
}

double FuzzyReverseGrade(double value, double x0, double x1)
{
    double result = 0;
    double x = value;
```

```
    if(x <= x0)
        result = 1;
    else if(x >= x1)
        result = 0;
    else
        result = (-x/(x1-x0))+(x1/(x1-x0));

    return result;
}

double    FuzzyTriangle(double value, double x0,
                        double x1, double x2)
{
    double result = 0;
    double x = value;

    if(x <= x0)
        result = 0;
    else if(x == x1)
        result = 1;
    else if((x>x0) && (x<x1))
        result = (x/(x1-x0))-(x0/(x1-x0));
    else
        result = (-x/(x2-x1))+(x2/(x2-x1));

    return result;
}

double    FuzzyTrapezoid(double value, double x0, double x1,
                         double x2, double x3)
{
    double result = 0;
    double x = value;

    if(x <= x0)
        result = 0;
    else if((x>=x1) && (x<=x2))
        result = 1;
    else if((x>x0) && (x<x1))
        result = (x/(x1-x0))-(x0/(x1-x0));
    else
        result = (-x/(x3-x2))+(x3/(x3-x2));

    return result;
}
```

To determine the membership of a given input value in a particular set, you simply call one of the functions in Example 10-1, passing the value and parameters that define the shape of the function. For example, FuzzyTrapezoid(value, x0, x1, x2, x3) determines the degree of membership of value in the set defined by x0, x1, x2, x3 with a shape, as shown in Figure 10-7.

Hedges

Hedge functions are sometimes used to modify the degree of membership returned by a membership function. The idea behind hedges is to provide additional linguistic constructs that you can use in conjunction with other logical operations. Two common hedges are VERY and NOT_VERY, which are defined as follows:

$$VERY(Truth(A)) = Truth(A)^2$$

$$NOT\_VERY(Truth(A)) = Truth(A)^{0.5}$$

Here, *Truth(A)* is the degree of membership of *A* in some fuzzy set. Hedges effectively change the shape of membership functions. For example, these hedges applied to piecewise linear membership functions will result in the linear portions of those membership functions becoming nonlinear.

Hedges are not required in fuzzy systems. You can construct membership functions to suit your needs without the additional hedges. We mention them here for completeness, as they often appear in fuzzy logic literature.

Fuzzy Rules

After fuzzifying all input variables for a given problem, what we'd like to do next is construct a set of rules, combining the input in some logical manner, to yield some output. In an if-then style rule such as *if A then B*, the "if A" part is called the *antecedent*, or the premise. The "then B" part is called the *consequent*, or conclusion. We want to combine fuzzy input variables in a logical manner to form the premise, which will yield a fuzzy conclusion. The conclusion effectively will be the degree of membership in some predefined output fuzzy set.

Fuzzy Axioms

If we're going to write logical rules given fuzzy input, we'll need a way to apply the usual logical operators to fuzzy input much like we would do for Boolean input. Specifically, we'd like to be able to handle *conjunction* (logical *AND*), *disjunction* (logical *OR*), and *negation* (logical *NOT*). For fuzzy variables, these logical operators typically are defined as follows:

Disjunction

   $Truth(A\ OR\ B) = MAX(Truth(A), Truth(B))$

Conjunction

   $Truth(A\ AND\ B) = MIN(Truth(A), Truth(B))$

Negation

   $Truth(NOT\ A) = 1 - Truth(A)$

Here, again, *Truth(A)* means the degree of membership of *A* in some fuzzy set. This will be a real number between 0 and 1. The same applies for *Truth(B)* as well. As you can see, the logical *OR* operator is defined as the maximum of the operands, the *AND* operator is defined as the minimum of the operands, and *NOT* is simply 1 minus the given degree of membership.

Let's consider an example. Given a person is *overweight* to a degree of 0.7 and *tall* to a degree of 0.3, the logical operators defined earlier result in the following:

$$\text{overweight AND tall} = \text{MIN}(0.7, 0.3) = 0.3$$
$$\text{overweight OR tall} = \text{MAX}(0.7, 0.3) = 0.7$$
$$\text{NOT overweight} = 1 - 0.7 = 0.3$$
$$\text{NOT tall} = 1 - 0.3 = 0.7$$
$$\text{NOT(overweight AND tall)} = 1 - \text{MIN}(0.7, 0.3) = 1 - 0.3 = 0.7$$

In code, these logical operations are fairly trivial, as shown in Example 10-2.

Example 10-2. Fuzzy logical operator functions

```
double FuzzyAND(double A, double B) {
    return MIN(A, B);
}

double FuzzyOR(double A, double B) {
    return MAX(A, B);
}

double FuzzyNOT(double A) {
    return 1.0 - A;
}
```

These are not the only definitions used for *AND*, *OR*, and *NOT*. Some specific applications use other definitions—for example, you can define *AND* as the product of two degrees of membership, and you can define *OR* as the *probabilistic-OR*, as follows:

$$\text{probabilistic - OR} = \text{Truth}(A) + \text{Truth}(B) - \text{Truth}(A)\text{Truth}(B)$$

Some third-party fuzzy logic tools even facilitate user-defined logical operators, making the possibilities endless. For most applications, however, the definitions presented here work well.

Rule Evaluation

In a traditional Boolean logic application, rules such as *if A AND B then C* evaluate to absolutely `true` or `false` 1 or 0. After reading the previous section, you can see that this clearly is not the case using fuzzy logic. *A AND B* in fuzzy logic can evaluate to any number between 0 and 1, inclusive. This fact makes a fundamental difference in how fuzzy rules are evaluated versus Boolean logic rules.

In a traditional Boolean system, each rule is evaluated in series until one evaluates to `true` and it fires, so to speak—that is, its conclusion is processed. In a fuzzy rules system, all rules are evaluated in parallel. Each rule always fires; however, they fire to various degrees, or strengths. The result of the logical operations in each rule's premise yields the strength of the rule's conclusion. In other words, the strength of each rule represents the degree of membership in the output fuzzy set.

Let's say you have a video game and are using a fuzzy system to evaluate whether a creature should attack a player. The input variables are range, creature health, and opponent ranking. The membership functions for each variable might look something like those shown in Figure 10-10.

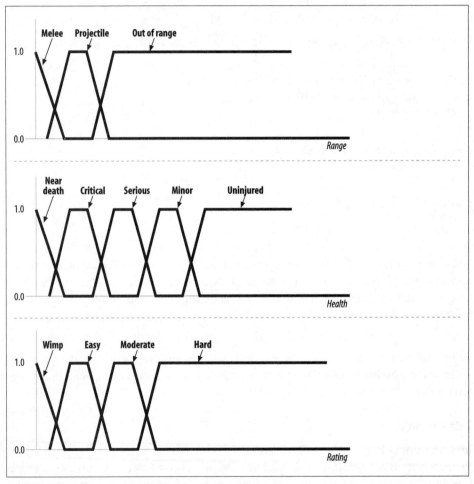

Figure 10-10. Input variable membership functions

The output actions in this example can be *flee*, *attack*, or *do nothing*. We can write some rules that look something like the following:

> if (in melee range AND uninjured) AND NOT hard then attack

if (NOT in melee range) AND uninjured then do nothing

if (NOT out of range AND NOT uninjured) AND (NOT wimp) then flee

You can set up several more rules to handle more possibilities. In your game, all these rules would be evaluated to yield a degree of membership for each output action. Given specific degrees for the input variables, you might get outputs that look something like this:

attack to degree 0.2

do nothing to degree 0.4

flee to degree 0.7

In code, evaluation of these rules would look something like that shown in Example 10-3, where you can see a distinct difference from traditional if-then style rules.

Example 10-3. Fuzzy rules

```
degreeAttack = MIN(MIN (degreeMelee, degreeUninjured),
                   1.0 - degreeHard);

degreeDoNothing = MIN ( (1.0 - degreeMelee),
                        degreeUninjured);

degreeFlee = MIN (MIN ((1.0 - degreeOutOfRange),
                       (1.0 - degreeUninjured)),
                       (1.0 - degreeWimp));
```

The output degrees represent the strength of each rule. The easiest way to interpret these outputs is to take the action associated with the highest degree. In this example, the resulting action would be to *flee*.

In some cases, you might want to do more with the output than execute the action with the highest degree. For example, in the threat assessment case we discussed earlier in this chapter, you might want to use the fuzzy output to determine the number, a crisp number, of defensive units to deploy. To get a crisp number as an output, you have to defuzzify the results from the fuzzy rules.

Defuzzification

Defuzzification is required when you want a crisp number as output from a fuzzy system. As we mentioned earlier, each rule results in a degree of membership in some output fuzzy set. Let's go back to our previous example. Say that instead of determining some finite action—do nothing, flee, or attack—you also want to use the output to determine the speed to which the creature should take action. For example, if the output action is to *flee*, does the creature walk away or run away, and how fast does it go? To get a crisp number, we need to aggregate the output strengths somehow and we need to define output membership functions.

For example, we might have output membership functions such as those shown in Figure 10-11.

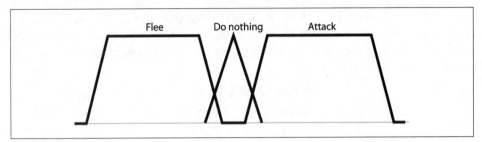

Figure 10-11. Output fuzzy sets

With the numerical output we discussed already—0.2 degree attack, 0.4 degree do nothing, and 0.7 degree flee—we'd end up with a composite membership function, as shown in Figure 10-12.

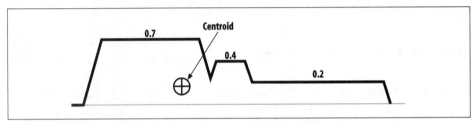

Figure 10-12. Output membership function

To arrive at such a composite membership function, each output set is truncated to the output degree of membership for that set as determined by the strength of the rules. Then all output sets are combined using disjunction.

At this point, we still have only an output membership function and no single crisp number. We can arrive at a crisp number from such an output fuzzy set in many ways. One of the more common methods involves finding the geometric centroid of the area under the output fuzzy set and taking the corresponding horizontal axis coordinate of that center as the crisp output. This yields a compromise between all the rules—that is, the single output number is a weighted average of all the output memberships.

To find the center of area for such an output function, you have to integrate the area under the curve using numerical techniques. Or you can consider it a polygon and use computational geometry methods to find the center. There are other schemes as well. In any case, finding the center of area is computationally expensive, especially considering the large number of times such a calculation would be performed in a game. Fortunately, there's an easier way that uses so-called *singleton* output membership functions.

A singleton output function is really just a spike and not a curve. It is essentially a predefuzzified output function. For our example, we can assign speeds to each output action, such as −10 for *flee*, 1 for *do nothing*, and 10 for *attack*. Then, the resulting speed for *flee*, for example, would be the preset value of −10 times the degree to which the output action *flee* is true. In our example, we'd have −10 times 0.7, or −7 for the flee speed. (Here, the negative sign simply indicates *flee* as opposed to *attack*.) Considering the aggregate of all outputs requires a simple weighted average rather than a center of gravity calculation.

In general, let μ be the degree to which an output set is true and let x be the crisp result, singleton, associated with the output set. The aggregate, defuzzified output would then be:

$$output = \frac{\sum_{i=1}^{n} \mu_i x_i}{\sum_{i=1}^{n} \mu_i}$$

In our example, we might have something such as:

Output = [(0.7)(−10) + (0.4)(1)+(0.3)(10)] / (0.7+0.4+0.3) = −2.5

Such an output when used to control the motion of the creature would result in the creature fleeing, but not necessarily in earnest.

To reinforce all the concepts we've discussed so far, let's consider a few examples in greater detail.

Control Example

In the control example at the beginning of this chapter we wanted to use fuzzy control to steer a computer-controlled unit toward some objective. This objective could be a waypoint, an enemy unit, and so on. To achieve this, we'll set up several fuzzy sets that describe the relative heading between the computer-controlled unit and its objective. The relative heading is simply the angle between the computer-controlled unit's velocity vector and the vector connecting the positions of the computer-controlled unit and the objective. Using techniques we've discussed in earlier examples—namely, the chase and evade examples—you can determine this relative heading angle, which will be a scalar angle in degrees.

What we now aim to do is use that relative heading as input to a fuzzy control system to determine the appropriate amount of steering force to apply to guide the computer-controlled unit to the target. This is a very simple example, as there is only one input variable and thus only one set of fuzzy membership functions to define. For this example, we set up the membership functions and fuzzy sets illustrated in Figure 10-13.

We have five fuzzy sets in this case. Reading from left to right, each set represents relative headings qualitatively as *Far Left*, *Left*, *Ahead*, *Right*, and *Far Right*. The *Far Left* and *Far Right* membership functions are grade functions, while the *Left* and

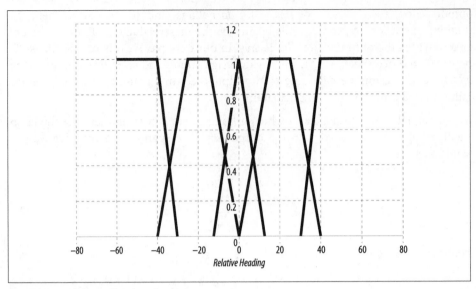

Figure 10-13. Relative heading fuzzy sets

Right functions are trapezoids. The *Ahead* function is a triangle. Given any relative heading angle, you can use the C functions shown in Example 10-1 to calculate membership in each fuzzy set.

Let's say that at some given time in the game, the relative heading angle is found to be a positive 33 degrees. Now we need to calculate the degree to which this relative heading falls within each of the five fuzzy sets. Clearly, the degree will be 0 for all sets, with the exception of the *Right* and *Far Right* sets. However, we'll go ahead and show code for all membership calculations for completeness. Example 10-4 shows the code.

Example 10-4. Relative heading membership calculations

```
mFarLeft   = FuzzyReverseGrade(33, -40, -30);
mLeft      = FuzzyTrapezoid(33, -40, -25, -15, 0);
mAhead     = FuzzyTriangle(33, -10, 10);
mRight     = FuzzyTrapezoid(33, 0, 15, 25, 40);
mFarRight  = FuzzyGrade(33, 30, 40);
```

In this example, the variables mFarLeft, mLeft, and so on, store the degree of membership of the relative heading value of 33 degrees in each predefined fuzzy set. The results are summarized in Table 10-1.

Now, to use these resulting degrees of membership to control our unit, we're going to simply apply each degree as a coefficient in a steering force calculation. Let's assume that the maximum left steering force is some constant, FL, and the maximum right steering force is another constant, FR. We'll let FL = − 100 pounds of force,

Table 10-1. Membership calculation results

Fuzzy Set	Degree of Membership
Far Left	0.0
Left	0.0
Ahead	0.0
Right	0.47
Far Right	0.3

and FR = 100 pounds of force. Now we can calculate the total steering force to apply, as shown in Example 10-5.

Example 10-5. Steering force calculation

```
NetForce= mFarLeft * FL + mLeft * FL + mRight * FR + mFarRight * FR;
```

The result of this calculation is 77 pounds of steering force. Notice that we didn't include mAhead in the calculation. This means that any membership in *Ahead* does not require steering action. Technically, we could have done away with the *Ahead* membership function; however, we put it in there for emphasis.

In a physics-based simulation such as the examples we saw earlier in this book, this steering force would get applied to the unit for the cycle through the game loop within which the relative heading was calculated. The action of the steering force would change the heading of the unit for the next cycle through the game loop and a new relative heading would be calculated. This new relative heading would be processed in the same manner as discussed here to yield a new steering force to apply. Eventually the resultant steering force would smoothly decrease as the relative heading goes to 0. Or in fuzzy terms, as the degree of membership in the *Ahead* set goes to 1.

Threat Assessment Example

In the threat assessment example we discussed at the beginning of this chapter, we wanted to process two input variables, enemy force and the size of force, to determine the level of threat posed by this force. Ultimately, we want to determine the appropriate number for defensive units to deploy as protection against the threatening force. This example requires us to set up several fuzzy rules and defuzzify the output to obtain a crisp number for the number of defensive units to deploy. The first order of business, however, is to define fuzzy sets for the two input variables. Figures 10-14 and 10-15 show what we've put together for this example.

Referring to Figure 10-14 and going from the left to the right, these three membership functions represent the sets *Close*, *Medium*, and *Far*. The range can be specified in any units appropriate for your game. Let's assume here that the range is specified in hexes.

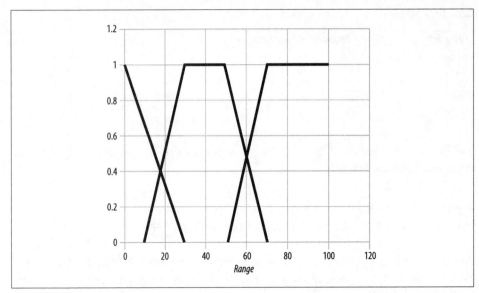

Figure 10-14. Range fuzzy sets

Referring to Figure 10-15 and going from left to right, these membership functions represent the fuzzy sets *Tiny*, *Small*, *Moderate*, and *Large*. With these fuzzy sets in hand, we're ready to perform some calculations.

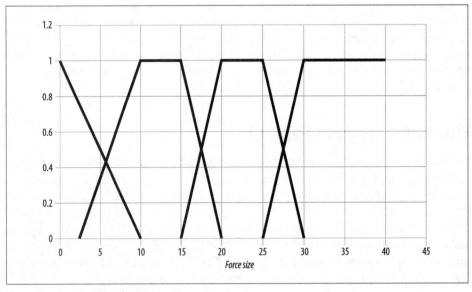

Figure 10-15. Force size fuzzy sets

Let's assume that during a given cycle through the game loop this fuzzy system is called upon to assess the threat posed by an enemy force eight units strong at a range of 25 hexes. So, now we need to fuzzify these crisp input values, determining the degree to which these variables fall within each predefined fuzzy set. Example 10-6 shows the code for this step.

Example 10-6. Fuzzification of range and force size variables

```
mClose    = FuzzyTriangle(25, -30, 0, 30);
mMedium   = FuzzyTrapezoid(25, 10, 30, 50, 70);
mFar      = FuzzyGrade(25, 50, 70);

mTiny     = FuzzyTriangle(8, -10, 0, 10);
mSmall    = FuzzyTrapezoid(8, 2.5, 10, 15, 20);
mModerate = FuzzyTrapezoid(8, 15, 20, 25, 30);
mLarge    = FuzzyGrade(8, 25, 30);
```

The results for this example are summarized in Table 10-2.

Table 10-2. Summary of fuzzification results

Fuzzy Set	Degree of Membership
Close	0.17
Medium	0.75
Far	0.0
Tiny	0.2
Small	0.73
Moderate	0.0
Large	0.0

Before we consider any rules, let's address output actions. In this case, we want the fuzzy output to be an indication of the threat level posed by the approaching force. We'll use singleton output functions in this example, and the output, or action, fuzzy sets *Low*, *Medium*, and *High* for the threat level. Let's define the singleton output values for each set to be 10 units, 30 units, and 50 units to deploy for *Low*, *Medium*, and *High*, respectively.

Now we can address the rules. The easiest way to visualize the rules in this case is through the use of a table, such as Table 10-3.

Table 10-3. Rule matrix

	Close	Medium	Far
Tiny	Medium	Low	Low
Small	High	Low	Low
Moderate	High	Medium	Low
Large	High	High	Medium

The top row represents the *range* fuzzy sets, while the first column represents the *force size* fuzzy sets. The remaining cells in the table represent the threat level given the conjunction of any combination of range and force size. For example, if the force size is *Tiny* and the range is *Close*, the threat level is *Medium*.

We can set up and process the rules in this case in a number of ways. By inspecting Table 10-3, it's clear that we can combine the input variables using various combinations of the AND and OR operators to yield one rule for each output set. However, this will result in rather unwieldy code with many nested logical operations. At the other extreme we can process one rule for each combination of input variables and pick the highest degree for each output set; however, this results in a bunch of rules. Nonetheless, it's the simplest, most readable way to proceed, so we'll sort of take that approach here. To simplify things further, we'll show only combinations of input sets with nonzero degrees of membership, and we'll make at least one nested operation. These are illustrated in Example 10-7.

Example 10-7. Nested and non-nested fuzzy rules

```
        .
        .
        .

mLow = FuzzyOr(FuzzyAND(mMedium, mTiny), FuzzyAND(mMedium, mSmall));

mMedium = FuzzyAND(mClose, mTiny);

mHigh = FuzzyAND(mClose, mSmall);
        .
        .
        .
```

For our example, the results of these rule evaluations are `mLow` = 0.73, `mMedium` = 0.17, and `mHigh` = 0.17. These are the degrees of membership in the respective output fuzzy sets. Now we can defuzzify the results using the singleton output membership functions we defined earlier to get a single number representing the number of defensive forces to deploy. This calculation is simply a weighted average, as discussed earlier. Example 10-8 shows the code for this example.

Example 10-8. Defuzzification

```
nDeploy = ( mLow * 10 + mMedium * 30 + mHigh * 50) /
          (mLow + mMedium + mHigh);
```

The resulting number of units to deploy, `nDeploy`, comes to 19.5 units, or 20 if you round up. This seems fairly reasonable given the small size of the force and their proximity. Of course, all of this is subject to tuning. For example, you easily can adjust the results by changing the singleton values we used in this example. Also, the shapes of the various input membership functions are good candidates for tuning— you can try different shapes for each fuzzy set or use more or fewer fuzzy sets. Once everything is tuned, you'll find that no matter what input values go in, the response always will vary smoothly from one set of input variables to another. Further, the results will be much harder for the player to predict because there are no clearly defined cutoffs, or breakpoints, at which the number of units to deploy would change sharply. This makes for much more interesting gameplay.

CHAPTER 11

Rule-Based AI

In this chapter we're going to study *rule-based AI systems*. Rule-based AI systems are probably the most widely used AI systems for both real-world and game AI applications. In their simplest form, rule-based systems consist of a set of if-then style rules that are used to make inferences or action decisions. Technically, we've already looked at one form of rule-based system in Chapter 9 on finite state machines. There we used rules to handle state transitions. We also looked at another type of rule-based system in the previous chapter on fuzzy logic, Chapter 10.

In this chapter, we're going to look specifically at rule-based systems that commonly are used in so-called *expert systems*. Examples of real-world, rule-based expert systems include medical diagnosis, fraud protection, and engineering fault analysis. One advantage of rule-based systems is that they mimic the way people tend to think and reason given a set of known facts and their knowledge about the particular problem domain. Another advantage of this sort of rule-based system is that it is fairly easy to program and manage because the knowledge encoded in the rules is modular and rules can be coded in any order. This gives some flexibility both when coding the system and modifying the system at a later time. These advantages hopefully will become clearer to you as we move through the material in this chapter. Before we get into the details, though, let's discuss a couple of game examples that can use rule-based systems.

Imagine you're writing a real-time strategy simulation game involving the typical technology tree, whereby players must train peasants, build facilities, and harvest resources. An illustrative technology tree is shown in Figure 11-1.

What we aim to do here is enable the computer opponent to keep track of the player's current state of technology so that the computer opponent can plan and deploy offensive and defensive resources accordingly. Now, you could cheat and give the computer opponent perfect knowledge of the player's state of technology. However, it would be fair and more realistic to have the computer gain knowledge and

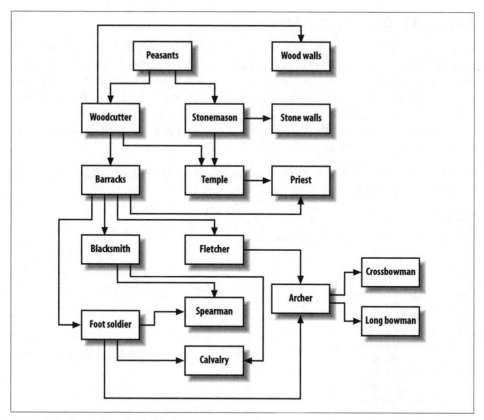

Figure 11-1. Example technology tree

make inferences on the state of the player's technology in much the same way that the player will have to so that she can assess the computer opponent's state of technology. Both player and computer will have to send out scouts to collect information and then make inferences given the information as it is received. We can achieve this using a fairly simple rule-based system, as you'll see in this chapter.

Let's consider another example. Say you're writing a martial arts fighting game and you want to give the computer the ability to anticipate the player's next strike so that the computer opponent can make the appropriate countermove, such as a counter strike, a dodge, or a parry. The trick here is to somehow keep track of the player's strike patterns—combinations of kicks and punches—and to learn which strike most likely will follow an observed set of previous strikes. For example, if during the fight the player throws a punch, punch combination, what will the player most likely throw next: a punch, a low kick, or a high kick? We can use a rule-based system to achieve such anticipation. We'll come back to this example in much more detail later in this chapter.

Rule-Based System Basics

Rule-based systems have two main components: the *working memory* and the *rules memory*. The working memory stores known facts and assertions made by the rules. The rules memory, or rules, for short, contains if-then style rules that operate over the facts stored in working memory. As rules are triggered, or *fired* in rule-based system lingo, they can trigger some action or state change, such as in a finite state machine, or they can modify the contents of the working memory by adding new information called *assertions*.

Example 11-1 shows how the working memory for a real-time, strategy-game technology tree might look.

Example 11-1. Example working memory

```
enum TMemoryValue{Yes, No, Maybe, Unknown};

TMemoryValue    Peasants;
TMemoryValue    Woodcutter;
TMemoryValue    Stonemason;
TMemoryValue    Blacksmith;
TMemoryValue    Barracks;
TMemoryValue    Fletcher;
TMemoryValue    WoodWalls;
TMemoryValue    StoneWalls;
TMemoryValue    Cavalry;
TMemoryValue    FootSoldier;
TMemoryValue    Spearman;
TMemoryValue    Archer;
TMemoryValue    Temple;
TMemoryValue    Priest;
TMemoryValue    Crossbowman;
TMemoryValue    Longbowman;
```

For this example, we made each element in working memory a TMemoryValue type that can take on any one of four values: Yes, No, Maybe, or Unknown. The idea here is to keep track of the computer opponent's current perception of the state of technology of the player opponent. A value of Yes implies that the player has the particular technology, whereas a value of No implies that she does not. If the player meets all the criteria to gain or posses a certain technology, but the state has yet to be confirmed by a scout, the value of Maybe is used. If the computer knows nothing about a particular technology capability for the player, Unknown is used.

The computer can gather facts on the player's current state of technology by sending out scouts and making observations. For example, if the computer sends out a scout and sees that the player has built a temple, Temple would be set to Yes. Using a set of if-then style rules, the player can infer the state of technology for the player, before a scout confirms it, given some known facts. For example, referring to

Figure 11-1, if the player has woodcutters and stonemasons, she is capable of having a temple. In this case, `Temple` is set to `Maybe`. A rule for this scenario might look like that shown in Example 11-2.

Example 11-2. Example temple rule

```
if(Woodcutter == Yes && Stonemason == Yes &&
    Temple == Unknown)
        Temple = Maybe;
```

Inference can work the other way as well. For example, if the player has been observed to have a priest, the computer can infer that the player also must have a temple, and therefore also must have a barracks, a woodcutter, and a stonemason. A rule for this scenario might look like that shown in Example 11-3.

Example 11-3. Example priest rule

```
if(Priest == Yes)
{
    Temple = Yes;
    Barracks = Yes;
    Woodcutter= Yes;
    Stonemason= Yes;
}
```

You can have many more rules for this type of technology tree. Example 11-4 shows a handful of other rules you can write.

Example 11-4. More example rules

```
if(Peasants == Yes && Woodcutter == Unknown)
    Woodcutter = Maybe;

if(Peasants == Yes && Stonemason == Unknown)
    Stonemason = Maybe;

if(Woodcutter == Yes && Barracks == Unknown)
    Barracks = Maybe;

if(Woodcutter == Yes && Stonemason == Yes &&
   Temple == Unknown)
    Temple = Maybe;

if(Barracks == Yes && Blacksmith == Unknown)
    Blacksmith = Maybe;

if(Fletcher == Yes && FootSoldier == Yes &&
   Archer == Unknown)
    Archer = Maybe;

if(Woodcutter == Yes && WoodWalls == Unknown)
    WoodWalls = Maybe;
```

```
if(Stonemason == Yes && StoneWalls == Unknown)
        StoneWalls = Maybe;

if(Archer == Yes && Crossbowman == Unknown)
        Crossbowman = Maybe;

if(Archer == Maybe && Longbowman == Unknown)
        Longbowman = Maybe;

if(Longbowman == Yes)
{
        Archer = Yes;
        Fletcher = Yes;
        FootSoldier = Yes;
        Barracks = Yes;
        Woodcutter = Yes;
}

if(Cavalry == Yes)
{
        Blacksmith = Yes;
        FootSoldier = Yes;
        Barracks = Yes;
        Woodcutter = Yes;
}

if(StoneWalls == Yes)
        Stonemason = Yes;
```

As we stated already, these aren't the only rules you can write for this example. You can develop several more, covering all possible technologies shown in Figure 11-1. The idea here is that you can write such rules and execute them continuously during the game—that is, each iteration through the game loop—to maintain an up-to-date picture of the computer opponent's view of the player's technology capabilities. In this example, the computer can use this knowledge in other AI subsystems to decide how to deploy its attack forces and defenses.

This example should give you a basic idea of how a rule-based system works. It really comes down to a set of if-then style rules and a set of facts and assertions. Note, however, that very often developers do not build rule-based systems using actual if-statements such as those shown in this section. We discuss alternatives a little later, but basically hardcoding the if-statements makes a certain type of inference hard to achieve. Further, developers often use scripting languages or shells so that they can create and modify rules without having to change source code and recompile.

Inference in Rule-Based Systems

In the previous section we took a look at the main components of rule-based systems and showed how you can use such a system to make inferences in a real-time strategy game. In this section we're going to take a slightly more formal look at making inferences using rule-based systems. Our aim here is to distinguish between the two basic algorithms for making inferences and to introduce some standard rule-based system lingo in case you decide to dig further in the technical literature for more information on rule-based systems. (We give some references at the end of this chapter.)

Forward Chaining

The most common inference algorithm for rule-based systems is called *forward chaining*. This algorithm consists of three basic phases. The first phase involves matching rules to facts stored in working memory. You do this by checking the if-parts of each rule to see if they match the given set of facts or assertions in working memory. For example, in our technology tree example, if the working memory indicates that Peasants = Yes and Woodcutter = Unknown, we know the first rule shown in Example 11-4 matches and potentially can be fired. When a rule is fired, its then-part is executed. Potentially, more than one rule can match a given set of facts in working memory. In this case, we have to figure out which rule to fire. This leads to the so-called *conflict resolution* phase.

In the conflict resolution phase we have to examine all the matching rules and figure out which one we want to fire. We can make this decision in many ways. A common approach is to fire the first matching rule. Sometimes you can pick one at random. In other cases, the rules are weighted and the one with the highest weight is selected. We're going to take this latter approach in our fighting example.

After the conflict resolution phase is executed and a rule is selected, we fire the rule. Firing a rule simply means executing its then-part. The rule might assert some new facts in working memory, such as in the rules in Example 11-4. It might trigger some event or call some other function that does some sort of processing.

After these three phases are executed, the whole process is repeated until no more rules can be fired. When this happens the working memory should contain everything the rule-based system can infer given the starting facts. Don't worry if this is a bit nebulous at this point. Things will become clearer when we get to the fighting example.

Backward Chaining

Backward chaining is sort of the opposite of forward chaining. We still have working memory and rules memory, but instead of trying to match if-parts of rules to working memory, we try to match the then-parts. In other words, in backward chaining we start with some outcome, or goal, and we try to figure out which rules must be fired to arrive at that outcome or goal. Consider the technology tree example one more time. Let's say the outcome is that the player has cavalry units—that is, `Cavalry = Yes`. To figure out how the player arrived at acquiring cavalry we can backward-chain to see which rules must be fired to set `Cavalry` to `Yes`.

Looking at Figure 11-1, we see that to have cavalry, the player must have had a blacksmith. A rule for this situation might look like the code shown in Example 11-5.

Example 11-5. Cavalry rule

```
if(Blacksmith == Yes)
     Cavalry =Yes
```

Continuing, if the player has a blacksmith, she must have had barracks. If the player had barracks, she must have had a woodcutter, and so on. We can continue this sort of logic backward up the technology tree from the goal, `Cavalry = Yes`, through all the rules and facts that are required to arrive at that goal. This is backward chaining.

In practice, backward chaining is recursive and more difficult to implement than forward chaining. Further, hardcoding if-statements such as those in our illustrative examples makes it difficult to match the then-parts of rules to facts stored in working memory during backward chaining. In the fighting example, we'll look at how to implement rule-based systems without actually hardcoding if-then style rules.

Fighting Game Strike Prediction

In this example, we aim to predict a human opponent's next strike in a martial arts fighting game. The basic assumption is that the player will try to use combinations of strikes to find the most effective combination. These combinations can be something such as low kick, low kick, high kick; or punch, punch, power kick; and so on. We want the computer opponent to somehow learn to anticipate which strike the player will throw next given the most recently thrown strikes and some history of the player's strike patterns. If the computer can anticipate the next strike, it can throw an appropriate counter strike, or block, or take evasive action such as side-stepping or back-stepping. This will add a higher level of realism to the combat simulation and present new challenges for the player.

To achieve this, we're going to implement a rule-based system with a learning capability. We will achieve this learning by weighting each rule to reinforce some while suppressing others. In Chapter 13 we'll look at an alternative approach to this problem whereby instead of rules, we'll use conditional probabilities to help predict the next strike.

To keep this example manageable for discussion purposes, we're going to simplify things a bit. We'll assume that the player's strikes can be classified as punch, low kick, or high kick. And we're going to track three-strike combinations. Even with these simplifications we still end up with 27 rules to capture all possible three-strike combinations of punch, low kick, and high kick. We'll look at the rules in a moment, but first let's take a look at the structures and classes we need to implement the working memory and rules memory.

Working Memory

Example 11-6 shows how the working memory is implemented.

Example 11-6. Working memory

```
enum TStrikes {Punch, LowKick, HighKick, Unknown};

struct TWorkingMemory {
    TStrikes     strikeA; // previous, previous strike (data)
    TStrikes     strikeB; // previous strike (data)
    TStrikes     strikeC; // next, predicted, strike (assertion)
    // note: can add additional elements here for things such as which counter
to throw, etc....
};

TWorkingMemory  WorkingMemory;  // global working memory variable
```

TStrikes is just an enumerated type for the possible strikes. Note that we include Unknown for the case when the computer does not know what strike will be thrown.

TWorkingMemory is the structure defining the working memory. Here we have three elements: strikeA, strikeB, and strikeC. strikeC will store the predicted next strike to be thrown. This will be asserted by forward chaining through the rules given the observed facts, strikeA and strikeB. strikeB represents the most recently thrown strike while strikeA represents the strike thrown before strikeB. The three-strike combinations are strikeA, then strikeB, then strikeC, in that order, where strikeC is predicted by the rule system.

We can add more facts or assertions to the working memory if desired. For example, we can include a counter strike element that can be asserted given the predicted next strike. If the predicted next strike is, say, low kick, we can have rules that assert an appropriate counter such as back step, and so on. Given the way we're implementing the working memory and rules in this example, you easily can add new elements in the working memory as well as new rules.

Rules

Example 11-7 shows the rules class for this example. Note that we are not going to hardcode if-then rules. Instead, we'll keep an array of TRule objects to represent the rules memory. We easily could have used if-then constructs; however, the approach we're taking here makes it easier to add or delete rules and facilitates backward chaining, which we're going to use to a limited extent. We'll come back to this subject a little later.

Example 11-7. Ruleclass

```
class TRule {
public:
TRule();
void SetRule(TStrikes A, TStrikes B, TStrikes C);

TStrikes      antecedentA;
TStrikes      antecedentB;
TStrikes      consequentC;

bool          matched;
int           weight;
};
```

The TRule object contains five members. The first two are antecedentA and antecedentB. These members correspond to the previous two strikes thrown by the player. The next member, consequentC, corresponds to the predicted next strike—the strike that we'll assert using the rules. If we were using standard if-statements for the rules, we'd have rules that look something like this:

if antecedentA AND antecedentB then consequentC

In an if-then style rule such as *if X then Y*, the "if X" part is the antecedent, or the premise. The "then Y" part is the consequent, or conclusion. In our example, we're assuming that our rules consist of the conjunction (logical *AND*) of two parameters: antecedentA and antecedentB. The then-part in our rules, consequentC, is the expected strike given the two previous strikes.

The next member in TRule is matched. This flag is set to true if the antecedents in the rule match the facts stored in working memory. More specifically, for a given rule, if antecedentA equals WorkingMemory.strikeA and antecedentB equals WorkingMemory.strikeB, the rule is matched. It's possible that more than one rule will match a given set of facts. This matched member helps us keep track of those that do match so that we can pick one to fire during the conflict resolution phase.

The final member in TRule is weight. This is a weighting factor that we can adjust to reinforce or inhibit rules. In a sense it represents the strength of each rule. Looking at it from a different angle, the weight represents the computer's belief that a given rule is more or less applicable relative to other potentially matching rules. During the conflict resolution phase where more than one rule matches, we'll fire the one rule with the highest weight to make a strike prediction. If after the next strike is thrown, we see that we fired the wrong rule—that is, we made a wrong prediction—we'll decrement the fired rule's weight to suppress it. Further, we'll figure out which rule should have been fired and increment its weight to reinforce it.

TRule contains only two methods, SetRule and the constructor. The constructor simply initializes matched to false and weight to 0. We use SetRule to set the other members—antecedentA, antecedentB, and consequentC—therefore defining a rule. SetRule is illustrated in Example 11-8.

Example 11-8. SetRule method

```
void TRule::SetRule(TStrikes A, TStrikes B, TStrikes C)
{
      antecedentA = A;
      antecedentB = B;
      consequentC = C;
}
```

We need a few global variables for this example. The first is WorkingMemory, as we showed in Example 11-6. Example 11-9 shows the others.

Example 11-9. Global variables

```
TRule       Rules[NUM_RULES];
int         PreviousRuleFired;

TStrikes    Prediction;
TStrikes    RandomPrediction;

int         N;
int         NSuccess;
int         NRandomSuccess;
```

Here, Rules is an array of TRule objects. The size of the Rules array is set to NUM_RULES, which is defined as 27 for this example. PreviousRuleFired is an integer type that we'll use to store the index to the rule fired during the previous game cycle. Prediction keeps track of the strike prediction the rule system makes. Technically we don't need this because the prediction also is stored in working memory.

We're going to use RandomPrediction to store a randomly generated prediction to compare with our rule-based prediction. What we'll really compare is the success rate for our rule-based predictions versus the success rate for random guesses. The global variable N will store the number of predictions made. NSuccess will store the number of successful predictions made by our rule-based systems, while NRandomSuccess will store the number of successes for the random guesses. We calculate the success rates by dividing the number of successes by the total number of predictions.

Initialization

At the start of this simulation, or at the start of the game, we need to initialize all the rules and working memory. The Initialize function shown in Example 11-10 takes care of this for us.

Example 11-10. Initialize function

```
void TForm1::Initialize(void)
{
    Rules[0].SetRule(Punch, Punch, Punch);
    Rules[1].SetRule(Punch, Punch, LowKick);
    Rules[2].SetRule(Punch, Punch, HighKick);
    Rules[3].SetRule(Punch, LowKick, Punch);
    Rules[4].SetRule(Punch, LowKick, LowKick);
    Rules[5].SetRule(Punch, LowKick, HighKick);
    Rules[6].SetRule(Punch, HighKick, Punch);
    Rules[7].SetRule(Punch, HighKick, LowKick);
    Rules[8].SetRule(Punch, HighKick, HighKick);
    Rules[9].SetRule(LowKick, Punch, Punch);
    Rules[10].SetRule(LowKick, Punch, LowKick);
    Rules[11].SetRule(LowKick, Punch, HighKick);
    Rules[12].SetRule(LowKick, LowKick, Punch);
    Rules[13].SetRule(LowKick, LowKick, LowKick);
    Rules[14].SetRule(LowKick, LowKick, HighKick);
    Rules[15].SetRule(LowKick, HighKick, Punch);
    Rules[16].SetRule(LowKick, HighKick, LowKick);
    Rules[17].SetRule(LowKick, HighKick, HighKick);
    Rules[18].SetRule(HighKick, Punch, Punch);
    Rules[19].SetRule(HighKick, Punch, LowKick);
    Rules[20].SetRule(HighKick, Punch, HighKick);
    Rules[21].SetRule(HighKick, LowKick, Punch);
    Rules[22].SetRule(HighKick, LowKick, LowKick);
    Rules[23].SetRule(HighKick, LowKick, HighKick);
    Rules[24].SetRule(HighKick, HighKick, Punch);
    Rules[25].SetRule(HighKick, HighKick, LowKick);
    Rules[26].SetRule(HighKick, HighKick, HighKick);

    WorkingMemory.strikeA = sUnknown;
    WorkingMemory.strikeB = sUnknown;
    WorkingMemory.strikeC = sUnknown;
    PreviousRuleFired = -1;

    N = 0;
    NSuccess = 0;
    NRandomSuccess = 0;
    UpdateForm();
}
```

Here we have 27 rules corresponding to all possible three-strike combinations of punch, low kick, and high kick. For example, the first rule, Rules[0], can be read as follows:

> if WorkingMemory.strikeA = AND WorkingMemory.strikeB=Punch
>
> then WorkingMemory.strikeC=Punch

Examining these rules, it's clear that more than one can match the facts stored in working memory at any given time. For example, if strikes *A* and *B* are punch, punch, respectively, the first three rules will match and the prediction could be punch, or low kick, or high kick. This is where the weight factor comes into play to help select which matching rule to fire. We simply select the rule with the highest weight. We pick the first rule encountered in the event that two or more rules have the same weight.

After all the rules are set, the working memory is initialized. Basically, everything in working memory is initialized to Unknown.

Strike Prediction

While the game is running we need to make a strike prediction after every strike the player throws. This will allow the computer opponent to anticipate the next strike the player will throw, as we've already discussed. In our example, we have one function, ProcessMove, to process each strike the player throws and to predict the next strike. Example 11-11 shows the ProcessMove function.

Example 11-11. ProcessMove function

```
TStrikes TForm1::ProcessMove(TStrikes move)
{
    int    i;
    int    RuleToFire = -1;

  // Part 1:
    if(WorkingMemory.strikeA == sUnknown)
    {
            WorkingMemory.strikeA = move;
            return sUnknown;
    }

    if(WorkingMemory.strikeB == sUnknown)
    {
            WorkingMemory.strikeB = move;
            return sUnknown;
    }

  // Part 2:
  // Process previous prediction first
    // Tally and adjust weights
    N++;
    if(move == Prediction)
    {
            NSuccess++;
            if(PreviousRuleFired != -1)
                Rules[PreviousRuleFired].weight++;
    } else {
            if(PreviousRuleFired != -1)
                Rules[PreviousRuleFired].weight--;

            // Backward chain to increment the rule that
            // should have been fired:
            for(i=0; i<NUM_RULES; i++)
```

```
                    {
                            if(Rules[i].matched && (Rules[i].consequentC == move))
                            {
                                    Rules[i].weight++;
                                    break;
                            }
                    }
            }

            if(move == RandomPrediction)
                    NRandomSuccess++;

            // Roll back
            WorkingMemory.strikeA = WorkingMemory.strikeB;
            WorkingMemory.strikeB = move;

    // Part 3:
    // Now make new prediction
            for(i=0; i<NUM_RULES; i++)
            {
                    if(Rules[i].antecedentA == WorkingMemory.strikeA &&
                       Rules[i].antecedentB == WorkingMemory.strikeB)
                            Rules[i].matched = true;
                    else
                            Rules[i].matched = false;
            }

            // Pick the matched rule with the highest weight...
            RuleToFire = -1;
            for(i=0; i<NUM_RULES; i++)
            {
                    if(Rules[i].matched)
                    {
                            if(RuleToFire == -1)
                                RuleToFire = i;
                            else if(Rules[i].weight > Rules[RuleToFire].weight)
                                RuleToFire = i;
                    }
            }

            // Fire the rule
            if(RuleToFire != -1) {
                    WorkingMemory.strikeC = Rules[RuleToFire].consequentC;
                    PreviousRuleFired = RuleToFire;
            } else {
                    WorkingMemory.strikeC = sUnknown;
                    PreviousRuleFired = -1;
            }

            return WorkingMemory.strikeC;
}
```

You can break this function into three distinctive parts, as indicated by the comments // Part 1, // Part 2, and // Part 3. Let's consider each part in turn.

Part 1

The first part populates the working memory. At the start of the game, after working memory is initialized and before any strikes are thrown, the working memory contains only Unknown values. This is insufficient to make a prediction, so we want to collect some data from the player as he begins to throw strikes. The first strike thrown is stored in WorkingMemory.strikeA and ProcessMoves simply returns Unknown without attempting a prediction. After the second strike is thrown, ProcessMoves is called again and this time the second strike is stored in WorkingMemory.strikeB. ProcessMoves returns Unknown one more time.

Part 2

The second part in ProcessMoves takes care of processing the previous prediction—that is, the prediction returned the previous time ProcessMoves was called. The first task in part 2 is to determine whether the previous prediction was accurate. ProcessMoves takes move as a parameter. move is the strike the player threw most recently. Therefore, if move equals the previous prediction stored in Prediction, we have a success. In this case, we increment NSuccess so that we can update our success rate. Then we reinforce the previously fired rule because it was the correct one to fire given the strike history stored in working memory. To reinforce a rule we simply increment the rule's weight.

If the previous prediction was wrong—that is, if move does not equal Prediction—we need to inhibit the previously fired rule. To do this we simply decrement the previously fired rule's weight. At the same time we want to reinforce the rule that should have been fired. To do this we have to figure out which rule should have been fired the last time ProcessMoves was called. To this end, we need to backward-chain a bit. Essentially, we know the move; therefore, we know what consequent should have been returned for the previous prediction. So, all we have to do is cycle through the last set of matched rules and pick the one who's consequentC equals move. Once we find the rule, we increment its weight and we're done.

The remaining tasks in part 2 of ProcessMoves are relatively simple. The next task is to see if the previous random prediction was correct and, if so, to increment the number of successful random predictions, NRandomSuccess.

Finally, we need to update the strikes in working memory in preparation for making a new prediction. To this end, we simply shift the strikes in working memory and add the most recent move. Specifically, WorkingMemory.strikeB becomes WorkingMemory.strikeA and move becomes WorkingMemory.strikeB. Now we're ready to make a new prediction for the new series of strikes stored in working memory.

Part 3

Referring to // Part 3 in Example 11-11, the first task in the prediction process is to find the rules that match the facts stored in working memory. We take care of this in the first for loop under the // Part 3 comment. Note that this is the so-called *match* phase of the forward chaining algorithm. Matching occurs when a rule's antecedentA and antecedentB equal WorkingMemory.strikeA and WorkingMemory.strikeB, respectively.

After the match phase, we need to pick one rule to fire from those that were matched during the matching phase. This is the conflict resolution phase. Basically, all we do is cycle through the matched rules and pick the one with the highest weight. We take care of this in the second for loop after the // Part 3 comment in Example 11-11. After this loop does its thing, the index to the selected rule is stored in RuleToFire. To actually fire the rule we simply copy consequentC of Rules[RuleToFire] to WorkingMemory.strikeC.

ProcessMoves stores the index to the fired rule, RuleToFire, in PreviousRuleFired, which will be used in part 2 the next time ProcessMoves is called. Finally, ProcessMoves returns the predicted strike.

That's pretty much all there is to this example. Upon running the example and simulating thrown strikes, by pressing buttons corresponding to punch, low kick, and high kick, we see that the rule-based system is pretty good at predicting the next strike. Our experiments saw success rates from 65% up to 80%. Comparing this to the roughly 30% success rate we achieved by guessing randomly, it's clear that such a rule-based system works very well.

Further Information

We've only scratched the surface of rule-based systems in this chapter. Although we covered all the fundamental concepts and showed how effective rule-based systems are, other aspects to rule-based systems are worthwhile investigating if you plan to implement them for large-scale systems.

Optimization is one area that deserves attention. For small rule sets, forward chaining does not take much processing time; however, for larger sets of rules where many rules can match a given set of facts, it's wise to optimize the conflict resolution phase. The most common algorithm for this is the so-called *Rete algorithm*. (Check out the article "Rete: A Fast Algorithm for the Many Pattern/Many Object Pattern Match Problem," by C. L. Forgy, Artificial Intelligence, 1982.) Most textbooks on rule-based, or expert, systems cover the Rete algorithm.

As you saw with our fighting example, you don't have to use if-then statements in a rule-based system. You don't even have to use the sort of enumerated types or other types, such as integers, Booleans, and so on. You can use strings to represent facts in working memory and string matching routines to determine if the antecedents of a rule (also, strings) match facts stored in working memory. This approach opens the door to scripting rules outside of the compiled program, which paves the way for designers to script AI rules. Indeed, developers have been using scripting languages, such as the well-known Prolog, Lisp, and CLIPS languages, for scripting rule-based systems for decades now. (There's even a relatively new Java-based language called JESS.) Another advantage to using a scripting language to implement rule-based systems is that it's easy to change, delete, or expand upon the rules without having to modify the compiled game code.

Instead of using a third-party scripting language, you can write your own; however, caution is in order here. Writing a scripted rule system to handle facts that can take on a range of values, along with rules with compound antecedents and consequents that might even trigger other events, is far more complicated than writing a rule system with only Boolean facts and simple rule structures. If you'd like to see how you might go about such a task, check out Chapter 8 of *AI Application Programming* by M. Tim Jones (Charles River Media). Note that the author's example is not a general-purpose scripting language such as Prolog and the others mentioned earlier, but it does show how to implement a simple rules-scripting algorithm from scratch. Recall that we covered basic scripting in Chapter 8 of this book. You can apply those same techniques to writing rule-based systems, as we discussed in this chapter.

As for other sources of information, the Internet is replete with web pages on rule-based systems and scripting shells. If you conduct an Internet search on rule-based systems, often abbreviated RBS, you're sure to find tons of links to pages that discuss rule-based systems in some context or another. Here are some Web sites that we find helpful for beginners:

- *http://www.aaai.org/AITopics/html/expert.html*
- *http://ai-depot.com/Tutorial/RuleBased.html*
- *http://www.igda.org/ai/*

CHAPTER 12

Basic Probability

Developers use probability in games for such things as hit probabilities, damage probabilities, and personality (e.g., propensity to attack, run, etc.). Games use probabilities to add a little uncertainty. In this chapter, we review elementary principles of probability and discuss how you can apply these basic principles to give the game AI some level of unpredictability. A further aim of this chapter is to serve as a primer for the next chapter, which covers decisions under uncertainty and Bayesian analysis.

How Do You Use Probability in Games?

Bayesian analysis for decision making under uncertainty is fundamentally tied to probability. Genetic algorithms also use probability to some extent—for example, to determine mutation rates. Even neural networks can be coupled with probabilistic methods. We cover these rather involved methods to various extents later in this book.

Randomness

Because the examples we discuss rely heavily on generating random numbers, let's look at some code to generate random numbers. The standard C function to generate a random number is rand(), which generates a random integer in the range from 0 to RAND_MAX. Typically RAND_MAX is set to 32727. To get a random integer between 0 and 99, use rand() %100. Similarly, to get a random number between 0 and any integer *N-1*, use rand() % N. Don't forget to seed the random number generator once at the start of your program by calling srand (*seed*). Note that srand takes a single unsigned int parameter as the random seed with which to initialize the random number generator.

In a very simple example, say you decide to program a little randomness to unit movement in your game. In this case, you can say the unit, when confronted, will move left with a 25% probability or will move right with a 25% probability or will back up with a 50% probability. Given these probabilities, you need only generate a random number between 0 and 99 and perform a few tests to determine in which direction to move the unit. To perform these tests, we'll assign the range 0 to 24 as the possible range of values for the move-left event. Similarly, we'll assign the range of values 75 to 99 as the possible range of values for the move-right event. Any other value between 25 and 74 (inclusive) indicates the backup event. Once a random number is selected, we need only test within which range it falls and then make the appropriate move. Admittedly, this is a very simple example, and one can argue that this is not intelligent movement; however, developers commonly use this technique to present some uncertainty to the player, making it more difficult to predict where the unit will move when confronted.

Hit Probabilities

Another common use of probabilities in games involves representing a creature or player's chances to hit an opponent in combat. Typically, the game developer defines several probabilities, given certain characteristics of the player and his opponent. For example, in a role-playing game you can say that a player with a moderate dexterity ranking has a 60% probability of striking his opponent with a knife in melee combat. If the player's dexterity ranking is high, you might give him better odds of successfully striking with a knife; for example, you can say he has a 90% chance of striking his opponent. Notice that these are essentially conditional probabilities. We're saying that the player's probability of success is 90% given that he is highly dexterous, whereas his probability of success is 60% given that he is moderately dexterous. In a sense, all probabilities are conditional on some other event or events, even though we might not explicitly state the condition or assign a probability to it, as we did formally in the previous section. In fact, it's common in games to make adjustments to such hit probabilities given other factors. For example, you can say that the player's probability of successfully striking his opponent is increased to 95% given that he possesses a "dagger of speed." Or, you can say the player's chances of success are reduced to 85% given his opponent's magic armor. You can come up with any number of these and list them in what commonly are called *hit probability tables* to calculate the appropriate probability given the occurrence or nonoccurrence of any number of enumerated events.

Character Abilities

Yet another example of using probabilities in games is to define abilities of character classes or creature types. For example, say you have a role-playing game in which the player can take on the persona of a wizard, fighter, rouge, or ranger. Each class has its own strengths and weaknesses relative to the other classes, which you can enumerate in a table of skills with probabilities assigned so as to define each class's characteristics. Table 12-1 gives a simple example of such a character class ability table.

Table 12-1. Character class ability

Ability	Wizard	Fighter	Rouge	Ranger
Use magic	0.9	0.05	0.2	0.1
Wield sword	0.1	0.9	0.7	0.75
Harvest wood	0.3	0.5	0.6	0.8
Pick locks	0.15	0.1	0.05	0.5
Find traps	0.13	0.05	0.2	0.7
Read map	0.4	0.2	0.1	0.8
...	...	...	...	...

Typically such character class tables are far more expansive than the few skills we show here. However, these serve to illustrate that each skill is assigned a probability of success, which is conditional on the character class. For example, a wizard has a 90% chance of successfully using magic, a fighter has a mere 5% chance, and so on. In practice these probabilities are further conditioned on the overall class level for each individual player. For example, a first-level wizard might have only a 10% chance of using magic. Here, the idea is that as the player earns levels, his proficiency in his craft will increase and the probabilities assigned to each skill will reflect this progress.

On the computer side of such a game's AI, all creatures in the world will have similar sets of probability tables defining their abilities given their type. For example, dragons would have a different set of proficiencies than would giant apes, and so on.

State Transitions

You can take creature abilities a step further by combining probabilities with state transitions in the finite state machine that you can use to manage the various creature states. (See Chapter 9 for a discussion of finite state machines.) For example, Figure 12-1 illustrates a few states that a creature can assume.

Let's assume that this is one branch within a finite state machine that will be executed when the computer-controlled creature encounters the player. In the figure, *Conditions* are the necessary conditions that are checked in the finite state machine that would cause this set of states—Attack, Flee, Hide, etc.—to be considered. A condition could be something such as "the player is within range and has a weapon drawn." Instead of deterministically selecting a state for the creature, we can assign certain probabilities to each applicable state. For illustration purposes we show that there's a 50% chance the creature will attack the player. However, there's a 20% chance the creature will flee the scene, and there's a 10% chance it will try to hide. For even more variability, you can assign different probabilities to different types of creatures, making some more or less aggressive than others, and so on. Furthermore,

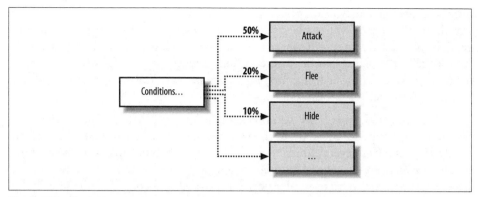

Figure 12-1. Creature states

within each creature type you can assign individual creatures different probabilities, giving each one their own distinct personality.

To select a state given probabilities such as these, you pick a random number between, say, 0 and 99, and check to see if it falls within specific ranges corresponding to each probability. Alternatively, you can take a lottery-type approach. In this case, you enumerate each state—for example, 0 for attack, 1 for flee, 2 for hide, and so on—and fill an array with these values in proportion to their probability. For example, for the attack state you'd fill half of the array with 0s. Once the array is populated, you simply pick a random number from 0 to the maximum size of the array minus 1, and you use that as an index to the array to get the chosen state.

Adaptability

A somewhat more compelling use of probability in games involves updating certain probabilities as the game is played in an effort to facilitate computer-controlled unit learning or adapting. For example, during a game you can collect statistics on the number and outcomes of confrontations between a certain type of creature and a certain class of player—for example, a wizard, fighter, and so on. Then you can calculate in real time the probability that the encounter results in the creature's death. This is essentially the relative frequency approach to determining probabilities. Once you have this probability, you can use it—rather, the creature can—when deciding whether to engage players of this class in combat. If the probability is high that a certain class of player will kill this type of creature, you can have creatures of this type start to avoid that particular class. On the other hand, if the probability suggests that the creature might do well against a particular type of player class, you can have the creature seek out players of that class.

We look at this type of analysis in the next chapter, where we show you how to calculate such things as given the probability that the player is of a certain class and the probability that death results from encounters with this class, what is the probability that death will result? You could take this a step further by not assuming that the creature knows in what class the player belongs. Instead, the creature's knowledge of the player can be uncertain, and it will have to infer what class he is facing to make a decision. Being able to collect statistics during gameplay and use probabilities for decisions clearly offers some interesting possibilities.

So far we discussed probability without actually giving it a formal definition. We need to do so before we move on to the next chapter on Bayesian methods. Further, we need to establish several fundamental rules of probability that you must know to fully appreciate the material in the next chapter. Therefore, in the remainder of this chapter we cover fundamental aspects of probability theory. If you're already up to speed on this material, you can skip right to the next chapter.

What is Probability?

The question posed here—what is probability?—is deceptively simple to answer in that there's no single definition of probability. One can interpret probability in several different ways, depending on the situation being considered and who's doing the considering. In the following sections, we consider three common interpretations of probability, all of which have a place in games in some form or another. We keep these discussions general in nature to keep them easy to understand.

Classical Probability

Classical probability is an interpretation of probability that refers to events and possibilities, or possible outcomes. Given an event, E, which can occur in n ways out of a total of N possible outcomes, the probability, p, of occurrence of the event is:

$$p = P(E) = n/N$$

Here, *P(E)* is the probability of event E, which is equal to the number of ways E occurs out of N possible ways. *P(E)* usually is called the *probability of success* of the event. The *probability of failure* of the event is *1-P(E)*. In summary:

$$\text{Probability of success, } p_s = n/N$$
$$\text{Probability of failure, } p_f = 1 - p_s$$

Note that probabilities range in value from 0 to 1 and the sum of the probabilities of success and failure, $p_s + p_f$, must equal 1.

Let's consider a simple example. Say you roll a six-sided die; the probability that a four will show up is 1/6 because there's only one way in which a four can show up out of six possible outcomes in a single roll. In this example, the event, E, is the event that a four will show up. For the roll of a single die, a four can show up in only one way; therefore, $n = 1$. The total number of possible outcomes, N, is six in this case; therefore, *P(E = 4) = 1/6*. Clearly, in this case the probability of any given number showing up is 1/6 because each number can show up in only one possible way out of six ways.

Now, consider two six-sided dice, both rolled at the same time. What is the probability that the sum of the numbers that show up is equal to, say, five? Here, the event we're interested in is a sum of five being rolled. In this case, there are four possible ways in which the sum of five can result. These are illustrated in Figure 12-2.

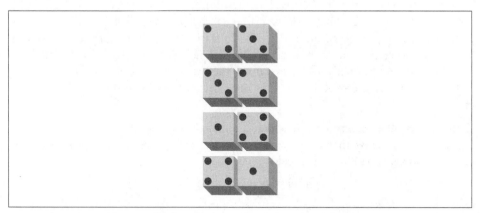

Figure 12-2. Sums of five in roll of two dice

Note that the outcome of the first die showing a two and the second showing a three is distinctly different from the outcome of the first die showing a three and the second showing a two. In this case, $N = 36$—that is, there are 36 possible outcomes of the roll of two dice. The probability, then, that the sum of five will appear is four divided by 36, with 36 being the total number of possible outcomes for two six-sided dice. This results in a probability of 4/36 or 1/9.

You can find the probability that any sum can show up in a similar manner. For example, the possible ways in which the sum of seven can occur are summarized in Table 12-2.

Table 12-2. Sums of seven in roll of two dice

Die 1	Die 2
1	6
6	1
2	5
5	2
3	4
4	3

In this case, the probability of a sum of seven is 6/36 or 1/6. Stated another way, the probability of a sum of seven is 16.7%. We can express probability as percentages by taking the probability value, which will be between 0 and 1, and multiplying it by 100.

Frequency Interpretation

The *frequency interpretation* of probability, also known as *relative frequency* or *objective probability*, considers events and samples or *experiments*. If an experiment is conducted N times and some event, E, occurs n times, the probability of E occurring is:

$$P(E) = n/N, \text{ as } N \rightarrow \infty$$

Note here the caveat that $P(E)$ is n/N as the number of experiments conducted gets very large. For a finite number of experiments, the resulting probability will be approximate, or empirical, because it is derived statistically. Empirical probability can be slightly different from theoretical probability if it can, indeed, be calculated for a given event. Additionally, we're assuming the experiments are independent—that is, the outcome of one experiment does not affect the outcome of any other experiment.

Consider a simple experiment in which a coin is tossed 1000 times. The results of this experiment show that heads came up 510 times. Therefore, the probability of getting heads is 510/1000, which yields:

$$P(\text{heads}) = 0.51, \text{ or } 51\%$$

Of course, in this example we know that *P(heads)* is 0.5 or 50% and were we to continue with these experiments for a larger number of tosses we would expect our empirically derived *P(heads)* to approach 0.5.

Subjective Interpretation

Subjective probability is a measure, on a scale from zero to one, of a person's degree of belief that a particular event will occur given their knowledge, experience, or judgment. This interpretation is useful when the event, or experiment, in question is not repeatable—that is, we can't use a frequency measure to calculate a probability.

Subjective probabilities are found everywhere—we can say "it probably will rain tomorrow" or "I have a good chance of passing this test" or "the Saints probably will win tomorrow." In each case, we base our belief in the outcome of these events on our knowledge of the events, whether it is complete or incomplete knowledge, and on our judgment considering a potential variety of relevant factors. For example, the fact that it is raining today might lead us to believe that it probably will rain tomorrow. We believe the Saints might win tomorrow's football game with a better-than-usual probability because we know the other team's star quarterback is suffering from an injury.

Consider this example: let's assume you're up for the lead game designer promotion in your company. You might say, "I have a 50% chance of getting the promotion," knowing that someone else in your group with identical qualifications also is being considered for the job. One the other hand, you might say, "I have about a

75% chance of getting the promotion," knowing that you've been with this company longer than your colleague who also is being considered. If in this case you also learn that the other candidate has notoriously missed milestone deadlines on various game projects, you might be inclined to revise your belief that you'll get the promotion to something like a 90% chance. Formally, Bayesian analysis enables us to update our belief of some event given such new information. We discuss this in much greater detail in the next chapter.

Subjective probabilities very often are difficult to pin down, even when one has a fairly good intuitive feeling about a particular event. For example, if you say you probably will pass that test, what would you say is the actual probability: 60%, 80%, or 90%? You can employ some techniques to help pin down subjective probabilities, and we go over two of them shortly. Before we do that, however, we need to cover two other fundamental topics: odds and expectation.

Odds

Odds show up commonly in betting scenarios. For example, Sunflower Petals might be the long shot to win next week's horse race, and the odds against her winning are 20 to 1; a football fan might take 3 to 1 odds on a bet in favor of the Giants winning Sunday's game; and so on. For many, it's easier or more intuitive to think of probabilities in terms of odds rather than in terms of some number between 0 and 1, or in terms of percentages. Odds reflect probabilities, and you can convert between them using a few simple relations.

If we say the odds in favor of the success of some event, E, are a to b, the probability of success of that event, P(E), is:

$$P(E) = a/(a + b)$$

We can work in the other direction from probability to odds too. If you are given the probability of success of some event, P(E), the odds in favor of the event succeeding are P(E) to (1-P(E)). For example, if the odds are 9 to 1 that you'll pass a test, the probability that you'll pass is 0.9 or 90%. If, however, the probability you'll pass is only 0.6, or 60%, because you didn't study as much as you would have liked, the odds in favor of you passing are 60 to 40 or 1.5 to 1.

Expectation

Often it is useful in probability problems to think in terms of expectation. *Mathematical expectation* is the expected value of some discrete random variable, X, that can take on any values, x_0, x_1, x_2, ..., x_n, with corresponding probabilities, p_0, p_1, p_2, ..., p_n. You calculate the expectation for such a distribution of outcomes as follows:

$$E(X) = x_0 p_0 + x_1 p_1 + x_2 p_2 + x_3 p_3 + \cdots + x_n p_n$$

For distributions such as this, you can think of the expectation as an average value. Statisticians think of expectation as a measure of central tendency. Decision theorists think of expectation as some measure of payoff.

As a very simple example, if you stand to win $100 with a probability of 0.12, your expectation is $12—that is, $100 times 0.12.

As another example, say you have a perpetual online role-playing game in which you monitor the number of players who gather at the local tavern each evening. Let's assume from this monitoring you establish the probabilities shown in Table 12-3 for the number of players in the tavern each evening. Let's further assume that the samples you used to calculate these frequency-based probabilities were all taken at about the same time of day; for example, you might have a spy casing the tavern every night collecting intelligence for an upcoming invasion.

Table 12-3. Probabilities of number of players in tavern each evening

# Players	Probability
0	0.02
2	0.08
4	0.20
6	0.24
8	0.17
10	0.13
12	0.10
14	0.05
16	0.01

Note that this distribution forms a mutually exclusive, exhaustive set. That is, there can't be, say, zero and eight players there at the same time—it has to be one or the other—and the sum of probabilities for all these outcomes must be equal to 1. In this case, the expectation, the expected number of players in the tavern in the evening, is equal to 7.1. You can calculate this by taking the sum of the products of each pair of numbers appearing in each row of the table. Therefore, in any given evening, one can expect to find about seven players in the tavern, on average. Note that using this kind of analysis, an invading force could estimate how many units to send toward the tavern to take control of it.

Techniques for Assigning Subjective Probability

As we stated earlier, it is often very difficult to pin subjective probabilities to a specific number. Although you might have a good feel for the probability of some event, you might find it difficult to actually assign a single number to the probability of that event. To help in this regard, several commonly used metaphors are available to assist you in assigning numbers to subjective probabilities. We briefly discuss two of them here.

The first technique we can use to assign subjective probabilities is a betting metaphor. Let's return to the promotion example we discussed earlier. Let's say that another co-worker asked if you're willing to make a wager on whether you'll get the promotion. If the co-worker takes the side that you won't get the promotion and is willing to put up $1 on the bet, but then asks for 9 to 1 odds, you'll have to pay $9 if you lose and you'll gain $1 if you win. Would you accept this bet? If you would, you consider this a fair bet and you essentially are saying you believe you'll get the promotion with a probability of 90%. You can calculate this by considering the odds to which you agreed and using the relationship between odds and probability we discussed earlier. If you rejected these odds but instead offered 4 to 1 odds in favor of you getting the promotion, you essentially are saying you believe the probability that you'll get the promotion is 4/5 or 80%.

Underlying this approach is the premise that you believe that the agreed-upon odds constitute a fair bet. Subjectively, a fair bet is one in which the expected gain is 0 and it does not matter to you which side of the bet you choose. Let's say you took the 9 to 1 odds and you thought this was a fair bet. In this case, you expect to win ($1)(0.9) or 90 cents. This is simply the amount you will win times the probability that you will win. At the same time you expect to lose ($9)(0.1) or 90 cents—the amount you are wagering times the probability that you will lose. Therefore, the net gain you expect is your expected winnings minus your expected loss, which is clearly 0. Now, if you took this bet with 9 to 1 odds, but you really felt that your probability of successfully getting the promotion was only 80% as compared to 90%, your expected gain would be:

$$(\$1)(0.8) - (\$9)(0.2) = -\$1$$

In this case you'd expect to lose $1, which indicates that this would not be a fair bet.

The betting metaphor we described here is the so-called *put up or shut up* approach in which you're required to really think about the probability in terms of what you'd be willing to wager on the outcome. The idea is that you should get a pretty good sense of your true belief about a particular outcome.

There's a problem with this approach, however, that is due to individual tolerances for risk. When we're talking about $1 versus $9, the idea of losing $9 might not be that significant to you and you might have a greater propensity to take these odds. However, what if the bets were $100 and $900, or perhaps even $1000 and $9000? Certainly, most rational people who don't own a money tree would think a little harder about their belief in some outcome occurring when larger sums of money are at stake. In some cases, the risk of losing so much money would override their belief in a certain outcome occurring, even if their subjective probability were well founded. And therein lies the problem in using this technique when perceived risk becomes significant: a person's subjective probability could be biased by the risk they perceive.

An alternative to the betting metaphor is the so-called *fair price* metaphor whereby instead of betting on the outcome of an event, you ask yourself to put a fair price on some event. For example, let's consider an author of a book who stands to earn $30,000 in royalties if the book he wrote is successful. Further, suppose that he will get nothing if the book fails. Now suppose the author is given the option by his publisher of taking an upfront, guaranteed payment of $10,000, but if he accepts he forfeits any further royalty rights. The question now is, what is the author's subjective probability, his belief, that the book will be successful?

If the author accepts the deal, we can infer that $10,000 is greater than his expectation—that is, $10,000 \geq (\$30,000)(p)$, where p is his assigned subjective probability of the book's success. Therefore, in this case his belief that the book will be successful as expressed by p is less than 0.33 or 33%. To get this we simply solve for p—that is, $p \geq \$10,000/\$30,000$. If the author rejects the deal, he evidently feels the book has greater than a 33% chance of success—that is, his expectation is greater than $10,000.

To narrow down what the author feels the probability of success of the book actually is, we can simply ask him what he would take up front—we ask him what he thinks is a fair price for the rights to the book. From his reply we can calculate the subjective probability that he has assigned for the book's success using the formula for expectation as before. If U is the amount he would accept up front, the subjective probability of the book's success, p, is simply $U/\$30,000$.

You can come up with various versions of this fair-price metaphor yourself depending on for what it is you're trying to estimate a subjective probability. The idea here is to eliminate any bias that might be introduced when considering scenarios in which your own money is at risk, as in the betting technique.

Probability Rules

Formal probability theory includes several rules that govern how probabilities are calculated. We'll go over these rules here to lay some groundwork for the next chapter. Although we've already discussed a few of these rules, we'll restate them again here for completeness. In the discussion that follows, we state the rules in general terms and don't provide specific examples. We will, however, see these rules in action in the next chapter. If you're interested in seeing specific examples of each rule, you can refer to any introductory-level book on probability.

Rule 1

This rule states the probability of an event, $P(A)$, must be a real number between 0 and 1, inclusive. This rule serves to constrain the range of values assigned to probabilities. On one end of the scale we can't have a negative probability, while on the other end the probability of an event can't be greater than 1, which implies absolute certainty that the event will occur.

Rule 2

As sort of an extension of rule 1, if *S* represents the entire sample space for the event, the probability of *S* equals 1. This says that because the sample space includes all possible outcomes, there is a 100% probability that one of the outcomes therein will occur. Here, it helps to visualize the sample space and events using *Venn diagrams*. Figure 12-3 illustrates a Venn diagram for the sample space *S* and events *A* and *B* within that sample space.

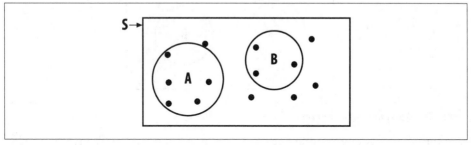

Figure 12-3. Venn diagram

The dots represent samples taken within the space, and the relative sizes of the circles for *A* and *B* indicate their relative probabilities—more specifically, their areas indicate their probabilities.

Rule 3

If the probability that an event, *A*, will occur is *P(A)* and the event that *A* will not occur is designated *A'*, the probability of the event not occurring, *P(A')*, is *1-P(A)*. This rule simply states that an event either occurs or does not occur and the probability of this event either occurring or not occurring is 1—that is, we can say with certainty the event either will occur or will not occur. Figure 12-4 illustrates events *A* and *A'* on a Venn diagram.

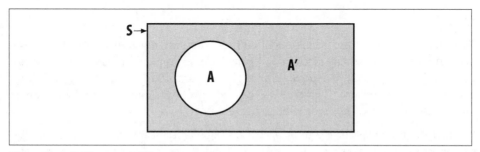

Figure 12-4. P(A) versus P(A')

Clearly, event *A'* covers all of the area within the sample space *S* that falls outside of event *A*.

Rule 4

This rule states that if two events *A* and *B* are mutually exclusive, only one of them can occur at a given time. For example, in a game, the events *creature is dead* and *creature is alive* are mutually exclusive. The creature cannot be both dead and alive at the same time. Figure 12-5 illustrates two mutually exclusive events *A* and *B*.

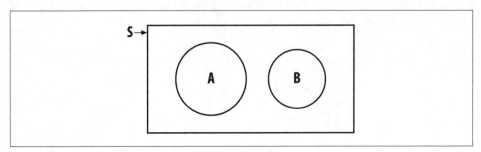

Figure 12-5. Mutually exclusive events

Note that the areas representing these two events do not overlap. For two mutually exclusive events, *A* and *B*, the probability of event *A* or event *B* occurring is as follows:

$$P(A \cup B) = P(A) + P(B)$$

where $P(A \cup B)$ is the probability of event *A* or event *B*, the probability that one or the other occurs, and *P(A)* and *P(B)* are the probabilities of events *A* and *B*, respectively.

You can generalize this rule for more than two mutually exclusive events. For example, if *A*, *B*, *C*, and *D* are four mutually exclusive events, the probability that *A* or *B* or *C* or *D* occurs is:

$$P(A \cup B \cup C \cup D) = P(A) + P(B) + P(C) + P(D)$$

Theoretically you can generalize this to any number of mutually exclusive events.

Rule 5

This rule states that if the events under consideration are not mutually exclusive, we need to revise the formulas discussed in rule 4. For example, in a game a given creature can be *alive*, *dead*, or *injured*. Although *alive* and *dead* are mutually exclusive, *alive* and *injured* are not. The creature can be alive and injured at the same time. Figure 12-6 shows two nonmutually exclusive events.

In this case, the areas for events *A* and *B* overlap. This means that event *A* can occur or event *B* can occur or both events *A* and *B* can occur simultaneously. The shaded area in Figure 12-5 indicates the probability that both *A* and *B* occur together. Therefore, to calculate the probability of event *A* or event *B* occurring in this

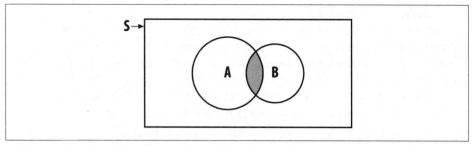

Figure 12-6. Nonmutually exclusive events

case, we use the following formula:

$$P(A \cup B) = P(A) + P(B) - P(A \cap B)$$

In this formula, $P(A \cup B)$ is the probability that both A and B occur.

You also can generalize this formula to more than two nonmutually exclusive events. Figure 12-7 illustrates three events, A, B, and C, that are not mutually exclusive.

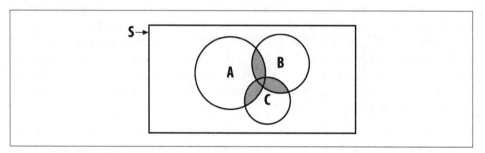

Figure 12-7. Three nonmutually exclusive events

To calculate the probability of A or B or C we need to calculate the probability corresponding to the shaded region in Figure 12-7. The formula that achieves this is as follows:

$$P(A \cup B \cup C) =$$
$$\{P(A) + P(B) + P(C)\} - \{P(A \cap B) + P(A \cap C) + P(B \cap C)\} + P(A \cap B \cap C)$$

Rule 6

This rule states that if two events, A and B, are independent—that is, the occurrence of one event does not depend on the occurrence or nonoccurrence of the other event—the probability of events A and B both occurring is as follows:

$$P(A \cap B) = P(A) \, P(B)$$

For example, two independent events in a game can be *player encounters a wandering monster* and *player is building a fire*. The occurrence of either of these events is independent of the occurrence of the other event. Now consider another event, *player is chopping wood*. In this case, the event *player encounters a wandering monster* might very well depend on whether the *player is chopping wood*. These events are not independent. By chopping wood, the player presumably is in a forest, which increases the likelihood of him encountering a wandering monster.

Referring to Figure 12-6, this probability corresponds to the shaded region shared by events *A* and *B*.

If events *A* and *B* are not independent, we must deal with the so-called conditional probability of these events. The preceding formula does not apply in the conditional case. The rule governing conditional probabilities is so important, especially in the context of Bayesian analysis, we're going to discuss it next in its own section.

Conditional Probability

When events are not independent, they are said to be *conditional*. For example, if you arrive home one day to find your lawn wet, what is the probability that it rained while you were at work? It is possible that someone turned on your sprinkler system while you were at work, so the outcome of your grass being wet is conditional upon whether it rained or whether someone turned on your sprinkler. You can best solve this sort of scenario using Bayesian analysis, which we cover in the next chapter. But as you'll see in a moment, Bayesian analysis is grounded in conditional probability.

In general, if event *A* depends on whether event *B* occurred, we can't use the formula shown earlier in rule 6 for independent events. Given these two dependent events, we denote the probability of *A* occurring given that *B* has occurred as *P(A|B)*. Likewise, the probability of *B* occurring given that *A* has occurred is denoted as *P(B|A)*. Note that *P(A|B)* is not necessarily equal to *P(B|A)*.

To find the compound probability of both *A* and *B* occurring, we use the following formula:

$$P(A \cap B) = P(A)\,P(B|A)$$

This formula states that the probability of both dependant events *A* and *B* occurring at the same time is equal to the probability of event *A* occurring times the probability of event *B* occurring given that event *A* has occurred.

We can extend this to three dependent events, *A*, *B*, and *C*, as follows:

$$P(A \cap B \cap C) = P(A)\,P(B|A)\,P(C|A,B)$$

This formula states that the probability of events *A*, *B*, and *C* all occurring at once is equal to the probability of event *A* occurring times the probability of event *B* occurring given that A has occurred times the probability of event C occurring given that both events A and B have occurred.

Often we are more interested in the probability of an event given that some other condition or event has occurred. Therefore, we'll often write:

$$P(B|A) = P(A \cap B)/P(A)$$

This formula states that the conditional probability of event B occurring given that A has occurred is equal to the probability of both A and B occurring divided by the probability of event A occurring. We note that $P(A \cap B)$ also is equal to $P(B)$ $P(A|B)$, and we can make a substitution for $P(A \cap B)$ in the formula for $P(B|A)$ as follows:

$$P(B|A) = P(B)P(A|B)/P(A)$$

This is known as *Bayes' rule*. We'll generalize Bayes' rule in the next chapter, where we'll also see some examples.

CHAPTER 13

Decisions Under Uncertainty— Bayesian Techniques

This chapter introduces Bayesian inference and Bayesian networks and shows how you can use these techniques in games. Specifically, we'll show you how to use these techniques to enable nonplayer characters (NPCs) to make decisions when the states of the game world are uncertain. We'll also show you how simple Bayesian models enable your computer-controlled characters to adapt to changing situations. We'll make heavy use of probability, so if that subject is not fresh in your mind, you might want to read Chapter 12 first and then come back to this chapter.

Before getting into the details of Bayesian networks, let's discuss a hypothetical example. Suppose you're writing a role-playing game in which you enable players to store valuables in chests located around the game world. Players can use these chests to store whatever they want, but they run the risk of NPCs looting the chests. To deter looting, players can trap the chests if they have the skill and materials to set such traps. Now, as a game developer, you're faced with the issue of how to code NPC thieves for them to decide whether to open a given chest that they discover.

One option is to have NPCs always attempt to open any given chest. Although simple to implement, this option is not so interesting and has some undesirable consequences. First, having the NPCs always open the chest defeats the purpose of players trapping chests as a deterrent. Second, if players catch on that NPCs always will attempt to open a chest no matter what, they might try to exploit this fact by trapping empty chests for the sole purpose of weakening or even killing NPCs without having to engage them in direct combat.

Your other option is to cheat and give NPCs absolute knowledge that any given chest is trapped (or not) and have them avoid trapped chests. Although this might render traps adequate deterrents, it can be viewed as unfair. Further, there's no variety, which can get boring after a while.

A potentially better alternative is to give NPCs some knowledge, though not perfect, and to enable them to reason given that knowledge. Further, if we enable NPCs to have some sort of memory, they potentially can learn or adapt, thus avoiding such exploits as the trapped empty chest we discussed a moment ago. We'll take a closer look at this example later in this chapter. When we do, we'll use probabilities and statistical data collected in-game as NPC memory and Bayesian models as the inference or decision-making mechanism for NPCs.

Note that in this example, we actually can give NPCs perfect knowledge, but we introduce uncertainty to make things more interesting. In other game scenarios, you might not be able to give NPCs perfect knowledge because you yourself might not have it to give! For example, in a fighting game you can't know for sure what strike a player will throw next. Therefore, NPC opponents can't know either. However, you can use Bayesian techniques and probabilities to give NPC opponents the ability to predict the next strike—that is, to anticipate the next strike—at a success rate more than twice what otherwise can be achieved by just guessing. We'll take a closer look at this example, and others, later in this chapter. First, let's go over the fundamentals of Bayesian analysis.

What is a Bayesian Network?

Bayesian networks are graphs that compactly represent the relationship between random variables for a given problem. These graphs aid in performing reasoning or decision making in the face of uncertainty. Such reasoning relies heavily on Bayes' rule, which we discussed in Chapter 12. In this chapter, we use simple Bayesian networks to model specific game scenarios that require NPCs to make decisions given uncertain information about the game world. Before looking at some specific examples, let's go over the details of Bayesian networks.

Structure

Bayesian networks consist of nodes representing random variables and arcs or links representing the causal relationship between variables. Figure 13-1 shows an example Bayesian network. Imagine a game in which an NPC can encounter a chest that can be locked or unlocked. Whether it is locked depends on whether it contains treasure or whether it is trapped.

In this example, the nodes labeled *T*, *Tr*, and *L* represent random variables (often referred to as events in the probabilistic sense). The arrows connecting each node represent causal relationships. You can think of nodes at the tail of the arrows as parents and nodes at the head of the arrows as children. Here, parents cause children. For example, Figure 13-1 shows that *Locked* is caused by *Trapped* or *Treasure* or both *Trapped* and *Treasure*. You should be aware that this causal relationship is probabilistic and not certain. For example, the chest being *Trapped* does not necessarily always cause the chest to be *Locked*. There's a certain probability that *Trapped* might cause *Locked*, but it's possible that *Trapped* might not cause *Locked*.

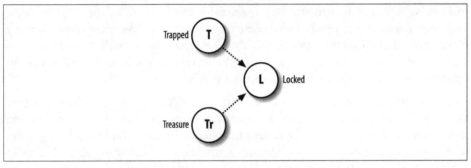

Figure 13-1. Example Bayesian network

You measure the strength of the connections between events in terms of probabilities. Each node has an associated conditional probability table that gives the probability of any outcome of the child event given all possible combinations of outcomes of its parents. For our purposes, we're going to consider discrete events only. What we mean here is that any event, any variable, can take on any one of a set of discrete values. These values are assumed to be mutually exclusive and exhaustive. For example, *Locked* can take on values of *TRUE* or *FALSE*.

Let's assume that *Trapped* can be either *TRUE* or *FALSE*. Let's also assume *Treasure* can be either *TRUE* or *FALSE*. If *Locked* can take on the values *TRUE* or *FALSE*, we need a conditional probability table for *Locked* that gives the probability of *Locked* being *TRUE* given every combination of values for *Trapped* and *Treasure*, and the probability of *Locked* being false given every combination of values for *Trapped* and *Treasure*. Table 13-1 summarizes the conditional probability table for *Locked* in this case.

Table 13-1. Example conditional probability table

		Probability of *Locked*	
Value of *Trapped*	Value of *Treasure*	L = TRUE	L = FALSE
T	T	$P(L|T \cap Tr)$	$P(\sim L|T \cap Tr)$
T	F	$P(L|T \cap \sim Tr)$	$P(\sim L|T \cap \sim Tr)$
F	T	$P(L|\sim T \cap Tr)$	$P(\sim L|\sim T \cap Tr)$
F	F	$P(L|\sim T \cap \sim Tr)$	$P(\sim L|\sim T \cap \sim Tr)$

In this table, the first two columns show all combinations of values for *Trapped* and *Treasure*. The third column shows the probability that *Locked=TRUE* given each combination of values for *Trapped* and *Treasure*, while the last column shows the probability that *Locked=FALSE* given each combination of values for *Trapped* and *Treasure*. The tilde symbol, $\sim$, as used here indicates the conjugate of a binary event. If $P(T)$ is the probability of *Trapped* being equal to *TRUE*, $P(\sim T)$ is the probability of *Trapped* being equal to *FALSE*. Note that each of the three events considered here are binary in that they each can take on only one of two values. This yields the 2 × 4 set of conditional probabilities for *Locked*, as shown in Table 13-1.

As the number of possible values for these events gets larger, or as the number of parent nodes for a given child node goes up, the number of entries in the conditional probability table for the child node increases exponentially. This is one of the biggest deterrents for using Bayesian methods in games. Not only does it become difficult to determine all of these conditional probabilities, but also as the size of the network increases, the computational requirements become prohibitive for real-time games. (Technically Bayesian networks are considered NP-hard, which means they are computationally too expensive for large numbers of nodes.)

Keep in mind that every child node will require a conditional probability table. So-called *root nodes*, nodes that don't have parents—events *Trapped* and *Treasure* in this example—don't have conditional probability tables. Instead, they have what are called *prior probability tables* which contain the probabilities of these events taking on each of their possible values. The term *prior* used here means that these are probabilities for root nodes before we make adjustments to the probabilities given new information somewhere else in the network. Updated probabilities given new information are called *posterior probabilities*. We'll see examples of this sort of calculation later.

The complexity we discussed here is a major incentive for keeping Bayesian networks for use in games simple and specific. For example, theoretically you could construct a Bayesian network to control every aspect of an NPC unit. You could have nodes in the network representing decisions to chase or evade, and still other nodes to represent turn left, turn right, and so on. The trouble with this approach is that the networks become incredibly complex and difficult to set up, solve, and test. Further, the required conditional probability tables become so large that you'd have to resort to some form of training to figure them out rather than specify them. We don't advocate this approach.

As we mentioned in Chapter 1, and as we'll discuss in Chapter 14 on neural networks, we recommend that you use Bayesian methods for very specific decision-making problems and leave the other AI tasks to other methods that are better suited for them. Why use a Bayesian network to steer a chasing unit when reliable, easy, and robust deterministic methods are available for that task? Use the Bayesian network to decide whether to chase or evade and let other algorithms take over to handle the actual chasing or evading.

Inference

You can make three basic types of reasoning or inference using Bayesian networks. For this discussion, we'll refer to the simple networks shown in Figure 13-2.

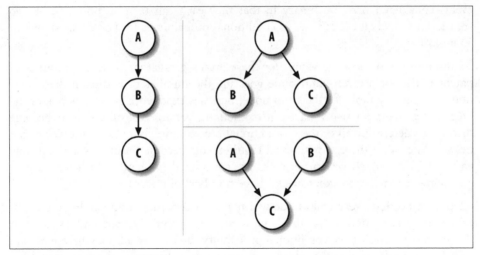

Figure 13-2. Simple networks

The network on the left is called a *causal chain*, in this case a three-node chain. The network on the upper right is called a *common cause network*. It's also more commonly referred to as a *naïve Bayesian network* or *Bayesian classifier*. The network on the lower right is called a *common effect network*. The three basic types of reasoning are as follows:

Diagnostic reasoning

Diagnostic reasoning is probably the most common type of reasoning using Bayesian networks. This sort of reasoning, along with Bayesian classifier networks, is used heavily in medical diagnostics. For example, referring to the network on the upper right in Figure 13-2, *A* would be a disease and *B* and *C* symptoms. Given the symptoms presented, the doctor could make inferences as to the probability of the disease being present.

Predictive reasoning

Predictive reasoning involves making inferences about effects given information on causes. For example, referring to the network on the left in Figure 13-2, if we know something about *A*, which causes *B*, we can make some inferences about the probability of *B* occurring.

Explaining away

Explaining away involves common cause networks, as shown on the lower right in Figure 13-2. Let's assume the nodes are all binary—that is, true or false. If we know *C* is true and we know *A* and *B* cause *C*, given that *C* is true we would raise the probability that *A* and *B* also are true. However, say we later learn that *B* is true; this implies that the probability of *A* occurring actually decreases. This brings up some interesting characteristics of Bayesian networks—namely, independence and conditional dependence.

The structure on the lower right in Figure 13-2 implies that events A and B are independent of each other. There's no causal link between A and B. However, if we learn something about C and then something about A or B, we do affect the probability of A or B. In our example, learning that C is true and that B also is true lowers the probability that A is true even though A and B are independent events.

Now consider the network shown on the left in Figure 13-2. In this case, we see that A causes B which in turn causes C. If we learn the state of B, we can make inferences on the state of C irrespective of the state of A. A has no influence on our belief of event C if we know the state of B. In Bayesian lingo, node B blocks A from affecting C.

Another form of independence present in Bayesian networks is *d-separation*. Look back at the network shown in Figure 13-1. Instead of one node blocking another node, as in the previous discussion, you could have a situation in which a node blocks clusters of nodes. In Figure 13-1, C causes D and D causes E and F, but A and B cause C. However, if we learn the state of C, A and B have no effect on D and thus no effect on E and F. Likewise, if we learn something about the state of D, nodes A, B, and C become irrelevant to E and F. Identifying these independence situations is helpful when trying to solve Bayesian networks because we can treat parts of a network separately, simplifying some computations.

Actually solving, or making inferences, using Bayesian networks involves calculating probabilities using the rules we discussed in Chapter 12. We're going to show you how to do this for simple networks in the examples that follow. We should point out, though, that some general-purpose methods for solving complex Bayesian networks we aren't going to cover. These networks include the popular message passing algorithm (see the second reference cited at the end of this chapter) as well as other approximate stochastic methods. Many of these methods don't seem appropriate for real-time games because computation requirements are large. Here, again, we recommend that you keep Bayesian networks simple if you're going to use them in games. Of course, you don't have to listen to us, but by keeping them simple, you can use them where they are best suited for specific tasks and let other methods do their job. This will make your testing and debugging job easier because you can isolate the complicated AI code from the rest of your AI code.

Trapped?

Let's say you're writing a game in which NPCs can loot chests potentially filled with players' treasure and other valuables. Players can put their valuables in these chests for storage and they have the option of trapping the chests (if they have the skill) along with the option of locking the chests. NPCs can attempt to loot such chests as they find them. An NPC can observe the chest and determine whether it is locked, but he can't make a direct observation as to whether any given chest is trapped. The NPC must decide whether to attempt to loot the chest. If success-ful, he keeps the loot. If the chest is trapped, he incurs damage, which could kill him. We'll use a simple Bayesian network along with some fuzzy rules to make the decision for the NPC.

The Bayesian network for this is among the simplest possible. The network is a two-node chain, as illustrated in Figure 13-3.

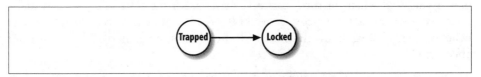

Figure 13-3. Two-node chain

Each event, *Trapped* and *Locked*, can take on one of two discrete states: true or false. Therefore, we have the following probability tables, shown in Tables 13-2 and 13-3, associated with each event node.

Table 13-2. Trapped probabilities

P(Trapped)	
True	**False**
p_T	$(1-p_T)$

Table 13-3. Locked conditional probabilities

	P(Locked | Trapped)	
Trapped	**True**	**False**
True	p_{Lt}	$(1-p_{Lt})$
False	p_{Lf}	$(1-p_{Lf})$

In Table 13-2, p_T is the probability that the chest is trapped, while *(1-p_T)* is the probability that the chest is not trapped. Table 13-3 shows the conditional proba-bilities that the chest is locked given each possible state of the chest being trapped. In Table 13-3, p_{Lt} represents the probability that the chest is locked given that it is trapped; p_{Lf} represents the probability that the chest is locked given that it is not trapped; *(1-p_{Lt})* represents the probability that the chest is not locked given that it is trapped; and *(1-p_{Lf})* represents the probability that the chest is not locked given that it is not trapped.

Tree Diagram

Sometimes it's helpful to look at problems in the form of tree diagrams as well. The tree diagram for this problem is very simple, as shown in Figure 13-4.

Looking at this tree diagram, it is clear that a chest can be locked in two possible ways and can be unlocked in two possible ways. Each branch in the tree has a cor-responding probability associated with it. These are the same probabilities shown in

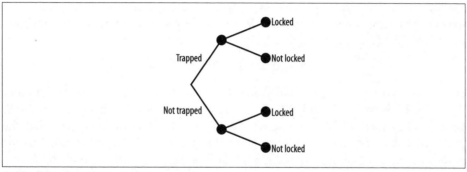

Figure 13-4. Tree diagram

Tables 13-2 and 13-3. This diagram illustrates the compactness of Bayesian network-style graphs as opposed to tree diagrams for visualizing causal relationships. This is important for more complicated problems with greater numbers of events and possible states for each event. In such cases, tree diagrams can become unwieldy in terms of visualizing the relationships between each event.

Determining Probabilities

We can determine the probabilities we need—those shown in Tables 13-2 and 13-3—by gathering statistics during the game. For example, every time an NPC encounters a chest and opens it, the frequencies of the chest being trapped versus not trapped can be updated. The NPC effectively learns these probabilities through experience. You can have each NPC learn based on its own experience, or you can have groups of NPCs learn collectively. You also can collect statistics on the frequencies of chests being locked given they are trapped and locked given they are not trapped to determine the conditional probabilities. Because we are using discrete probabilities and because each event has two states, you'll have to develop a four-element conditional probability table as we discussed earlier. In a game, it is plausible that any given chest can exist in any one of the four states we illustrated in Figure 13-4. For example, a player can put his valuables in a chest and lock it without trapping it because he might not have the skill or materials required to set traps. Or a player can possess skill and materials to trap the chest as well as lock it, and so on. Therefore, we can't assume that a chest always will be trapped or always will be locked, and so forth.

Making Inferences

In this example, we're going to use diagnostic inference. What we aim to do is answer the question, given an NPC encounters a chest what is the probability that the chest is trapped? If the NPC does not observe that the chest is locked, the probability that the chest is trapped is simply p_T. However, if the NPC observes the state of the chest being locked, we can revise the probability of the chest being trapped given this new information. We'll use Bayes' rule to make this revision. Bayes' rule yields the following:

$$P(T|L) = P(L|T) P(T)/P(L)$$

Here *P(T)* represents the probability that *Trapped=TRUE*, *P(L)* represents the probability of *Locked=TRUE*, and *P(L|T)* represents the probability that *Locked=TRUE* given that *Trapped=TRUE*. In English, Bayes' rule for this problem says that the probability that the chest is trapped given that the chest is locked is equal to the probability that the chest is locked given that it is trapped times the probability that the chest is trapped divided by the probability that the chest is locked. *P(L|T)* is taken from the conditional probability table. *P(T)* also is known from the probability table. However, we must calculate *P(L)*—the probability that the chest is locked. Looking at the tree diagram in Figure 13-4, we see that the chest can be locked in two ways: 1) given the chest is trapped; or 2) given the chest is not trapped. We can use probability rule 4 from Chapter 12 to determine *P(L)*. In this case, *P(L)* is as follows:

$$P(L) = P(L|T) P(T) + P(L|{\sim}T) P({\sim}T)$$

Again, in words, this says that the probability of the chest being locked is equal to the probability of the chest being locked given that it is trapped times the probability of the chest being trapped plus the probability of the chest being locked given that it is not trapped times the probability of the chest being not trapped. Here the tilde symbol, $\sim$, indicates the conjugate state. For example, if *P(T)* represents the probability that the event *Trapped=TRUE*, *P($\sim$T)* represents the probability that the event *Trapped=FALSE*.

Notice that we use rule 6 from Chapter 12 to determine the probability of *Locked=TRUE* and *Trapped=TRUE*—that is, *P(L|T) P(T)*. The same rule applies when determining the probability of *Locked=TRUE* and *Trapped=FALSE*—that is, *P(L|$\sim$T) P($\sim$T)*. This also is the conditional probability formula we saw in Chapter 12 in the section "Conditional Probability."

Let's consider some real numbers now. Say a given NPC in your game has experience opening 100 chests and of those 100 chests 37 were trapped. Of the 37 trapped chests, 29 were locked. Of the 63 chests that were not trapped, 18 were locked. With this information we can calculate the following probabilities:

$$P(T) = 37/100 = 0.37$$
$$P({\sim}T) = 63/100 = 0.63$$
$$P(L|T) = 29/37 = 0.78$$
$$P(L|{\sim}T) = 18/63 = 0.29$$

Given these probabilities, we can see that there's a 37% chance that a given chest is trapped. Now, if the NPC also notices that the chest is locked—that is,

Locked=TRUE—the probability that the chest is trapped is revised as follows:

$$P(T|L) = (0.78)(0.37)/\{(0.78)(0.37) + (0.29)(0.63)\} = 0.61$$

Thus, the observation that the chest is indeed locked increases the NPC's belief that the chest is trapped. In this case, *P(T)* goes from 37% to 61%. In Bayesian network lingo, the 37% probability is the prior probability, while the revised probability of 61% is the posterior probability.

Now suppose the NPC observes that the chest was not locked. In this case, we have:

$$P(T|{\sim}L) = P({\sim}L|T)\,P(T)/P({\sim}L)$$

where:

$$P({\sim}L|T) = 1 - 0.78 = 0.22$$
$$P(T) = 0.37 \text{ (as before)}$$
$$P({\sim}L) = 1 - P(L) = 0.53$$

therefore:

$$P(T|{\sim}L) = (0.22)(0.37)/(0.53) = 0.15$$

This implies that the chest is less likely to be trapped because the NPC was able to observe that it was unlocked.

Now that you have these probabilities, how can your NPC use them to decide whether to open the chest? Let's go back to the first scenario in which the NPC observed that the chest was locked and the posterior probability of the chest being trapped was determined to be 0.61. Does 61% imply a high probability that the chest is trapped, or perhaps a moderate probability, or maybe even a low probability? We could set up some Boolean logic if-then rules to decide, but clearly this is a good job for fuzzy rules, as we discussed in detail in Chapter 10.

Using Fuzzy Logic

We can set up fuzzy membership functions such as the ones shown in Figure 13-5 for the probability that the chest is trapped.

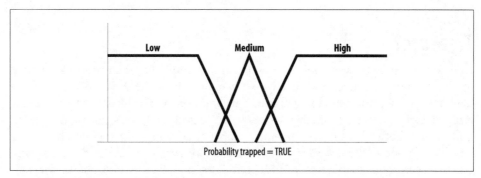

Figure 13-5. Trapped membership functions

Then we can use fuzzy rules to determine what to do. For example, we can have rules to account for conditions and actions such as the following:

- If High Probability Trapped then don't open chest.
- If Low Probability Trapped then open chest.

Even better, however, is to consider other relevant information as well. For example, presumably a trapped chest causes some damage to the NPC if it is triggered; therefore, it seems reasonable to consider the NPC's health in his decision as to whether to open the chest given his belief that it is trapped. Taking this approach, we can set up rules such as the following:

- If High Probability Trapped and Low Health then don't open.
- If Low Probability Trapped and High Health then open.
- If Medium Probability Trapped and High Health then open.
- If Medium Probability Trapped and Moderate Health then don't open.

These are just a few examples of the sort of rules you can set up. The benefit of using this Bayesian approach in conjunction with fuzzy rules is that you can give the NPCs the ability to make rational decisions without having to cheat. Further, you give them the ability to make decisions in the face of uncertainty. Moreover, NPCs can adapt to players' actions using this approach. For example, initially players can lock their chests without trapping them. However, proficient thief NPCs might learn to loot aggressively given the low risk of being hurt while opening a chest. If players start trapping their chests, NPCs can adapt to be less aggressive at looting and more selective as to which chests they open. Further, players might attempt to bluff NPCs by locking chests but not trapping them, or vice versa, and the NPC will adapt accordingly. This brings up another possibility: what if players try to fool NPCs by locking and trapping chests without putting anything of value in the chests? Players might do this to weaken NPCs before attacking them. Because stealing loot is the incentive for opening a chest, it would be cool to allow NPCs to assess the likelihood of the chest being trapped and it containing loot. NPCs could take both factors into account before deciding to open a chest. We'll consider this case in the next example.

Treasure?

In this next example, we're going to build on the simple Bayesian network we used in the previous example. Specifically, we want to allow the NPC to consider the likelihood of a chest containing treasure in addition to the likelihood of it being trapped before deciding whether to open it. To this end, let's add a new event node to the network from the previous problem to yield a three-node chain. The new event node is the *Treasure* event—that is, *Treasure* is *TRUE* if the chest contains treasure and *Treasure* is *FALSE* if it does not. Figure 13-6 shows the new network.

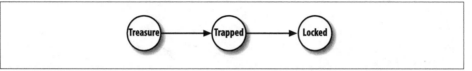

Figure 13-6. Three-node chain

In this case, we're assuming that whether a chest is locked is an indication of the state of the chest being trapped and the state of the chest being trapped is an indication of whether the chest contains treasure.

Each event—*Treasure*, *Trapped*, and *Locked*—can take on one of two discrete states: true or false. Therefore, we have the following probability tables, Tables 13-4, 13-5, and 13-6, associated with each event node.

Table 13-4. Treasure probabilities

P(Treasure)	
True	**False**
p_{Tr}	$(1-p_{Tr})$

Table 13-5. Trapped conditional probabilities

	P(Trapped | Treasure)	
Treasure	**True**	**False**
True	p_{Tt}	$(1-p_{Tt})$
False	p_{Tf}	$(1-p_{Tf})$

Table 13-6. Locked conditional probabilities

	P(Locked | Trapped)	
Trapped	**True**	**False**
True	p_{Lt}	$(1-p_{Lt})$
False	p_{Lf}	$(1-p_{Lf})$

Notice that in this case, the table for the probabilities of the chest being trapped is a conditional probability table dependent on the states of the chest containing treasure. For the *Locked* event, the table is basically the same as in the previous example.

Alternative Model

We should point out that the model shown in Figure 13-6 is a simplified model. It is plausible that a chest can be locked given that it contains treasure independent of whether the chest is trapped. This implies a causal link from the *Treasure* node to the *Locked* node as well. This is illustrated in Figure 13-7.

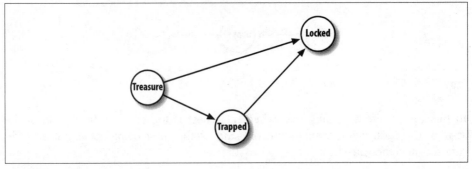

Figure 13-7. Alternative model

In this alternative case, you also have to set up conditional probabilities of the chest being locked given the various states of it containing treasure. Although you easily can do this and still solve the network by hand calculations, we're going to stick with the simple model in our discussion.

Making Inferences

We're going to stick with the model shown in Figure 13-6 for the remainder of this example. To determine the probability that the chest is trapped given it is locked, we proceed in a manner similar to the previous example. However, now we have conditional probabilities for the *Trapped* event—namely, the probabilities that the chest is trapped given that it contains treasure and that it does not contain treasure. With this in mind, we apply Bayes' rule as follows:

$$P(T|L) = P(L|T) \, P(T)/P(L)$$

P(L|T), the probability that the chest is locked given it is trapped, comes from the conditional probability table for the *Locked* event. This time, however, *P(T)* is not given, but we can calculate it as follows:

$$P(T) = P(T|Tr) \, P(Tr) + P(T| \sim Tr) \, P(\sim Tr)$$

In words, the probability of the chest being trapped is equal to the probability of it being trapped given it contains treasure plus the probability it is trapped given it does not contain treasure. Now, *P(L)* is as follows:

$$P(L) = P(L|T) \, P(T) + P(L| \sim T) \, P(\sim T)$$

We've already calculated *P(T)*, and *P(~T)* is simply *1-P(T)*, so all we need to do now is look up *P(L|T)* and *P(L|~T)* in the conditional probability table for *Locked* to determine *P(L)*. Then we can substitute these values in Bayes' rule to determine *P(T|L)*.

To find the probability of treasure given that the chest is locked, we need to apply Bayes' rule again as follows:

$$P(Tr|L) = P(L|Tr) \, P(Tr)/P(L)$$

Notice, however, that *Locked* is blocked from *Treasure* given *Trapped*. Therefore, we can write *P(L|Tr)* as follows:

$$P(L|Tr) = P(L|T)\,P(T|Tr) + P(L|\sim T)\,P(\sim T|Tr)$$

This is the case because our simple model assumes that a trapped chest causes a locked chest.

We've already calculated *P(L)* from the previous step, and *P(Tr)* is given, so we have everything we need to determine *P(Tr|L)*.

Numerical Example

Let's consider some numbers now. Say a given NPC in your game has experience opening 100 chests, and of those, 50 of them contained treasure. Out of these 50, 40 of them were trapped and of these 40 trapped chests, 28 were locked. Now, of the 10 untrapped chests, three were locked. Further, of the 50 chests containing no treasure, 20 were trapped. With this information, we can calculate the following probabilities:

$$P(Tr) = 50/100 = 0.5$$
$$P(\sim Tr) = 50/100 = 0.5$$
$$P(T|Tr) = 40/50 = 0.8$$
$$P(T|\sim Tr) = 20/50 = 0.4$$
$$P(\sim T|Tr) = 10/50 = 0.2$$
$$P(\sim T|\sim Tr) = 30/50 = 0.6$$
$$P(L|T) = 28/40 = 0.7$$
$$P(L|\sim T) = 3/10 = 0.3$$
$$P(\sim L|T) = 12/40 = 0.3$$
$$P(\sim L|\sim T) = 7/10 = 0.3$$

Let's assume your NPC approaches a chest. Without observing whether the chest is locked, the NPC would believe that there's a 50% chance that the chest contained treasure. Now let's assume the NPC observes that the chest is locked. What is the probability that the chest is trapped and what is the probability that it contains treasure? We can use the formulas shown earlier to determine these probabilities. In this case, we have:

$$P(T) = P(T|Tr)\,P(Tr) + P(T|\sim Tr)\,P(\sim Tr) = (0.8)\,(0.5) + (0.4)\,(0.5) = 0.6$$
$$P(L) = P(L|T)\,P(T) + P(L|\sim T)\,P(\sim T) = (0.7)\,(0.6) + (0.3)\,(1 - 0.6) = 0.54$$
$$P(T|L) = (0.7)\,(0.6)/(0.54) = 0.78$$

Now we can find *P(Tr|L)* as follows:

$$P(Tr) = 0.5$$
$$P(L) = 0.54$$

$$P(L|Tr) = P(L|T) P(T|Tr) + P(L|\sim T) P(\sim T|Tr) = (0.7)(0.8) + (0.3)(0.2) = 0.62$$
$$P(Tr|L) = (0.62)(0.5)/(0.54) = 0.57$$

In this example, we see that the observation of the chest being locked raises the probability of the chest being trapped from 60% to 78%. Further, the probability of the chest containing treasure is raised from 50% to 57%.

With this information, you can use fuzzy logic in a manner similar to the previous example to decide for the NPC whether to open the chest. For example, you can set up fuzzy membership functions for the events that the chest is trapped and has treasure and then construct a set of rules along these lines:

- If High Probability Trapped and High Probability Treasure and Low Health then don't open.

- If Low Probability Trapped and High Probability Treasure and not Low Health then open.

These are just a couple of the cases you'd probably want to include in your rules set. Using this approach, your NPC can make decisions considering several factors, even in the face of uncertainty.

By Air or Land

For this next example, let's assume you're writing a war simulation in which the player can attack the computer-controlled army by land, by air, or by land and air. Our goal here is to estimate the chances of the player winning a battle given how he chooses to attack. We then can use the probabilities of the player winning to determine what sort of targets and defense should be given higher priority by the computer-controlled army. For example, say that after every game played you have the computer keep track of who won, the player or computer, along with how the player attacked—that is, by air, land, or both air and land. You then can keep a running count of these statistics to determine the conditional probability of the player winning given his attack mode. Suppose your game finds that the player is most likely to win if he attacks by air. Perhaps he found a weakness in the computer's air defenses or has come up with some other winning tactic. If this is the case, it would be wise for the computer to make construction of air defenses a higher priority. Further, the computer might give enemy aircraft production facilities higher target priority. Such an approach would allow the computer to adjust its defensive and offensive strategies as it learns from past battles.

The Model

The Bayesian network for this simple example looks like that shown in Figure 13-8.

Notice that we have two causes for the player-winning result: air and land attacks. We assume these events are not mutually exclusive—that is, the player can make

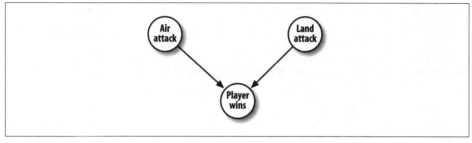

Figure 13-8. Attack mode network

a land attack, or an air attack, or both. Each event node can take on one of two values: true or false. For example, *Air Attack* could be true or false, *Land Attack* could be true or false, and so on.

If instead we allowed only a land or air attack but not both, the network would look like that shown in Figure 13-9.

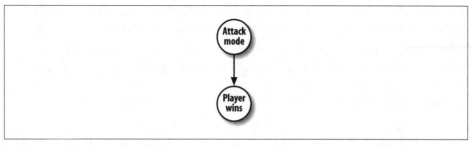

Figure 13-9. Alternative attack network

In this case, *Attack Mode* could take on values such as *Air Attack* or *Land Attack*. Here, the values are mutually exclusive. For this discussion, we'll stick with the more general case shown earlier.

Calculating Probabilities

As we mentioned earlier, we'll have to collect some statistics to estimate the probabilities we're going to need for our inference calculations. The statistics we need to collect as the game is played over and over are as follows:

- Total number of games played, N
- Total number of games won by player, Nw
- Number of games won by player in which he launched an air attack only, Npa
- Number of games won by player in which he launched a land attack only, Npl
- Number of games played in which the player launched an air attack, Na

- Number of games played in which the player launched a land attack, Nl
- Number of games won by player in which he launched an attack by air and land, Npla

We can use this data to calculate the following probabilities:

$$P(A) = Na/N$$
$$P(L) = N1/N$$
$$P(Pw|A \cap \sim L) = Npla/Nw$$
$$P(Pw|A \cap \sim L) = Npa/Nw$$
$$P(Pw| \sim A \cap L) = Npl/Nw$$
$$P(Pw| \sim A \cap \sim L) = 0$$

The first two probabilities are the probabilities that the player launches an air attack and the player launches a land attack, respectively. The last four probabilities are conditional probabilities that the player wins the game given all combinations of the *Air Attack* and *Land Attack* events. In these formulas, *L* represents *Land Attack*, *A* represents *Air Attack*, and *Pw* represents *Player Wins*. Note also that we assume the probability of the player winning a game is 0 if he does not launch any attack.

With this information, we can determine the probability of the player winning a new game. To do this, we sum the probabilities of all the ways in which a player can win. In this case, the player can win in any of four different ways. These calculations use the joint probability formula for each scenario. The formula is as follows:

$$P(Pw \cap A \cap L) = P(A)\, P(L)\, P(Pw|A \cap L)$$

The possible ways in which the player can win are summarized in Table 13-7, along with all relevant probability data.

Table 13-7. Conditional probability table for Player Wins

Air Attack	Land Attack	P(Pw| A∩L)	P(Pw)	Normalized P(Pw)
$P(A) = N_a/N$	$P(L) = N_l/N$	N_{pla}/Nw	$N_a N_l N_{pla}/N_w N^2$	$P(Pw)/\Sigma P(Pw)$
$P(A) = N_a/N$	$P(\sim L) = 1 - P(L)$	N_{pa}/Nw	$(N_a N_{pa}/N_w N)(1-N_l/N)$	$P(Pw)/\Sigma P(Pw)$
$P(\sim A) = 1 - P(A)$	$P(L) = N_l/N$	N_{pl}/Nw	$(N_l N_{pl}/N_w N)(1-N_a/N)$	$P(Pw)/\Sigma P(Pw)$
$P(\sim A) = 1 - P(A)$	$P(\sim L) = 1 - P(L)$	0	0	0
			$\Sigma P(Pw)$	1.0

This table looks a little complicated, but it's really fairly straightforward. The first two columns represent the possible combinations of state for *Air Attack* and *Land Attack*. The first column contains the probabilities for each state of *Air Attack*—true or false—while the second column contains the probabilities for each state of *Land Attack*—true or false. The third column shows the conditional probability that *Player Wins* = TRUE given each combination of states for *Air Attack* and *Land Attack*. The fourth column, *P(Pw)*, represents the joint probability of the events *Air Attack*, *Land Attack*, and *Player Wins*. You find each entry in this column by simply multiplying the values contained in the first three columns and placing the product in the fourth column. Summing the entries in the fourth column yields the marginal probability of the player winning.

Take a look at the fifth column. The fifth column contains the *normalized* probabilities for *Player Wins*. You find the entries in this column by dividing each entry in the fourth column by the sum of the entries in the fourth column. This makes the sum of all the entries in the fifth column add up to 1. (It's like normalizing a vector to make a vector of unit length.) The results contained in the fifth column basically tell us which combination of states of *Air Attack* and *Land Attack* is most likely given that the player wins.

Numerical Example

Let's consider some numbers. We'll assume we have enough statistics to generate the probabilities shown in the first three columns of Table 13-8.

Table 13-8. Example conditional probability table for Player Wins

Air Attack	Land Attack	P(Pw|A∩L)	P(Pw)	Normalized P(Pw)
P(A) = 0.6	P(L) = 0.4	0.167	0.04	0.15
P(A) = 0.6	P(~L) = 0.6	0.5	0.18	0.66
P(~A) = 0.4	P(L) = 0.4	0.33	0.05	0.2
P(~A) = 0.4	P(~L) = 0.6	0	0	0
			0.27	1.0

These numbers indicate that the player wins about 27% of the games played. (This is taken from the sum of the fourth column.) Also, inspection of the fifth column indicates that if the player wins, the most probable mode of attack is an air attack without a land attack. Thus, it would be prudent in this example for the computer to give priority to its air defense systems and to target the player's aircraft construction resources.

Now let's assume that for a new game, the player will attack by air and we want to find the probability that he will win in this case. Our probability table now looks like that shown in Table 13-9.

Table 13-9. Revised probability table

Air Attack	Land Attack	P(Pw|A∩L)	P(Pw)	Normalized P(Pw)
P(A) = 1.0	P(L) = 0.4	0.167	0.07	0.18
P(A) = 1.0	P(~L) = 0.6	0.5	0.3	0.82
P(~A) = 0.0	P(L) = 0.4	0.33	0.00	0.0
P(~A) = 0.0	P(~L) = 0.6	0	0	0
			0.37	1.0

All we've done here is replace *P(A)* by 1.0 and *P(~A)* by 0.0 and recalculate the fourth and fifth columns. In this case, we get a new marginal probability that the player wins reflecting our assumption that the player attacks by air. Here, we see the probability that the player wins increases to 37%. Moreover, we see that if the player wins, there's an 82% chance he won by launching an air attack. This further reinforces our conclusion earlier that the computer should give priority to air defenses and target the player's air offensive resources. We can make further what-if scenarios if we want. We can, for example, set $P(L)$ to 1.0 and get a new $P(Pw)$ corresponding to an assumed land attack, and so on.

Kung Fu Fighting

For our final example we're going to assume we're writing a fighting game and we want to try to predict the next strike the player will throw. This way, we can have the computer-controlled opponents try to anticipate the strike and defend or counter accordingly. To keep things simple, we're going to assume the player can throw one of three types of strikes: punch, low kick, or high kick. Further, we're going to keep track of three-strike combinations. For every strike thrown we're going to calculate a probability for that strike given the previous two strikes. This will enable us to capture three-strike combinations. You easily can keep track of more, but you will incur higher memory and calculation costs because you'll end up with larger conditional probability tables.

The Model

The Bayesian network we're going to use for this example is shown in Figure 13-10.

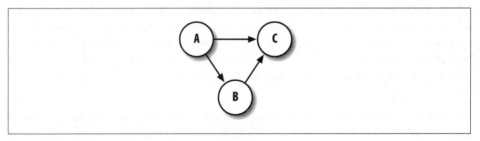

Figure 13-10. Strike network

In this model, we call the first strike in the combination event A, the second strike event B, and the third strike event C. We assume that the second strike thrown, event B, in any combination is dependent on the first strike thrown, event A. Further, we assume that the third strike thrown, event C, is dependant on both the first and second strikes thrown, events A and B. Combinations can be anything—punch, punch, high kick; or low kick, low kick, high kick; and so on.

Calculating Probabilities

Ordinarily we would need to calculate probabilities for A and conditional probabilities for B given A, and conditional probabilities for C given A and B. However, in this example we're always going to observe A and B rendering their prior probabilities irrelevant. Therefore, we need only calculate conditional probabilities for C given every combination of A and B. Because three states exist for each strike event A and B, we'll have to track nine possible combinations of A and B.

We'll again take a frequency approach to determining these conditional probabilities. After every strike thrown by the player, we'll increment a counter for that strike given the two prior strikes thrown. We'll end up with a conditional probability table that looks like the one shown in Table 13-10.

Table 13-10. Conditional probability table for strikes thrown

		Probability of Strike C being:		
Strike A	**Strike B**	**Punch**	**Low Kick**	**High Kick**
Punch	Punch	p_{00}	p_{01}	p_{02}
Punch	Low Kick	p_{10}	p_{11}	p_{12}
Punch	High Kick	p_{20}	p_{21}	p_{22}
Low Kick	Punch	p_{30}	p_{31}	p_{32}
Low Kick	Low Kick	p_{40}	p_{41}	p_{42}
Low Kick	High Kick	p_{50}	p_{51}	p_{52}
High Kick	Punch	p_{60}	p_{61}	p_{62}
High Kick	Low Kick	p_{70}	p_{71}	p_{72}
High Kick	High Kick	p_{80}	p_{81}	p_{82}

This table shows the probability of strike C taking on each of the three values—punch, low kick, or high kick—given every combination of strikes thrown in A and B. The probabilities shown here are subscripted with indices indicating rows and columns to a lookup matrix. We're going to use these indices in the example code we'll present shortly.

To calculate these probabilities, we need to keep track of the total number of strikes thrown. We then can calculate probabilities such as these:

$$P(A = Punch) = N_{punch}/N$$

$$P(B = Punch|A = Punch) = N_{punch\text{-}punch}/N$$

$$P(B = Punch|A = LowKick) = N_{LowKick\text{-}Punch}/N$$

$$P(C = Punch|A = Punch, B = Punch) = N_{punch\text{-}punch\text{-}punch}/N_{AB}$$

These are just a few examples; we can calculate all the conditional probabilities in this manner. In these equations, N represents the number of strikes thrown and N with a subscript represents the number of a particular strike thrown given previously thrown strikes. For example, $N_{punch\text{-}punch\text{-}punch}$ is the number of times A, B, and C all equal punch.

In practice you don't have to store probabilities; the frequencies are sufficient to use to calculate probabilities when required. In this case, we'll store the frequencies of strike combinations in a 9×3 matrix. This matrix will represent counters for all outcomes of C corresponding to all nine combinations of A and B. We'll also need a nine-element array to store counters for all nine combinations of A and B.

Strike Prediction

Now, to make a prediction for the next strike, *C*, look at which two strikes, *A* and *B*, were thrown most recently and then look up the combination in the conditional probability table for *C*. Basically, use *A* and *B* to establish which row to consider in the conditional probability matrix, and then simply pick the strike for *C* that has the highest probability. That is, pick the column with the highest conditional probability.

We've put together a little example program to test this approach. We have a window with three buttons on it corresponding to punch, low kick, and high kick. The user can press these in any order to simulate fighting moves. As he throws these strikes, the conditional probabilities we discussed earlier are updated and a prediction for the next strike to be thrown is made. Example 13-1 shows the core function that performs the calculations for this program.

Example 13-1. Strike prediction

```
TStrikes ProcessMove(TStrikes move)
{
        int    i, j;

        N++;
        if(move == Prediction) NSuccess++;

        if((AB[0] == Punch) && (AB[1] == Punch)) i = 0;
        if((AB[0] == Punch) && (AB[1] == LowKick)) i = 1;
        if((AB[0] == Punch) && (AB[1] == HighKick)) i = 2;

        if((AB[0] == LowKick) && (AB[1] == Punch)) i = 3;
        if((AB[0] == LowKick) && (AB[1] == LowKick)) i = 4;
        if((AB[0] == LowKick) && (AB[1] == HighKick)) i = 5;

        if((AB[0] == HighKick) && (AB[1] == Punch)) i = 6;
        if((AB[0] == HighKick) && (AB[1] == LowKick)) i = 7;
        if((AB[0] == HighKick) && (AB[1] == HighKick)) i = 8;

        if(move == Punch) j = 0;
        if(move == LowKick) j = 1;
        if(move == HighKick) j = 2;

        NAB[i]++;
        NCAB[i][j]++;

        AB[0] = AB[1];
        AB[1] = move;


        if((AB[0] == Punch) && (AB[1] == Punch)) i = 0;
        if((AB[0] == Punch) && (AB[1] == LowKick)) i = 1;
        if((AB[0] == Punch) && (AB[1] == HighKick)) i = 2;
```

```
      if((AB[0] == LowKick) && (AB[1] == Punch)) i = 3;
      if((AB[0] == LowKick) && (AB[1] == LowKick)) i = 4;
      if((AB[0] == LowKick) && (AB[1] == HighKick)) i = 5;

      if((AB[0] == HighKick) && (AB[1] == Punch)) i = 6;
      if((AB[0] == HighKick) && (AB[1] == LowKick)) i = 7;
      if((AB[0] == HighKick) && (AB[1] == HighKick)) i = 8;

      ProbPunch = (double) NCAB[i][0] / (double) NAB[i];
      ProbLowKick = (double) NCAB[i][1] / (double) NAB[i];
      ProbHighKick = (double) NCAB[i][2] / (double) NAB[i];

      if((ProbPunch > ProbLowKick) &&
         (ProbPunch > ProbHighKick))
           return Punch;
      if((ProbLowKick > ProbPunch) &&
         (ProbLowKick > ProbHighKick))
           return LowKick;
      if((ProbHighKick > ProbPunch) &&
         (ProbHighKick > ProbLowKick))
           return HighKick;

      return (TStrikes) rand() % 3; // Last resort
}
```

This function takes a TStrikes variable called move as a single parameter. TStrikes is simply an enumerated type defined as shown in Example 13-2.

Example 13-2. TStrikes

```
enum TStrikes {Punch, LowKick, HighKick};
```

The move parameter represents the most recent strike thrown by the player. The ProcessMove function also returns a value of type TStrikes representing the predicted next strike to be thrown by the player.

Bookkeeping

Upon entering ProcessMove, the global variable, N, is incremented. N represents the total number of strikes thrown by the player. Further, if the most recently thrown strike, move, is equal to the previously predicted strike, Prediction, the number of successful predictions, NSuccess, gets incremented.

The next task performed in ProcessMove is to update the conditional probability table given the most recently thrown strike, move, and the two preceding strikes stored in the two-element array AB. AB is defined as shown in Example 13-3.

Example 13-3. Global variables

```
      int          NAB[9];
      int          NCAB[9][3];
```

```
TStrikes        AB[2];
double          ProbPunch;
double          ProbLowKick;
double          ProbHighKick;
TStrikes        Prediction;
TStrikes        RandomPrediction;

int             N;
int             NSuccess;
```

Because the conditional probability table is stored in a 9 × 3 array, NCAB, we need to find the appropriate row and column for the entry with which we'll increment given the most recent strike and the previous two strikes. Calling NCAB a conditional probability table is not exactly correct. We don't store probabilities. Instead we store frequencies and then use these frequencies to calculate probabilities when we need to do so.

At any rate, the first set of nine if-statements in ProcessMove checks all possible combinations of the strikes stored in AB to determine which row in the NCAB matrix we need to update. The next set of three if-statements determines which column in NCAB we need to update. Now we can increment the element in NCAB corresponding to the row and column just determined. We also increment the element in NAB corresponding to the row we just determined. NAB stores the number of times any given combination of A and B strikes was thrown.

The next step is to shift the entries in the AB array. We want to shift the strike stored in the B position (array index 1) to the A position (array index 0), bumping off the value that was previously stored in the A position. Then we put the most recently thrown strike, move, in the B position to make our prediction and for the next go around through this function.

Making the Prediction

At this point, we're ready to make a prediction for the next strike to be thrown. The next set of nine if-statements determines which row in the NCAB matrix we need to consider given the new pattern of strikes stored in AB. We use the row thus determined to look up the frequencies in the NCAB matrix corresponding to each of the three possible strikes that can be thrown. Keep in mind these frequencies are conditional given the pattern of strikes stored in AB.

The next step is to calculate the actual probabilities, ProbPunch, ProbLowKick, and ProbHighKick, by simply dividing the retrieved frequency for each particular strike by the total number of times the combination of strikes stored in AB have been thrown. Finally, the function makes its prediction of the next strike by returning the strike with the highest probability. For the unlikely case in which all the probabilities are equal, we simply return a random guess. Technically speaking, we probably should have put a few more checks in place to capture cases in which two of the three strikes had equal probabilities that were higher than the third. In this case, a random guess between the two strikes with equal probability could be made.

Through repeated testing we found that the computer, using this method, achieves a success rate for predicting the next strike to be thrown of 60% to 80%. This is as opposed to a 30% success rate if the computer just makes random guesses every time a strike is thrown. Also, if the player happens to find a favorite combination and uses it frequently, the computer will catch on fairly quickly and its success rate will increase. As the player adjusts his combinations in light of the computer getting better at defending his other combinations, the success rate will drop initially and then pick up again as the player continues to use the new combinations. This cycle will continue, forcing the player to keep changing his techniques as the computer opponent adapts.

Further Information

Hopefully we've achieved our objective in this chapter of introducing Bayesian techniques and showing you how you can use simple Bayesian models in game AI for making decisions under uncertainty and for achieving some level of adaptation using probabilities. We've really only scratched the surface of these powerful methods and a wealth of additional information is available to you should you decide to learn more about these techniques. To set you on your way, we've compiled a short list of references that we find to be very useful. They are as follows:

- *Bayesian Inference and Decision,* Second Edition by Robert Winkler (Probabilistic Publishing)
- *Probabilistic Reasoning in Intelligent Systems: Networks of Plausible Inference* by Judea Pearl (Morgan Kaufmann Publishers, Inc.)
- *Bayesian Artificial Intelligence* by Kevin Korb and Ann Nicholson (Chapman & Hall/CRC)

The first reference shown here is particularly exceptional in that it covers probability, Bayesian inference, and decision making under uncertainty thoroughly and in plain English. If you decide to pursue complex Bayesian models that are not easily solved using simple calculations, you'll definitely want to check out the second reference, as it presents methods for solving more complicated Bayesian networks for general inference.

Numerous Bayesian resources also are available on the Internet. Here are some links to resources that we find useful:

- *http://bndev.sourceforge.net/*
- *http://www.niedermayer.ca/papers/bayesian/*
- *http://www.cs.ualberta.ca/~greiner/bn.html*
- *http://www.research.microsoft.com/research/dtg/*

The first link points to the "Bayesian Network Tools in Java" web site that contains tools and information on the open source Java toolkit for Bayesian analysis (for more information on the Open Source Initiative, visit *http://www.opensource.org*). The second link points to a page that contains a brief introduction to Bayesian networks for nongame applications. This page also contains links to other Internet resources on Bayesian networks. The third link points to a page containing several tutorials and many online links to other resources. The fourth link points to Microsoft's Decision Theory and Adaptive Systems research page, which contains many links to resources on uncertainty and decision support technologies including, but not limited to, Bayesian networks. You can find many other resources on the Internet aside from these four links. You need only perform a search using the keywords "Bayesian networks" to find hundreds of additional links.

CHAPTER 14

Neural Networks

Our brains are composed of billions of neurons, each one connected to thousands of other neurons to form a complex network of extraordinary processing power. Artificial neural networks, hereinafter referred to simply as neural networks or networks, attempt to mimic our brain's processing capability, albeit on a far smaller scale.

Information, so to speak, is transmitted from one neuron to another via the *axon* and *dendrites*. The axon carries the voltage potential, or action potential, from an activated neuron to other connected neurons. The action potential is picked up from receptors in the dendrites. The *synaptic gap* is where chemical reactions take place, either to excite or inhibit the action potential input to the given neuron. Figure 14-1 illustrates a neuron.

The adult human brain contains about 10^{11} neurons and each neuron receives synaptic input from about 10^4 other neurons. If the combined effect of all these inputs is of sufficient strength, the neuron will fire, transmitting its action potential to other neurons.

The artificial networks we use in games are quite simple by comparison. For many applications artificial neural networks are composed of only a handful, a dozen or so, neurons. This is far simpler than our brains. Some specific applications use networks composed of perhaps thousands of neurons, yet even these are simple in comparison to our brains. At this time we can't hope to approach the processing power of the human brain using our artificial networks; however, for specific problems our simple networks can be quite powerful.

This is the biological metaphor for neural networks. Sometimes it's helpful to think of neural networks in a less biological sense. Specifically, you can think of a neural network as a mathematical function approximator. Input to the network represents independent variables, while output represents the dependant variable(s). The network itself is a function giving one unique set of output for the given input. The

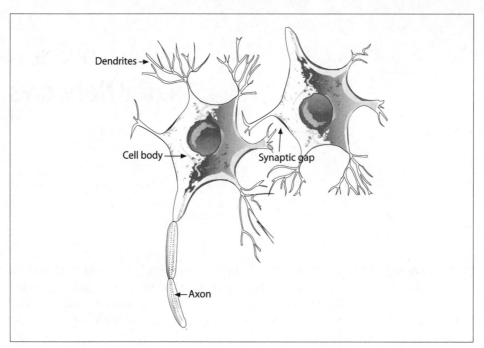

Figure 14-1. Neuron

function in this case is difficult to write in equation form and fortunately we don't need to do so. Further, the function is highly nonlinear. We'll come back to this way of thinking a little later.

For games, neural networks offer some key advantages over more traditional AI techniques. First, using a neural network enables game developers to simplify coding of complex state machines or rules-based systems by relegating key decision-making processes to one or more trained neural networks. Second, neural networks offer the potential for the game's AI to adapt as the game is played. This is a rather compelling possibility and is a very popular subject in the game AI community at the time of this writing.

In spite of these advantages, neural networks have not gained widespread use in video games. Game developers have used neural networks in some popular games; but by and large, their use in games is limited. This probably is due to several factors, of which we describe two key factors next.

First, neural networks are great at handling highly nonlinear problems; ones you cannot tackle easily using traditional methods. This sometimes makes understanding exactly what the network is doing and how it is arriving at its results difficult to follow, which can be disconcerting for the would-be tester. Second, it's difficult at times to predict what a neural network will generate as output, especially if the network is programmed to learn or adapt within a game. These two factors make testing and debugging a neural network relatively difficult compared to testing and debugging a finite state machine, for example.

Further, some early attempts at the use of neural networks in games have tried to tackle complete AI systems—that is, massive neural networks were assembled to handle the most general AI tasks that a given game creature or character could encounter. The neural network acted as the entire AI system—the whole brain, so to speak. We don't advocate this approach, as it compounds the problems associated with predictability, testing, and debugging. Instead, just like our own brains have many areas that specialize in specific tasks, we suggest that you use neural networks to handle specific game AI tasks as part of an integrated AI system that uses traditional AI techniques as well. In this way, the majority of the AI system will be relatively predictable, and the hard AI tasks or the ones which you want to take advantage of learning and adapting will use specific neural networks that were trained strictly for that one task.

The AI community uses many different kinds of neural networks to solve all sorts of problems, from financial to engineering problems and many in between. Neural networks often are combined with other techniques such as fuzzy systems, genetic algorithms, and probabilistic methods, to name a few. This subject is far too vast to treat in a single chapter, so we're going to narrow our focus on a particularly useful class of neural networks. We're going to concentrate our attention on a type of neural network called a *multilayer, feed-forward network*. This type of network is quite versatile and is capable of handling a wide variety of problems. Before getting into the details of such a network, let's first explore in general terms how you can apply neural networks in games.

Control

Neural networks often are used as neural controllers for robotics applications. In these cases, the robot's sensory system provides relevant inputs to the neural controller, and the neural controller's output, which can consist of one or more output nodes, sends the proper responses to the robot's motor control system. For example, a neural controller for a robot tank might take three inputs, each indicating whether an obstacle is sensed in front of or to either side of the robot. (The range to each sensed obstacle also can be input.) The neural controller can have two outputs that control the direction of motion of its left and right tracks. One output node can set the left track to move forward or backward, while the other can set the right track to move forward or backward. The combination of the resulting outputs has the robot either move forward, move backward, turn left, or turn right. The neural network might look something such as that illustrated in Figure 14-2.

Very similar situations arise in games. You can, in fact, have a computer-controlled, half-track mechanized unit in your game. Or perhaps you want to use a neural

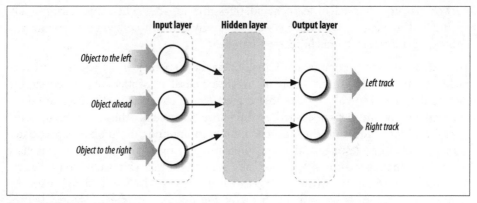

Figure 14-2. Example robot control neural network

network to handle the flight controls for a spaceship or aircraft. In each case, you'll have one or more input neurons and one or more output neurons that will control the unit's thrust, wheels, tracks, or whatever means of locomotion you're simulating.

Threat Assessment

As another example, say you're writing a strategy simulation-type game in which the player has to build technology and train units to fend off or attack the computer-controlled base. Let's say you decide to use a neural network to give the computer-controlled army some means of predicting the type of threat presented by the player at any given time during gameplay. One possible neural network is illustrated in Figure 14-3.

The inputs to this network include the number of enemy (the player) ground units, the number of enemy aerial units, an indication as to whether the ground units are on the move, an indication as to whether the aerial units are on the move, the range to the ground units, and the range to the aerial units. The outputs consist of neurons that indicate one of four possible threats, including an aerial threat, a ground threat, both an aerial and a ground threat, or no threat. Given appropriate data during gameplay and a means of assessing the performance of the network (we'll talk about training later), you can use such a network to predict what, if any, sort of attack is imminent. Once the threat is assessed, the computer can take the appropriate action. This can include deployment of ground or aerial forces, shoring up defenses, putting foot soldiers on high alert, or carrying on as usual, assuming no threat.

This approach requires in-game training and validation of the network, but potentially can tune itself to the playing style of the player. Further, you are alleviated of

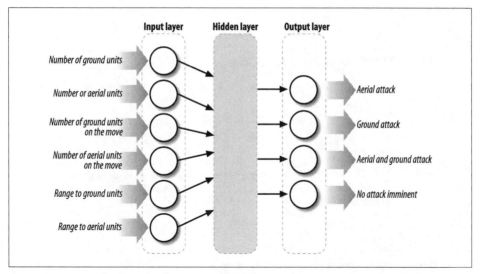

Figure 14-3. Example threat-level assessment neural network

the task of figuring out all the possible scenarios and thresholds if you were to use a rules-based or finite state machine-type architecture for this task.

Attack or Flee

As a final example, let's say you have a persistent role-playing game and you decide to use a neural network to control how certain creatures in the game behave. Now let's assume you're going to use a neural network to handle the creature's decision-making process—that is, whether the creature will attack, evade, or wander, depending on whether an enemy (a player) is in the creature's proximity. Figure 14-4 shows how such a neural network might look. Note that you would use this network only to decide whether to attack, evade, or wander. You would use other game logic, such as the chasing and evading techniques we discussed earlier, to execute the desired action.

We have four inputs in this example: the number of like creatures in proximity to the creature who's making the decision (this is an indication of whether the creature is traveling in a group or alone); a measure of the creature's hit points or health; an indication as to whether the enemy is engaged in combat with another creature; and finally, the range to the enemy.

We can make this example a little more sophisticated by adding more inputs, such as the class of the enemy, whether the enemy is a mage or a fighter, and so on. Such a consideration would be important to a creature whose attack strategies and defenses are better suited against one type of class or another. You could determine the enemy's class by "cheating," or better yet, you could predict the enemy's class

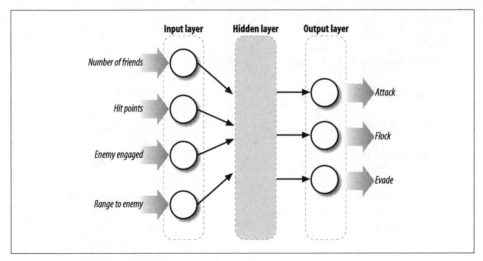

Figure 14-4. Example attack decision neural network

by using another neural network or Bayesian analysis, adding a bit more uncertainty to the whole process.

Dissecting Neural Networks

In this section we're going to dissect a three-layer feed-forward neural network, looking at each of its components to see what they do, why they are important, and how they work. The aim here is to clearly and concisely take the mystery out of neural networks. We'll take a rather practical approach to this task and leave some of the more academic aspects to other books on the subject. We will give references to several such books throughout this chapter.

Structure

We focus on three-layer feed-forward networks in this chapter. Figure 14-5 illustrates the basic structure of such a network.

A three-layer network consists of one *input layer*, one *hidden layer*, and one *output layer*. There's no restriction on the number of neurons within each layer. Every neuron from the input layer is connected to every neuron in the hidden layer. Further, every neuron in the hidden layer is connected to every neuron in the output layer. Also, every neuron, with the exception of the input layer, has an additional input called the *bias*. The numbers shown in Figure 14-5 serve to identify each node in the three layers. We'll use this numbering system later when we write the formulas for calculating the value of each neuron.

Calculating the output value(s) for a network starts with some input provided to each input neuron. Then these inputs are weighted and passed along to the

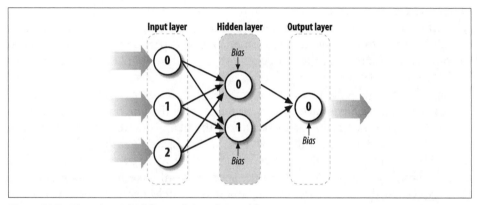

Figure 14-5. Three-layer feed-forward neural network

hidden-layer neurons. This process repeats, going from the hidden layer to the output layer, where the output of the hidden-layer neurons serves as input to the output layer. This process of going from input to hidden to output layer is the feed-forward process. We'll look at each component of this type of network in more detail in the following sections.

Input

Inputs to a neural network obviously are very important; without them there's nothing for the neural network to process. Clearly we need them, but what should you choose as inputs? How many do you need? And what form should they take?

Input: What and How Many?

The question of what to choose as input is very problem-specific. You have to look at the problem you're trying to solve and select what game parameters, data, and environment characteristics are important to the task at hand. For example, say you're designing a neural network to classify player characters in a role-playing game so that the computer-controlled creatures can decide whether they want to engage the player. Some inputs you might consider include some indication of the player's attire, his drawn weapon if present, and perhaps any witnessed actions—for example, whether his just cast a spell.

Your job of training the neural network, which we'll discuss later, will be easier if you keep the number of input neurons to a minimum. However, in some situations the inputs to select won't always be obvious to you. In such cases, the general rule is to include what inputs you think might be important and let the neural network sort out for itself which ones are important. Neural networks excel at sorting out the relative importance of inputs to the desired output. Keep in mind, however, that the more inputs you throw in, the more data you're going to have to prepare to train the network, and the more computations you'll have to make in the game.

Often you can reduce the number of inputs by combining or transforming important information into some other, more compact form. As a simple example, let's say you're trying to use a neural network to control a spacecraft landing on a planet in your game. The mass of the spacecraft, which could be variable, and the acceleration due to gravity on the planet clearly are important factors, among others, that you should provide as input to the neural network. You could, in fact, create one input neuron for each parameter—one for the mass and another for the acceleration due to gravity. However, this approach forces the neural network to perform extra work in figuring out a relationship between the spacecraft's mass and the acceleration due to gravity. A better input capturing these two important parameters is a single neuron that takes the weight of the spacecraft—the product of its mass times the acceleration due to gravity—as an input to a single neuron. There would, of course, be other input neurons besides this one, for example, you probably would have altitude and speed inputs as well.

Input: What Form?

You can use a variety of forms of data as inputs to a neural network. In games, such input generally consists of three types: boolean, enumerated, and continuous types. Neural networks work with real numbers, so whatever the type of data you have, it must be converted to a suitable real number for use as input.

Consider the example shown in Figure 14-4. The "enemy engaged" input is clearly a boolean type—true if the enemy is engaged and false otherwise. However, we can't pass true or false to a neural network input node. Instead, we input a 1.0 for true and a 0.0 for false.

Sometimes your input data might be enumerated. For example, say you have a network designed to classify an enemy, and one consideration is the kind of weapon he is wielding. The choices might be something such as dagger, bastard sword, long sword, katana, crossbow, short bow, or longbow. The order does not matter here, and we assume that these possibilities are mutually exclusive. Typically you handle such data in neural networks using the so-called *one-of-n* encoding method. Basically, you create an input for each possibility and set the input value to 1.0 or 0.0 corresponding to whether each specific possibility is true. If, for example, the enemy was wielding a katana, the input vector would be {0, 0, 0, 1, 0, 0, 0} where the 1 is set for the katana input node and the 0s are set for all other possibilities.

Very often your data will, in fact, be a floating-point number or an integer. In either case this type of data generally can take on any number of values between some practical upper and lower bounds. You simply can input these values directly into the neural network (which game developers often do).

This can cause some problems, however. If you have input values that vary widely in terms of order of magnitude, the neural network might give more weight to the larger-magnitude input. For example, if one input ranges from 0 to 20 while another ranges from 0 to 20,000, the latter likely will swamp out the influence of the former. Thus, in these cases it is important to scale such input data to ranges that are comparable in terms of order of magnitude. Commonly, you can scale such data in terms of percentage values ranging from 0 to 100, or to values ranging from 0 to 1. Scaling in this way levels the playing field for the various inputs. You must be careful how you scale, however. You need to make sure the data used to train your network is scaled in the exact same way as the data the network will see in the field. For example, if you scale a distance input value by the screen width for your training data, you must use the same screen width to scale your input data when the network is functioning in your game.

Weights

Weights in a neural network are analogous to the synaptic connection in a biological neural network. The weights affect the strength of a given input and can be either inhibitory or excitatory. It is the weights that truly define the behavior of a neural network. Further, the task of determining the value of these weights is the subject of *training* or *evolving* a neural network.

Every connection from one neuron to another has an associated weight. This is illustrated in Figure 14-5. The input to a neuron is then the sum of the products of each input's weight connecting that neuron times its input value plus a bias term, which we'll discuss later. The net result is called the *net input* to a neuron. The following equation shows how the net input to a given neuron, neuron *j*, is calculated from a set of input, *i*, neurons.

$$n_j = \sum n_i w_{ij} + b_j w_j$$

Referring to Figure 14-5, you can see that every input to a neuron is multiplied by the weight of the connection between those two neurons plus the bias. Let's look at a simple example (we'll take a look at source code for these calculations later).

Let's say we want to calculate the net input to the 0th neuron in the hidden layer shown in Figure 14-5. Applying the previous equation, we get the following formula for the net input to the 0th neuron in the hidden layer:

$$n^h{}_0 = n^i{}_0 w_{00} + n^i_1 w_{10} + n^i{}_2 w_{20} + b^h{}_0 w_{b0}$$

In this formula the *n*s represents the value of the neuron. In the case of the input neurons, these are the input values. In the case of the hidden neurons, they are the net input values. The superscripts *h* and *i* represent to which layer the neuron belongs—*h* for the hidden layer and *i* for the input layer. The subscripts indicate the node within each layer.

Notice here that the net input to a given neuron is simply a linear combination of weighted inputs from other neurons. If this is so, how does a neural network approximate highly nonlinear functions such as those we mentioned earlier? The key lies in how the net input is transformed to an output value for a neuron. Specifically, *activation functions* map the net input to a corresponding output in a nonlinear way.

Activation Functions

An activation function takes the net input to a neuron and operates on it to produce an output for the neuron. Activation functions should be nonlinear (except in one case, which we'll discuss shortly). If they are not, the neural network is reduced to a linear combination of linear functions and is rendered incapable of approximating nonlinear functions and relationships.

The most commonly used activation function is the *logistic* function or *sigmoid* function. Figure 14-6 illustrates this S-shaped function.

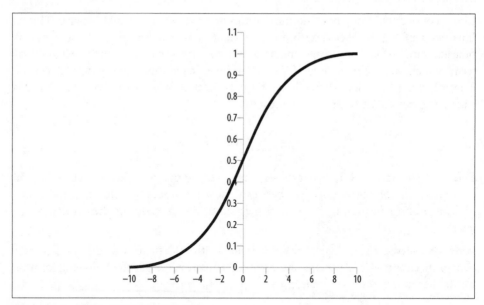

Figure 14-6. Logistic activation function

The formula for the logistic function is as follows:

$$f(x) = \frac{1}{(1 + e^{-x})}$$

Sometimes this function is written in this form:

$$f(x) = \frac{1}{(1 + e^{-x/c})}$$

In this case, the c term is used to alter the shape of the function—that is, either stretching or compressing the function along the horizontal axis.

Note that the input lies along the horizontal axis and the output from this function ranges from 0 to 1 for all values of x. In practice the working range is more like 0.1 to 0.9, where a value of around 0.1 implies the neuron is unactivated and a value of around 0.9 implies the neuron is activated. It is important to note that no matter how large (positive or negative) x gets, the logistic function will never actually reach 1.0 or 0.0; it asymptotes to these values. You must keep this in mind when training. If you attempt to train your network so that it outputs a value of 1 for a given output neuron, you'll never get there. A more reasonable value is 0.9, and shooting for this value will speed up training immensely. The same applies if you are trying to train a network to output a value of 0. Use something such as 0.1 instead.

Other activation functions are at your disposal as well. Figures 14-7 and 14-8 show two other well-known activation functions: the step function and the hyperbolic tangent function.

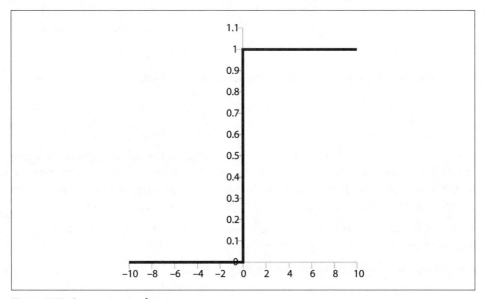

Figure 14-7. Step activation function

The formula for the step function is as follows:

$$f(x) = \begin{cases} 0; x <= 0 \\ 1; x > 0 \end{cases}$$

Step functions were used in early neural network development, but their lack of a derivative made training tough. Note that the logistic function has an easy-to-evaluate derivative, which is needed for training the network, as we'll see shortly.

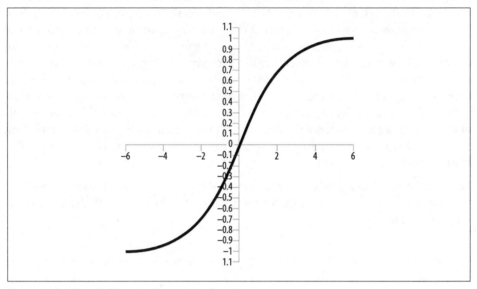

Figure 14-8. Hyperbolic activation tangent function

The formula for the hyperbolic tangent function is as follows:

$$f(x) = \frac{(e^x - e^{-x})}{(e^x + e^{-x})}$$

The hyperbolic tangent function is sometimes used and is said to speed up training. Other activation functions are used in neural networks for various applications; however, we won't get into those here. In general, the logistic function seems to be the most widely used and is applicable to a large variety of applications.

Figure 14-9 shows yet another activation function that sometimes is used—a linear activation function.

The formula for the linear activation function is simply:

$$f(x) = x$$

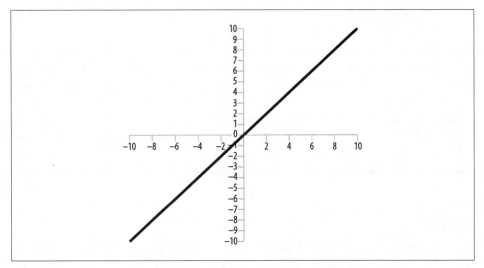

Figure 14-9. Linear activation function

This means that the output of a neuron is simply the net input—that is, the sum of the weighted inputs from all connected input neurons plus the bias term.

Linear activation functions sometimes are used as the activation functions for output neurons. Note that nonlinear activation functions must be used for the hidden neurons if the network is not to be reduced to a linear combination of linear functions. Employing such a linear output neuron is sometimes useful when you don't want the output confined to an interval between 0 and 1. In such cases, you still can use a logistic output activation function, so long as you scale the output to the full range of values for which you're interested.

Bias

When we discussed how to calculate the net input to a neuron earlier, we mentioned that each neuron has a bias associated with it. This is represented as a bias value and a bias weight for each neuron and shows up in the net input formula we showed earlier and are showing again here for convenience:

$$n_j = \sum n_i w_{ij} + b_j w_j$$

b_j is the bias value and w_j is the bias weight.

To understand what the bias does, you have to look at the activation functions used to generate output for a neuron given the net input. Basically, the bias term shifts the net input along the horizontal axis of the activation function, which effectively changes the threshold at which a neuron activates. The bias value always is set to 1 or −1 and its weight is adjusted through training, just like all other weights. This essentially allows the neural network to learn the appropriate thresholds for each neuron's activation.

Some practitioners always set the bias value to 1, while others always use −1. In our experience it really doesn't matter whether you use 1 or −1 because, through training, the network will adjust its bias weights to suit your choice. Weights can be either positive or negative, so if the neural network thinks the bias should be negative, it will adjust the weight to achieve that, regardless of your choice of 1 or −1. If you choose 1, it will find a suitable negative weight, whereas if you choose −1, it will find a suitable positive weight. Of course, you achieve all of this through training or evolving the network, as we'll discuss later in this chapter.

Output

Just like input, your choice of output neurons for a given network is problem-specific. In general, it's best to keep the number of output neurons to a minimum to reduce computation and training time.

Consider a network in which, given certain input, you desire output that classifies that input. Perhaps you want to determine whether a given set of input falls within a certain class. In this case, you would use one output neuron. If it is activated, the result is true, whereas if it is not activated, the result is false—the input does not fall within the class under consideration. If you were using a logistic function as your output activation, an output of around 0.9 would indicate activated, or true, whereas an output of around 0.1 would indicate not activated, or false. In practice, you might not actually get output values of exactly 0.9 or 0.1; you might get 0.78 or 0.31, for example. Therefore, you have to define a threshold that will enable you to assess whether a given output value indicates activation. Generally, you simply choose an output threshold midway between the two extremes. For the logistic function, you can use 0.5. If the output is greater than 0.5, the result is activated or true, otherwise it's false.

When you're interested in whether certain input falls within more than a single class, you have to use more than a single output neuron. Consider the network shown in Figure 14-3. Here, essentially we want to classify the threat posed by an enemy; the classes are aerial threat, ground threat, both aerial and ground threats, or no threat. We have one output neuron for each class. For this type of output we assume that high output values imply activated, while low output values imply not activated. The actual output values for each node can cover a range of values, depending on how the network was trained and on the kind of output activation function used. Given a set of input values and the resulting value at each output node, one way to figure out which output is activated is to take the neuron with the highest output value. This is the so-called *winner-take-all* approach. The neuron with highest activation indicates the resulting class. We'll see an example of this approach later in this chapter.

Often, you want a neural network that will generate a single value given a set of input. Time-series prediction, whereby you try to predict the next value given historical values over time, is one such situation in which you'll use a single output neuron. In this case, the value of the output neuron corresponds to the predicted value of interest. Keep in mind, however, you might have to scale the result if you're using an output activation function that generates bounded values, such as the logistic function, and if the value of the quantity you're trying to predict falls within some other range.

In other cases, such as that illustrated in Figure 14-2, you might have more than one output neuron that's used to directly control some other system. In the case of the example shown in Figure 14-2, the output values control the motion of each track for a half-track robot. In that example, it might be useful to use the hyperbolic tangent function for the output neurons so that the output value will range between -1 and $+1$. Then, negative values could indicate backward motion while positive values could indicate forward motion.

Sometimes you might require a network with as many output neurons as input neurons. Such networks commonly are used for autoassociation (pattern recognition) and data compression. Here, the aim is that the output neurons should echo the input values. For pattern recognition, such a network would be trained to output its input. The training set would consist of many sample patterns of interest. The idea here is that when presented with a pattern that's either degraded somewhat or does not exactly match a pattern that was included in the training set, the network should produce output that represents the pattern included in its training set that most closely matches the one being input.

The Hidden Layer

So far we've discussed input neurons, output neurons, and how to calculate net inputs for any neuron, but we've yet to discuss the hidden layer specifically. In our three-layer feed-forward network, we have one hidden layer of neurons sandwiched between the input and output layers.

As illustrated in Figure 14-5, every input is connected to every hidden neuron. Further, every hidden neuron sends its output to every output neuron. By the way, this isn't the only neural network structure at your disposal; there are all sorts—some with more than one hidden layer, some with feedback, and some with no hidden layer at all, among others. However, it is one of the most commonly used configurations. At any rate, the hidden layer is crucial for giving the network facility to process features in the input data. The more hidden neurons, the more features the network can handle; conversely, the fewer hidden neurons, the fewer features the network can handle.

So, what do we mean by features? To understand what we mean here, it's helpful to think of a neural network as a function approximator. Say you have a function that looks very noisy, as illustrated in Figure 14-10.

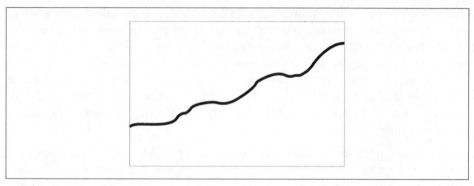

Figure 14-10. Noisy function

If you were to train a neural network to approximate such a function using too few hidden neurons, you might get something such as that shown in Figure 14-11.

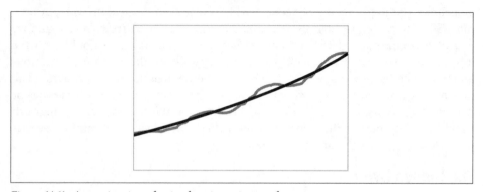

Figure 14-11. Approximation of noisy function using too few neurons

Here, you can see that the approximated function captures the trend of the input data but misses the local noisy features. In some cases, such as for signal noise reduction applications, this is exactly what you want; however, you might not want this for other problems. If you go the other route and choose too many hidden neurons, the approximated function likely will pick up the local noisy features in addition to the overall trend of the function. In some cases, this might be what you want; however, in other cases, you might end up with a network that is overtrained and unable to generalize given new input data that was not part of the training set.

Exactly how many hidden neurons to use for a given application is hard to say with certainty. Generally, you go about it by trial and error. However, here's a rule of thumb that you might find useful. For three-layer networks in which you're not interested in autoassociation, the appropriate number of hidden neurons is approximately equal to the square root of the product of the number of input and output neurons. This is just an approximation, but it's as good a place to start as any. The thing to keep in mind, particularly for games in which CPU usage is critical, is that the larger the number of hidden neurons, the more time it will take to compute the output of the network. Therefore, it's beneficial to try to minimize the number of hidden neurons.

Training

So far, we've repeatedly mentioned training a neural network without actually giving you the details as to how to do this. We'll tackle that now in this section.

The aim of training is to find the values for the weights that connect all the neurons such that the input data generates the desired output values. As you might expect, there's more to training than just picking some weight values. Essentially, training a neural network is an optimization process in which you are trying to find optimal weights that will allow the network to produce the right output.

Training can fall under two categories: *supervised* training and *unsupervised* training. Covering all or even some of the popular training approaches is well beyond a single chapter, so we'll focus on one of the most commonly used supervised training methods: *back-propagation*.

Back-Propagation Training

Again, the aim of training is to find the values for the weights that connect all the neurons such that the input data generates the desired output values. To do this, you need a training set, which consists of both input data and the desired output values corresponding to that input. The next step is to iteratively, using any of a number of techniques, find a set of weights for the entire network that causes the network to produce output matching the desired output for each set of data in the training set. Once you do this, you can put the network to work and present it with new data, not included in the training set, to produce output that is reasonable.

Because training is an optimization process, we need some measure of merit to optimize. In the case of back-propagation, we use a measure of error and try to minimize the error. Given some input and the generated output, we need to compare the generated output with the known, desired output and quantify how well the results match—i.e., calculate the error. Many error measures are available for you to use, and we'll use one of the most common ones here: the mean square error, which is simply the average of the square of the differences between the calculated output and the desired output.

If you've studied calculus you might recall that to minimize or maximize a function you need to be able to calculate the function's derivative. Because we're trying to optimize weights by minimizing the error measure, it's no surprise that we need to calculate a derivative somewhere. Specifically, we need the derivative of the activation function, and this is why the logistic function is so nice—we easily can determine its derivative analytically.

As we mentioned earlier, finding the optimum weights is an iterative process, and it goes something like this:

1. Start with a training set consisting of input data and corresponding desired outputs.
2. Initialize the weights in the neural network to some small random values.
3. With each set of input data, feed the network and calculate the output.
4. Compare the calculated output with the desired output and compute the error.
5. Adjust the weights to reduce the error, and repeat the process.

You can execute the process in two ways. One way is to calculate the error measure, adjust the weights for each set of input and desired output data, and then move on to the next set of input/output data. The other way is to calculate the cumulative error for all sets of input and desired output data in the training set, then adjust the weights, and then repeat the process. Each iteration is known as an *epoch*.

Steps 1 through 3 are relatively straightforward and we'll see an example implementation a little later. Now, though, let's examine steps 4 and 5 more closely.

Computing Error

To train a neural network, you feed it a set of input, which generates some output. To compare this calculated output to the desired output for a given set of input, you need to calculate the error. This enables you to not only determine whether the calculated output is right or wrong, but also to determine the degree to which it is right or wrong. The most common error to use is the mean-square error, which is the average of the square of the difference between the desired and calculated output:

$$\varepsilon = \frac{\sum (n_c - n_d)^2}{m}$$

In this equation, ε is the mean square error for the training set. n_c and n_d are the calculated and desired output values, respectively, for all output neurons, while m is the number of output neurons for each epoch.

The goal is to get this error value as small as is practical by iteratively adjusting the weight values connecting all the neurons in the network. To know how much the weights need adjusting, each iteration requires that we also calculate the error associated with each neuron in the output and hidden layers. We calculate the error for output neurons as follows:

$$\delta_i^o = \Delta n_i^o f' \left(n_{ci}^o \right)$$

Here, $\delta_i{}^o$ is the error for the i th output neuron, $\Delta n_i{}^o$ is the difference between the calculated and desired output for the i th output neuron, and $f'(n_{ci}{}^o)$ is the derivative of the activation function for the ith output neuron. Earlier we told you that we'd need to calculate a derivative somewhere, and this is where to do it. This is why the logistic function is so useful; its derivative is quite simple in form, and it's easy to calculate it analytically. Rewriting this equation using the derivative of the logistic function yields the following equation for output neuron error:

$$\delta_i^o = \left(n_{di}^{\;o} - n_{ci}^{\;o}\right) n_{ci}^{\;o} \left(1 - n_{ci}^{\;o}\right)$$

In this equation, $n_{di}^{\;o}$ is the desired output value for the ith neuron, and $n_{ci}^{\;o}$ is the calculated output value for the ith neuron.

For hidden-layer neurons, the error equation is somewhat different. In this case, the error associated with each hidden neuron is as follows:

$$\delta_i^{\;h} = \left(\sum \delta_j^o w_{ij}\right) f'\left(n_{ci}^{\;h}\right)$$

Notice here that the error for each hidden-layer neuron is a function of the error associated with each output-layer neuron to which the hidden neuron connects times the weight for each connection. This means that to calculate the error and, subsequently, to adjust weight, you need to work backward from the output layer toward the input layer.

Also notice that the activation function derivative is required again. Assuming the logistic activation function yields the following:

$$\delta_i^{\;h} = \left(\sum \delta_j^o w_{ij}\right) n_{ai}^{\;h} \left(1 - n_{ai}^{\;h}\right)$$

Lastly, no error is associated with input layer neurons because those neuron values are given.

Adjusting Weights

With calculated errors in hand, you can proceed to calculate suitable adjustments for each weight in the network. The adjustment to each weight is as follows:

$$\Delta w = \rho \delta_i n_i$$

In this equation, ρ is the learning rate, δ_i is the error associated with the neurons being considered, and n_i is the value of the neuron being considered. The new weight is simply the old weight plus Δw.

Keep in mind that the weight adjustments will be made for each weight and the adjustment will be different for each weight. When updating the weights connecting output to hidden-layer neurons, the errors and values for the output neurons calculate the weight adjustment. When updating the weights connecting the hidden-to-input-layer neurons, the errors and values for the hidden-layer neurons are used.

The learning rate is a multiplier that affects how much each weight is adjusted. It's usually set to some small value such as 0.25 or 0.5. This is one of those parameters that you'll have to tune. If you set it too high, you might overshoot the optimum weights; if you set it too low, training might take longer.

Momentum

Many back-propagation practitioners use a slight modification to the weight adjustments we just discussed. This modified technique is called *adding momentum*. Before showing you how to add momentum, let's first discuss why you might want to add momentum.

In any general optimization process the goal is to either minimize or maximize some function. More specifically, we're interested in finding the global minimum or maximum of the given function over some range of input parameters. The trouble is that many functions exhibit what are called *local minima* or *maxima*. These are basically hollows and humps in the function, as illustrated in Figure 14-12.

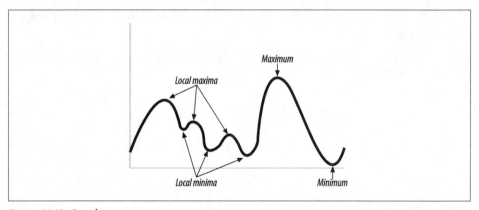

Figure 14-12. Local extrema

In this example, the function has a global minimum and maximum over the range shown; but it also has several local minima and maxima, characterized by the smaller bumps and hollows.

In our case, we're interested in minimizing the error of our network. Specifically we're interested in finding the optimum weights that yield the global minimum error; however, we might run into a local minimum instead of a global minimum.

When network training begins, we initialize the weights to some small random values. We have no idea at that point how close those values are to the optimum weights; thus, we might have initialized the network near a local minimum rather than a global minimum. Without going into calculus, the technique by which we update the weights is called a *gradient descent* type of technique, whereby we use the derivative of the function in an attempt to steer toward a minimum value, which in our case is a minimum error value. The trouble is that we don't know if we get to a global minimum or a local minimum, and typically the *error-space*, as it's called for neural networks, is full of local minima.

This sort of problem is common among all optimization techniques and many different methods attempt to alleviate it. The momentum technique is one such technique used for neural networks. It does not eliminate the possibility of converging on a local minimum, but it is thought to help get out of them and head toward the global minimum, which is where it derives its name. Basically, we add a small additional fraction to the weight adjustment that is a function of the previous iteration's weight adjustment. This gives the weight adjustments a little push so that if a local minimum is being approached, the algorithm will, hopefully, overshoot the local minimum and proceed on toward the global minimum.

So, using momentum, the new formula that calculates the weight adjustment is as follows:

$$\Delta w = \rho \delta_i n_i + \alpha(\Delta w')$$

In this equation, $\Delta w'$ is the weight adjustment from the previous iteration, and α is the momentum factor. The momentum factor is yet another factor that you'll have to tune. It typically is set to some small fractional number between 0.0 and 1.0.

Neural Network Source Code

At last it's time to look at some actual source code that implements a three-layer feed-forward neural network. The following sections present two C++ classes that implement such a network. Later in this chapter, we'll look at an example implementation of these classes. Feel free to skip to the section entitled "Chasing and Evading with Brains" if you prefer to see how the neural network is used before looking at its internal details.

We need to implement two classes in the three-layer feed-forward neural network. The first class represents a generic layer. You can use it for input, hidden, and output layers. The second class represents the entire neural network composed of three layers. The following sections present the complete source code for each class.

The Layer Class

The class `NeuralNetworkLayer` implements a generic layer in a multilayer feed-forward network. It is responsible for handling the neurons contained within the layer. The tasks it performs include allocating and freeing memory to store neuron values, errors, and weights; initializing weights; calculating neuron values; and adjusting weights. Example 14-1 shows the header for this class.

Example 14-1. NeuralNetworkLayer class

```cpp
class NeuralNetworkLayer
{
public:
    int             NumberOfNodes;
    int             NumberOfChildNodes;
    int             NumberOfParentNodes;
    double**        Weights;
    double**        WeightChanges;
    double*         NeuronValues;
    double*         DesiredValues;
    double*         Errors;
    double*         BiasWeights;
    double*         BiasValues;
    double          LearningRate;

    bool            LinearOutput;
    bool            UseMomentum;
    double          MomentumFactor;

    NeuralNetworkLayer*    ParentLayer;
    NeuralNetworkLayer*    ChildLayer;

    NeuralNetworkLayer();

    void    Initialize(int NumNodes,
                       NeuralNetworkLayer* parent,
                       NeuralNetworkLayer* child);
    void    CleanUp(void);
    void    RandomizeWeights(void);
    void    CalculateErrors(void);
    void    AdjustWeights(void);
    void    CalculateNeuronValues(void);
};
```

Layers are connected to each other in a parent-child relationship. For example, the input layer is the parent layer for the hidden layer, and the hidden layer is the parent layer for the output layer. Also, the output layer is a child layer to the hidden layer, and the hidden layer is a child layer to the input layer. Note that the input layer has no parent and the output layer has no child.

The members of this class primarily consist of arrays to store neuron weights, values, errors, and bias terms. Also, a few members store certain settings governing the behavior of the layer. The members are as follows:

NumberOfNodes

This member stores the number of neurons, or nodes, in a given instance of the layer class.

NumberOfChildNodes

This member stores the number of neurons in the child layer connected to a given instance of the layer class.

NumberOfParentNodes

This member stores the number of neurons in the parent layer connected to a given instance of the layer class.

Weights

This member is a pointer to a pointer to a double value. Basically, this represents a two-dimensional array of weight values connecting nodes between parent and child layers.

WeightChanges

This member also is a pointer to a pointer to a double value, which accesses a dynamically allocated two-dimensional array. In this case, the values stored in the array are the adjustments made to the weight values. We need these to implement momentum, as we discussed earlier.

NeuronValues

This member is a pointer to a double value, which accesses a dynamically allocated array storing the calculated values, or activations, for the neurons in the layer.

DesiredValues

This member is a pointer to a double value, which accesses a dynamically allocated array storing the desired, or target, values for the neurons in the layer. We use this for the output array where we calculate errors given the calculated outputs and the target outputs from the training set.

Errors

This member is a pointer to a double value, which accesses a dynamically allocated array storing the errors associated with each neuron in the layer.

BiasWeights

This member is a pointer to a double value, which accesses a dynamically allocated array storing the bias weights connected to each neuron in the layer.

BiasValues

This member is a pointer to a double value, which accesses a dynamically allocated array storing the bias values connected to each neuron in the layer. Note that this member is not really required because we usually set the bias values to either +1 or −1 and leave them alone.

LearningRate

This member stores the learning rate, which calculates weight adjustments.

LinearOutput

This member stores a flag indicating whether to use a linear activation function for the neurons in the layer. You use this only if the layer is an output layer. If this flag is false, use the logistic activation function instead. The default value is false.

UseMomentum

> This member stores a flag indicating whether to use momentum when adjusting weights. The default value is `false`.

MomentumFactor

> This member stores the momentum factor, as we discussed earlier. Use it only if the `UseMomentum` flag is `true`.

ParentLayer

> This member stores a pointer to an instance of a `NeuralNetworkLayer` representing the parent layer connected to the given layer instance. This pointer is set to `NULL` for input layers.

ChildLayer

> This member stores a pointer to an instance of a `NeuralNetworkLayer` representing the child layer connected to the given layer instance. This pointer is set to `NULL` for output layers.

The `NeuralNetworkLayer` class contains seven methods. Let's go through each one in detail, starting with the constructor shown in Example 14-2.

Example 14-2. NeuralNetworkLayer constructor

```
NeuralNetworkLayer::NeuralNetworkLayer()
{
    ParentLayer = NULL;
    ChildLayer = NULL;
    LinearOutput = false;
    UseMomentum = false;
    MomentumFactor = 0.9;
}
```

The constructor is very simple. All it does is initialize a few settings that we've already discussed. The `Initialize` method, shown in Example 14-3, is somewhat more involved.

Example 14-3. Initialize method

```
void NeuralNetworkLayer::Initialize(int NumNodes,
                                    NeuralNetworkLayer* parent,
                                    NeuralNetworkLayer* child)
{
    int    i, j;

    // Allocate memory
    NeuronValues = (double*) malloc(sizeof(double) *
                                    NumberOfNodes);
    DesiredValues = (double*) malloc(sizeof(double) *
                                    NumberOfNodes);
    Errors = (double*) malloc(sizeof(double) * NumberOfNodes);

    if(parent != NULL)
    {
```

```c
        ParentLayer = parent;
    }

    if(child != NULL)
    {
        ChildLayer = child;


        Weights = (double**) malloc(sizeof(double*) *
                                NumberOfNodes);
        WeightChanges = (double**) malloc(sizeof(double*) *
                                    NumberOfNodes);
        for(i = 0; i<NumberOfNodes; i++)
        {
            Weights[i] = (double*) malloc(sizeof(double) *
                                    NumberOfChildNodes);
            WeightChanges[i] = (double*) malloc(sizeof(double) *
                                        NumberOfChildNodes);
        }

        BiasValues = (double*) malloc(sizeof(double) *
                            NumberOfChildNodes);
        BiasWeights = (double*) malloc(sizeof(double) *
                            NumberOfChildNodes);
    } else {
        Weights = NULL;
        BiasValues = NULL;
        BiasWeights = NULL;
        WeightChanges = NULL;
    }

    // Make sure everything contains 0s
    for(i=0; i<NumberOfNodes; i++)
    {
        NeuronValues[i] = 0;
        DesiredValues[i] = 0;
        Errors[i] = 0;

        if(ChildLayer != NULL)
            for(j=0; j<NumberOfChildNodes; j++)
            {
                Weights[i][j] = 0;
                WeightChanges[i][j] = 0;
            }
    }

    // Initialize the bias values and weights
    if(ChildLayer != NULL)
        for(j=0; j<NumberOfChildNodes; j++)
        {
            BiasValues[j] = -1;
            BiasWeights[j] = 0;
        }
}
```

The Initialize method is responsible for allocating all memory for the dynamic arrays used to store weights, values, errors, and bias values and weights for the neurons in the layer. It also handles initializing all these arrays.

The method takes three parameters: the number of nodes, or neurons, in the layer; a pointer to the parent layer; and a pointer to the child layer. If the layer is an input layer, NULL should be passed in for the parent layer pointer. If the layer is an output layer, NULL should be passed in for the child layer pointer.

Upon entering the method, memory for the NeuronValues, DesiredValues, and Errors arrays is allocated. All of these arrays are one-dimensional, with the number of entries defined by the number of nodes in the layer.

Next, the parent and child layer pointers are set. If the child layer pointer is not NULL, we have either an input layer or a hidden layer and memory for connection weights must be allocated. Because Weights and WeightChanges are two-dimensional arrays, we need to allocate the memory in steps. The first step involves allocated memory to hold pointers to double arrays. The number of entries here corresponds to the number of nodes in the layer. Next, for each entry we allocate another chunk of memory to store the actual array values. The size of these additional chunks corresponds to the number of nodes in the child layer. Every neuron in an input or hidden layer connects to every neuron in the associated child layer; therefore, the total size of the weight and weight adjustment arrays is equal to the number of neurons in the layer times the number of neurons in the child layer.

We also go ahead and allocate memory for the bias values and weights arrays. The sizes of these arrays are equal to the number of neurons in the connected child layer.

After all the memory is allocated, the arrays are initialized. For the most part we want everything to contain 0s, with the exception of the bias values, where we set all the bias value entries to −1. Note that you can set these all to +1, as we discussed earlier.

Example 14-4 shows the CleanUp method, which is responsible for freeing all memory allocated in the Initialization method.

Example 14-4. CleanUp method

```
void NeuralNetworkLayer::CleanUp(void)
{
    int    i;

    free(NeuronValues);
    free(DesiredValues);
    free(Errors);

    if(Weights != NULL)
    {
        for(i = 0; i<NumberOfNodes; i++)
```

```
    {
        free(Weights[i]);
        free(WeightChanges[i]);
    }

    free(Weights);
    free(WeightChanges);
}

if(BiasValues != NULL) free(BiasValues);
if(BiasWeights != NULL) free(BiasWeights);
}
```

The code here is pretty self-explanatory. It simply frees all dynamically allocated memory using free.

Earlier we mentioned that neural network weights are initialized to some small random numbers before training begins. The RandomizeWeights method, shown in Example 14-5, handles this task for us.

Example 14-5. RandomizeWeights method

```
void NeuralNetworkLayer::RandomizeWeights(void)
{
    int    i,j;
    int    min = 0;
    int    max = 200;
    int    number;

    srand( (unsigned)time( NULL ) );

    for(i=0; i<NumberOfNodes; i++)
    {
        for(j=0; j<NumberOfChildNodes; j++)
        {
            number = (((abs(rand())%(max-min+1))+min));

            if(number>max)
                number = max;

            if(number<min)
                number = min;

            Weights[i][j] = number / 100.0f - 1;
        }
    }

    for(j=0; j<NumberOfChildNodes; j++)
    {
            number = (((abs(rand())%(max-min+1))+min));

            if(number>max)
                number = max;
```

```
        if(number<min)
            number = min;

        BiasWeights[j] = number / 100.0f - 1;
    }
}
```

All this method does is simply calculate a random number between −1 and +1 for each weight in the Weights array. It does the same for the bias weights stored in the BiasWeights array. You should call this method at the start of training only.

The next method, CalculateNeuronValues, is responsible for calculating the activation or value of each neuron in the layer using the formulas we showed you earlier for net input to a neuron and the activation functions. Example 14-6 shows this method.

Example 14-6. CalculateNeuronValues method

```
void NeuralNetworkLayer::CalculateNeuronValues(void)
{
    int      i,j;
    double   x;

    if(ParentLayer != NULL)
    {
        for(j=0; j<NumberOfNodes; j++)
        {
            x = 0;
            for(i=0; i<NumberOfParentNodes; i++)
            {
                x += ParentLayer->NeuronValues[i] *
                    ParentLayer->Weights[i][j];
            }
            x += ParentLayer->BiasValues[j] *
                ParentLayer->BiasWeights[j];

            if((ChildLayer == NULL) && LinearOutput)
                NeuronValues[j] = x;
            else
                NeuronValues[j] = 1.0f/(1+exp(-x));
        }
    }
}
```

In this method, all the weights are cycled through using the nested for statements. The j loop cycles through the layer nodes (the child layer), while the i loop cycles through the parent layer nodes. Within these nested loops, the net input is calculated and stored in the x variable. The net input for each node in the layer is the weighted sum of all connections from the parent layer (the i loop) feeding into each node, the jth node, plus the weighted bias for the jth node.

After you have calculated the net input for each node, you calculate the value for each neuron by applying an activation function. You use the logistic activation function for all layers, except for the output layer, in which case you use the linear activation function depending on the LinearOutput flag.

The CalculateErrors method shown in Example 14-7 is responsible for calculating the errors associated with each neuron using the formulas we discussed earlier.

Example 14-7. CalculateErrors method

```
void NeuralNetworkLayer::CalculateErrors(void)
{
    int       i, j;
    double    sum;

    if(ChildLayer == NULL) // output layer
    {
        for(i=0; i<NumberOfNodes; i++)
        {
            Errors[i] = (DesiredValues[i] - NeuronValues[i]) *
                        NeuronValues[i] *
                        (1.0f - NeuronValues[i]);
        }
    } else if(ParentLayer == NULL) { // input layer
        for(i=0; i<NumberOfNodes; i++)
        {
            Errors[i] = 0.0f;
        }
    } else { // hidden layer
        for(i=0; i<NumberOfNodes; i++)
        {
            sum = 0;
            for(j=0; j<NumberOfChildNodes; j++)
            {
                sum += ChildLayer->Errors[j] * Weights[i][j];
            }
            Errors[i] = sum * NeuronValues[i] *
                        (1.0f - NeuronValues[i]);
        }
    }
}
```

If the layer has no child layer, which happens only if the layer is an output layer, the formula for output layer errors is used. If the layer has no parent, which happens only if the layer is an input layer, the errors are set to 0. If the layer has both a parent layer and a child layer, it is a hidden layer and the formula for hidden-layer errors is applied.

The AdjustWeights method, shown in Example 14-8, is responsible for calculating the adjustments to be made to each connection weight.

Example 14-8. AdjustWeights method

```
void NeuralNetworkLayer::AdjustWeights(void)
{
    int      i, j;
    double   dw;

    if(ChildLayer != NULL)
    {
        for(i=0; i<NumberOfNodes; i++)
        {
            for(j=0; j<NumberOfChildNodes; j++)
            {
                dw = LearningRate * ChildLayer->Errors[j] *
                    NeuronValues[i];
                if(UseMomentum)
                {
                    Weights[i][j] += dw + MomentumFactor *
                                        WeightChanges[i][j];
                    WeightChanges[i][j] = dw;
                } else {
                    Weights[i][j] += dw;
                }
            }
        }

        for(j=0; j<NumberOfChildNodes; j++)
        {
            BiasWeights[j] += LearningRate *
                            ChildLayer->Errors[j] *
                            BiasValues[j];
        }
    }
}
```

Weights are adjusted only if the layer has a child layer—that is, if the layer is an input layer or a hidden layer. Output layers have no child layer and therefore no connections and associated weights to adjust. The nested for loops cycle through the nodes in the layer and the nodes in the child layer. Remember that each neuron in a layer is connected to every node in a child layer. Within these nested loops, the weight adjustment is calculated using the formula shown earlier. If momentum is to be applied, the momentum factor times the previous epoch's weight changes also are added to the weight change. The weight change for this epoch is then stored in the WeightChanges array for the next epoch. If momentum is not used, the weight change is applied without momentum and there's no need to store the weight changes.

Finally, the bias weights are adjusted in a manner similar to the connection weights. For each bias connected to the child nodes, the adjustment is equal to the learning rate times the child neuron error times the bias value.

The Neural Network Class

The NeuralNetwork class encapsulates three instances of the NeuralNetworkLayer class, one for each layer in the network: the input layer, the hidden layer, and the output layer. Example 14-9 shows the class header.

Example 14-9. NeuralNetwork class

```
class NeuralNetwork
{
public:
    NeuralNetworkLayer    InputLayer;
    NeuralNetworkLayer    HiddenLayer;
    NeuralNetworkLayer    OutputLayer;

    void    Initialize(int nNodesInput, int nNodesHidden,
                       int nNodesOutput);
    void    CleanUp();
    void    SetInput(int i, double value);
    double  GetOutput(int i);
    void    SetDesiredOutput(int i, double value);
    void    FeedForward(void);
    void    BackPropagate(void);
    int     GetMaxOutputID(void);
    double  CalculateError(void);
    void    SetLearningRate(double rate);
    void    SetLinearOutput(bool useLinear);
    void    SetMomentum(bool useMomentum, double factor);
    void    DumpData(char* filename);
};
```

Only three members in this class correspond to the layers comprising the class. However, this class contains 13 methods, which we'll go through next.

Example 14-10 shows the Initialize method.

Example 14-10. Initialize method

```
void NeuralNetwork::Initialize(int nNodesInput,
                               int nNodesHidden,
                               int nNodesOutput)
{
    InputLayer.NumberOfNodes = nNodesInput;
    InputLayer.NumberOfChildNodes = nNodesHidden;
    InputLayer.NumberOfParentNodes = 0;
    InputLayer.Initialize(nNodesInput, NULL, &HiddenLayer);
    InputLayer.RandomizeWeights();

    HiddenLayer.NumberOfNodes = nNodesHidden;
    HiddenLayer.NumberOfChildNodes = nNodesOutput;
    HiddenLayer.NumberOfParentNodes = nNodesInput;
    HiddenLayer.Initialize(nNodesHidden,&InputLayer,&OutputLayer);
    HiddenLayer.RandomizeWeights();
```

```
OutputLayer.NumberOfNodes = nNodesOutput;
OutputLayer.NumberOfChildNodes = 0;
OutputLayer.NumberOfParentNodes = nNodesHidden;
OutputLayer.Initialize(nNodesOutput, &HiddenLayer, NULL);

}
```

Initialize takes three parameters corresponding to the number of neurons contained in each of the three layers comprising the network. These parameters initialize the instances of the layer class corresponding to the input, hidden, and output layers. Initialize also handles making the proper parent-child connections between layers. Further, it goes ahead and randomizes the connection weights.

The CleanUp method, shown in Example 14-11, simply calls the CleanUp methods for each layer instance.

Example 14-11. CleanUp method

```
void NeuralNetwork::CleanUp()
{
    InputLayer.CleanUp();
    HiddenLayer.CleanUp();
    OutputLayer.CleanUp();
}
```

SetInput is used to set the input value for a specific input neuron. Example 14-12 shows the SetInput method.

Example 14-12. SetInput method

```
void    NeuralNetwork::SetInput(int i, double value)
{
    if((i>=0) && (i<InputLayer.NumberOfNodes))
    {
        InputLayer.NeuronValues[i] = value;
    }
}
```

SetInput takes two parameters corresponding to the index to the neuron for which the input will be set and the input value itself. This information is then used to set the specific input. You use this method both during training to set the training set input, and during field use of the network to set the input data for which outputs will be calculated.

Once a network generates some output, we need a way to get at it. The GetOutput method is provided for that purpose. Example 14-13 shows the GetOutput method.

Example 14-13. GetOutput method

```
double    NeuralNetwork::GetOutput(int i)
{
    if((i>=0) && (i<OutputLayer.NumberOfNodes))
    {
        return OutputLayer.NeuronValues[i];
    }

    return (double) INT_MAX; // to indicate an error
}
```

GetOutput takes one parameter, the index to the output neuron for which we desire the output value. The method returns the value, or activation, for the specified output neuron. Note that if you specify an index that falls outside of the range of valid output neurons, INT_MAX will be returned to indicate an error.

During training we need to compare calculated output to desired output. The layer class facilitates the calculations along with storage of the desired output values. The SetDesiredOutput method, shown in Example 14-14, is provided to facilitate setting the desired output to the values corresponding to a given set of input.

Example 14-14. SetDesiredOutput method

```
void NeuralNetwork::SetDesiredOutput(int i, double value)
{
    if((i>=0) && (i<OutputLayer.NumberOfNodes))
    {
        OutputLayer.DesiredValues[i] = value;
    }
}
```

SetDesiredOutput takes two parameters corresponding to the index of the output neuron for which the desired output is being set and the value of the desired output itself.

To actually have the network generate output given a set of input, we need to call the FeedForward method shown in Example 14-15.

Example 14-15. FeedForward method

```
void NeuralNetwork::FeedForward(void)
{
    InputLayer.CalculateNeuronValues();
    HiddenLayer.CalculateNeuronValues();
    OutputLayer.CalculateNeuronValues();
}
```

This method simply calls the CalculateNeuronValues method for the input, hidden, and output layers in succession. Once these calls are complete, the output layer will contain the calculated output, which then can be inspected via calls to the GetOutput method.

During training, once output has been calculated, we need to adjust the connection weights using the back-propagation technique. The BackPropagate method handles this task. Example 14-16 shows the BackPropagate method.

Example 14-16. BackPropagate method

```
void NeuralNetwork::BackPropagate(void)
{
    OutputLayer.CalculateErrors();
    HiddenLayer.CalculateErrors();

    HiddenLayer.AdjustWeights();
    InputLayer.AdjustWeights();
}
```

BackPropagate first calls the CalculateErrors method for the output and hidden layers, in that order. Then it goes on to call the AdjustWeights method for the hidden and input layers, in that order. The order is important here and it must be the order shown in Example 14-16—that is, we work backward through the network rather than forward, as in the FeedForward case.

When using a network with multiple output neurons and the winner-takes-all approach to determine which output is activated, you need to figure out which output neuron has the highest output value. GetMaxOutputID, shown in Example 14-17, is provided for that purpose.

Example 14-17. GetMaxOutputID method

```
int     NeuralNetwork::GetMaxOutputID(void)
{
    int        i, id;
    double     maxval;

    maxval = OutputLayer.NeuronValues[0];
    id = 0;

    for(i=1; i<OutputLayer.NumberOfNodes; i++)
    {
        if(OutputLayer.NeuronValues[i] > maxval)
        {
            maxval = OutputLayer.NeuronValues[i];
            id = i;
        }
    }

    return id;
}
```

`GetMaxOutputID` simply iterates through all the output-layer neurons to determine which one has the highest output value. The index to the neuron with the highest value is returned.

Earlier we discussed the need to calculate the error associated with a given set of output. We need to do this for training purposes. The `CalculateError` method takes care of the error calculation for us. Example 14-18 shows the `CalculateError` method.

Example 14-18. CalculateError method

```
double NeuralNetwork::CalculateError(void)
{
    int      i;
    double   error = 0;

    for(i=0; i<OutputLayer.NumberOfNodes; i++)
    {
        error += pow(OutputLayer.NeuronValues[i] -
                OutputLayer.DesiredValues[i], 2);
    }

    error = error / OutputLayer.NumberOfNodes;

    return error;
}
```

`CalculateError` returns the error value associated with the calculated output values and the given set of desired output values using the mean-square error formula we discussed earlier.

For convenience, we provide the `SetLearningRate` method, shown in Example 14-19. You can use it to set the learning rate for each layer comprising the network.

Example 14-19. SetLearningRate method

```
void NeuralNetwork::SetLearningRate(double rate)
{
    InputLayer.LearningRate = rate;
    HiddenLayer.LearningRate = rate;
    OutputLayer.LearningRate = rate;
}
```

`SetLinearOutput`, shown in Example 14-20, is another convenience method. You can use it to set the `LinearOutput` flag for each layer in the network. Note, however, that only the output layer will use linear activations in this implementation.

Example 14-20. SetLinearOutput method

```
void    NeuralNetwork::SetLinearOutput(bool useLinear)
{
    InputLayer.LinearOutput = useLinear;
    HiddenLayer.LinearOutput = useLinear;
    OutputLayer.LinearOutput = useLinear;
}
```

You use `SetMomentum`, shown in Example 14-21, to set the `UseMomentum` flag and the momentum factor for each layer in the network.

Example 14-21. SetMomentum method

```
void    NeuralNetwork::SetMomentum(bool useMomentum, double factor)
{
    InputLayer.UseMomentum = useMomentum;
    HiddenLayer.UseMomentum = useMomentum;
    OutputLayer.UseMomentum = useMomentum;

    InputLayer.MomentumFactor = factor;
    HiddenLayer.MomentumFactor = factor;
    OutputLayer.MomentumFactor = factor;

}
```

`DumpData` is a convenience method that simply streams some important data for the network to an output file. Example 14-22 shows the `DumpData` method.

Example 14-22. DumpData method

```
void NeuralNetwork::DumpData(char* filename)
{
    FILE*    f;
    int      i, j;

    f = fopen(filename, "w");

    fprintf(f, "----------------------------------------------\n");
    fprintf(f, "Input Layer\n");
    fprintf(f, "----------------------------------------------\n");
    fprintf(f, "\n");
    fprintf(f, "Node Values:\n");
    fprintf(f, "\n");
    for(i=0; i<InputLayer.NumberOfNodes; i++)
        fprintf(f, "(%d) = %f\n", i, InputLayer.NeuronValues[i]);
    fprintf(f, "\n");
    fprintf(f, "Weights:\n");
    fprintf(f, "\n");
    for(i=0; i<InputLayer.NumberOfNodes; i++)
        for(j=0; j<InputLayer.NumberOfChildNodes; j++)
            fprintf(f, "(%d, %d) = %f\n", i, j,
                    InputLayer.Weights[i][j]);
    fprintf(f, "\n");
    fprintf(f, "Bias Weights:\n");
    fprintf(f, "\n");
    for(j=0; j<InputLayer.NumberOfChildNodes; j++)
        fprintf(f, "(%d) = %f\n", j, InputLayer.BiasWeights[j]);

    fprintf(f, "\n");
    fprintf(f, "\n");
    fprintf(f, "----------------------------------------------\n");
```

```
fprintf(f, "Hidden Layer\n");
fprintf(f, "----------------------------------------------\n");
fprintf(f, "\n");
fprintf(f, "Weights:\n");
fprintf(f, "\n");
for(i=0; i<HiddenLayer.NumberOfNodes; i++)
    for(j=0; j<HiddenLayer.NumberOfChildNodes; j++)
        fprintf(f, "(%d, %d) = %f\n", i, j,
                HiddenLayer.Weights[i][j]);
fprintf(f, "\n");
fprintf(f, "Bias Weights:\n");
fprintf(f, "\n");
for(j=0; j<HiddenLayer.NumberOfChildNodes; j++)
    fprintf(f, "(%d) = %f\n", j, HiddenLayer.BiasWeights[j]);

fprintf(f, "\n");
fprintf(f, "\n");

fprintf(f, "----------------------------------------------\n");
fprintf(f, "Output Layer\n");
fprintf(f, "----------------------------------------------\n");
fprintf(f, "\n");
fprintf(f, "Node Values:\n");
fprintf(f, "\n");
for(i=0; i<OutputLayer.NumberOfNodes; i++)
    fprintf(f, "(%d) = %f\n", i, OutputLayer.NeuronValues[i]);
fprintf(f, "\n");


    fclose(f);
}
```

The data that is sent to the given output file consists of weights, values, and bias weights for the layers comprising the network. This is useful when you want to examine the internals of a given network. This is helpful when debugging and in cases in which you might train a network using a utility program and want to hardcode the trained weights in an actual game instead of spending the time in-game performing initial training. For this latter purpose, you'll have to revise the NeuralNetwork class shown here to facilitate loading weights from an external source.

Chasing and Evading with Brains

The example we're going to discuss in this section is a modification of the flocking and chasing example we discussed in Chapter 4. In that chapter we discussed an example in which a flock of units chased the player-controlled unit. In this modified example, the computer-controlled units will use a neural network to decide whether to chase the player, evade him, or flock with other computer-controlled units. This example is an idealization or approximation of a game scenario in which you have creatures or units within the game that can engage the player in battle. Instead of having the creatures always attack the player and instead of using a finite state machine "brain," you want to use a neural network to not only make decisions for the creatures, but also to adapt their behavior given their experience with attacking the player.

Here's how our simple example will work. About 20 computer-controlled units will move around the screen. They will attack the player, run from the player, or flock with other computer-controlled units. All of these behaviors will be handled using the deterministic algorithms we presented in earlier chapters; however, here the decision as to what behavior to perform is up to the neural network. The player can move around the screen as he wishes. When the player and computer-controlled units come within a specified radius of one another, we're going to assume they are engaged in combat. We won't actually simulate combat here and will instead use a rudimentary system whereby the computer-controlled units will lose a certain number of hit points every turn through the game loop when in combat range of the player. The player will lose a certain number of hit points proportional to the number of computer-controlled units within combat range. When a unit's hit points reach zero, he dies and is respawned automatically.

All computer-controlled units share an identical brain—the neural network. We're also going to have this brain evolve as the computer-controlled units gain experience with the player. We'll achieve this by implementing the back-propagation algorithm in the game itself so that we can adjust the network's weights in real time. We're assuming that the computer-controlled units evolve collectively.

We hope to see the computer-controlled units learn to avoid the player if the player is overwhelming them in combat. Conversely, we hope to see the computer-controlled units become more aggressive as they learn they have a weak player on their hands. Another possibility is that the computer-controlled units will learn to stay in groups, or flock, where they stand a better chance of defeating the player.

Initialization and Training

Using the flocking example from Chapter 4 as a starting point, the first thing we have to do is add a new global variable, called TheBrain, to represent the neural network, as shown in Example 14-23.

Example 14-23. New global variable

```
NeuralNetwork    TheBrain;
```

We must initialize the neural network at the start of the program. Here, initialization includes configuring and training the neural network. The Initialize function taken from the earlier example is an obvious place to handle initializing the neural network, as shown in Example 14-24.

Example 14-24. Initialization

```
void    Initialize(void)
{
    int i;

    .
    .
    .

    for(i=0; i<_MAX_NUM_UNITS; i++)
    {
        .
        .
        .

        Units[i].HitPoints = _MAXHITPOINTS;
        Units[i].Chase = false;
        Units[i].Flock = false;
        Units[i].Evade = false;
    }

    .
    .
    .

    Units[0].HitPoints = _MAXHITPOINTS;

    TheBrain.Initialize(4, 3, 3);
    TheBrain.SetLearningRate(0.2);
    TheBrain.SetMomentum(true, 0.9);
    TrainTheBrain();
}
```

Most of the code in this version of Initialize is the same as in the earlier example, so we omitted it from the code listing in Example 14-24. The remaining code is what we added to handle incorporating the neural network into the example.

Notice we had to add a few new members to the rigid body structure, as shown in Example 14-25. These new members include the number of hit points, and flags to indicate whether the unit is chasing, evading, or flocking.

Example 14-25. RigidBody2D class

```
class RigidBody2D {
public:
    .
    .
    .

    double  HitPoints;
    int     NumFriends;
    int     Command;
    bool    Chase;
    bool    Flock;
    bool    Evade;
    double  Inputs[4];
};
```

Notice also that we added an Inputs vector. This is used to store the input values to the neural network when it is used to determine what action the unit should take.

Getting back to the Initialize method in Example 14-24, after the units are initialized it's time to deal with TheBrain. The first thing we do is call the Initialize method for the neural network, passing it values representing the number of neurons in each layer. In this case, we have four input neurons, three hidden neurons, and three output neurons. This network is similar to that illustrated in Figure 14-4.

The next thing we do is set the learning rate to a value of 0.2. We tuned this value by trial and error, with the aim of keeping the training time down while maintaining accuracy. Next we call the SetMomentum method to indicate that we want to use momentum during training, and we set the momentum factor to 0.9.

Now that the network is initialized, we can train it by calling the function TrainTheBrain. Example 14-26 shows the TrainTheBrain function.

Example 14-26. TrainTheBrain function

```
void    TrainTheBrain(void)
{
    int        i;
    double     error = 1;
    int        c = 0;

    TheBrain.DumpData("PreTraining.txt");

    while((error > 0.05) && (c<50000))
    {
        error = 0;
        c++;
        for(i=0; i<14; i++)
        {
            TheBrain.SetInput(0, TrainingSet[i][0]);
            TheBrain.SetInput(1, TrainingSet[i][1]);
            TheBrain.SetInput(2, TrainingSet[i][2]);
            TheBrain.SetInput(3, TrainingSet[i][3]);

            TheBrain.SetDesiredOutput(0, TrainingSet[i][4]);
            TheBrain.SetDesiredOutput(1, TrainingSet[i][5]);
            TheBrain.SetDesiredOutput(2, TrainingSet[i][6]);

            TheBrain.FeedForward();
            error += TheBrain.CalculateError();
            TheBrain.BackPropagate();

        }
        error = error / 14.0f;
    }

    TheBrain.DumpData("PostTraining.txt");
}
```

Before we begin training the network, we dump its data to a text file so that we can refer to it during debugging. Next, we enter a while loop that trains the network using the back-propagation algorithm. The while loop is cycled through until the calculated error is less than some specified value, or until the number of iterations reaches a specified maximum threshold. This latter condition is there to prevent the while loop from cycling forever in the event the error threshold is never reached.

Before taking a closer look at what's going on within the while loop, let's look at the training data used to train this network. The global array called TrainingSet is used to store the training data. Example 14-27 shows the training data.

Example 14-27. Training data

```
double TrainingSet[14][7] = {
//#Friends, Hit points, Enemy Engaged, Range, Chase, Flock, Evade
 0,        1,          0,         0.2,   0.9,   0.1,   0.1,
 0,        1,          1,         0.2,   0.9,   0.1,   0.1,
 0,        1,          0,         0.8,   0.1,   0.1,   0.1,
 0.1,      0.5,        0,         0.2,   0.9,   0.1,   0.1,
 0,        0.25,       1,         0.5,   0.1,   0.9,   0.1,
 0,        0.2,        1,         0.2,   0.1,   0.1,   0.9,
 0.3,      0.2,        0,         0.2,   0.9,   0.1,   0.1,
 0,        0.2,        0,         0.3,   0.1,   0.9,   0.1,
 0,        1,          0,         0.2,   0.1,   0.9,   0.1,
 0,        1,          1,         0.6,   0.1,   0.1,   0.1,
 0,        1,          0,         0.8,   0.1,   0.9,   0.1,
 0.1,      0.2,        0,         0.2,   0.1,   0.1,   0.9,
 0,        0.25,       1,         0.5,   0.1,   0.1,   0.9,
 0,        0.6,        0,         0.2,   0.1,   0.1,   0.9
};
```

The training data consists of 14 sets of input and output values. Each set consists of values for the four input nodes representing the number of friends for a unit, its hit points, whether the enemy is engaged already, and the range to the enemy. Each set also contains data for three output nodes corresponding to the behaviors chase, flock, and evade.

Notice that all the data values are within the range from 0.0 to 1.0. All the input data is scaled to the range 0.0 to 1.0, as we discussed earlier, and because the logistic output function is used, each output value will range from 0.0 to 1.0. We'll see how the input data is scaled a little later. As for the output, it's impractical to achieve 0.0 or 1.0 for output, so we use 0.1 to indicate an inactive output and 0.9 to indicate an active output. Also note that these output values represent the desired output for the corresponding set of input data.

We chose the training data rather empirically. Basically, we assumed a few arbitrary input conditions and then specified what a reasonable response would be to that input and set the output values accordingly. In practice you'll probably give this more thought and likely will use more training sets than we did here for this simple example.

Now, let's get back to that `while` loop that handles back-propagation training shown in Example 14-26. Upon entering the `while` loop, the error is initialized to 0. We're going to calculate the error for each epoch, which consists of all 14 sets of input and output values. For each set of data, we set the input neuron values and desired output neuron values and then call the `FeedForward` method for the network. After that, we can calculate the error. To do this we call the `CalculateError` method for the network and accumulate the result in the error variable. We then proceed to adjust the connection weights by calling the `BackPropagate` method. After these steps are complete for an epoch, we calculate the average error for the epoch by dividing the error by 14—the number of data sets in the epoch. At the end of training, the network's data is dumped to a text file for later inspection.

At this point, the neural network is ready to go. You can use it with the trained connection weights, as is. This will save you the trouble of having to code a finite state machine, or the like, to handle all the possible input conditions. A more compelling application of the network is to allow it to learn on the fly. If the units are performing well given the decisions made by the network, we can reinforce that behavior. On the other hand, if the units are performing poorly, we can retrain the network to suppress poor decisions.

Learning

In this section we're going to continue looking at code that implements the neural network, including the ability to learn in-game using the back-propagation algorithm. Take a look at the `UpdateSimulation` function shown in Example 14-28. This is a modified version of the `UpdateSimulation` function we discussed in Chapter 4. For clarity, Example 14-28 shows only the modifications to the function.

Example 14-28. Modified UpdateSimulation function

```
void    UpdateSimulation(void)
{
    .
    .
    .
    int     i;
    Vector  u;
    bool    kill = false;

    .
    .
    .

    // calc number of enemy units currently engaging the target
    Vector d;
    Units[0].NumFriends = 0;
```

```
for(i=1; i<_MAX_NUM_UNITS; i++)
{
    d = Units[i].vPosition - Units[0].vPosition;
    if(d.Magnitude() <= (Units[0].fLength *
                    _CRITICAL_RADIUS_FACTOR))
        Units[0].NumFriends++;
}

// deduct hit points from target
if(Units[0].NumFriends > 0)
{
    Units[0].HitPoints -= 0.2 * Units[0].NumFriends;
    if(Units[0].HitPoints < 0)
    {
        Units[0].vPosition.x = _WINWIDTH/2;
        Units[0].vPosition.y = _WINHEIGHT/2;
        Units[0].HitPoints = _MAXHITPOINTS;
        kill = true;
    }
}

// update computer-controlled units:
for(i=1; i<_MAX_NUM_UNITS; i++)
{
    u = Units[0].vPosition - Units[i].vPosition;
    if(kill)
    {
        if((u.Magnitude() <= (Units[0].fLength *
                        _CRITICAL_RADIUS_FACTOR)))
        {
            ReTrainTheBrain(i, 0.9, 0.1, 0.1);
        }
    }

    // handle enemy hit points, and learning if required
    if(u.Magnitude() <= (Units[0].fLength *
                    _CRITICAL_RADIUS_FACTOR))
    {
        Units[i].HitPoints -= DamageRate;
        if((Units[i].HitPoints < 0))
        {
          Units[i].vPosition.x=GetRandomNumber(_WINWIDTH/2
                            -_SPAWN_AREA_R,
                            _WINWIDTH/2+_SPAWN_AREA_R,
                            false);

            Units[i].vPosition.y=GetRandomNumber(_WINHEIGHT/2
                            -_SPAWN_AREA_R,
                            _WINHEIGHT/2+_SPAWN_AREA_R,
                            false);
            Units[i].HitPoints = _MAXHITPOINTS/2.0;
            ReTrainTheBrain(i, 0.1, 0.1, 0.9);
        }
    } else {
```

```
        Units[i].HitPoints+=0.01;
        if(Units[i].HitPoints > _MAXHITPOINTS)
            Units[i].HitPoints = _MAXHITPOINTS;
    }

    // get a new command
    Units[i].Inputs[0] = Units[i].NumFriends/_MAX_NUM_UNITS;
    Units[i].Inputs[1] = (double) (Units[i].HitPoints/
                              _MAXHITPOINTS);
    Units[i].Inputs[2] = (Units[0].NumFriends>0 ? 1:0);
    Units[i].Inputs[3] = (u.Magnitude()/800.0f);

    TheBrain.SetInput(0, Units[i].Inputs[0]);
    TheBrain.SetInput(1, Units[i].Inputs[1]);
    TheBrain.SetInput(2, Units[i].Inputs[2]);
    TheBrain.SetInput(3, Units[i].Inputs[3]);
    TheBrain.FeedForward();

    Units[i].Command = TheBrain.GetMaxOutputID();
    switch(Units[i].Command)
    {
        case 0:
            Units[i].Chase = true;
            Units[i].Flock = false;
            Units[i].Evade = false;
            Units[i].Wander = false;
            break;

        case 1:
            Units[i].Chase = false;
            Units[i].Flock = true;
            Units[i].Evade = false;
            Units[i].Wander = false;
            break;

        case 2:
            Units[i].Chase = false;
            Units[i].Flock = false;
            Units[i].Evade = true;
            Units[i].Wander = false;
            break;
    }

    DoUnitAI(i);
    .
    .
    .

} // end i-loop

kill = false;
.
.
.
}
```

The first new thing we do in the modified UpdateSimulation function is to calculate the number of computer-controlled units currently engaging the target. In our simple example, a unit is considered to be engaging the target if it is within a specified distance from the target.

Once we determine the number of engaging units, we deduct a number of hit points from the target proportional to the number of engaging units. If the number of target hit points reaches zero, the target is considered killed and it is respawned in the middle of the screen. Also, the kill flag is set to true.

The next step is to handle the computer-controlled units. For this task, we enter a for loop to cycle through all the computer-controlled units. Upon entering the loop, we calculate the distance from the current unit to the target. Next we check to see if the target was killed. If it was, we check to see where the current unit was in relation to the target—that is, whether it was in engagement range. If it was, we retrain the neural network to reinforce the chase behavior. Essentially, if the unit was engaging the target and the target died, we assume the unit is doing something right and we reinforce the chase behavior to make it more aggressive.

Example 14-29 shows the function that handles retraining the network.

Example 14-29. ReTrainTheBrain function

```
void    ReTrainTheBrain(int i, double d0, double d1, double d2)
{
    double    error = 1;
    int       c = 0;

    while((error > 0.1) && (c<5000))
    {
        c++;
        TheBrain.SetInput(0, Units[i].Inputs[0]);
        TheBrain.SetInput(1, Units[i].Inputs[1]);
        TheBrain.SetInput(2, Units[i].Inputs[2]);
        TheBrain.SetInput(3, Units[i].Inputs[3]);
        TheBrain.SetDesiredOutput(0, d0);
        TheBrain.SetDesiredOutput(1, d1);
        TheBrain.SetDesiredOutput(2, d2);
        //TheBrain.SetDesiredOutput(3, d3);

        TheBrain.FeedForward();
        error = TheBrain.CalculateError();
        TheBrain.BackPropagate();
    }
}
```

ReTrainTheBrain simply implements the back-propagation training algorithm again, but this time the stored inputs for the given unit and specified target outputs are used as training data. Note here that you don't want to set the maximum iteration

---

threshold for the while loop too high. If you do, a noticeable pause could occur in the action as the retraining process takes place. Also, if you try to retrain the network to achieve a very small error, it will adapt too rapidly. You can control somewhat the rate at which the network adapts by varying the error and maximum iteration thresholds.

The next step in the UpdateSimulation function is to handle the current unit's hit points. If the current unit is in engagement range of the target, we deduct a prescribed number of hit points from the unit. If the unit's hit points reach zero, we assume it died in combat, in which case we respawn it at some random location. We also assume that the unit was doing something wrong, so we retrain the unit to evade rather than chase.

Now we go ahead and use the neural network to make a decision for the unit—that is, under the current set of conditions, should the unit chase, flock, or evade. To do this we first set the input to the neural network. The first input value is the number of friends for the current unit. We scale the number of friends by dividing the maximum number of units constant into the number of friends for the unit. The second input is the number of hit points for the unit, which is scaled by dividing the maximum number of hit points into the unit's hit point count. The third input is an indication as to whether the target is engaged. This value is set to 1.0 if the target is engaged or 0.0 if it is not engaged. Finally, the fourth input is the range to the target. In this case, the distance from the current unit to the target is scaled by dividing the screen width (assumed to be 800 pixels) into the range.

Once all the inputs are set, the network is propagated by calling the FeedForward method. After this call, the output values of the network can be examined to derive the proper behavior. For this, we select the output with the highest activation, which is determined by making a call to the GetmaxOutputID method. This ID is then used in the switch statement to set the appropriate behavior flag for the unit. If the ID is 0, the unit should chase. If the ID is 1, the unit should flock. If the ID is 2, the unit should evade.

That takes care of the modified UpdateSimulation function. If you run this example program, which is available from this book's Web site (*http://www. oreilly.com/catalog/ai*), you'll see that the computer-controlled unit's behavior does indeed adapt as the simulation runs. You can use the number keys to control how much damage the target inflicts on the units. The 1 key corresponds to little or no damage, while the 8 key corresponds to massive damage. If you let the target die without inflicting damage on the units, you'll see that they soon adapt to attack more often. If you set the target so that it inflicts massive damage, you'll see that the units start adapting to avoid the target more. They also start engaging in groups more often as opposed to engaging as individuals. Eventually, they adapt to avoid the target at all costs. An interesting emergent behavior resulting from this example is that the units tend to form flocks and leaders tend to emerge. Often a flock will form, and the leading units might chase or evade while the intermediate and trailing units follow their lead.

Further Information

As we stated at the beginning of this chapter, the subject of neural networks is far too vast to treat in one chapter. Therefore, we've compiled a short list of pretty good references that you might find useful should you decide to pursue this subject further. The list is as follows:

- *Practical Neural Network Recipes in C++* (Academic Press)
- *Neural Networks for Pattern Recognition* (Oxford University Press)
- *AI Application Programming* (Charles River Media)

Many other books on neural networks also are available; however, the ones we list above proved very useful to us, especially the first one, *Practical Neural Network Recipes in C++*. This book provides a wealth of practical tips and advice on the programming and use of neural networks for a variety of applications.

CHAPTER 15

Genetic Algorithms

It is the game designer's job to create a challenging game environment for the player. In fact, a large part of game development involves balancing the game world. It needs to be challenging enough for the players, or the game will seem too easy and they will lose interest. On the other hand, if it's too difficult, the players will become frustrated. Sometimes players can discover loopholes, or exploits, with which they essentially can cheat. This can be a result of a game design issue that the developers simply overlooked. Another game design problem stems from the fact that the skill levels of different players can vary greatly. Creating a truly balanced and challenging game for players of different skill levels can be a daunting task. Fortunately, genetic algorithms can help.

In this chapter, we are not going to attempt to model a true genetic system. A true genetic model probably wouldn't be practical or beneficial in a real computer game. Instead, the system we are going to discuss is merely inspired by a biological genetic system. In some ways it will be similar, but we won't hesitate to bend the rules if it benefits the game design process.

In the real world, species constantly evolve in an attempt to better adapt to their environments. Those that are most fit continue to survive. Charles Darwin proposed this phenomenon in 1859 in his famous work entitled "On the Origin of Species." Those that are most able to survive in their environments are able to pass on their traits to the next generation. The individual traits are encoded in chromosomes. In the next generation, these chromosomes are combined in a process called *crossover*. Crossover is a recombination of the chromosomes in the offspring. Figure 15-1 illustrates this process.

In Figure 15-1 we used random letters to represent chromosomes. As you can see, each parent passes half of its genetic material on to the child. However, in the real world this crossover process might not be exact. Random mutations also can take place. This is illustrated in Figure 15-2.

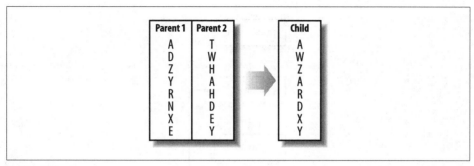

Figure 15-1. Crossover

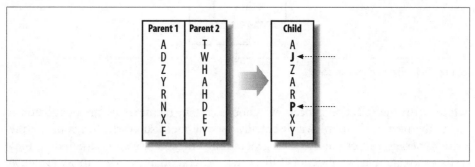

Figure 15-2. Random mutations

Random mutations are nature's way of trying new things. If a random mutation improves the species, it gets passed on to future generations. If not, it doesn't get passed on.

This constant recombination of chromosomes from the most successful members of the previous generation, combined with random mutations, creates future generations that are better adapted to survive and flourish in their environments. You can apply this same concept in games. Just as in the biological world, the elements in a game world can be made to evolve and adapt to changing situations.

Evolutionary Process

You can break down the implementation of genetic algorithms in games into four steps. Figure 15-3 illustrates this four-step process.

As Figure 15-3 shows, the first step involves creating the first generation. The entire population is seeded with a set of starting traits. Once the population starts interacting with its environment, we need a way to rank the individual members. This is the process of ranking fitness. This tells us which members of the population are the most successful. The process of ranking fitness aids us in the next step, which is

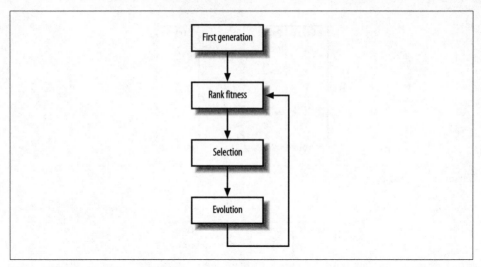

Figure 15-3. Evolutionary process

selection. In the selection process we choose certain members of the population to create the next generation. We essentially use the most successful traits of the previous generation to create the next generation. The actual step of combining these traits to create a new, and hopefully fitter, generation is referred to as *evolution*. Genetic algorithms are essentially optimization processes in which we're trying to find the fittest set of traits—we're looking for the optimum solution to a specific problem.

First Generation

Each individual in the first generation represents a possible solution to the problem at hand. One way to approach the creation of the first generation is to arrange the chromosomes randomly. In a game environment, however, randomly arranging chromosomes might not always be the best solution. If the game designer already knows which combinations of chromosomes are likely to produce a fit individual, a true random combination probably won't be necessary. However, it is still important to create an initial diverse population. If the individuals are too much alike, the genetic process will be less effective.

Encoding is the process of storing the chromosomes in a structure that can be stored in a computer. This, of course, can be any type of structure the programmer chooses to use. Genetic algorithms frequently use strings of bits, but arrays, lists, and trees also commonly are used.

Figure 15-4 shows an example of a first generation of flowers. These hypothetical flowers would include random chromosomes that would affect how well they thrive in their environments.

Figure 15-4. First generation

Ranking Fitness

This step in the evolutionary process involves evaluating each member of the population. This is where we attempt to identify the most successful members of the population, and typically we accomplish this using a *fitness function*. The purpose of the fitness function is to rank the individuals in the population. This tells us which individuals are best at solving the problem at hand.

Figure 15-5 shows how the flowers would be ranked. We assume the flowers that grow the tallest are the fittest.

Figure 15-5. Ranking fitness

Selection

In the selection step we choose the individuals whose traits we want to instill in the next generation. In the selection process typically we call the fitness function to identify the individuals that we use to create the next generation. In the biological world, usually two parents contribute chromosomes to the offspring. Of course, in game development, we are free to use any combination of parents. For example, we are free to combine the traits of the top two, five, 10, or any other number of individuals.

Figure 15-6 shows how we use rankings calculated by the fitness function to determine which individuals to use when creating the next generation. In this case, we selected the two tallest flowers.

Figure 15-6. Flower selection

Evolution

In the final step we create new individuals to place into the game environment. We do this by using individuals from the selection process. We take the individual chromosomes from the fittest members of the population and begin combining their chromosomes. At this point it is also important to introduce random mutations. Once the evolutionary process is complete, we return to the fitness ranking step.

The evolutionary step is where crossover occurs. This is where we combine the chromosomes of the fittest individuals. In this case, we combine the chromosomes of the two tallest flowers to create a new flower. We also introduce two random mutations. This is illustrated in Figure 15-7.

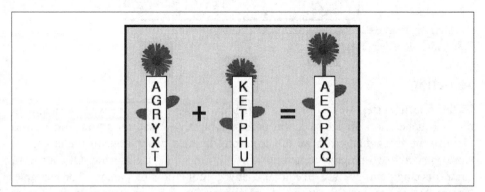

Figure 15-7. Flower evolution

Evolving Plant Life

This first example shows how to apply a genetic algorithm to successive generations of flowers as they attempt to thrive in their environment. We define a series of hypothetical environmental conditions in which the flowers must grow. Each flower then contains genetic information that indicates its ideal growing environment. Flowers whose ideal growing environments most closely match the actual conditions grow the tallest. The tallest flowers will be considered the most fit and have their genetic information passed on to successive generations. This should result in a general increase in flower height as generations progress.

Encoding the Flower Data

We start by defining the six hypothetical environmental conditions, which we consider to be the actual conditions of the flower world. These are shown in Example 15-1.

Example 15-1. Encoding

```
Class ai_World
{
public:

    int currentTemperature;
    int currentWater;
    int currentSunlight;
    int currentNutrient;
    int currentBeneficialInsect;
    int currentHarmfulInsect;

    ai_World();
    ~ai_World();
};
```

As Example 15-1 shows, the six conditions are `currentTemperature`, `currentWater`, `currentSunlight`, `currentNutrient`, `currentBeneficialInsect`, and `currentHarmfulInsect`.

Encoding is the process of storing the chromosomes in a structure that can be stored in a computer. This, of course, can be any type of structure of the programmer's choosing. Example 15-2 shows the structure that we use in the flower evolution example.

Example 15-2. Conditions

```
#define kMaxFlowers   11

Class ai_World
{
```

```
public:

    int temperature[kMaxFlowers];
    int water[kMaxFlowers];
    int sunlight[kMaxFlowers];
    int nutrient[kMaxFlowers];
    int beneficialInsect[kMaxFlowers];
    int harmfulInsect[kMaxFlowers];

    int currentTemperature;
    int currentWater;
    int currentSunlight;
    int currentNutrient;
    int currentBeneficialInsect;
    int currentHarmfulInsect;

    ai_World();
    ~ai_World();
};
```

As Example 15-2 shows, we use six arrays to represent the six environmental conditions. These include temperature, water, sunlight, nutrient, beneficialInsect, and harmfulInsect. Each contains a chromosome that indicates the ideal conditions for each flower.

First Flower Generation

As with all genetic algorithms, first we must populate the world with the initial generation. If we consider the genetic process as searching for the optimum solution to a problem, the first generation consists of a group of our best guesses at a solution. We also need to ensure that we have a diverse set of possible solutions. Example 15-3 shows the creation of the first generation.

Example 15-3. First flower generation

```
void ai_World::Encode(void)

{
  int i;

  for (i=1;i<kMaxFlowers;i++)
    {
      temperature[i]=Rnd(1,75);
      water[i]=Rnd(1,75);
      sunlight[i]=Rnd(1,75);
      nutrient[i]=Rnd(1,75);
      beneficialInsect[i]=Rnd(1,75);
      harmfulInsect[i]=Rnd(1,75);
    }
```

```
currentTemperature=Rnd(1,75);
currentWater=Rnd(1,75);
currentSunlight=Rnd(1,75);
currentNutrient=Rnd(1,75);
currentBeneficialInsect=Rnd(1,75);
currentHarmfulInsect=Rnd(1,75);
```

}

As Example 15-3 shows, we begin by randomly encoding the chromosomes of the flowers. We use six arrays to indicate the ideal growing conditions for each member of the flower population. The arrays include temperature, water, sunlight, nutrient, beneficialInsect, and harmfulInsect. Each array contains a value from 1 to 75. This range was tuned for this example. A number smaller than 75 makes evolution occur more quickly. However, if evolution takes place over just a few generations, there won't be much to observe. Likewise, using a higher number slows the evolution process, requiring more generations before an optimum solution is found.

The flowers grow best when the actual conditions closely match the ideal growing conditions encoded in their chromosomes. We use a for loop to set the values randomly in each array. This will ensure a diverse population of flowers. Once the for loop has executed, we assign the values of the current conditions; these include currentTemperature, currentWater, currentSunlight, currentNutrient, currentBeneficialInsect, and currentHarmfulInsect.

Ranking Flower Fitness

For the purpose of this genetic simulation, we assume the fittest flowers are those that are most capable of flourishing in the current environmental conditions. The chromosomes in each individual flower are encoded with their own ideal growing conditions. We essentially measure how close each flower's ideal conditions are to the actual conditions. Those that are closest grow the tallest. This is shown in Figure 15-8.

Figure 15-8 shows the initial deviation among the flower population. Those that are best suited to grow in the current conditions are the tallest. As the figure shows, some are noticeably better at flourishing in their environment. Next we look at how we actually determine the fittest members of the population. This is shown in Example 15-4.

Example 15-4. Flower fitness function

```
int ai_World::Fitness(int flower)

{
    int theFitness=0;
```

Figure 15-8. Initial flower population

```
theFitness = fabs(temperature[flower] - currentTemperature);
theFitness = theFitness+fabs(water[flower] - currentWater);
theFitness = theFitness+fabs(sunlight[flower] -
                            currentSunlight);
theFitness = theFitness+fabs(nutrient[flower] -
                            currentNutrient);
theFitness = theFitness+fabs(beneficialInsect[flower] -
                            currentBeneficialInsect);
theFitness = theFitness+fabs(harmfulInsect[flower] -
                            currentHarmfulInsect);

return (theFitness);
}
```

As Example 15-4 shows, we use the Fitness function to calculate the total deviation between the current environmental conditions and the ideal conditions needed for each individual flower to flourish. We begin by initializing the variable theFitness to 0. We then increase the value in theFitness by the absolute value of the difference between each flower's ideal condition and the current condition. This gives us a sum of the total deviation of all the growing conditions.

Evolving the Flowers

The ultimate goal of any genetic algorithm is to produce offspring that are more fit than their parents. Our first step was to create the initial population and then determine the fitness of each individual. The fitness ranking process enabled us to select the best members of the population. The final step is the actual creation of the new generation using the traits of the most successful members of the previous generation. Besides crossing over the traits of the fittest flowers, we also introduce random mutations. The Evolve function in Example 15-5 shows both the crossover step and the introduction of random mutations.

Example 15-5. Flower evolution

```
void ai_World::Evolve(void)

{
    int fitTemperature[kMaxFlowers];
    int fitWater[kMaxFlowers];
    int fitSunlight[kMaxFlowers];
    int fitNutrient[kMaxFlowers];
    int fitBeneficialInsect[kMaxFlowers];
    int fitHarmfulInsect[kMaxFlowers];
    int fitness[kMaxFlowers];
    int i;
    int leastFit=0;
    int leastFitIndex;

    for (i=1;i<kMaxFlowers;i++)
        if (Fitness(i)>leastFit)
            {
                leastFit=Fitness(i);
                leastFitIndex=i;
            }

    temperature[leastFitIndex]=temperature[Rnd(1,10)];
    water[leastFitIndex]=water[Rnd(1,10)];
    sunlight[leastFitIndex]=sunlight[Rnd(1,10)];
    nutrient[leastFitIndex]=nutrient[Rnd(1,10)];
    beneficialInsect[leastFitIndex]=beneficialInsect[Rnd(1,10)];
    harmfulInsect[leastFitIndex]=harmfulInsect[Rnd(1,10)];

    for (i=1;i<kMaxFlowers;i++)
        {
            fitTemperature[i]=temperature[Rnd(1,10)];
            fitWater[i]=water[Rnd(1,10)];
            fitSunlight[i]=sunlight[Rnd(1,10)];
            fitNutrient[i]=nutrient[Rnd(1,10)];
            fitBeneficialInsect[i]=beneficialInsect[Rnd(1,10)];
            fitHarmfulInsect[i]=harmfulInsect[Rnd(1,10)];
        }
```

```
for (i=1;i<kMaxFlowers;i++)
    {
        temperature[i]=fitTemperature[i];
        water[i]=fitWater[i];
        sunlight[i]=fitSunlight[i];
        nutrient[i]=fitNutrient[i];
        beneficialInsect[i]=fitBeneficialInsect[i];
        harmfulInsect[i]=fitHarmfulInsect[i];
    }

for (i=1;i<kMaxFlowers;i++)
    {
        if (tb_Rnd(1,100)==1)
            temperature[i]=Rnd(1,75);
        if (tb_Rnd(1,100)==1)
            water[i]=Rnd(1,75);
        if (tb_Rnd(1,100)==1)
            sunlight[i]=Rnd(1,75);
        if (tb_Rnd(1,100)==1)
            nutrient[i]=Rnd(1,75);
        if (tb_Rnd(1,100)==1)
            beneficialInsect[i]=Rnd(1,75);
        if (tb_Rnd(1,100)==1)
            harmfulInsect[i]=Rnd(1,75);
    }

}
```

You can implement a crossover function in many ways. Game developers are not burdened by the limits of the biological world. In the biological world the crossover would involve the chromosomes to two fit parents. In game development, crossover can involve any number of parents. In the case of this flower evolution example, we are going to identify the least fit member of the population. The first for loop calls the Fitness function to identify the least fit member of the population. We then reassign the traits of the least fit flower to those of random members of the flower population. The next two for loop blocks randomly mix up the traits of the flower population. Essentially we already reassigned the traits of the least fit flower, so at this point the flower population as a whole should be an improvement over the previous generation. Unfortunately, no individual trait can be any better than it was in the previous generation because the same traits were passed on. We now need a way to try to surpass the previous generation. We accomplish this through random mutations. In the last for loop block, each trait of each flower has a 1% chance of randomly mutating. If the mutation is a success, the trait probably will be passed on to the next generation. If the mutation results in a flower being the least fit member of the population, it will be dropped. Figure 15-9 shows the end result of multiple generations.

As Figure 15-9 shows, all the flowers are at or near their maximum heights. The area beneath the flowers also graphs the fitness of each generation. As the graph

Figure 15-9. Resulting flower population

shows, there is a general upward trend in the fitness of each generation. However, not every generation was an improvement over the one before it. The graph does show some downturns. This is due to the random mutations introduced into the population. However, as the graph shows, the genetic process eventually will find the best solution to the problem.

Genetics in Game Development

In games, genetic algorithms are simply a method of finding an optimum solution to a problem. Of course, there are lots of problems to be solved in game AI, and not all of them are good candidates for a genetic algorithm. Pathfinding, for example, can be solved with a genetic algorithm, however it's usually a problem better suited to something such as the A* algorithm. Genetic algorithms work best when the elements of the problem are somewhat unpredictable. This allows the game AI to adapt to a situation the game designer might not have been able to predict. In game design, the most unpredictable element of the game environment is the player. To some degree, the game designer must be able to predict the player's behavior to create a challenging adversary. Unfortunately, it can be difficult to predict and account for every possible player behavior.

Genetic algorithms basically involve a trial-and-error approach. You essentially populate the game world with many possible solutions and then determine which solutions work the best. Of course, the solutions won't always be the same for every player. That's the beauty of genetic algorithms. The game AI will adapt to individual players.

Role-Playing Example

Genetic algorithms are useful in any scenario in which a computer-controlled adversary must respond and change due to player behavior. For example, consider a hypothetical multiplayer role-playing game. In this game the players would be able to choose from many different types of character classes and abilities. This means the computer-controlled characters would have to be able to present a challenge to many types of player-controlled characters. A player could choose to play a warrior character that would fight mainly with brute force. Of course, with this class the player would be able to choose from a multitude of weapons. The player could attack with a sword, axe, or any number of other weapons. The fighter class also would be able to wear an assortment of armor. On the other hand, the player might choose a totally different class. A magical class would produce a totally different player behavior. The various combinations of class and weapon types would make it difficult for a game designer to create a single type of computer-controlled individual that would be a challenge to every type of player-controlled character. It could be even more complicated in a multiplayer game. In this type of game the computer will have to be a challenge to a group of diverse players working in combination. The number of possible combinations quickly would become more than a game designer could account for.

Encoding the Data

We are searching for a type of computer-controlled character that will be a challenge to a player or group of players. This isn't a search that you can precalculate. Each player or group of players would behave differently. We need to determine the situations and responses that will either increase or decrease the level of fitness in the population. For example, one possible situation could be when the player attacks a computer-controlled character with a magic weapon. We can create several possible responses to this player action. The computer-controlled character could attack the player in response, attempt to flee, or attempt to hide. We could assign this situation and response to a chromosome. If this chromosome is set to create an attack response in this situation, the player will be attacked when using a magic weapon. However, what if this scenario always leads to the defeat of the computer-controlled character? In that case, the computer-controlled character would be deemed less fit, and therefore, less likely to pass on that trait. In successive generations this scenario would lead to a different behavior, such as a retreat whenever the player wields a magic weapon. Example 15-6 lists some of the possible scenarios we address in our hypothetical example.

Example 15-6. Possible scenarios

```
#define kAttackedbyFighter              0
#define kAttackedbyWizard               1
#define kAttackedbyGroup                2
#define kHealerPresent                  3
#define kAttackedByBlade                4
#define kAttackedByBlunt                5
#define kAttackedByProjectile           6
#define kAttackedByMagic                7
#define kAttackerWearingMetalArmor      8
#define kAttackerWearingLeatherArmor    9
#define kAttackerWearingMagicArmor      10
#define kImInGroup                      11
```

Figure 15-5 shows the possible situations in which members of the population will behave differently. We use a different chromosome to store the response to each situation. We begin with the kAttackedbyFighter constant. This chromosome will store the response whenever the computer-controlled character is attacked by a player-controlled fighter character. Some creature types might be more or less effective when doing battle against fighter characters. Similarly, the kAttackedbyWizard chromosome will store the response to being attacked by a player-controlled wizard character. The kAttackedbyGroup chromosome will indicate the behavioral response to being attacked by a group of player characters. The kHealerPresent chromosome indicates which behavior should be used when a player healer is present. If the players can be healed repeatedly, it might be a futile situation in which retreat would be most appropriate.

The next four chromosomes, kAttackedByBlade, kAttackedByBlunt, kAttackedByProjectile, and kAttackedByMagic, determine which response to give for each type of weapon the player can wield. The next three, kAttackerWearingMetalArmor, kAttackerWearing-LeatherArmor, and kAttackerWearingMagicArmor, determine the best response to the various types of protective armor the player can wear. Some computer-controlled characters can choose from a selection of weapons. For example, a blade weapon might be more effective against leather armor. The final chromosome, kImInGroup, is used to determine the best response when the computer-controlled character is fighting in a group. Some types of creatures, such as wolves, can be more effective when fighting in a pack.

A real game probably would have a much more thorough list of possible scenarios, but for this example our list should suffice. Example 15-7 shows the possible responses to each scenario.

Example 15-7. Possible behaviors

```
#define kRetreat            0
#define kHide               1
#define kWearMetalArmor     2
#define kWearMagicArmor     3
#define kWearLeatherArmor   4
#define kAttackWithBlade    5
#define kAttackWithBlunt    6
#define kAttackWithMagic    7
```

Each constant shown in Example 15-7 defines a possible character behavior; they each assign a behavior to one scenario shown in Example 15-6, and we start with the kRetreat constant. As the name implies, this behavior causes the computer-controlled character to run from player characters. The second constant, kHide, makes the computer-controlled character enter a state in which it will attempt to elude detection. The next three constants, kWearMetalArmor, kWearMagicArmor, and kWearLeatherArmor, make the computer-controlled character switch to each respective type of armor. The final three constants, kAttackWithBlade, kAttackWithBlunt, and kAttackWithMagic, define the type of attack the computer-controlled character should use against the player.

Now we create an array that contains a behavioral response for each possible scenario shown in Example 15-6. We will use one array element for each possible scenario. We accomplish this with a simple C++ class structure, as shown in Example 15-8.

Example 15-8. Encoding structure

```
#define kChromosomes   12

Class ai_Creature
{
    public:

    int chromosomes[kChromosomes];

    ai_ Creature ();
    ~ai_ Creature ();
};
```

As Example 15-8 shows, we create an ai_Creature class that contains an array of chromosomes. Each element of the array represents a trait, or behavior, for the computer-controlled character. We define each possible behavior and then we link each chromosome to each behavior. We use an array size of 12 because Example 15-6 shows 12 possible situations.

The First Generation

So far we have defined the possible scenarios that we use for the genetic tests, defined the possible behaviors associated with each scenario, and created a structure to store the genetic data. The next step is to create the population. We start by expanding on the code shown in Example 15-8. Example 15-9 shows the modifications.

Example 15-9. Defining the population

```
#define kChromosomes      12
#define kPopulationSize   100

Class ai_Creature
{
public:

    int chromosomes[kChromosomes];

    ai_ Creature ();
    ~ai_ Creature ();
};

ai_Creature   population[kPopulationSize];
```

As Example 15-9 shows, we added the constant kPopulationSize to define the size of the creature population. We also added an array of ai_Creature whose bounds are set to the values assigned to kPopulationSize. The next step is to begin linking individual behaviors to each possible situation shown in Example 15-6. We start by adding a new function to the ai_Creature class. Example 15-10 shows the modified ai_Creature class.

Example 15-10. Defining createIndividual

```
#define kChromosomes      12
#define kPopulationSize   100

Class ai_Creature
{
public:

    int chromosomes[kChromosomes];

    void createIndividual (int i);

    ai_ Creature ();
    ~ai_ Creature ();

};

ai_Creature   population[kPopulationSize];
```

The new function, ai_createIndividual, initializes a new member of the population. However, we don't want to initialize each individual using a set of predefined constants. We want the population to be as diverse as possible. A population that isn't diverse won't be as effective at finding the best solution. The best way to create a diverse population is to assign the behaviors in a random fashion. However, we can't simply randomly assign the behaviors shown in Example 15-7 to the situations shown in Example 15-6. Some of the behaviors don't apply to the listed situations. We solve this problem by using a block of conditional statements, as shown in Example 15-11.

Example 15-11. Randomly assigning chromosomes

```
void ai_ Creature::createIndividual(int i)

{

    switch (Rnd(1,5)) {
        case 1:
            ai_Creature[i].chromosomes[kAttackedbyGroup]=kRetreat;
         break;

        case 2:
            ai_Creature[i].chromosomes[kAttackedbyGroup]=kHide;
        break;

        case 3:
            ai_Creature[i].chromosomes[kAttackedbyGroup]=
                                            kAttackWithBlade;
        break;

        case 4:
            ai_Creature[i].chromosomes[kAttackedbyGroup]=
                                            kAttackWithBlunt;
        break;

        case 5:
          ai_Creature[i].chromosomes[kAttackedbyGroup]=
                                            kAttackWithMagic;
        break;
        }
    switch (Rnd(1,5)) {
        case 1:
            ai_Creature[i].chromosomes[kHealerPresent]=kRetreat;
        break;

        case 2:
            ai_Creature[i].chromosomes[kHealerPresent]=kHide;
        break;

        case 3:
            ai_Creature[i].chromosomes[kHealerPresent]=
                                            kAttackWithBlade;
        break;
```

```
case 4:
  ai_Creature[i].chromosomes[kHealerPresent]=
                                 kAttackWithBlunt;
break;

case 5:
  ai_Creature[i].chromosomes[kHealerPresent]=
                                 kAttackWithMagic;
break;
}
```

The first case statement assigns a random behavior to the kAttackedbyGroup chromosome. For this chromosome we choose from five possible behaviors (kRetreat, kHide, kAttackWithBlade, kAttackWithBlunt, and kAttackWithMagic). The idea is to try to determine if any of these actions provide a noticeable advantage or disadvantage when a group of player characters attacks the computer-controlled character. For example, the process of evolution might show that retreating is the best course of action when attacked by a group of players.

The second case statement sets the value in the kHealerPresent chromosome. Again, we want to determine if creating a diverse population, in which the response to this situation varies among the members, will give some individuals an advantage or disadvantage. As in the case of the kAttackedbyGroup chromosome, we use the following five responses: kRetreat, kHide, kAttackWithBlade, kAttackWithBlunt, and kAttackWithMagic.

Now we consider the possible behaviors to link to the various types of attacks the player could use. Again, we randomly assign appropriate behaviors to each possible attack method. This is shown in Example 15-12.

Example 15-12. Attack responses

```
switch (Rnd(1,5)) {
    case 1:
      ai_Creature[i].chromosomes[kAttackedByBlade]=kRetreat;
    break;

    case 2:
      ai_Creature[i].chromosomes[kAttackedByBlade]=kHide;
    break;

    case 3:
      ai_Creature[i].chromosomes[kAttackedByBlade]=
                                      kWearMetalArmor;
    break;

    case 4:
      ai_Creature[i].chromosomes[kAttackedByBlade]=
                                      kWearMagicArmor;
    break;
```

```
      case 5:
        ai_Creature[i].chromosomes[kAttackedByBlade]=
                                      kWearLeatherArmor;
      break;
    }

    switch (Rnd(1,5)) {
      case 1:
        ai_Creature[i].chromosomes[kAttackedByBlunt]=kRetreat;
      break;

      case 2:
        ai_Creature[i].chromosomes[kAttackedByBlunt]=kHide;
      break;

      case 3:
        ai_Creature[i].chromosomes[kAttackedByBlunt]=
                                      kWearMetalArmor;
      break;

      case 4:
        ai_Creature[i].chromosomes[kAttackedByBlunt]=
                                      kWearMagicArmor;
      break;

      case 5:
        ai_Creature[i].chromosomes[kAttackedByBlunt]=
                                      kWearLeatherArmor;
      break;
    }

    switch (Rnd(1,5)) {
      case 1:
        ai_Creature[i].chromosomes[kAttackedByProjectile]=
                                      kRetreat;
      break;

      case 2:
        ai_Creature[i].chromosomes[kAttackedByProjectile]=kHide;
      break;

      case 3:
        ai_Creature[i].chromosomes[kAttackedByProjectile]=
                                      kWearMetalArmor;
      break;

      case 4:
        ai_Creature[i].chromosomes[kAttackedByProjectile]=
                                      kWearMagicArmor;
      break;

      case 5:
        ai_Creature[i].chromosomes[kAttackedByProjectile]=
                                      kWearLeatherArmor;
```

```
        break;
    }

switch (Rnd(1,5)) {
    case 1:
      ai_Creature[i].chromosomes[kAttackedByMagic]=kRetreat;
    break;

    case 2:
      ai_Creature[i].chromosomes[kAttackedByMagic]=kHide;
    break;

    case 3:
      ai_Creature[i].chromosomes[kAttackedByMagic]=
                                    kWearMetalArmor;
    break;

    case 4:
      ai_Creature[i].chromosomes[kAttackedByMagic]=
                                    kWearMagicArmor;
    break;

    case 5:
      ai_Creature[i].chromosomes[kAttackedByMagic]=
                                    kWearLeatherArmor;
    break;
}
```

As Example 15-12 shows, we consider four possible attack methods by the player (kAttackedByBlade, kAttackedByBlunt, kAttackedByProjectile, and kAttackedByMagic). Each possible attack is linked to its own chromosome and is assigned in a separate case statement. Each will be randomly assigned one of five possible responses: kRetreat, kHide, kWearMetalArmor, kWearMagicArmor, and kWearLeatherArmor.

These chromosomes will help us determine which types of armor are better suited for each possible player attack. They also will tell us if retreating or hiding is the best response to some attacks. For example, if members of the population are repeatedly defeated when attacked by magic, retreat might end up being the best response.

Now we consider the possible effects resulting from the various types of armor the player might be wearing. We follow a similar case statement structure, as shown in Example 15-13.

Example 15-13. Armor responses

```
switch (Rnd(1,5)) {
    case 1:
      ai_Creature[i].chromosomes[kAttackerWearingMetalArmor]=
                                            kRetreat;
    break;
```

```
          case 2:
            ai_Creature[i].chromosomes[kAttackerWearingMetalArmor]=
                                            kHide;
        break;

          case 3:
            ai_Creature[i].chromosomes[kAttackerWearingMetalArmor]=
                                            kAttackWithBlade;
        break;

          case 4:
            ai_Creature[i].chromosomes[kAttackerWearingMetalArmor]=
                                            kAttackWithBlunt;
        break;

          case 5:
            ai_Creature[i].chromosomes[kAttackerWearingMetalArmor]=
                                            kAttackWithMagic;
        break;
    }

    switch (Rnd(1,5)) {
        case 1:
            ai_Creature[i].chromosomes[kAttackerWearingLeatherArmor]=
                                            kRetreat;
        break;

          case 2:
            ai_Creature[i].chromosomes[kAttackerWearingLeatherArmor]=
                                            kHide;
        break;

        case 3:
            ai_Creature[i].chromosomes[kAttackerWearingLeatherArmor]=
                                            kAttackWithBlade;
        break;

          case 4:
            ai_Creature[i].chromosomes[kAttackerWearingLeatherArmor]=
                                            kAttackWithBlunt;
        break;

          case 5:
            ai_Creature[i].chromosomes[kAttackerWearingLeatherArmor]=
                                            kAttackWithMagic;
        break;
    }

    switch (Rnd(1,5)) {
        case 1:
            ai_Creature[i].chromosomes[kAttackerWearingMagicArmor]=
                                            kRetreat;
        break;
```

```
   case 2:
      ai_Creature[i].chromosomes[kAttackerWearingMagicArmor]=
                                    kHide;
   break;

   case 3:
      ai_Creature[i].chromosomes[kAttackerWearingMagicArmor]=
                                    kAttackWithBlade;
   break;

   case 4:
      ai_Creature[i].chromosomes[kAttackerWearingMagicArmor]=
                                    kAttackWithBlunt;
   break;

   case 5:
      ai_Creature[i].chromosomes[kAttackerWearingMagicArmor]=
                                    kAttackWithMagic;
   break;
   }
}
```

Example 15-13 uses three case statements to assign responses randomly to the various types of armor the player can wear. Hopefully, this will help us determine the best type of attack to use against the various types of armor. The type of armor we consider includes kAttackerWearingMetalArmor, kAttackerWearingLeatherArmor, and kAttackerWearingMagicArmor. Each will be randomly assigned one of five possible responses, including kRetreat, kHide, kAttackWithBlade, kAttackWithBlunt, and kAttackWithMagic.

Ranking Fitness

At some point we need to try to determine which members of the population are the fittest. Remember, we are searching for members of the population that are the greatest challenge to the players. We need some way to quantify and measure the level of challenge. We can consider several different approaches. Role-playing games typically assign hit points to each character. These hit points are reduced as the character is injured during battle. The character dies once the hit points reach zero. So, one way to quantify the level of challenge is to keep a cumulative total of the amount of hit-point damage done to the players. Each member of the population would track its total damage inflicted. Conversely, we also could track the amount of damage done by the players to the members of the population. Example 15-14 shows how we would expand the ai_Creature class to include variables to track the damage done and damage received.

Example 15-14. Tracking hit-point damage

```
#define kChromosomes      12
#define kPopulationSize   100
```

```
Class ai_Creature
{
public:

    int chromosomes[kChromosomes];
    float totalDamageDone;
    float totalDamageReceived;

    void createIndividual (int i);

    ai_ Creature ();
    ~ai_ Creature ();
};

ai_Creature   population[kPopulationSize];
```

As Example 15-14 shows, we added two new variables to the ai_CreatureClass. The first, totalDamageDone, will be increased each time the computer-controlled character inflicts damage to a player; it will be increased by the amount of the hit-point damage done. Conversely, the totalDamageReceived variable would be increased whenever the player injured the computer-controlled character. As in the case of totalDamageDone, the amount of the increase would be equal to the hit-point damage done.

Of course, you should consider other game elements when determining the fitness of the individuals in the population. For example, the total player kills would be another good indicator.

Selection

The next step in the evolutionary process is to search for the fittest members of the population. These individuals will exhibit traits we want to pass on to the next generation. Once again we expand on the ai_Creature class. We calculate the ratio of damage done to damage received. We keep a running total of damage done and damage received in the totalDamageDone and totalDamageReceived variables. The fitness variable will contain the ratio of damage done to damage received. Example 15-15 shows the updated class.

Example 15-15. Adding fitness tracking

```
#define kChromosomes      12
#define kPopulationSize   100

Class ai_Creature
{
public:

    int chromosomes[kChromosomes];
    float totalDamageDone;
```

```
    float totalDamageReceived;
    float fitness;

    void createIndividual (int i);
    void sortFitness (void);

    ai_ Creature ();
    ~ai_ Creature ();
};

ai_Creature   population[kPopulationSize];
```

As Example 15-15 shows, now we have a variable to quantify the actual fitness of each individual. We use the fitness variable to calculate the fitness of each individual and then sort the population from most successful to least successful. We also added the sortFitness function to the ai_Creature class. This calculation and sorting are shown in Example 15-16.

Example 15-16. Sorting fitness

```
void ai_ Creature:: sortFitness (void)

{
int   i
int   j;
int   k;
float temp;

for (i=0;i<kPopulationSize;i++)
   ai_Creature[i].fitness = ai_Creature[i].totalDamageDone /
                            ai_Creature[i].totalDamageReceived;

for (i = (kPopulationSize - 1); i >= 0; i-)
   {
     for (j = 1; j <= i; j++)
        {
          if (ai_Creature[j-1].fitness < ai_Creature[j].fitness)
             {
               temp = ai_Creature[j-1].fitness;
               ai_Creature[j-1].fitness=ai_Creature[j].fitness;
               ai_Creature[j].fitness = temp;

               temp = ai_Creature[j-1].totalDamageDone;
               ai_Creature[j-1].totalDamageDone =
                            ai_Creature[j].totalDamageDone;
               ai_Creature[j].totalDamageDone = temp;

               temp = ai_Creature[j-1].totalDamageReceived;
               ai_Creature[j-1].totalDamageReceived =
                          ai_Creature[j].totalDamageReceived;
               ai_Creature[j].totalDamageReceived = temp;
```

```
        for (k=0;k<kChromosomes;k++)
          {
            temp = ai_Creature[j-1].chromosomes[k];
            ai_Creature[j-1].chromosomes[k] =
                    ai_Creature[j].chromosomes[k];
            ai_Creature[j].chromosomes[k] = temp;
          }
      }
    }
  }
```

The sortFitness function begins by calculating the damage done to damage received ratio for each individual in the population. This is accomplished in the first for loop. The actual ratio is stored in the fitness variable. Once we have calculated the fitness ratio for each individual, we can sort the entire population array. The sort is handled by the nested for loops. This is just a standard bubble sort algorithm. The end result is that we sort the entire population array by the fitness variable, from most fit to least fit.

Evolution

Now we have an easy way to identify the most successful individuals in the population. Calling the sortFitness function will ensure that the lower positions in the ai_Creature array will be the fittest individuals. We then can use the traits of the individuals in the lower array elements to create the next generation. Figure 15-10 shows how the chromosomes in each array will be combined to create a new individual.

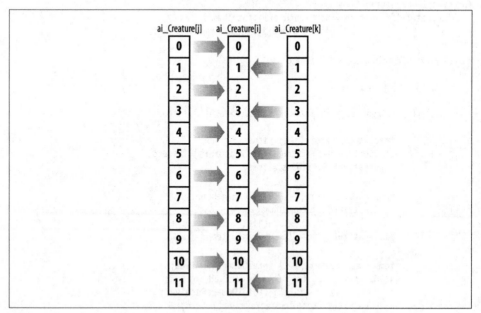

Figure 15-10. Crossover

As Figure 15-10 shows, we use the crossover process when creating the new individual. Now we update the ai_Creature class to include a new crossover function. Example 15-17 shows the updated ai_Creature class.

Example 15-17. Adding the crossover function

```
#define kChromosomes     12
#define kPopulationSize  100

Class ai_Creature
{
public:

    int chromosomes[kChromosomes];
    float totalDamageDone;
    float totalDamageReceived;
    float fitness;

    void createIndividual (int i);
    void sortFitness (void);
    void crossover(int i, int j, int k);

    ai_ Creature ();
    ~ai_ Creature ();
};

ai_Creature   population[kPopulationSize];
```

The new crossover function will take the traits of two individuals and combine them to create a third. Example 15-18 shows this function.

Example 15-18. Crossover

```
void ai_ Creature:: crossover (int i, int j, int k)

    {
        ai_Creature[i].chromosomes[0]=ai_Creature[j].chromosomes[0];
        ai_Creature[i].chromosomes[1]=ai_Creature[k].chromosomes[1];
        ai_Creature[i].chromosomes[2]=ai_Creature[j].chromosomes[2];
        ai_Creature[i].chromosomes[3]=ai_Creature[k].chromosomes[3];
        ai_Creature[i].chromosomes[4]=ai_Creature[j].chromosomes[4];
        ai_Creature[i].chromosomes[5]=ai_Creature[k].chromosomes[5];
        ai_Creature[i].chromosomes[6]=ai_Creature[j].chromosomes[6];
        ai_Creature[i].chromosomes[7]=ai_Creature[k].chromosomes[7];
        ai_Creature[i].chromosomes[8]=ai_Creature[j].chromosomes[8];
        ai_Creature[i].chromosomes[9]=ai_Creature[k].chromosomes[9];
        ai_Creature[i].chromosomes[10]=ai_Creature[j].chromosomes[10];
        ai_Creature[i].chromosomes[11]=ai_Creature[k].chromosomes[11];
        ai_Creature[i].totalDamageDone=0;
        ai_Creature[i].totalDamageReceived=0;
        ai_Creature[i].fitness=0;
    }
```

As Example 15-18 shows, three variables are passed into the crossover function. There are three array indexes. The first two are the parents whose chromosomes will be combined to create a new individual. The third variable is the array index of the new individual. On each line we alternate between the j and k array indexes. This essentially mixes the chromosome of the parents when creating the offspring.

Although mixing the chromosomes of two fit parents should create a new fit individual, we also want to try to improve on the previous generation. We do this by introducing random mutations. We start by updating the ai_Creature class to include a random mutation function. This is shown in Example 15-19.

Example 15-19. Adding the random mutation function

```
#define kChromosomes      12
#define kPopulationSize   100

Class ai_Creature
{
public:

    int chromosomes[kChromosomes];
    float totalDamageDone;
    float totalDamageReceived;
    float fitness;

    void createIndividual (int i);
    void sortFitness (void);
    void crossover(int i, int j, int k);
    void randomMutation(int i);

    ai_ Creature ();
    ~ai_ Creature ();
};

ai_Creature   population[kPopulationSize];
```

As the updated ai_Creature class in Example 15-19 shows, now we need to add a random mutation function. A random mutation enables us to build a fit individual with what is essentially a guess at what might make it a little bit better. Example 15-20 shows the random mutation function.

Example 15-20. Random mutations

```
void ai_ Creature::randomMutation(int i)

{
  if (Rnd(1,20)==1)
    switch (Rnd(1,5)) {
        case 1:
           ai_Creature[i].chromosomes[kAttackedbyGroup]=kRetreat;
        break;
```

```
        case 2:
          ai_Creature[i].chromosomes[kAttackedbyGroup]=kHide;
        break;

        case 3:
          ai_Creature[i].chromosomes[kAttackedbyGroup]=
                                          kAttackWithBlade;
        break;

        case 4:
          ai_Creature[i].chromosomes[kAttackedbyGroup]=
                                          kAttackWithBlunt;
        break;

        case 5:
          ai_Creature[i].chromosomes[kAttackedbyGroup]=
                                          kAttackWithMagic;
        break;
        }

  if (Rnd(1,20)==1)
     switch (Rnd(1,5)) {
        case 1:
          ai_Creature[i].chromosomes[kHealerPresent]=kRetreat;
        break;

        case 2:
          ai_Creature[i].chromosomes[kHealerPresent]=kHide;
        break;

        case 3:
          ai_Creature[i].chromosomes[kHealerPresent]=
                                             kAttackWithBlade;
        break;

        case 4:
          ai_Creature[i].chromosomes[kHealerPresent]=
                                             kAttackWithBlunt;
        break;

        case 5:
          ai_Creature[i].chromosomes[kHealerPresent]=
                                             kAttackWithMagic;
        break;
        }

  if (Rnd(1,20)==1)
     switch (Rnd(1,5)) {
        case 1:
          ai_Creature[i].chromosomes[kAttackedByBlade]=kRetreat;
        break;

        case 2:
          ai_Creature[i].chromosomes[kAttackedByBlade]=kHide;
        break;
```

```
        case 3:
          ai_Creature[i].chromosomes[kAttackedByBlade]=
                                        kWearMetalArmor;
      break;

        case 4:
          ai_Creature[i].chromosomes[kAttackedByBlade]=
                                        kWearMagicArmor;
      break;

        case 5:
          ai_Creature[i].chromosomes[kAttackedByBlade]=
                                        kWearLeatherArmor;
      break;
    }

  if (Rnd(1,20)==1)
    switch (Rnd(1,5)) {
        case 1:
          ai_Creature[i].chromosomes[kAttackedByBlunt]=kRetreat;
      break;

        case 2:
          ai_Creature[i].chromosomes[kAttackedByBlunt]=kHide;
      break;

        case 3:
          ai_Creature[i].chromosomes[kAttackedByBlunt]=
                                        kWearMetalArmor;
      break;

        case 4:
          ai_Creature[i].chromosomes[kAttackedByBlunt]=
                                        kWearMagicArmor;
      break;

        case 5:
          ai_Creature[i].chromosomes[kAttackedByBlunt]=
                                        kWearLeatherArmor;
      break;
    }

  if (Rnd(1,20)==1)
    switch (Rnd(1,5)) {
        case 1:
          ai_Creature[i].chromosomes[kAttackedByProjectile]=
                                        kRetreat;
      break;

        case 2:
          ai_Creature[i].chromosomes[kAttackedByProjectile]=
                                        kHide;
      break;
```

```
        case 3:
          ai_Creature[i].chromosomes[kAttackedByProjectile]=
                                        kWearMetalArmor;

        break;

        case 4:
          ai_Creature[i].chromosomes[kAttackedByProjectile]=
                                        kWearMagicArmor;

        break;

        case 5:
          ai_Creature[i].chromosomes[kAttackedByProjectile]=
                                        kWearLeatherArmor;

        break;
    }

  if (Rnd(1,20)==1)
    switch (Rnd(1,5)) {
        case 1:
          ai_Creature[i].chromosomes[kAttackedByMagic]=
                                              kRetreat;

        break;

        case 2:
          ai_Creature[i].chromosomes[kAttackedByMagic]=kHide;
        break;

        case 3:
          ai_Creature[i].chromosomes[kAttackedByMagic]=
                                        kWearMetalArmor;

        break;

        case 4:
          ai_Creature[i].chromosomes[kAttackedByMagic]=
                                        kWearMagicArmor;

        break;

        case 5:
          ai_Creature[i].chromosomes[kAttackedByMagic]=
                                        kWearLeatherArmor;

        break;
    }

  if (Rnd(1,20)==1)
    switch (Rnd(1,5)) {
        case 1:
          ai_Creature[i].chromosomes[kAttackerWearingMetalArmor]=
                                              kRetreat;

        break;

        case 2:
          ai_Creature[i].chromosomes[kAttackerWearingMetalArmor]=
                                              kHide;

        break;
```

```
                case 3:
                    ai_Creature[i].chromosomes[kAttackerWearingMetalArmor]=
                                                    kAttackWithBlade;
            break;

                case 4:
                    ai_Creature[i].chromosomes[kAttackerWearingMetalArmor]=
                                                    kAttackWithBlunt;
            break;

                case 5:
                    ai_Creature[i].chromosomes[kAttackerWearingMetalArmor]=
                                                    kAttackWithMagic;
            break;
        }

    if (Rnd(1,20)==1)
        switch (Rnd(1,5)) {
                case 1:
                    ai_Creature[i].chromosomes[kAttackerWearingLeatherArmor]=
                                                    kRetreat;
            break;

                case 2:
                    ai_Creature[i].chromosomes[kAttackerWearingLeatherArmor]=
                                                        kHide;
            break;

                case 3:
                    ai_Creature[i].chromosomes[kAttackerWearingLeatherArmor]=
                                                    kAttackWithBlade;
            break;

                case 4:
                    ai_Creature[i].chromosomes[kAttackerWearingLeatherArmor]=
                                                    kAttackWithBlunt;
            break;

                case 5:
                    ai_Creature[i].chromosomes[kAttackerWearingLeatherArmor]=
                                                    kAttackWithMagic;
            break;
        }

    if (Rnd(1,20)==1)
        switch (Rnd(1,5)) {
                case 1:
                    ai_Creature[i].chromosomes[kAttackerWearingMagicArmor]=
                                                    kRetreat;
            break;

                case 2:
                    ai_Creature[i].chromosomes[kAttackerWearingMagicArmor]=
                                                        kHide;
            break;
```

```
      case 3:
        ai_Creature[i].chromosomes[kAttackerWearingMagicArmor]=
                                      kAttackWithBlade;
      break;

      case 4:
        ai_Creature[i].chromosomes[kAttackerWearingMagicArmor]=
                                      kAttackWithBlunt;
      break;

      case 5:
        ai_Creature[i].chromosomes[kAttackerWearingMagicArmor]=
                                      kAttackWithMagic;
      break;
    }

}
```

Example 15-20 will reassign chromosomes randomly. Each trait has a 5% chance of randomly mutating. This is accomplished with each conditional line if (Rnd(1,20)==1). Like the createIndividual function, there are limits to the values we can assign to each trait. We use the switch statements to ensure that only legitimate values are assigned to each trait.

You can incorporate genetic algorithms into a multiplayer role-playing game in other ways as well. The previous example focused mainly on changing behavior in response to player actions; however, other areas of game design can benefit from genetic algorithms. For example, role-playing games typically categorize character abilities and assign a point level to each. A troll might have 100 opportunity points to divide over several attributes, such as strength, magical ability, dexterity, and a magic resistance. Instead of assigning the same values to each troll in the population, it might be better to use some diversity. For example, some would be physically stronger while others would have a greater resistance to magic. Varying the point distribution and then ranking the fitness of the population would help determine the best balance of point distribution. Successive generations of trolls then could evolve into more challenging adversaries for the players.

Further Information

As we stated earlier, many strategies are available for implementing crossover and mutation. Further, many other game problems besides the ones we've discussed could use genetic algorithms effectively. If you're interested in pursuing genetic algorithms further and would like alternative strategies and additional examples, we encourage you to check out the following references:

- *AI Application Programming* (Charles River Media)

- *AI Techniques for Game Programming* (Premier Press)
- *AI Game Programming Wisdom* (Charles River Media)

Mat Buckland's book, *AI Techniques for Game Programming*, covers both genetic algorithms and neural networks and even shows how to use genetic algorithms to evolve, or train, neural networks. This is an interesting alternative to the back-propagation training method we discussed in Chapter 14.

Vector Operations

This appendix implements a class called Vector that encapsulates all of the vector operations that you need when writing 2D or 3D rigid body simulations. Although, Vector represents 3D vectors, you can easily reduce it to handle 2D vectors by eliminating all of the z-terms or simply constraining the z-terms to zero where appropriate in your implementation.

Vector Class

The Vector class is defined with three components, x, y, and z, along with several methods and operators that implement basic vector operations. The class has two constructors, one of which initializes the vector components to zero and the other of which initializes the vector components to those passed to the constructor.

```
// - - - - - - - - - - - - - - - - - - - - - - - - - - - - - - - - - - - - - - - - - - -
// Vector Class and vector functions
// - - - - - - - - - - - - - - - - - - - - - - - - - - - - - - - - - - - - - - - - - - -
class Vector {
public:
    float x;
    float y;
    float z;

    Vector(void);
    Vector(float xi, float yi, float zi);

    float Magnitude(void);
    void  Normalize(void);
    void  Reverse(void);

    Vector& operator+=(Vector u);
    Vector& operator-=(Vector u);
    Vector& operator*=(float s);
    Vector& operator/=(float s);

    Vector operator-(void);

};
```

```
// Constructor
inline Vector::Vector(void)
{
    x = 0;
    y = 0;
    z = 0;
}

// Constructor
inline Vector::Vector(float xi, float yi, float zi)
{
    x = xi;
    y = yi;
    z = zi;
}
```

Magnitude

The `Magnitude` method simply calculates the scalar magnitude of the vector according to the formula

$$|\mathbf{v}| = \sqrt{x^2 + y^2 + z^2}$$

This is for a zero-based vector in which the components are specified relative to the origin. The magnitude of a vector is equal to its length, as illustrated in Figure A-1.

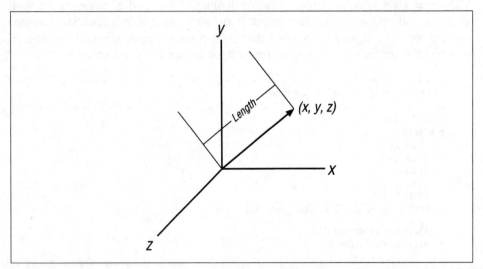

Figure A-1. Vector Length (Magnitude)

Here's the code that calculates the vector magnitude for our Vector class:

```
inline      float Vector::Magnitude(void)
{
    return (float) sqrt(x*x + y*y + z*z);
}
```

Note that you can calculate the components of a vector if you know its length and direction angles. *Direction angles* are the angles between each coordinate axis and the vector, as shown in Figure A-2.

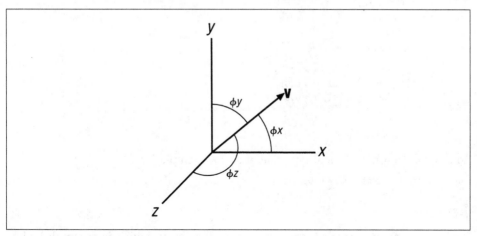

Figure A-2. Direction Angles

The components of the vector shown in this figure are as follows:

$$v_x = |\mathbf{v}|\cos\varphi_x$$
$$v_y = |\mathbf{v}|\cos\varphi_y$$
$$v_z = |\mathbf{v}|\cos\varphi_z$$

The cosines of the direction angles seen in these equations are known as *direction cosines*. The sum of the squares of the direction cosines is always equal to 1:

$$\cos^2\varphi_x + \cos^2\varphi_y + \cos^2\varphi_z = 1$$

Normalize

The `Normalize` method normalizes the vector, or converts it to a unit vector satisfying the following equation:

$$|\mathbf{v}| = \sqrt{x^2 + y^2 + z^2} = 1$$

In other words, the length of the normalized vector is 1 unit. If **v** is a nonunit vector with components x, y, and z, then the unit vector **u** can be calculated from **v** as follows:

$$\mathbf{u} = \mathbf{v}/|\mathbf{v}| = (x/|\mathbf{v}|)\mathbf{i} + (y/|\mathbf{v}|)\mathbf{j} + (z/|\mathbf{v}|)\mathbf{k}$$

Here, $|\mathbf{v}|$ is simply the magnitude, or length, of vector **v** as described earlier.

Here's the code that converts our `Vector` class vector to a unit vector:

```
inline      void   Vector::Normalize(void)
{
    float m = (float) sqrt(x*x + y*y + z*z);
    if(m <= tol) m = 1;
    x /= m;
    y /= m;
    z /= m;

    if (fabs(x) < tol) x = 0.0f;
    if (fabs(y) < tol) y = 0.0f;
    if (fabs(z) < tol) z = 0.0f;


}
```

In this function `tol` is a float type tolerance, for example,

```
float      const tol = 0.0001f;
```

Reverse

The `Reverse` method reverses the direction of the vector, which is accomplished by simply taking the negative of each component. After calling `Reverse`, the vector will point in a direction opposite to the direction in which it was pointing before `Reverse` was called.

```
inline      void Vector::Reverse(void)
{
    x = -x;
    y = -y;
    z = -z;
}
```

This operation is illustrated in Figure A-3.

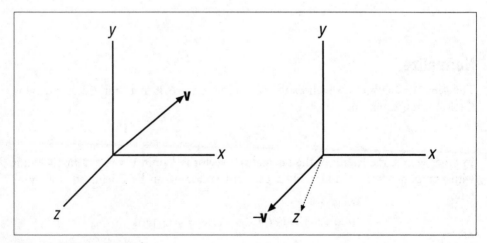

Figure A-3. Vector Reversal

Vector Addition: The += Operator

This summation operator is used for vector addition, whereby the passed vector is added to the current vector component by component. Graphically, vectors are added in tip-to-tail fashion as illustrated in Figure A-4.

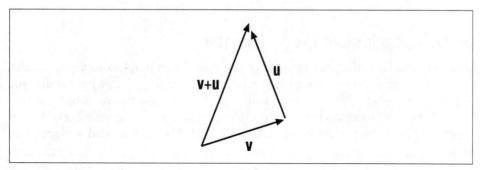

Figure A-4. Vector Addition

Here's the code that adds the vector **u** to our Vector class vector:

```
inline Vector& Vector::operator+= (Vector u)
    {
        x += u.x;
        Y += u.y;
        z += u.z;
        return *this;
    }
```

Vector Subtraction: The −= Operator

This subtraction operator is used to subtract the passed vector from the current one, which is performed on a component-by-component basis. Vector subtraction is very similar to vector addition except that you take the reverse of the second vector and add it to the first as illustrated in Figure A-5.

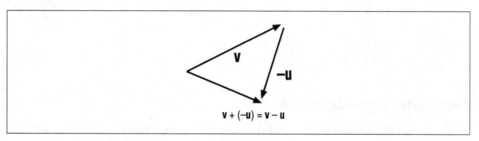

Figure A-5. Vector Subtraction

Here's the code that subtracts vector **u** from our Vector class vector:

```
inline  Vector& Vector::operator-=(Vector u)
{
    x -= u.x;
    y -= u.y;
    z -= u.z;
    return *this;
}
```

Scalar Multiplication: The *= Operator

This is the scalar multiplication operator that's used to multiply a vector by a scalar, effectively scaling the vector's length. When you multiply a vector by a scalar, you simply multiply each vector component by the scalar quantity to obtain the new vector. The new vector points in the same direction as the unsealed one, but its length will be different (unless the scale factor is 1). This is illustrated in Figure A-6.

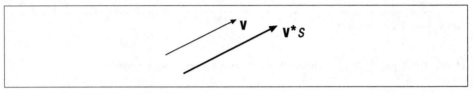

Figure A-6. Scalar Multiplication

Here's the code that scales our Vector class vector:

```
inline       Vector& Vector::operator*=(float s)
{
    x *=s;
    y *=s;
    z *=s;
    return *this;
}
```

Scalar Division: The /= Operator

This scalar division operator is similar to the scalar multiplication operator except that each vector component is divided by the passed scalar quantity.

```
inline      Vector& Vector::operator/=(float s)
{
    x /=s;
    y /=s;
    z /=s;
    return *this;
}
```

Conjugate: The — Operator

The conjugate operator simply takes the negative of each vector component and can be used when subtracting one vector from another or for reversing the direction of the vector. Applying the conjugate operator is the same as reversing a vector, as discussed earlier.

```
inline    Vector Vector::operator-(void)
{
    return Vector(-x, -y, -z);
}
```

Vector Functions and Operators

The functions and overloaded operators that follow are useful in performing operations with two vectors, or with a vector and a scalar, where the vector is based on the Vector class.

Vector Addition: The + Operator

This addition operator adds vector **v** to vector **u** according to the formula

$$\mathbf{u} + \mathbf{v} = (u_x + v_x)\mathbf{i} + (u_y + v_y)\mathbf{j} + (u_z + v_z)\mathbf{k}$$

Here's the code:

```
inline  Vector operator+ (Vector u, Vector v)
{
    return Vector(u.x + v.x, u.y + v.y, u.z + v.z);
}
```

Vector Subtraction: The — Operator

This subtraction operator subtracts vector **v** from vector **u** according to the formula

$$\mathbf{u} - \mathbf{v} = (u_x - v_x)\mathbf{i} + (u_y - v_y)\mathbf{j} + (u_z - v_z)\mathbf{k}$$

Here's the code:

```
inline  Vector operator-(Vector u, Vector v)
{
    return Vector(u.x - v.x, u.y - v.y, u.z - v.z);
}
```

Vector Cross Product: The ^Operator

This cross product operator takes the vector cross product between vectors **u** and **v**, **u** × **v**, and returns a vector perpendicular to both **u** and **v** according to the formula

$$\mathbf{u} \times \mathbf{v} = (u_y {}^*v_z - u_z {}^*v_y)\mathbf{i} + (-u_x {}^*v_z + u_z {}^*v_x)\mathbf{j} + (u_x {}^*v_y - u_y {}^*v_x)\mathbf{k}$$

The resulting vector is perpendicular to the plane that contains vectors **u** and **v**. The direction in which this resulting vector points can be determined by the righthand rule. If you place the two vectors, **u** and **v**, tail to tail as shown in Figure A-7 and curl your fingers (of your right hand) in the direction from **u** to **v**, your thumb will point in the direction of the resulting vector.

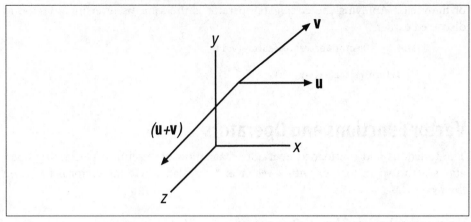

Figure A-7. Vector Cross Product

In this case the resulting vector points out of the page along the z-axis, since the vectors **u** and **v** lie in the plane formed by the x- and y-axes.

If two vectors are parallel, then their cross product will be zero. This is useful when you need to determine whether or not two vector are indeed parallel.

The cross product operation is distributive; however, it is not commutative:

$$\mathbf{u} \times \mathbf{v} \neq \mathbf{v} \times \mathbf{u}$$

$$\mathbf{u} \times \mathbf{v} = -(\mathbf{v} \times \mathbf{u})$$

$$s(\mathbf{u} \times \mathbf{v}) = (s)(\mathbf{u}) \times \mathbf{v} = \mathbf{u} \times (s)(\mathbf{v})$$

$$\mathbf{u} \times (\mathbf{v} + \mathbf{p}) = (\mathbf{u} \times \mathbf{v}) + (\mathbf{u} \times \mathbf{p})$$

Here's the code that takes the cross product of vectors **u** and **v**:

```
inline       Vector operator^ (Vector u, Vector v)
{
      return Vector(      u.y*v.z - u.z*v.y,
                         -u.x*v.z + u.z*v.x,
                          u.x*v.y - u.y*v.x );
}
```

Vector cross products are handy when you need to find normal (perpendicular) vectors. For example, when performing collision detection, you often need to find the vector normal to the face of a polygon. You can construct two vectors in the plane of the polygon using the polygon's vertices and then take the cross product of these two vectors to get normal vector.

Vector Dot Product: The * Operator

This operator takes the vector dot product between the vectors **u** and **v**, according to the formula

$$\mathbf{u} \cdot \mathbf{v} = (u_x {}^* v_x) + (u_y {}^* v_y) + (u_z {}^* v_z)$$

The dot product represents the projection of the vector **u** onto the vector **v** as illustrated in Figure A-8.

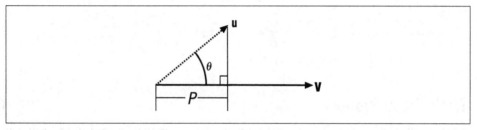

Figure A-8. Vector Dot Product

In this figure, P is the result of the dot product, and it is a scalar. You can also calculate the dot product if you the know the angle between the vectors:

$$P = \mathbf{u} \cdot \mathbf{v} = |\mathbf{u}|\,|\mathbf{v}|\cos\theta$$

Here's the code that takes the dot product of **u** and **v**:

```
// Vector dot product
inline      float operator*(Vector u, Vector v)
{
      return (u.x*v.x + u.y*v.y + u.z*v.z);
}
```

Vector dot products are handy when you need to find the magnitude of a vector projected onto another one. Going back to collision detection as an example, you often have to determine the closest distance from a point, which may be a polygon vertex on one body (body 1), to a polygon face on another body (body 2). If you construct a vector from the face under consideration on body 2, using any of its vertices, to the point under consideration from body 1, then you can find the closest distance of that point from the plane of body 2's face by taking the dot product of that point with the normal vector to the plane. (If the normal vector is not of unit length, you'll have to divide the result by the magnitude of the normal vector.)

Scalar Multiplication: The * Operator

This operator multiplies the vector **u** by the scalar s on a component-by-component basis. There are two versions of this overloaded operator depending on the order in which the vector and scalar are encountered:

```
inline      Vector operator*(float s, Vector u)
{
      return Vector(u.x*s, u.y*s, u.z*s);
}

inline   Vector operator*(Vector u, float s)
{
      return Vector(u.x*s, u.y*s, u.z*s);
}
```

Scalar Division: The / Operator

This operator divides the vector **u** by the scalar s on a component-by-component basis:

```
inline      Vector operator/(Vector u, float s)
{
    return Vector(u.x/s, u.y/s, u.z/s);
}
```

Triple Scalar Product

This function takes the triple scalar product of the vectors **u**, **v**, and **w** according to the formula

$$s = \mathbf{u} \cdot (\mathbf{v} \times \mathbf{w})$$

Here, the result, s, is a scalar. The code is as follows:

```
inline      float TripleScalarProduct(Vector u, Vector v, Vector w)
{
    return float(    (u.x * (v.y*w.z - v.z*w.y)) +
                     (u.y * (-v.x*w.z + v.z*w.x)) +
                     (u.z * (v.x*w.y - v.y*w.x)) );
}
```

Index

P

Parent tile, 130
    linking to, 132
Parsing
    basic script, 151–154
Path
    array initialization
        code, 30
    building, 122
    completed, 140
    direction calculation
        code, 14
    finding, 124
    following, 109–115
    following shortest, 108
    initialization code, 13–14
    initial tile scores, 133
    lowest-cost, 143, 145
        calculating, 144
    movement
        line of sight, 97
        over terrain elements,
            144
    road, 115
    score calculating, 133
    shortest vs. quickest,
        143–145
    simple movement, 97
    square, 49
    wall-tracing, 120
    zigzag, 50
Pathfinding, 1, 4
    A*, 126–148
    algorithm, 129
    basic, 96–98
    basic algorithm
        code, 96–97
    breadcrumb, 101–109
    workhorse method, 148
Patrolling pattern
    code
        complex, 35
        simple, 34
Pattern(s)
    arbitrary, 51
    rectangular
        code, 32–33
        movement, 33
    square, 50
    tile
        complex movement, 35
    zigzag, 50

Pattern array
    code
        declarations, 42
        processing, 29
Pattern definition, 42–45
Pattern execution, 45–46
Pattern function
    code, 33–34
Pattern initialization
    code, 28–29
    square patrol
        code, 42–43
    zigzag
        code, 44
Pattern matrix
    following
        code, 37–38
    initialization
        code, 36
Pattern movement, 27–51
    algorithm, 28–30
        arrays, 28
        control instruction, 28
        encoded instructions, 28
        lists, 28
    control data structure
        code, 28, 40
    physically stimulated environments, 38–39
    rectangular, 33
    scripted, 156
        code, 156
    stimulated environments, 38–39
    tiled environments, 30–38
    tracking, 37
Pattern results, 50–51
Pattern setup
    code, 36
Pearl, Judea, 267
Physics for Game Developers, 16, 72
Pixel-based environment
    line drawing, 12
Placing nodes, 121
Player input
    code, 160
Point-slope equation
    for straight line, 195
Population
    defining
        code, 331
Population explosion
    Ant Example, 186
Possible directions, 111

About the Authors

David M. Bourg performs computer simulations and develops analysis tools that measure such things as hovercraft performance and the effect of waves on the motion of ships and boats. He teaches at the University of New Orleans School of Naval Architecture and Marine Engineering. David is professionally involved in game development and consulting, and is also the author of *Physics for Game Developers* (O'Reilly). David also teaches the online course entitled, "Physics for Game Developers," for the Game Institute. Currently, David is nearing completion of his requirements for the degree of PhD in Engineering and Applied Sciences. His current research involves developing computer codes for computational fluid dynamics simulations and applying AI techniques to solve business and engineering problems.

Glenn Seemann is a veteran game programmer with over a dozen Mac and Windows systems games to his credit. He is a co-founder of Crescent Vision Interactive, a game development company specializing in cross-platform games.

Colophon

Our look is the result of reader comments, our own experimentation, and feedback from distribution channels. Distinctive covers complement our distinctive approach to technical topics, breathing personality and life into potentially dry subjects.

The animal on the cover of *AI for Game Developers* is a Ring-tailed lemur. Ring-tailed lemurs (*Lemur catta*) are found solely in Madagascar, an island off of southeast Africa.

Ring-tailed lemurs have a distinctive bushy tail with alternating bands of black and white rings. Their tails can reach lengths of up to 25 inches. They also have a black, pointed muzzle, which is typical among the various species of lemur.

These lemurs prefer more open areas, such as rocky plains and desert areas, and typically travel on the ground, although they will sometimes walk on large limbs in trees. This differentiates them from other lemur species, which prefer forested areas and travel almost exclusively in trees.

Similar to cats, Ring-tailed lemurs have a reflective layer in the back of their eyes. This allows them to have excellent night vision. Their tails are highly scented, and are used to warn other lemurs of approaching danger. The tails are also an integral part of the mating process. The males will use their scent to try and attract the females, and vicious "stink fights" can often erupt within the group.

Ring-tailed lemurs live in groups of between five and thirty members. They have distinct hierarchies that are enforced by frequent, aggressive confrontations between members. Females, who stay in the group for their entire lives, dominate the group. Males will often change groups at least once during their lifetime.

Living in arid habitats, Ring-tailed lemurs quench their thirst with juicy fruits. They will also eat leaves, flowers, insects, and tree gum.

Like most lemurs, Ring-tails have only one baby, although twins or even triplets are common when food is plentiful. Newborns are quite helpless and are carried around by the mother in her mouth until they can hold on to her fur by themselves. They will then ride around on the mother's back. They first begin to climb after about three weeks, and are usually independent after six months. They can live for up to 27 years in the wild.

Darren Kelly was the production editor, Audrey Doyle was the copyeditor, and Kathryn Geddie was the proofreader for *AI for Game Developers*. Claire Cloutier provided quality control. TechBooks, Inc. provided production services and Ronald Prottsman wrote the index.

Ellie Volckhausen designed the cover of this book, based on a series design by Edie Freedman. The cover image is a 19th-century engraving from *Royal Natural History*. Emma Colby produced the cover layout with QuarkXPress 4.1 using Adobe's ITC Garamond font.

David Futato designed the interior layout. Techbooks, Inc. implemented the design. This book was converted by Andrew Savikas to FrameMaker 5.5.6 with a format conversion tool created by Erik Ray, Jason McIntosh, Neil Walls, and Mike Sierra that uses Perl and XML technologies. The text font is Linotype Birka; the heading font is Adobe Myriad Condensed; and the code font is LucasFont's TheSans Mono Condensed. The illustrations that appear in the book were produced by Robert Romano and Jessamyn Read using Macromedia FreeHand 9 and Adobe Photoshop 6. The tip and warning icons were drawn by Christopher Bing. This colophon was written by Darren Kelly.

Related Titles Available from O'Reilly

Hacks

Amazon Hacks

BSD Hacks

Digital Photography Hacks

eBay Hacks

Excel hacks

Google Hacks

Harware Hacking Projects for Geeks

Linux Server Hacks

Mac OS X Hacks

Mac OS X Panther Hacks

Spidering Hacks

TiVo Hacks

Windows Server Hacks

Windows XP Hacks

Wireless Hacks

Keep in touch with O'Reilly

1. Download examples from our books

To find example files for a book, go to:

www.oreilly.com/catalog

select the book, and follow the "Examples" link.

2. Register your O'Reilly books

Register your book at *register.oreilly.com*

Why register your books?
Once you've registered your O'Reilly books you can:

- Win O'Reilly books, T-shirts or discount coupons in our monthly drawing.
- Get special offers available only to registered O'Reilly customers.
- Get catalogs announcing new books (US and UK only).
- Get email notification of new editions of the O'Reilly books you own.

3. Join our email lists

Sign up to get topic-specific email announcements of new books and conferences, special offers, and O'Reilly Network technology newsletters at:

elists.oreilly.com

It's easy to customize your free elists subscription so you'll get exactly the O'Reilly news you want.

4. Get the latest news, tips, and tools

www.oreilly.com

- "Top 100 Sites on the Web"—PC Magazine
- CIO Magazine's Web Business 50 Awards

Our web site contains a library of comprehensive product information (including book excerpts and tables of contents), downloadable software, background articles, interviews with technology leaders, links to relevant sites, book cover art, and more.

5. Work for O'Reilly

Check out our web site for current employment opportunities:

jobs.oreilly.com

6. Contact us

O'Reilly & Associates
1005 Gravenstein Hwy North
Sebastopol, CA 95472 USA

TEL: 707-827-7000 or 800-998-9938
(6am to 5pm PST)

FAX: 707-829-0104

order@oreilly.com
For answers to problems regarding your order or our products. To place a book order online, visit:

www.oreilly.com/order_new

catalog@oreilly.com
To request a copy of our latest catalog.

booktech@oreilly.com
For book content technical questions or corrections.

corporate@oreilly.com
For educational, library, government, and corporate sales.

proposals@oreilly.com
To submit new book proposals to our editors and product managers.

international@oreilly.com
For information about our international distributors or translation queries. For a list of our distributors outside of North America check out:

international.oreilly.com/distributors.html

adoption@oreilly.com
For information about academic use of O'Reilly books, visit:

academic.oreilly.com